A Special Issue of
The European Journal of Cognitive Psychology

Verbalising Visual Memories

Guest Editors

Toby J. Lloyd-Jones
Swansea University, UK

Maria A. Brandimonte
Università Suor Orsola Benincasa (USOB), Napoli, Italy

and

Karl-Heinz Bäuml
Regensburg University, Germany

LONDON AND NEW YORK

First published 2008 by Psychology Press

Published 2018 by Routledge
2 Park Square, Milton Park, Abingdon, Oxon, OX14 4RN
52 Vanderbilt Avenue, New York, NY 10017

First issued in paperback 2018

Routledge is an imprint of the Taylor & Francis Group, an informa business

British Library Cataloguing in Publication Data
A catalogue record for this book is available from the British Library

Cover design by Anń Design, Tara, Co. Meath, Ireland
Typeset in Ireland by Datapage International, Dublin

ISBN 13: 978-1-138-87779-5 (pbk)
ISBN 13: 978-1-84169-853-3 (hbk)
ISSN 0954-1446

Contents*

Editorial: Verbalising visual memories
Toby J. Lloyd-Jones, Maria A. Brandimonte, and Karl-Heinz Bäuml 387

Why do words hurt? Content, process, and criterion shift accounts of verbal overshadowing
Jason M. Chin and Jonathan W. Schooler 396

A theoretical review and meta-analysis of the description-identification relationship in memory for faces
Christian A. Meissner, Siegfried L. Sporer, and Kyle J. Susa 414

Verbal overshadowing of multiple face recognition: Effects on remembering and knowing over time
Toby J. Lloyd-Jones and Charity Brown 456

The role of verbal processing at different stages of recognition memory for faces
Kazuyo Nakabayashi and A. Mike Burton 478

Person descriptions and person identifications: Verbal overshadowing or recognition criterion shift?
Melanie Sauerland, Franziska E. Holub, and Siegfried L. Sporer 497

Eliciting person descriptions from eyewitnesses: A survey of police perceptions of eyewitness performance and reported use of interview techniques
Charity Brown, Toby J. Lloyd-Jones, and Mark Robinson 529

Testing alternatives to Navon letters to induce a transfer-inappropriate processing shift in face recognition
Peter J. Hills and Michael B. Lewis 561

(*continued overleaf*)

* This book is also a special issue of *The European Journal of Cognitive Psychology*, and comprises pp. 387–654 of Volume 20 (2008). The page numbers are taken from the journal and so begin with p. 387.

The effect of verbal description and processing type on face identification
Lee H. V. Wickham and Karen Lander 577

Navon processing and verbalisation: A holistic/featural distinction
Nicola J. Weston, Timothy J. Perfect, Jonathan W. Schooler, and Ian Dennis 587

Verbal overshadowing in visual imagery is due to recoding interference
Maria A. Brandimonte and Simona Collina 612

Object naming induces viewpoint-independence in longer term visual remembering: Evidence from a simple object drawing task
Peter Walker, Helen Blake, and J. Gavin Bremner 632

EUROPEAN JOURNAL OF COGNITIVE PSYCHOLOGY
2008, 20 (3), 387–395

Verbalising visual memories

Toby J. Lloyd-Jones
Swansea University, Swansea, UK

Maria A. Brandimonte
Università Suor Orsola Benincasa (USOB), Napoli, Italy

Karl-Heinz Bäuml
Regensburg University, Regensburg, Germany

In this paper, we introduce a special issue on the role of verbalisation in visual memory. In particular, we provide an overview of research on: (a) verbal interference and facilitation in face and person recognition; (b) similarities and differences between effects of verbalisation and processing in the Navon task (i.e., global or local letter identification; Navon, 1977); and (c) effects of verbalisation in visual imagery and object memory. We argue that verbal processes influence the encoding, storage, and retrieval of visual information. Moreover, different forms of verbal interference and facilitation are likely to be due to different mechanisms in different contexts. The state of the art is that we are just beginning to understand the rich complexity of the problem.

> The cavernous interior of St. Paul's Cathedral instills a sense of awe; King Lear's dying words fill the audience with lofty emotion; the idea of infinity is beyond words. (Shaw, 2006, Introduction)

Our experience of *the sublime*, when the power of an object or event seems beyond reason and cannot be described fully in words, demonstrates that some cognitions cannot be captured by language (e.g., Burke, 1757/1990; Kant, 1789/1987). Although language may structure cognition, cognition may also extend beyond the constraints of language.

Two strands of research in cognitive psychology have made some progress towards understanding the more tractable problem of how verbally describing a cognition that is normally difficult to describe (such as one's

---

Correspondence should be addressed to Toby J. Lloyd-Jones, Department of Psychology, Swansea University, Singleton Park, Swansea SA2 8PP, UK.
E-mail: T.J.Lloyd-Jones@swansea.ac.uk.

http://www.psypress.com/ecp DOI: 10.1080/09541440701755543

memory of a face) may influence subsequent behaviour. On the one hand, there has been a resurgence of interest in verbal interference (or *verbal overshadowing*) whereby describing a face can interfere with subsequent visual recognition (e.g., Schooler, 2002; Schooler & Engstler-Schooler, 1990; Schooler, Fiore, & Brandimonte, 1997; and a special issue of *Applied Cognitive Psychology*, 2002). In a seminal study, Schooler and Engstler-Schooler (1990) presented participants with a 30 second video of a bank robbery, after which participants were assigned to either a description or no description control condition. Those in the description condition were instructed to use the next 5 minutes to describe the facial features of the bank robber, whilst control participants were given an unrelated filler task. Description condition participants were less able to subsequently identify the robber, as compared with the control group, when given a lineup comprising the robber and several potential suspects.

Verbal interference is not restricted to face recognition, however, as it occurs in other domains concerned with perceptual expertise, including visual imagery (e.g., Brandimonte & Gerbino, 1993), wine tasting (Melcher & Schooler, 1996), voice recognition (Perfect, Hunt, & Harris, 2002), problem solving (Schooler, Ohlsson, & Brooks, 1993), and analogical reasoning (Lane & Schooler, 2004).

On the other hand, a number of studies have demonstrated that describing a face can benefit subsequent recognition (e.g., Bloom & Mudd, 1991; Bower & Karlin, 1974; Brown & Lloyd-Jones, 2005, 2006; Mueller, Courtois, & Bailis, 1981). Surprisingly, however, research on this question has been neglected.

Examining the detrimental and beneficial influences of verbalisation on visual memory should advance our understanding of the complex relationship between language and cognition. Nevertheless, the parameters of these phenomena have not been clearly defined and there remain a number of competing explanations as to why verbal interference and facilitation may arise (for past reviews of interference and facilitation, see Schooler, 2002, and Brown & Lloyd-Jones, 2005, respectively).

In this special issue, Chin and Schooler provide a taxonomy and critical evaluation of the different accounts that have been used to explain verbal interference. They propose: (a) a content account, whereby the specific contents of verbalisation interfere with later performance; (b) a processing account, which refers to a shift in processing orientation caused by verbalisation; and (c) a criterion shift account, whereby verbalisation leads to a reliance on more conservative choosing of the target (see also Clare & Lewandowsky, 2004). A review of existing evidence provides some support for each account. Indeed, some of the studies of verbal interference in the present issue favour either content (Brandimonte & Collina; Meissner, Sporer, & Susa), processing (Lloyd-Jones & Brown; Weston, Perfect,

Schooler, & Dennis; Hills & Lewis), or criterion shift (Sauerland, Holub, & Sporer) accounts.

How might we reconcile these different explanations of verbal interference? Chin and Schooler argue that it is unlikely that a single mechanism will suffice. Rather, verbal interference is likely to be due to different mechanisms in different contexts (see also Lloyd-Jones & Brown; Sporer, Meissner, & Schooler, 2006).

Meissner et al. provide a review of both negative and positive effects of verbalisation on face recognition. In particular, they provide a meta-analysis of the relationship between verbal description and face identification across 33 research articles and a total of 4278 participants. Their findings provide evidence for a small but significant relationship between the description measures of accuracy, number of incorrect descriptors, and congruence (i.e., the degree of similarity between a description and the face that is described) with that of identification accuracy.

Moreover, particular conditions including the use of face recognition versus eyewitness identification paradigms and the length of delay between the relevant tasks were found to strengthen the magnitude of this relationship. Meissner et al.'s synthesis of previous findings also emphasises the need for rigorous methodology and reporting.

The majority of the remaining papers in the special issue are concerned with either face or person recognition (Brown, Lloyd-Jones, & Robinson; Hills & Lewis; Lloyd-Jones & Brown; Nakabayashi & Burton; Sauerland et al.; Weston et al.; Wickham & Lander).

Lloyd-Jones and Brown add to findings observed in their multiple-face presentation paradigm, where a series of faces are followed by a single face description (Brown & Lloyd-Jones, 2002, 2003; Lloyd-Jones, Brown, & Clarke, 2006). The remember/know procedure (Tulving, 1985) was used in examining the time course of verbal interference on recollection and familiarity-based recognition judgements. Verbal interference was evident at a short but not long lag between study and test and for both discrimination and false "know" judgements. They argue that verbalisation produces a shift in processing style which leads to an increase in confusability between targets and distractors, and hence false recognition. They also emphasise that although their findings share some similarities with those observed in previous studies, additional factors such as proactive and retroactive interference over multiple items or interference from similar distractors in a multiple-item forced two-choice task may come into play depending on the nature of the paradigm.

Nakabayashi and Burton take a broader approach and examine effects of verbalisation at both encoding and retrieval. Participants learned faces with or without articulatory suppression and then engaged in an old/new recognition task. The main finding was that articulatory suppression reduced recognition efficiency. This suggests that verbal processes are normally engaged during face encoding and benefit performance (see also Wickham & Swift, 2006). In addition, there was evidence of verbal interference when participants described a single face prior to recognition (replicating Brown & Lloyd-Jones, 2002, 2003). Together these findings demonstrate that verbalisation may have contrasting influences on performance at different stages of the face recognition process.

Sauerland et al. emphasise the importance of decision processes in observing verbal interference on person memory. Participants either gave no description or provided a written description after viewing a crime on video. Half of the describers reread their target descriptions prior to attempting to identify the perpetrator in either a target-absent or target-present lineup. Sauerland et al. found that rereaders were less likely to choose the target from the lineup. Moreover, choosing correctly was positively correlated with description accuracy and negatively correlated with the number of incorrect details reported. These findings are consistent with a criterion account and highlight the role of decision processes in both verbalisation and subsequent identification.

The only study in this issue to look at the implications of verbalisation in an applied setting is by Brown et al. (although see comments by Meissner et al. and Sauerland et al. in particular). They examined police perceptions of eyewitness performance and the methods they use to elicit person descriptions from witnesses. They also examined whether police procedures encourage verbal interference on eyewitness identification. It is concluded that although verbal interference is unlikely to be a major concern for most police officers, under some circumstances its potential impact should be considered. These include occasions when witnesses are encouraged to provide elaborate person descriptions and those situations in which they have been encouraged to lower their retrieval criterion to report information of which they are unsure. The other main point to emerge from this study is that it would be of benefit for future research to examine a number of variables relevant to the forensic setting. These include the postencoding retention interval, effects of repeated verbal description, and the delay between description and memory testing.

Three studies in particular (Hills & Lewis; Weston et al.; Wickham & Lander) touch upon research by Macrae and Lewis (2002) in examining the effects of a Navon task (i.e., global or local letter identification; Navon, 1977) at a particular stage of processing prior to face recognition. In the Macrae and Lewis study, participants viewed a video of a bank robbery and then, rather than providing a verbal description of the bank robber, viewed large letters composed of many small letters (i.e., Navon letters) and attended either to the large or the small letters. Those participants who attended to the small letters were less able than controls to identify the robber in a lineup task. However, those who attended to the large letters performed better than controls. One explanation of these findings is that effects of both Navon processing and verbalisation may be explained in terms of a shift in visual processing towards either more local featural processing which is detrimental to subsequent face recognition or more global visual processing which is beneficial for subsequent face recognition.

Hills and Lewis provide evidence that processing the local features of a Navon letter reduces subsequent face recognition performance and this effect generalises to a Navon task without a verbal component, namely processing Navon shapes (e.g., triangles, squares, and circles).

Wickham and Lander manipulated the kind of description (i.e., holistic, featural or no description) and also introduced a postdescription Navon task prior to participants identifying the target in a lineup. They found that describing faces holistically (i.e., describing personality, occupation and so on) benefited subsequent identification. In addition, the global Navon task produced better identification than the local Navon task. Thus, optimum performance was seen for holistic descriptions and global Navon processing and poorest performance was seen with featural descriptions and local Navon processing. It is clear from these findings that describing a face and processing letters in the Navon task influence face identification in an independent fashion.

Weston et al. also demonstrate that the interpretation of a processing shift induced by the Navon task is not straightforward. They compared face recognition following either global/local Navon processing or verbalisation. They also examined the extent to which the effects of these *interval tasks* (i.e., tasks presented after the series of faces to be memorised and prior to the forced two-choice recognition test) were influenced by prior encoding processes. Encoding was manipulated by using either a Navon task, personality judgement task (to induce holistic visual processing), or a physical feature judgement task (to induce featural encoding) prior to participants memorising faces. They found that both interval tasks influenced subsequent recognition, but a consistent global Navon advantage and local Navon/verbalisation disadvantage was not evident. Indeed, there was some evidence for all three interval tasks benefiting recognition. Moreover, the effects of encoding were different across subsequent Navon and verbalisation interval tasks. As with the study of Wickham and Lander, this research raises a number of questions concerning similarities and differences between Navon processing and verbalisation.

The final two studies examine effects of verbalisation in domains other than face and person processing, namely visual imagery and object memory. Previous work by Brandimonte and colleagues has shown that the ability to manipulate visual mental images is vulnerable to the negative effects of verbalisation (e.g., Brandimonte & Gerbino, 1993; Brandimonte, Hitch, &

Bishop, 1992a, 1992b, 1992c; Brandimonte, Schooler, & Gabbino, 1997; Hitch, Brandimonte, & Walker, 1995; Pelizzon, Brandimonte, & Favretto, 1999; Walker, Hitch, Dewhurst, Whitely, & Brandimonte, 1997). In this issue, Brandimonte and Collina explored the dynamics of verbal interference on visual imagery by manipulating the nature of stimulus processing at encoding and the presence of visual and verbal cues at retrieval. In particular, they focused on the role of self-generated names as retrieval cues.

Verbal interference on visual imagery, as assessed in an image transformation and discovery task, was attenuated by visual or verbal cues which re-presented the self-generated name of a drawing which was necessary to complete the task successfully. However, verbal interference was not attenuated by verbal labels which were presented with each drawing or self-generated words or nonwords that were not associated with the drawing. They argue that to be effective the cues needed to maintain some correspondence with particular features of the drawing. Consistent with this explanation, there was a positive correlation between imagery performance and the quality of the self-generated names as they related to parts of the visual drawing.

Brandimonte and Collina conclude that their findings support a content over a processing account of verbal interference. Verbal interference in this paradigm arises because of a conflict between representations: Verbalisation produces a verbally biased representation which interferes with, but does not eradicate, the original visual memory. In particular, verbalisation encourages a transition from featural to more global visual representations. Presenting appropriate retrieval cues alleviates verbal interference by allowing use of the original featural visual information.

In a similar vein, Walker, Blake, and Bremner examined the influence of verbalisation on visual object memory. Participants viewed a novel object from a viewpoint at which it would not normally be drawn from memory. The object was either named or not. Subsequently, participants drew the remembered object from immediate, short-term, or longer term memory. They found that, with the transition from immediate to longer term memory, object naming increased the probability that participants would depict the object from a new viewpoint rather than from the viewpoint at which it had been seen. They argue that two distinct types of representation are associated with short- and longer term memory: image-based representations (e.g., Tarr, 1995) and geon structural descriptions (GSDs, e.g., Biederman, 1987). However, GSDs are more likely to be used in long-term memory, when available. Thus, object naming may be an important determinant of the availability of GSDs and hence the extent to which memory is viewpoint-independent.

One of the implications of their model of these findings is that because distinct forms of visual processing support the derivation of distinct types of representation, content and processing accounts of verbalisation are compatible.

In summary, it is apparent from this brief overview of the role of verbalisation in visual memory that verbal processes influence the encoding, storage, and retrieval of visual information. Different forms of verbal interference and facilitation are likely to be due to different mechanisms in different contexts. The state of the art is that we are just beginning to understand the rich complexity of the problem.

REFERENCES

Biederman, I. (1987). Recognition by components: A theory of human image understanding. *Psychological Review, 94*, 115–145.

Bloom, L., & Mudd, S. A. (1991). Depth of processing approach to face recognition: A test of two theories. *Journal of Experimental Psychology: Learning, Memory, and Cognition, 17*, 556–565.

Bower, G. H., & Karlin, M. B. (1974). Depth of processing pictures of faces and recognition memory. *Journal of Experimental Psychology, 103*, 751–757.

Brandimonte, M. A., & Collina, S. (2008). Verbal overshadowing in visual imagery is due to recoding interference. *European Journal of Cognitive Psychology, 20*, 612–631.

Brandimonte, M. A., & Gerbino, W. (1993). Mental image reversal and verbal recoding: When ducks become rabbits. *Memory and Cognition, 21*, 23–33.

Brandimonte, M. A., Hitch, G. J., & Bishop, D. V. (1992a). Influence of short-term memory codes on visual image processing: Evidence from image transformation tasks. *Journal of Experimental Psychology: Learning, Memory, and Cognition, 18*, 157–156.

Brandimonte, M. A., Hitch, G. J., & Bishop, D. V. (1992b). Manipulation of visual mental images in children and adults. *Journal of Experimental Child Psychology, 53*, 300–312.

Brandimonte, M. A., Hitch, G. J., & Bishop, D. V. (1992c). Verbal recoding of visual stimuli impairs mental image transformations. *Memory and Cognition, 20*, 449–455.

Brandimonte, M. A., Schooler, J. W., & Gabbino, P. (1997). Attenuating verbal overshadowing through colour retrieval cues. *Journal of Experimental Psychology: Learning, Memory, and Cognition, 23*, 915–931.

Brown, C., & Lloyd-Jones, T. J. (2002). Verbal overshadowing in a multiple face presentation paradigm: Effects of description instruction. *Applied Cognitive Psychology, 16*, 873–885.

Brown, C., & Lloyd-Jones, T. J. (2003). Verbal overshadowing of multiple face and car recognition: Effects of within- versus across-category verbal descriptions. *Applied Cognitive Psychology, 17*, 183–201.

Brown, C., & Lloyd-Jones, T. J. (2005). Verbal facilitation of face recognition. *Memory and Cognition, 33*, 1442–1456.

Brown, C., & Lloyd-Jones, T. J. (2006). Beneficial effects of verbalization and visual distinctiveness on remembering and knowing faces. *Memory and Cognition, 34*, 277–286.

Brown, C., Lloyd-Jones, T. J., & Robinson, M. (2008). Eliciting person descriptions from eyewitnesses: A survey of police perceptions of eyewitness performance and reported use of interview techniques. *European Journal of Cognitive Psychology, 20*, 529–560.

Burke, E. (1990). *A philosophical inquiry into the origin of our ideas of the sublime and beautiful.* Oxford, UK: Oxford University Press. (Original work published 1757)

Chin, J. M., & Schooler, J. W. (2008). Why do words hurt? Content, process, and criterion shift accounts of verbal overshadowing. *European Journal of Cognitive Psychology, 20*, 396–413.

Clare, J., & Lewandowsky, S. (2004). Verbalizing facial memory: Criterion effects in verbal overshadowing. *Journal of Experimental Psychology: Learning, Memory, and Cognition, 30*, 739–755.

Hills, P. J., & Lewis, M. B. (2008). Testing alternatives to Navon letters to induce a transfer-inappropriate processing shift in face recognition. *European Journal of Cognitive Psychology, 20*, 561–576.

Hitch, G. J., Brandimonte, M. A., & Walker, P. (1995). Two types of representation in visual memory: Evidence from the effects of stimulus contrast in image combination. *Memory and Cognition, 23*, 147–154.

Kant, I. (1987). *Critique of judgement* (W. S. Pluhar, Trans.). Indianapolis, IN: Hackett. (Original work published 1789)

Lane, S. M., & Schooler, J. W. (2004). Skimming the surface: Verbal overshadowing of analogical retrieval. *Psychological Science, 15*, 715–719.

Lloyd-Jones, T. J., & Brown, C. (2008). Verbal overshadowing of multiple face recognition: Effects on remembering and knowing over time. *European Journal of Cognitive Psychology, 20*, 456–477.

Lloyd-Jones, T. J., Brown, C., & Clarke, S. (2006). Verbal overshadowing of perceptual discrimination. *Psychonomic Bulletin and Review, 13*, 269–274.

Macrae, C. N., & Lewis, H. L. (2002). Do I know you? Processing orientation and face recognition. *Psychological Science, 13*, 194–196.

Meissner, C. A., Sporer, S. L., & Schooler, J. W. (2007). Person descriptions as eyewitness evidence. In R. Lindsay, D. Ross, J. Read, & M. Toglia (Eds.), *Handbook of Eyewitness Psychology: Memory for People* (pp. 3–34). Mahwah, NJ: Lawrence Erlbaum Associates.

Meissner, C. A., Sporer, S. L., & Susa, K. J. (2008). A theoretical review and meta-analysis of the description-identification relationship in memory for faces. *European Journal of Cognitive Psychology, 20*, 414–455.

Melcher, J. M., & Schooler, J. W. (1996). Perceptual and conceptual training mediate the verbal overshadowing effect in an unfamiliar domain. *Memory and Cognition, 32*, 618–631.

Mueller, J. H., Courtois, M. R., & Bailis, K. L. (1981). Self-reference in facial recognition. *Bulletin on the Psychonomic Society, 17*, 85–88.

Nakabayashi, K., & Burton, A. M. (2008). The role of verbal processing at different stages of recognition memory for faces. *European Journal of Cognitive Psychology, 20*, 478–496.

Navon, D. (1977). Forest before trees: The precedence of global features in visual perception. *Cognitive Psychology, 9*, 353–383.

Pelizzon, L., Brandimonte, M. A., & Favretto, A. (1999). Imagery and recognition: Dissociable measures of memory? *European Journal of Cognitive Psychology, 3*, 429–443.

Perfect, T. J., Hunt, L. J., & Harris, C. M. (2002). Verbal overshadowing in voice recognition. *Applied Cognitive Psychology, 16*, 973–980.

Sauerland, M., Holub, F. E., & Sporer, S. L. (2008). Person descriptions and person identifications: Verbal overshadowing or recognition criterion shift? *European Journal of Cognitive Psychology, 20*, 497–528.

Schooler, J. W. (2002). Verbalization produces a transfer inappropriate processing shift. *Applied Cognitive Psychology, 16*, 989–997.

Schooler, J. W., & Engstler-Schooler, T. Y. (1990). Verbal overshadowing of visual memories: Some things are better left unsaid. *Cognitive Psychology, 22*, 36–71.

Schooler, J. W., Fiore, S. M., & Brandimonte, M. A. (1997). At a loss from words: Verbal overshadowing of perceptual memories. In D. L. Medin (Eds.), *Advances in research and theory: Vol. 37. The psychology of learning and motivation* (pp. 293–334). London: Academic Press.

Schooler, J. W., Ohlsson, S., & Brooks, K. (1993). Thoughts beyond words: When language overshadows insight. *Journal of Experimental Psychology: General, 122*, 166–183.

Shaw, P. (2006). *The sublime*. London: Routledge.

Tarr, M. J. (1995). Rotating objects to recognize them: A case study on the role of viewpoint dependency in the recognition of three-dimensional objects. *Psychonomic Bulletin and Review*, *2*, 55–82.

Tulving, E. (1985). Memory and consciousness. *Canadian Journal of Psychology*, *26*, 1–12.

Walker, P., Blake, H., & Bremner, J. G. (2008). Object naming induces viewpoint-independence in longer term visual remembering: Evidence from a simple object drawing task. *European Journal of Cognitive Psychology*, *20*, 632–648.

Walker, P., Hitch, G. J., Dewhurst, S., Whitely, H. E., & Brandimonte, M. A. (1997). The representation of non-structural information in visual memory: Evidence from image combination. *Memory and Cognition*, *25*, 484–491.

Wickham, L. H. V., & Swift, H. (2006). Articulatory suppression attenuates the verbal overshadowing effect: A role for verbal encoding in face identification. *Applied Cognitive Psychology*, *22*, 157–169.

Weston, N. J., Perfect, T. J., Schooler, J. W., & Dennis, I. (2008). Navon processing and verbalisation: a holistic/featural distinction. *European Journal of Cognitive Psychology*, *20*, 587–611.

Wickham, L. H. V., & Lander, K. (2008). The effect of verbal description and processing type on face identification. *European Journal of Cognitive Psychology*, *20*, 577–586.

EUROPEAN JOURNAL OF COGNITIVE PSYCHOLOGY
2008, 20 (3), 396–413

Why do words hurt? Content, process, and criterion shift accounts of verbal overshadowing

Jason M. Chin and Jonathan W. Schooler
University of British Columbia, Vancouver, BC, Canada

Verbal overshadowing describes the phenomenon in which verbalisation negatively affects performance on a task related to the verbalised material. Within the verbal overshadowing literature, three accounts exist which attempt to explain this phenomenon: content, processing, and criterion accounts. The content account refers to the notion that the specific contents of verbalisation interfere with later performance, processing refers to a proposed shift in processing caused by verbalisation, and criterion deals with the possibility that verbalisation leads to a reliance on more conservative choosing. The current manuscript reviews evidence for the existing accounts, while describing advantages and disadvantages of each account and attempting to reconcile these various accounts. The authors provide a framework for understanding verbal overshadowing as caused by one unified mechanism, or several. Finally, an outline for future research is suggested that should aid in reconciling the existing accounts for verbal overshadowing.

Theory, research, and general debate on the nature of the relationship between language and cognition has been in no short supply in past century (Hunt & Angoli, 1991; Watson, 1924; Whorf, 1956). Verbalisation—the simple act of translating one's thoughts into words—speaks quite directly to this debate and although verbalisation seems straightforward enough, its impact on cognition is far from clear. A phenomenon known as verbal overshadowing typifies the tenuous relationship between language and cognition. As the term implies, verbal overshadowing occurs when verbalisation proves detrimental to the task at hand. Originally demonstrated in the context of face recognition, the phenomenon has been found to be quite general, applying to such disparate domains as decision making (Wilson & Schooler, 1991), problem solving (Schooler, Ohlsson, & Brooks, 1993), analogical reasoning (Lane & Schooler, 2004), and visual imagery (Brandimonte, Hitch, & Bishop, 1992a, 1992b, 1992c). Despite, or perhaps because

Correspondence should be addressed to Jason M. Chin, Department of Psychology, University of British Columbia, 2136 West Mall, Vancouver, BC V6T 1Z4, Canada.
E-mail: jchin@psych.ubc.ca

http://www.psypress.com/ecp DOI: 10.1080/09541440701728623

of its pervasiveness, the sources of verbal overshadowing have remained in serious dispute.

In this paper we first review relevant existing evidence for verbal overshadowing and its generality to other domains. Next, we discuss three accounts for verbal overshadowing that have been proposed: a *content* account, which focuses on the content of verbalisation, a *processing* account, which focuses on a shift in processing orientation caused by verbalisation, and a *criterion shift* account, which focuses on the effect of verbalisation on recognition criteria. What we imply by the terms content, processing, and criterion will be explained in greater detail later. We will then propose a framework for understanding and integrating the three accounts, specifying situations in which one account is more applicable than another, as well as outline possible avenues for future research.

Verbal overshadowing was first documented by Schooler and Engstler-Schooler (1990) in a study of eyewitness memory. Participants viewed a video of a robbery perpetrated by a salient individual whom participants in the verbalisation condition subsequently described. The results indicated that participants who described the robber were poorer at picking him out of a lineup, as compared to control participants who read an unrelated text for the same amount of time. Since the initial series of studies by Schooler and Engstler-Schooler, verbal overshadowing of face recognition has been studied extensively, with many studies replicating the phenomenon (Dodson, Johnson, & Schooler, 1997; Fallshore & Schooler, 1995; Ryan & Schooler, 1998; Schooler, Ryan, & Reder, 1996; Sporer, 1989) and some failing to replicate the finding (Lovett, Small, & Engstrom, 1992; Yu & Geiselman, 1993). In a meta-analysis of verbal overshadowing studies, Meissner and Brigham (2001) found a small but statistically significant verbal overshadowing effect ($Zr = .12$). Within perceptual memory, verbal overshadowing has been shown to generalise to memory for colours (Schooler & Engstler-Schooler, 1990), music (Houser, Fiore, & Schooler, 1997), voices (Perfect, Hunt, & Harris, 2002), abstract figures (Brandimonte, Schooler, & Gabbino, 1997), wines (Melcher & Schooler, 1996), and mushrooms (Melcher & Schooler, 2004). In addition to being a reliable finding, verbal overshadowing effects have been shown to permeate several other areas of research.

With regards to visual imagery, several studies have demonstrated that verbalisation at the time of encoding can impair performance of such imagery tasks (Brandimonte & Gerbino, 1993; Brandimonte, Hitch, & Bishop, 1992a, 1992b, 1992c; Brandimonte et al., 1997; Hitch, Brandimonte, & Walker, 1995; Pelizzon, Brandimonte, & Favretto, 1999; Pelizzon, Brandimonte, & Luccio, 2002; Walker, Hitch, Dewhurst, Whiteley, & Brandimonte, 1997). In the prototypical experiment, participants are presented with visual stimuli and are either encouraged to covertly verbalise these stimuli or not, and then are asked to perform a mental rotation of the image to reveal underlying characteristics of these images. Verbalisation is sometimes encouraged through the use of easily named stimuli (and difficult to name stimuli in the control condition), or through naming of the stimuli by the participant (Brandimonte & Collina, 2008 this issue). Results of such studies indicate that verbalisation impairs performance on visual imagery tasks, a finding that is attenuated by the presence of visual or verbal cues prior to the mental rotation task (Brandimonte et al., 1997; Brandimonte & Collina, 2008 this issue). A significant literature therefore suggests that verbalisation impairs mental imagery.

In the problem-solving arena, Schooler and colleagues (1993) found that insight problems—problems that do not lend themselves well to analytic reasoning—are susceptible to verbal overshadowing. These researchers asked participants to verbalise their thought processes concurrent to solving several insight and analytic problems. They found that insight problem solving was impaired for verbalising participants, as opposed to participants who engaged in a control task. Further, analytic problem solving was not impaired by verbalisation. A similar effect was found in the domain of affective decision making. Wilson and Schooler (1991) performed a study to test whether verbalisation impairs the quality of people's judgements. In a study veiled as an enquiry into consumer judgements of strawberry jams, they asked some participants (verbalisers) to taste the jams and then list their reasons for liking or not liking the jams, as well as analysing their reasons. Control participants tasted the jams but did not list or analyse their thoughts about the jams. Schooler and Wilson found that participants who did not list and analyse their reasons made judgements that were more similar to that of expert jam raters (from consumer report magazines) as compared to verbalisers.

Similarly, verbalisation appears to impair both analogical reasoning and retrieval. Sieck, Quinn, and Schooler (1999), for instance, tested the influence of verbalisation on people's ability to evaluate the soundness of analogies. Participants were presented with stories that were similar either superficially (various aspects of the stories, such as names or places, were the same) or analogically. Participants then rated how sound they felt the match between stories was, either listing the reasons for their judgement (verbalisers) or not (control). The researchers found that verbalisers rated all stories as better matches, and did not discriminate between superficial and analogical matches as well as control participants. Subsequent research showed that verbalisation also influences the retrieval of analogies in that verbalisers are more likely to retrieve superficial/surface matches as opposed to actual analogical matches (Lane & Schooler, 2004). In short, verbal overshadowing is not limited to memory.

Given that a healthy number of studies have documented verbal overshadowing across several different areas of study, it is noteworthy that a single theory has not been accepted to explain what causes verbal overshadowing. Currently, three general accounts have been proposed to explain verbal overshadowing: a content account, a processing account, and a criterion shift account, which shall be explained next.

A CONTENT ACCOUNT

As the name suggests, the content account suggests that it is something about the specific contents of verbalisations that impairs memory. In other words, verbal overshadowing is caused by material within verbalisation interfering with the original memory, which in turn leads to poorer performance at recognition.

Schooler and Engstler-Schooler (1990) originally proposed a content-based account for verbal overshadowing in the form of a recoding interference explanation for the phenomenon. This original study dealt with visual stimuli that are not easily put to words: faces and colours. The recoding interference explanation suggests that memory for the original stimulus is impaired when subjects confuse the verbal memory created from the visual stimulus with the original visual memory. Moreover, recoding interference as a source of verbal overshadowing agrees well with standard theories of memory interference and misinformation effects (e.g., Schooler, Foster, & Loftus, 1988), in that the self-generated verbalisation may contain misinformation hampering future recognition. Recoding interference should not be a problem when the original stimulus is easily verbalised, or when the stimulus and distracters are qualitatively different, such that verbalisation aids in discrimination. In fact, recent research has demonstrated that under certain conditions, verbalisation does in indeed aid in discrimination (Brown & Lloyd-Jones, 2005). In line with the recoding interference explanation, research demonstrating that verbal overshadowing is especially likely when perceptual expertise exceeds verbal ability also provides evidence for the content account (Melcher & Schooler, 1996).

The recoding interference hypothesis predicts that individuals who possess a level of perceptual expertise that exceeds their verbal ability should be especially prone to verbal overshadowing. These individuals would be able to perceive and process various nuances of a stimulus, but would not be able to put theses perceptions into words. Therefore, subsequent verbalisation would be especially unrepresentative of the perceptual experience. In a study testing the effect varying levels of perceptual and linguistic expertise has on verbal overshadowing, Melcher and Schooler (1996) asked participants to taste a wine and either verbalise it or perform a control task prior to identifying the tasted wine among distractors. Participants were either nonwine drinkers, untrained wine drinkers, or trained wine experts (professionals, or those who had taken wine seminars).

Melcher and Schooler's results align well with the content account as they found that verbalisation only impaired untrained wine drinkers, but not trained wine drinkers or nonwine drinkers. Trained wine drinkers have the verbal ability to describe the various aspects of wine detected by their palates, and do not experience verbal overshadowing, ostensibly because their experiences and verbalisations match up. Similarly, nonwine drinkers have neither the expertise to perceive wines in depth, nor the verbal tools to describe them and so their experiences and verbalisations do not interfere with each other. Untrained wine drinkers' perceptual expertise in wine tasting exceeds their verbal expertise in describing wine, and thus they do not have the verbal tools to describe all of the nuances their palates detected. Thus, they create verbalisations that do not match up with experience—in other words, verbal overshadowing due to a mismatch between the content of verbalisations and perception.

Although Melcher and Schooler's (1996) study on memory for wine provided helpful insight on the role of expertise on verbal overshadowing, the results are only correlational because participants were not assigned to various levels of expertise. In an effort to remedy this shortcoming and build on previous findings, Melcher and Schooler (2004) performed a study in which participants were assigned to be trained as either perceptual or conceptual experts in the domain of mushroom recognition. Much like the study on wine recognition, they hypothesised that perceptual training (expertise) in the absence of conceptual training would lead to verbal overshadowing, while conceptual training in the absence of perceptual training would not result in verbal overshadowing, and potentially lead to verbal enhancement. They reasoned that conceptual training would benefit memory in the verbalisation condition, because conceptual training would emphasise verbalisable knowledge. Melcher and Schooler's hypotheses were largely supported by the data, with perceptual training leading to verbal overshadowing and conceptual training leading to verbal enhancement.

Recoding interference can also be understood in the context of individual differences. Ryan and Schooler (1998) performed a study in which they measured individual differences in verbal ability (through use of high school or college grade point average), as well as perceptual ability (through score on an independent face recognition task). In accordance with the previously discussed literature, Ryan and Schooler documented the strongest verbal overshadowing effect among those who were measured as having high perceptual ability and low verbal ability.

From this review, it appears that verbalisation can affect memory through the content of verbalisations. Thus far, the influence of content has been analysed through the expertise and training of the verbaliser. Content, however, may also play a role through the demands of the verbalisation task itself, specifically when participants are required to produce verbalisations that are beyond their abilities.

The influence of the verbalisation task falls under what Meissner, Brigham, and Kelley (2001) have termed, *retrieval-based effects.* In short, Meissner et al. find that the way in which verbalisation instructions are worded can influence the strength and even the existence of verbal overshadowing effects. They find strongest effects in what they call a *forced recall condition*, in which participants are asked to fill out 25 lines of descriptions, even if they feel they are guessing. Meissner et al. utilise a content-based explanation for their results, suggesting that forced recall participants are more apt to generate misinformation, which then interferes with recognition. Finger and Pezdek made a similar finding when they performed a verbal overshadowing study with a condition that involved a detailed and elaborate verbalisation task (a cognitive interview). They found that those in the elaborate verbalisation condition produced more incorrect details, which in turn predicted poorer recognition performance. Both Meissner et al. and Finger and Pezdek's research suggest that it is the content of verbalisations that overshadows memory for an original perceptual stimulus.

Research on the relationship between verbalisation and visual imagery is also in accord with the content account. In a recent study by Brandimonte and Collina (2008 this issue), they asked participants to generate a label for images they has just viewed. Brandimonte and Collina found that re-presenting these labels prior to retrieval improved performance on the visual imagery task. These researchers also found a correlation between quality of the labels in describing the parts of the image (local elements) and performance on the imagery task. There was no statistically significant correlation between the quality of the labels in describing the whole of the image and imagery performance. Brandimonte and Collina conclude that these results provide evidence for recoding interference, noting that re-presentation of the labels most likely aided participants by reactivating the visual code generated early in the study, which may well have been marked by focus on certain local characteristics of the image.

Despite a good deal of evidence implicating content effects as the cause of verbal overshadowing, there are situations in which it is an unlikely explanation.

Content account limitations

To be completely confident with a content account, a strong connection should exist between the quality of verbalisations and recognition accuracy. With face recognition, participants who create accurate and complete verbalisations should be more likely to recognise the verbalised face later in the study. Many studies, however, have not shown this correlation between verbalisation quality and recognition accuracy (Brown & Lloyd-Jones, 2003; Kitagami, Sato, & Yoshikawa, 2002; Fallshore & Schooler, 1995; Schooler & Engstler-Schooler, 1990). Besides its failure to explain the lack of correlation between verbalisation quality and recognition accuracy, the content account fails to explain other findings emerging from verbal overshadowing studies.

A growing number of studies indicate that overshadowing is not limited to the verbalised stimulus. Dodson et al. (1997), for instance, presented participants with two dissimilar faces (a male and female). The researchers found that verbalising one face, either the male or female face, not only impaired memory for that face, but for the other face presented. Similarly, Westerman and Larsen (1997) found that when participants viewed a photograph of a car and of a face, describing the car impaired memory for both the car and the face. Considering that in both studies, content was not generated for the non-verbalised face, yet verbalisation impaired accuracy for the face, it is highly doubtful that the content effects can account for the findings of these studies.

Brown and Lloyd-Jones (2002, 2003) found a similar effect when they presented participants with 13 faces and only asked that they describe the 13th face presented. They found that recognition accuracy was impaired not only for the verbalised face, but for the 12 faces presented prior to the verbalised face. Seeing as the content account relies on the recoding of content into a suboptimal form, the finding that verbal overshadowing occurs for content that is not verbalised makes it unlikely that this account can fully explain verbal overshadowing. Further research with a related paradigm (Lloyd-Jones, Brown, & Clarke, 2006) has supported this finding, demonstrating that verbalisation following encoding impairs participants' ability to discriminate between faces seen at encoding and nonfaces. This effect generalises to faces participants had not seen, an effect that further supports the notion that verbalisation can impair memory for nonverbalised faces.

Finally, the design of Meissner et al.'s (2001) study demonstrating verbal overshadowing only under forced-recall conditions lends itself to multiple alternative interpretations. Meissner et al. did not take measures of confidence, and it seems likely that requiring participants to fill 25 lines with descriptions, quite a difficult task, might also force participants to question their ability to remember the target face. This psychological change may have also led to a shift in criterion, as participants' level of confidence decreased. The potential for such a shift is discussed later in more detail. Further, such a difficult task might have caused more interference simply because it was more difficult than the control or standard verbalisation task.

These findings do suggest that, at least in part, verbal overshadowing may not be due to the specific content of verbalisations, but the simple fact that verbalisation occurs.

A PROCESSING ACCOUNT

To deal with the lack of explanatory power provided by the content account in certain situations, researchers have proposed a processing based account for verbal overshadowing (see Schooler, 2002, for a review). Past research has shown that memory for faces, insight problem solving, and certain kinds of decision making rely on holistic/global processing, as opposed to item-by-item analytic/local processing. For example, there is strong consensus in the face recognition literature that such featural processing could deprive the perceiver of holistic information important for face recognition (Valentine, 1988). In other words, when it comes to face recognition it is the way the face looks as a whole that matters, and not as much what each individual feature looks like. Considering it is often the features of a face that are verbalisable, it has been suggested that verbalisation causes a shift from a holistic/global processing orientation towards a more analytic/local processing orientation that is detrimental to face recognition. Drawing upon transfer appropriate processing research, creation of an environment in which processing orientations differ in encoding and retrieval can impair memory. In this vein, memory may be impaired when, after encoding, verbalisation shifts processing towards analytic/local, which may carry over into retrieval.

Support for the processing account within face recognition

A transfer inappropriate processing shift explains several aspects of previous facial memory studies that the content account cannot explain. For instance, Macrae and Lewis (2001) found that effects similar to verbal overshadowing could be found through substituting verbalisation with a task designed to shift processing from global to local. These researchers performed a face recognition study using the robbery video initially utilised by Schooler and Engstler-Schooler (1990), but in lieu of a verbalisation condition, presented participants with Navon (1977) letters (i.e., small letters which comprise a larger composite letter, for instance, a large letter "s" made up of smaller "j"s) and asked them to report either the larger global letter or the smaller local letters. Participants in the control condition read from a text unrelated to the study. Macrae and Lewis found that globally oriented participants were better at identifying the robber than control participants, who were in turn more accurate than locally oriented participants. To summarise, these researchers found that it is possible to create an effect similar to verbal overshadowing by inducing a processing shift from global to local.

Further evidence can be drawn from research on memory for same- and other-race faces. Fallshore and Schooler (1995) found that verbalisation interferes with memory for same-race faces, but not with memory for other-race faces. Given that researchers have found that other-race faces tend to be processed featurally (Rhodes, Tan, Brake, & Taylor, 1989), a processing shift towards local/featural processing should not have an effect on other-race faces, which are already being processed in such a manner.

The processing shift account is also applicable to some findings discussed as evidence for the content account. The Melcher and Schooler (2004) study on the effect of training on verbal overshadowing, for instance, is explained well by the processing account. Verbal overshadowing among perceptually trained participants is explained by how they may have learned to encode the stimulus mushroom in a more holistic manner, but were shifted away from this processing orientation by the verbalisation task, creating a mismatch between encoding and verbalisation. Conceptually trained participants, however, may have learned to process the stimulus in a more featural manner, which did not clash with the featural processing orientation potentially caused by verbalisation. Research on the effect of expertise and training, it seems, is also explainable through the lens of the processing account.

The fragility of verbal overshadowing

Numerous studies have shown the verbal overshadowing effect to be somewhat fragile, in that it may weaken, disappear, or even reverse across trials (Fallshore & Schooler, 1995; Melcher & Schooler, 1996; Schooler, Ryan, & Reder, 1996). This finding (or nonfinding), which was not easily reconcilable with the content account, fits well with the processing account. Generation of content that interferes with a memory does not seem as if it would necessarily be sensitive to time. However, seeing as the default processing orientation for humans appears to be more global than local (Kimchi, 1992; Navon, 1977), a processing shift accounts well for the fragility of verbal overshadowing. For instance, if verbalisation does indeed shift processing towards a more local orientation, time or other peripheral events may easily shift processing back to a more global orientation, thus eliminating the verbal overshadowing effect. Such an effect was demonstrated by Finger and Pezdek (1999) when they replicated the verbal overshadowing phenomenon, but found that when a significant delay is inserted between verbalisation and recognition, the verbal overshadowing effect is attenuated. They termed this finding, a "release" from verbal overshadowing. Finger (2002) later replicated this release, replacing the delay by either having participants listen to music, or working on a maze. According the processing account, listening to music or working on a maze may have allowed participants to shift back towards global processing more quickly, thus explaining the absence of verbal overshadowing.

Support for the processing account outside of face recognition

A processing shift has also been implicated in several studies altogether unrelated to facial memory. Forster, Friedman, and Liberman (2004), for instance, found evidence for both transfer appropriate and inappropriate processing shifts in their investigation into the effect of temporal construal on creativity and insight problem solving. Temporal construal refers to the time distance perspective one takes when imagining an event, a variable Forster et al. manipulated by asking participants to either imagine their life tomorrow or a year from tomorrow. With regards to creativity, they hypothesised that imagining their life a year from tomorrow would cause a transfer appropriate processing shift, activating mental processes related to more abstract representations, which would carry over to creativity tasks later in the experiment (e.g., creating more abstract solutions to problems or better performance on insight problem-solving tasks). Indeed, participants taking a distant time perspective demonstrated more creativity and solved more insight problems than participants taking the near time perspective. Forster et al. also found evidence for a transfer inappropriate processing shift in that participants taking a distant time perspective showed impaired performance on logic puzzles from the analytic section of the GRE (i.e., Graduate Record Exam, an entrance examination for graduate school), as compared to participants taking a near time perspective and participants in the control condition. As a result of these findings, they postulate that taking a distant time perspective shifts processing away from concrete thinking that is beneficial for analytic logic problems, in other words a transfer inappropriate processing shift.

Forster et al.'s (2004) findings map well onto Schooler et al.'s (1993) research on the effects of verbalisation on insight problem solving. Much as Forster et al. found that a near time perspective was not beneficial for insight problems, Schooler et al. found that verbalisation impairs solving of insight problems. If verbalisation does indeed induce an analytic/local processing shift, such processing should interfere with solving of insight problems, which benefit from more creative and abstract thinking. Research on verbalisation and insight problem solving demonstrates this connection well and provides more evidence in favour of the processing account (Schooler et al., 1993).

The processing account also helps explain the effects of verbalisation on cultural groups that have different levels of dependence on holistic or global information. That East Asians are both more dependent on and more prone to utilise holistic reasoning holds for the great preponderance of cross-cultural research findings (see Nisbett, Peng, Choi, & Norenzayan, 2001, for a review). For instance, Matsuda and Nisbett (described in Nisbett et al., 2001) asked Japanese and American participants to view an animated scene of fishes in an ocean environment and later recall what they had seen. Japanese participants made more statements about the environment, whereas Americans were more concerned with a focal fish. Further, Japanese participants were impaired on a later memory task when the focal fish was shown on a different background, but Americans were not, an effect that suggests that the Japanese were more dependent on background and contextual cues. Abel and Hsu (1949) performed a similar study in which they showed Rorschach cards to Chinese Americans and European Americans. European Americans based their responses more on part of the card, while Chinese Americans based their response more on the *gestalt* of the card. To apply these cross-cultural findings to the current discussion, it seems fair to say that compared to Europeans, East Asians are chronically globally oriented.

If East Asians are indeed more dependent on global information, a manipulation designed to shift their processing orientation towards a more local or analytic orientation should influence their performance more than Europeans who are more accustomed to such a processing orientation. Kim (2002) found such an effect while studying the effect of talking aloud while problem solving cross culturally. Specifically, Kim asked East Asian and European Americans (all native speakers) to either verbalise aloud their thought process or not while solving reasoning problems. Kim found that East Asian Americans participants were impaired by thinking aloud, while European Americans were not. Together with Schooler et al.'s (1993) finding that verbalisation impairs the performance of European Americans on insight problem-solving tasks, it seems likely that verbalisation shifted processing towards a more local/analytic processing orientation that East Asians were not accustomed to using, thus impairing their problem-solving performance. The research presented thus far is highly consistent with the notion that verbalisation causes a transfer inappropriate processing shift, which is at least partially responsible for verbal overshadowing effects.

To summarise, research has uncovered a general or related set of processes characterised by local, featural, and concrete thought, and another set of processes characterised by global, configural, and abstract thought. These two distinct sets of procedures have been shown to be predictably activated by a focus on global or local characteristics of unrelated stimuli, time perspective, mood (Gasper & Clore, 2002), and possibly verbalisation. The processing account for verbal overshadowing helps explain several findings not accounted for by content effects, as well as generalising to areas of research beyond perceptual memory.

A CRITERION SHIFT ACCOUNT

More recently, Clare and Lewandowsky (2004) have proposed a verbal overshadowing account that draws on neither content nor processing. These researchers suggested that verbalisation causes a shift in criterion towards more conservative choosing, causing participants to be more likely to choose a target not present option if available. In other words, if a lineup provides the option of reporting that none of the options are correct, verbalisers will be more prone to choose this option than nonverbalisers. Verbalisation, therefore, raises participants' response criterion, making them less likely to pick anyone out of the lineup. If the target individual is indeed present in the lineup, verbalisers will exhibit impaired performance—the verbal overshadowing effect.

Clare and Lewandowsky (2004) present strong evidence for the criterion shift account through two major findings. In a face recognition experiment, they find that when using a target absent lineup, verbalisers actually show improved accuracy due to declining to choose one of the options. A target present lineup, however, replicated the standard verbal overshadowing finding, with verbalisers showing poorer performance. Further, Clare and Lewandowsky find that when using a forced-choice paradigm (i.e., the absence of a target not present choice), they find no verbal overshadowing effect. Forcing participants to choose a face out of a lineup eliminates a criterion shift towards more conservative decision making, and so no verbal overshadowing in this condition is predicted by the criterion shift account.

In terms of comparison to prior theories, the criterion account seems to share more similarities with the process account, as opposed to the content account. Both the criterion and processing accounts seem to represent a shift in thinking, with a processing account dealing with global to local processing and a criterion dealing with a shift from more liberal to conservative criteria. Both processing and criterion accounts deal with the *way* one is thinking, while content deals with precisely *what* one is thinking. Regardless, the criterion shift account represents a unique approach for studying verbal overshadowing.

Although the criterion shift account provides an interesting new explanation for verbal overshadowing, as well as due focus on the oft-ignored effects the intricacies of the recognition task, a criterion shift does not readily account for several previous findings. For instance, despite Clare and Lewandowsky's (2004) demonstrated lack of verbal overshadowing with a forced-choice paradigm, other researchers have shown verbal overshadowing with this condition (e.g., Fallshore & Schooler, 1995; Ryan & Schooler, 1998). Furthermore, Brown and Lloyd-Jones' (2002, 2003) paradigm for studying verbal overshadowing allows for calculation of both signal detection and response criterion. Their results indicate that verbal overshadowing is caused by signal detection, and not response criterion. Still, criterion effects are quite important to a nuanced understanding of verbal overshadowing and they should certainly be considered in any sort of unified account.

RECONCILING THE ALTERNATIVE ACCOUNTS OF VERBAL OVERSHADOWING

As can be seen from the previous review, significant support exists for all three of the leading accounts of verbal overshadowing. The question thus arises as to how the three accounts can be reconciled. Ultimately it seems unlikely that a single account will be able to accommodate all of the extant verbal overshadowing findings. Indeed there are certain findings that seem inherently inexplicable with in the context of certain accounts. For example, the content account seems inherently incapable of explaining the finding that describing one face interferes with recognition of nonverbalised faces. Similarly, the criterion shift account has difficulty accounting for situations in which verbal overshadowing interferes with recognition performance even when a "not present" option is not included. And the transfer inappropriate processing account has difficulty explaining studies in which verbalisation during encoding impairs subsequent imagery performance (e.g., Brandimonte et al., 1992a, 1992b, 1992c) since images are initially encoded in a verbal manner, and thus verbalisation would not be expected to produce a conflict between the processing engaged in at encoding and test

Although there are some results which seem inherently challenging to account for with one or another perspective, there are a host of other findings which in principle might be accounted for by a single mechanism. As already noted, many key results that have been characterised as consistent with a content account can theoretically be accounted for by a processing account. The differential effects of verbalisation as a function of verbal expertise can be explained as occurring because a shift to verbal processing is not detrimental if verbal skills are sufficient (Schooler, Fiore, & Brandimonte, 1997). Similarly, the sometimes observed relationship between quality of verbal description and recognition performance can be accounted for by assuming that the impact of a shift to verbal processing will depend on the quality of the verbal representation that participants possess. Finally, the fact that extensive verbalisation produces the largest verbal overshadowing effect (Meissner et al., 2001) can be accounted for by assuming that the more extensive the verbalisation the more likely a processing shift is to occur. A processing shift account might also be able accommodate the occurrence of criterion shift if, as seems quite plausible, one of the consequences of a shift from visual to verbal processing is a more conservative criterion in recognising visual stimuli.

While it remains to be determined just how many of the verbal overshadowing findings can be explained by a single account, ultimately we think it quite likely that when the dust settles, verbal overshadowing will be seen to be due to different mechanisms in different situations (see Sporer, Meissner, & Schooler, 2006, for a similar argument). Although it is premature to speculate about what precise conditions should determine when one account versus another account is most viable, we can outline a line of investigation that should ultimately resolve this question. Specifically, the following set of criteria may reasonably be used to determine when each of three accounts apply.

Evidence supporting a content account. There are a variety of sources of evidence that could provide additional support for a content account. For example, if disruptive effects of verbalisation result from a reliance on specific inaccurately verbalised details, then it stands to reason that verbalisation should influence verbalised items more than nonverbalised items. To our knowledge no study has yet demonstrated a unique impact of verbalisation on verbalised items relative to nonverbalised ones; however, the majority of verbal overshadowing studies have not directly compared the two types of items. If future verbal overshadowing studies were to routinely include both verbalised and nonverbalised recognition items, it would become much easier to determine the precise situations in which content account is particularly likely to apply.

Although demonstrations of unique effects of verbalisation on verbalised versus nonverbalised stimuli provide the most direct evidence for content accounts, other sources of evidence also can support content accounts. For example, while there are ways of accommodating a relationship between description quality and accuracy within a processing account, a consistent and strong relationships between verbal descriptions and memory performance is most parsimoniously accounted for by the view that memory is being influenced by the verbal content of the description.

Evidence supporting a processing account. Several sources of evidence help to support the existence of processing shifts. As already noted, the demonstrations of the generalisability of verbalisation to nonverbalised stimuli implicate a processing shift. Processing shifts can also be assessed by examining the impact of processing manipulations. For example, if a nonverbal processing manipulation introduced at or immediately prior to retrieval attenuates the negative effects of verbalisation then this supports a role of processing shift (Finger & Pezdek, 1999). Alternatively, if the encouragement of verbal processing at test attenuates verbal overshadowing this argues against a processing shift account (Brandimonte & Collina, 2008 this issue)

Strikingly, although there is considerable evidence that is consistent with a processing account, surprisingly little research has attempted to directly establish the existence and nature of the hypothesised processing shift. If indeed verbalisation induces a processing shift, then this shift should be directly measurable by examining the concomitant impact of verbalisation on measures associated with the hypothesised shift. For example, if, as has been frequently speculated, verbalisation produces a shift from global to local processing, then it should be found that verbalisation shifts people's likelihood of focusing on the local versus global aspects of item arrays that can be viewed in either context (Chin & Schooler, 2006). For example, when given a Navon letter, verbalisation subjects should be more likely than controls to focus on the small letters relative to the large ones. Similarly, if verbalisation causes a shift in right versus left hemisphere processing (e.g., Schooler, 2002), this should be reflected by changes in hemispheric activation. By consistently including in verbal overshadowing studies measures that will assess hypothesised shifts in processing, it should be possible to establish both the extent of the processing shift account, as well as more precisely specify the nature of such a shift.

Evidence supportive of a criterion shift. Support for a criterion shift account would be revealed by conducting studies that either enable the separate determination of criterion and discrimination measures, and/or omitting not present options from experiments. If verbal overshadowing effects are found to be exclusively associated with criterion effects, this would (obviously) support criterion shift accounts. If verbal overshadowing effects are observed in contexts in which a not present option is omitted, then clearly criterion shift accounts are not tenable. Importantly, assessment of criterion shifts should be done concurrently with assessments of global processing shifts. This will enable us to establish whether criterion shifts, when observed, are a consequence of general global changes in processing, or some other yet to be established factor that could cause verbalisation to encourage participants to adopt a more stringent response criterion.

If the field is systematic in taking into account these considerations when conducting verbal overshadowing studies, it seems likely that we will soon become clearer about which mechanisms are operating under which conditions. And perhaps with time, we will be able to use this understanding to derive more general principles for predicting when verbalisation will cause a specific reliance on inaccurate verbalised details, a global shift in cognitive processing, or simply a criterion shift. We might even come to understand why verbal overshadowing, though observed on so many occasions and in so many contexts, continues to be such a fragile phenomenon.

REFERENCES

Abel, T. M., & Hsu, F. F. K. (1949). Chinese personality revealed by the Rorschach. *Rorschach Research Exchange, 13*, 285–301.

Brandimonte, M. A., & Collina, S. (2008). Verbal overshadowing in visual imagery is due to recoding interference. *European Journal of Cognitive Psychology, 20*, 612–631.

Brandimonte, M. A., & Gerbino, W. (1993). Mental image reversal and verbal recoding: When ducks become rabbits. *Memory and Cognition, 21*, 23–33.

Brandimonte, M. A., Hitch, G. J., & Bishop, D. V. M. (1992a). Influence of short-term memory codes on visual image processing: Evidence from image transformation tasks. *Journal of Experimental Psychology: Learning, Memory and Cognition, 18*, 157–165.

Brandimonte, M. A., Hitch, G. J., & Bishop, D. V. M. (1992b). Manipulation of visual mental images in children and adults. *Journal of Experimental Child Psychology, 53*, 300–312.

Brandimonte, M. A., Hitch, G. J., & Bishop, D. V. M. (1992c). Verbal recoding of visual stimuli impairs mental image transformations. *Memory and Cognition, 20*, 449–455.

Brandimonte, M. A., Schooler, J. W., & Gabbino, P. (1997). Attenuating verbal overshadowing through visual retrieval cues. *Journal of Experimental Psychology: Learning, Memory and Cognition, 23*, 915–931.

Brown, C., & Lloyd-Jones, T. J. (2002). Verbal overshadowing in a multiple face presentation paradigm: Effects of description instruction. *Applied Cognitive Psychology, 16*, 855–873.

Brown, C., & Lloyd-Jones, T. J. (2003). Verbal overshadowing of multiple faces and car recognition: Effects of within- versus across-category verbal descriptions. *Applied Cognitive Psychology, 17*, 183–201.

Brown, C., & Lloyd-Jones, T. J. (2005). Verbal facilitation of face recognition. *Memory and Cognition, 33*, 1442–1456.

Chin, J. M. & Schooler, J. W. (2006, January). *Verbal overshadowing and processing orientation: Does what we say affect how we think?* Poster session presented at the annual meeting of the Society for Personality and Social Psychology, Palm Springs.

Clare, J., & Lewandowsky, S. (2004). Verbalizing facial memory: Criterion effects in verbal overshadowing. *Journal of Experimental Psychology, 30*, 739–755.

Dodson, C. S., Johnson, M. D., & Schooler, J. W. (1997). The verbal overshadowing effect: Why descriptions impair face recognition. *Memory and Cognition, 25*, 129–139.

Fallshore, M., & Schooler, J. W. (1995). The verbal vulnerability of perceptual expertise. *Journal of Experimental Psychology: Learning, Memory and Cognition, 21*, 1608–1623.

Finger, K. (2002). Mazes and music: Using perceptual processing to release verbal overshadowing. *Applied Cognitive Psychology, 16*, 887–896.

Finger, K., & Pezdek, K. (1999). The effect of the cognitive interview on face identification accuracy: Release from verbal overshadowing. *Journal of Applied Psychology, 84*, 340–348.

Forster, J., Friedman, R., & Liberman, N. (2004). Temporal construal effects on abstract and concrete thinking: Consequences for insight and creative cognition. *Journal of Personality and Social Psychology, 88*, 263–275.

Gasper, K., & Clore, G. L. (2002). Attending to the big picture: Mood and global versus local processing of visual information. *Psychological Science, 13*, 34–40.

Hitch, G. J., Brandimonte, M. A., & Walker, P. (1995). Two types of representation in visual memory: Evidence from the effects of stimulus contrast in image combination. *Memory and Cognition, 23*, 147–154.

Houser, T. Fiore, S. M. & Schooler, J. W. (1997). *Verbal overshadowing of music memory: What happens when you describe that tune?* Unpublished manuscript.

Hunt, E., & Agnoli, F. (1991). The Whorfian hypothesis: A cognitive psychology perspective. *Psychological Review, 98*, 377–389.

Kim, H. S. (2002). We talk, therefore we think? A cultural analysis of the effect of talking on thinking. *Journal of Personality and Social Psychology, 83*, 828–842.

Kimchi, R. (1992). Primacy of wholistic processing and global/local paradigm: A critical review. *Psychological Bulletin, 112*, 24–38.

Kitagami, S., Sato, W., & Yoshikawa, S. (2002). The influence of test-set similarity in verbal overshadowing. *Applied Cognitive Psychology, 16*, 963–972.

Lane, S. M., & Schooler, J. W. (2004). Skimming the surface verbal overshadowing of analogical retrieval. *Psychological Science, 15*, 715–719.

Lloyd-Jones, T. J., Brown, C., & Clarke, S. (2006). Verbal overshadowing of perceptual discrimination. *Psychonomic Bulletin and Review, 13*, 269–274.

Lovett, S. B. Small, M. Y. & Engstrom, S. A. (1992, November). *The verbal overshadowing effect: Now you see it, now you don't.* Paper presented at the annual meeting of the Psychonomic Society, St Louis, MO.

Macrae, C. N., & Lewis, H. L. (2001). Do I know you? Processing orientation and face recognition. *Psychological Science, 13*, 194–196.

Meissner, C. A., & Brigham, J. C. (2001). A meta-analysis of the verbal overshadowing effect in face identification. *Applied Cognitive Psychology, 15*, 603–616.

Meissner, C. A., Brigham, J. C., & Kelley (2001). The influence of retrieval processes in verbal overshadowing. *Memory and Cognition, 29*, 176–186.

Meissner, C. M., Sporer, S., & Schooler, J. W. (2006). Person description as eyewitness evidence. In D. Ross, M. Toglia, J. D. Read, & R. C. Lindsay (Eds.), *Handbook of eyewitness psychology* (pp. 3–34). Chichester, UK: Wiley.

Melcher, J. M., & Schooler, J. W. (1996). The misremembrance of wines past: Verbal and perceptual expertise differentially mediate verbal overshadowing of taste memory. *Journal of Memory and Language, 35*, 231–245.

Melcher, J. M., & Schooler, J. W. (2004). Perceptual and conceptual training mediate the verbal overshadowing effect in an unfamiliar domain. *Memory and Cognition, 32*, 618–631.

Navon, D. (1977). Forest before trees: The precedence of global features in visual perception. *Cognitive Psychology, 9*, 353–383.

Nisbett, R. E., Peng, K., Choi, I., & Norenzayan, A. (2001). Culture and systems of thought: Holistic versus analytic cognition. *Psychological Review, 108*, 291–310.

Pelizzon, L., Brandimonte, M. A., & Favretto, A. (1999). Imagery and recognition: Dissociable measures of memory? *European Journal of Cognitive Psychology, 3*, 429–443.

Pelizzon, L., Brandimonte, M. A., & Luccio, R. (2002). The role of visual, spatial, and temporal cues in attenuating verbal overshadowing. *Applied Cognitive Psychology, 16*, 947–961.

Perfect, T. J., Hunt, L. J., & Harris, C. M. (2002). Verbal overshadowing in voice recognition. *Applied Cognitive Psychology, 16*, 973–980.

Rhodes, G., Tan, S., Brake, S., & Taylor, K. (1989). Expertise and configural coding in face recognition. *British Journal of Psychology, 80*, 313–331.

Ryan, S. R., & Schooler, J. W. (1998). Whom do words hurt? Individual differences in susceptibility to verbal overshadowing. *Applied Cognitive Psychology, 12*, S105–S125.

Schooler, J. W. (2002). Verbalization produces a transfer inappropriate processing shift. *Applied Cognitive Psychology, 16*, 989–997.

Schooler, J. W., & Engstler-Schooler, T. Y. (1990). Verbal overshadowing of visual memories: Some things are better left unsaid. *Cognitive Psychology, 22*, 36–71.

Schooler, J. W., Fiore, S. M., & Brandimonte, M. A. (1997). At a loss from words: Verbal overshadowing of perceptual memories. In D. L. Medin (Ed.), *Advances in research and theory: Vol. 37. The psychology of learning and motivation* (pp. 291–340). San Diego, CA: Academic Press.

Schooler, J. W., Foster, R. A., & Loftus, E. F. (1988). Some deleterious consequences of the act of recollection. *Memory and Cognition, 16*, 242–251.

Schooler, J. W., Ohlsson, S., & Brooks, K. (1993). Thoughts beyond words: When language overshadows insight. *Journal of Experimental Psychology: General, 122*, 166–183.

Schooler, J. W., Ryan, R. S., & Reder, L. M. (1996). The costs and benefits of verbally rehearsing memory for faces. In D. Herrmann, M. K. Johnson, C. McEvoy, C. Hertzog, & P. Hertel (Eds.), *Basic and applied memory: New findings* (pp. 51–65). Hillsdale, NJ: Lawrence Erlbaum Associates, Inc.

Sieck, W. R., Quinn, C. N., & Schooler, J. W. (1999). Justification effects on the judgment of analogy. *Memory and Cognition, 27*, 844–855.

Sporer, S. L. (1989). Verbal and visual processes in person identification. In H. Wegener, F. Lösel, & J. Haisch (Eds.), *Criminal behavior and the criminal justice system* (pp. 303–324). New York/ Berlin: Springer.

Valentine, T. (1988). Upside-down faces: A review of the effect of inversion up face recognition. *British Journal of Psychology, 79*, 471–491.

Walker, P., Hitch, G. J., Dewhurst, S., Whiteley, H. E., & Brandimonte, M. A. (1997). The representation of non-structural information in visual memory: Evidence from image combination. *Memory and Cognition, 25*, 484–491.

Watson, J. B. (1924). The place of kinesthetic, visceral and laryngeal organization in thinking. *Psychological Review, 31*, 339–347.

Westerman, D. L., & Larsen, J. D. (1997). Verbal overshadowing effect: Evidence for a general shift in processing. *American Journal of Psychology, 110*, 417–428.

Whorf, B. L. (1956). *Language, thought, and reality; selected writings.* Cambridge, MA: Technology Press of Massachusetts Institute of Technology.

Wilson, T. D., & Schooler, J. W. (1991). Thinking too much: Introspection can reduce the quality of preferences and decisions. *Journal of Personality and Social Psychology, 60*, 181–192.

Yu, C. J., & Geiselman, R. E. (1993). Effects of constructing identi-kit composites on photospread identification performance. *Criminal Justice and Behavior, 20*, 280–292.

EUROPEAN JOURNAL OF COGNITIVE PSYCHOLOGY
2008, 20 (3), 414–455

A theoretical review and meta-analysis of the description-identification relationship in memory for faces

Christian A. Meissner
University of Texas at El Paso, TX, USA

Siegfried L. Sporer
University of Giessen, Giessen, Germany

Kyle J. Susa
University of Texas at El Paso, TX, USA

Verbal descriptions can sometimes impair (or "overshadow") and other times facilitate subsequent attempts at perceptual identification of faces; however, understanding the relationship between these two tasks and the theoretical mechanisms that bridge this relationship has often proven difficult. Furthermore, studies that have attempted to assess the description-identification relationship have varied considerably in demonstrating significant and null results, often across a variety of paradigms and design parameters. In the present paper we review the relevant literatures and theoretical positions proposed to explain this relationship, and we present the first meta-analysis of this effect across 33 research papers and a total of 4278 participants. Our results suggest that there does appear to be a small, but significant, relationship between the description measures of accuracy, number of incorrect descriptors, and congruence with that of subsequent identification accuracy. Furthermore, certain conditions were found to strengthen the magnitude of this relationship, including the use of face recognition versus eyewitness identification paradigms and the length of delays between relevant tasks. We discuss both the theoretical and practical implications of this relationship for understanding memory for faces.

In 1972, the United States Supreme Court addressed the admissibility of eyewitness identification obtained under suggestive circumstances in *Neil v. Biggers*. Biggers, the defendant, was convicted of rape based primarily upon his identification by the victim who testified that she had "no doubt" that Biggers was the assailant. Shortly after the crime, the victim had provided

Correspondence should be addressed to Christian A. Meissner, Department of Psychology, University of Texas at El Paso, El Paso, TX 79968,USA. E-mail: cmeissner@utep.edu

The authors would like to thank Jasmine Koestler for her assistance with coding the data.

http://www.psypress.com/ecp DOI: 10.1080/09541440701728581

police with a description of the assailant and was administered several showups and lineups of individuals who matched her description. She was not able to identify anyone as the assailant. Seven months later, the police conducted another showup where the officers asked Biggers to say "shut up or I will kill you" to the victim. At this point the victim immediately identified Biggers as the assailant.

Lower Courts suppressed the victim's identification of the defendant, ruling that the identification process used by police was overly suggestive. Thereafter, the US Supreme Court was presented with the issue of determining whether or not the victim's identification of Biggers was reliable. In reversing the decisions of the lower Courts, the Court listed five factors that should be taken into account when evaluating the reliability of an identification, including: (1) the witness's opportunity to view the criminal during the crime; (2) the length of time between the crime and the subsequent identification; (3) the level of certainty demonstrated by the witness at the identification; (4) the witness's degree of attention directed toward the event/perpetrator; and (5) the (apparent) accuracy of the witness's prior description of the criminal. In the *Neil v. Biggers* case, the Court's emphasis appeared to shift from a concern with suggestivity to an overriding concern with the reliability of the identification, even if it was obtained under suggestive circumstances. At the time of this decision, little published scientific research on eyewitness memory existed. The Court could, therefore, make only "educated guesses" about the factors that might influence eyewitness accuracy; however, scientific research conducted over the past three decades has permitted a systematic evaluation of the validity of the five criteria enumerated by the Court.

In short, the Court's assumptions regarding the reliability of eyewitness testimony appear to have been overly simplistic. While research findings indicate that the first two of the five *Neil v. Biggers* factors are clearly related to accuracy in the way that the Court assumed (namely, the opportunity to view and the retention interval between the event and identification; for a review, see Tredoux, Meissner, Malpass, & Zimmerman, 2004; Wells & Olson, 2003), research on the remaining factors present a much more complex interpretation of the relationships assumed by the Court. For example, despite the fact that jurors rely quite heavily on the degree of confidence expressed by a witness (Brewer & Burke, 2002), meta-analyses conducted on the confidence-accuracy relationship suggest only a weak to medium correlation (Bothwell, Deffenbacher, & Brigham, 1987; Sporer, Penrod, Read, & Cutler, 1995), though this relationship is generally higher for choosers than for nonchoosers (Sporer et al., 1995), and has occasionally been found to be quite high under certain conditions (e.g., Lindsay, Read, & Sharma, 1998). We should emphasise, however, that the confidence-accuracy relationship mentioned here only holds for the original statement at the time of the identification, not for any later expression of confidence (e.g., in the courtroom) which is likely to be contaminated by feedback and other factors (see Wells & Olson, 2003). With regard to the attentiveness of the witness (the Court's fourth factor), research has found that witnesses who exude a moderate degree of attention to a situation are likely to be more accurate when compared to those who did not pay attention, or to those who were distracted because they were in a stressful crime situation (Deffenbacher, 1983). However, even if a witness were trying to be attentive, high fear or stress (induced, possibly, by the presence of a weapon) is likely to interfere with memory and impair the accuracy of subsequent identifications (Deffenbacher, Bornstein, Penrod, & McGorty, 2004).

The current paper provides the first empirical review of the US Supreme Court's fifth factor—namely, the relationship between the accuracy of the description provided by a witness and their subsequent identification of the perpetrator. Was the Court correct in assuming a relationship between verbal description and perceptual identification processes in memory for faces? Unfortunately, the available research presents a rather murky picture of this relationship, with correlational studies suggesting a wide variety of moderately strong to nonsignificant findings. Furthermore, studies investigating the influence of generating a verbal description on subsequent identification have shown that the former process can *impair* later attempts at identification (Schooler & Engstler-Schooler, 1990), while in contrast a handful of studies have shown that the act of describing can *enhance* later identification (Brown & Lloyd-Jones, 2005, 2006; Davids, Sporer, & McQuiston-Surrett, 2006; Meissner, Brigham, & Kelley, 2001).

In this paper we examine the variability of the description-identification relationship across studies in several ways. First, we provide a theoretical literature review of the relationship, including studies on the verbal overshadowing and verbal facilitation effects in face identification. Second, we present the first meta-analysis of studies that have estimated the relationship between description performance and identification accuracy on memory for faces. In this meta-analysis we consider a number of different performance measures associated with verbal descriptions, and examine the potential for moderator variables that might explain some of the variability across studies. In closing, we return to a theoretical framework that might assist in understanding the description-identification relationship based upon the findings of the meta-analysis, and discuss the practical implications of this relationship for eyewitness evidence.

VERBAL OVERSHADOWING VERSUS VERBAL FACILITATION EFFECTS IN FACE IDENTIFICATION

The ability of an eyewitness to verbally translate a perceptual memory is an important component of eyewitness evidence in our legal system. In fact, at numerous stages throughout the justice process an eyewitness may be asked to describe what s/he witnessed at the crime scene, and most importantly his/her perception of the culprit. It seems intuitive that an eyewitness who is capable of giving a verbal description of a perpetrator's face would also have an accurate recollection of their facial features, and subsequently be capable of identifying the perpetrator from a photo array. Research has shown, however, that verbal descriptions can sometimes interfere with subsequent attempts at perceptual identification (verbal overshadowing) and at other times enhance attempts at perceptual identification (verbal facilitation).

Referred to as *verbal overshadowing*, Schooler and Engstler-Schooler (1990) first demonstrated in a series of studies that providing a verbal description of another person's face can significantly impair our ability to recognise that face in a subsequent lineup identification task. In the years since Schooler and Engstler-Schooler's original demonstration of the verbal overshadowing phenomenon, a number of studies have replicated these results within the facial memory paradigm (Dodson, Johnson, & Schooler, 1997; Fallshore & Schooler, 1995; Ryan & Schooler, 1998; Schooler, Ryan & Reder, 1996; Sporer, 1989). Furthermore, researchers have shown the overshadowing phenomenon to occur in other domains involving "difficult to describe" perceptual experiences, including wine tasting (Melcher & Schooler, 1996), visual forms (Brandimonte, Hitch, & Bishop, 1992), and Euclidean distance estimations (Fiore & Schooler, 2002). While the phenomenon has been replicated many times within the facial memory domain, notable failures to replicate have also occurred (Davids et al., 2006; Lovett, Small, & Engstrom, 1992; Meissner et al., 2001; Sauerland, Holub, & Sporer, 2008 this issue; Yu & Geiselman, 1993).

As a manner in which to examine this variability across studies, Meissner and Brigham (2001a) conducted a meta-analysis of the verbal overshadowing effect in face identification studies. The authors located 15 research papers comprising 29 tests of the overshadowing hypothesis and more than 2000 participants. Across studies, Meissner and Brigham observed a small, yet significant, negative effect of verbalisation on subsequent identification. Taken together, participants who were asked to describe the target face were 1.27 times more likely to *misidentify* the target than participants who did not generate a verbal description. A handful of studies were excluded from Meissner and Brigham's meta-analysis due to failures in following the constraints of the typical overshadowing paradigm, including the use of multiple target faces or alternative identification procedures. The authors analysed these studies separately and found something rather interesting—namely, a *verbal facilitation* effect in which participants who generated a description (or series of descriptions across multiple faces) were 1.38 times more likely to *correctly identify* the target faces when compared with no-description control participants.

The facilitating effects of verbalisation are not novel; in fact, a number of published studies have demonstrated improvements in face identification following generation of a verbal description (Brown & Lloyd-Jones, 2005, 2006; Chance & Goldstein, 1976; Davids et al., 2006; Itoh, 2005; Mauldin & Laughery, 1981; McKelvie, 1976; Meissner, 2002; Meissner et al., 2001; Read, 1979; Wogalter, 1991, 1996). In a recent series of studies, Brown and Lloyd-Jones (2005) replicated this verbal facilitation using a face recognition paradigm in which participants viewed and, in some cases described, a series of faces. Across four experiments, Brown and Lloyd-Jones demonstrated that participants who described the faces performed significantly better when later attempting to perceptually discriminate between previously viewed and novel faces at test. These facilitating effects occurred regardless of the type of description task participants were provided (e.g., similarities vs. differences; holistic vs. featural), and could be localised to faces that had been described previously.

How might we understand the cognitive mechanisms that can lead to verbal overshadowing versus facilitation effects in memory for faces? A review of the literature suggests that several moderator variables may distinguish these studies. First, the majority of verbal facilitation studies have typically employed face recognition or multiple face paradigms, whereas studies in the classic overshadowing literature have involved perception and verbalisation of a single target face. Interestingly, studies within the overshadowing paradigm that have employed multiple study–test trials have found that the interfering effects of description occur only on the first trial, while subsequent trials generally demonstrate null effects of verbalisation (e.g., Fallshore & Schooler, 1995; see Schooler et al., 1996, for a discussion of this "trial effect"). In addition to the multiple face distinction, studies of verbal facilitation versus overshadowing also vary in the degree of delay between encoding and description of the target face, with studies using multiple face paradigms generally requesting a verbal description immediately following presentation of the target face (in the context of the encoding task) and those in the single face paradigms generally providing a delay prior to the description task.

A second moderator variable that appears to distinguish these studies involves the extent to which participants are provided an opportunity to generate a verbal description of each target face. For example, Schooler and Engstler-Schooler (1990) had participants generate a detailed verbal description of the target face for 5 min prior to attempting identification, and subsequent studies employing this paradigm have used similar procedures. In contrast, studies that have demonstrated verbal facilitation effects often vary in the type of description task they employed and the length of the description interval. In the studies conducted by Brown and Lloyd-Jones (2005, 2006), for example, participants were provided 15 s to generate a description of each face prior to the presentation of a subsequent face. A study by Meissner et al. (2001) also examined the influence of the description task by directly manipulating participants' criterion of responding on the description task via an instructional manipulation. The authors' found that participants encouraged to provide lengthy and detailed descriptions (loose criterion) performed more poorly on the identification task when compared with those given a free recall instruction and those that were instructed to provide very brief, but precise, descriptions (strict criterion). Interestingly, participants in the strict criterion condition actually demonstrated a verbal facilitation effect when contrasted with the no-description control condition.

Finally, it is noteworthy that a handful of studies have observed verbal facilitation effects following lengthy delays (2 or more days) between the description and identification tasks (e.g., Davids et al., 2006; Itoh, 2005), while other studies have noted attenuation of the verbal overshadowing effect following significant delays (e.g., Finger & Pezdek, 1999; see Meissner & Brigham, 2001a). We can only speculate why such a reversal of the verbal overshadowing effect may occur after such a long delay. Perhaps, when the original memory trace has faded remembering some aspect of a face may serve as an effective retrieval cue, even though this cue is only available in verbal form (see Sporer, 2007). This reasoning is akin to the outshining hypothesis, according to which context reinstatement cues at testing are more likely to be effective when the memory trace is degraded (but not when the memory is still strong), thus "outshining" the effect of other retrieval cues (Cutler, Penrod, & Martens, 1987; Smith, 1988). Alternatively, the description task could serve to preserve the memory trace over the extended delay when compared with a no-description control condition—a phenomenon consistent with the notion of "output encoding" (Humphreys & Bowyer, 1980; see also Meissner & Brigham, 2001a).

Based upon studies largely in the verbal overshadowing domain, several theoretical accounts have been proposed to explain the cognitive mechanisms leading to verbal overshadowing versus facilitation. First, in their original demonstration of the overshadowing effect, Schooler and Engstler-Schooler (1990) proposed that the product of verbal description may inappropriately "recode" participants' representation of the target face and thereby interfere with subsequent attempts at identification. This *retrieval-based interference* explanation is quite consistent with the influence of retrieval processes on memory across a range of studies in the cognitive literature, including the role of *output encoding* in basic memory studies of the recognition-recall relationship (Humphreys & Bowyer, 1980). As discussed in a review by Roediger and Guynn (1996), variation in individuals' initial retrieval processes can significantly influence subsequent attempts at recollection, including both positive effects that aid subsequent recollection and negative effects that result in forgetting, interference, or even false recollections. In their research on the instructional bias effect, Meissner and colleagues (Meissner, 2002; Meissner et al., 2001) explored whether the product of participants' verbal description might mediate the overshadowing versus facilitation effects observed. Prior research has provided mixed support for the relationship between the contents of verbal descriptions and participants' identification performance; however, the instructional manipulation employed by Meissner and colleagues provided a unique opportunity to examine this relationship in the absence of *range restrictions* that were often observed in prior studies. Across their studies, the authors found a consistent relationship between identification performance and both description accuracy and the frequency of inaccurate details (see also Finger & Pezdek, 1999, for similar results). However, other studies have not found such a description-identification relationship (Brown & Lloyd-Jones, 2002; Fallshore & Schooler 1995; Kitagami, Sato, & Yoshikawa, 2002; Schooler & Engstler-Schooler, 1990), and this has served as a major source of scepticism for a retrieval-based account.

Although a retrieval-based account provides a viable explanation for verbal overshadowing when a relationship exists between description accuracy and identification performance, it does little to explain why verbal overshadowing can occur when such a relationship does not exist. Furthermore, a retrieval-based processing account has difficulty explaining overshadowing effects that result from verbalisation of a different stimulus from that of the target (Brown & Lloyd-Jones, 2003; Dodson et al., 1997; Westerman & Larsen, 1997). As a result of these and other findings, Schooler and colleagues (Schooler, 2002; Schooler, Fiore, & Brandimonte, 1997) have suggested that verbal overshadowing effects may be the result of separable cognitive processes mediating attempts at verbal description and perceptual identification. Referred to as *transfer inappropriate processing*, this theory posits that verbal descriptions instantiate a *featural* process orientation that carries over to the perceptual identification task and thereby conflicts with the *configural* or *holistic* process orientation that was likely employed at encoding. As a result, the processing orientation at retrieval fails to match that used at encoding and thereby disrupts attempts at identification (or more likely, undermines any potential facilitation that might be gained by matching processes; e.g., encoding specificity or transfer appropriate processing). This notion of processing differences is quite consistent with a variety of models that have proposed separable memory systems responsible for verbal vs. visual processing (e.g., Tulving, 1985; Tulving & Schacter, 1990) and those suggesting independent coding of verbal versus visual information in the cognitive system (Paivio, 1971; Woodhead & Baddeley, 1981).

Debate regarding the mechanisms underlying the effects of verbal description on face recognition has also recently seen the addition of a third perspective suggesting that verbalisation rather simply induces a *criterion shift*—that is, individuals who provide a description (regardless of its accuracy) are subsequently less likely to make a positive identification (regardless of accuracy) when compared with no-description control participants. In testing this hypothesis, Clare and Lewandowsky (2004) found that verbal description of a previously presented face impaired performance on target-present lineups only when participants were provided a "not present" option. Moreover, on target-absent lineups, verbalisation actually improved performance as the conservative shift led to fewer false identifications. Although a study by Sauerland and colleagues (2008 this issue) has recently confirmed this result, other studies have been less successful in replicating these findings. For example, researchers have found verbal overshadowing effects with paradigms that did not include a "not present" option (e.g., Fallshore & Schooler, 1995) and with the use of target-absent lineups (e.g., Meissner, 2002). In addition, use of a recognition paradigm introduced by Brown and Lloyd-Jones (2002, 2003) demonstrated verbal overshadowing (and verbal facilitation effects, see Brown & Lloyd-Jones, 2005, 2006) on signal detection measures of discrimination, but not on measures of response criterion.

Finally, researchers that have focused on verbal facilitation effects have often employed a *levels of processing* framework (Craik & Lockhart, 1972) to suggest that deeper encoding strategies (e.g., trait judgements regarding a target face) should facilitate later memory performance when compared with more shallow encoding strategies (e.g., categorical judgements of target race or gender) (however, see Sporer, 1991). Generally speaking, researchers have distinguished between those deeper processing strategies involving greater quantity/quality of visual processing (e.g., Wells & Hryciw, 1984; Winograd, 1981) and those involving greater semantic encoding (e.g., Anderson & Reder, 1979). While a recent study by Brown and Lloyd-Jones (2006) favours the semantic encoding alternative, further studies examining this approach appear warranted. Importantly, however, one must consider that studies invoking this approach have generally involved the use of multiple faces at encoding and have generally requested descriptions immediately following presentation of a target face (and preceding the presentation of a subsequent target face). Thus, descriptions are elicited as part of the encoding task in such studies rather than as a distinct memory phase of the experiment (as in most verbal overshadowing studies). One way in which to reconcile this distinction across studies may be to consider the extent to which the product of the description task might influence subsequent identification performance. For example, consistent with both the notion of retrieval-based processing (Meissner et al., 2001) and output encoding (Humphreys & Bowyer, 1980), descriptions with greater richness and accuracy may be more likely to facilitate subsequent memory performance when compared with those that lack detail or include inaccurate aspects.

Taken together, it appears that retrieval-based processing, transfer inappropriate processing, and levels of processing frameworks can account for a variety of conditions that lead to verbal overshadowing versus verbal facilitation. Given recent suggestions that the encoding and recognition of faces involve both verbal/featural and visual/holistic processing elements, it is possible that multiple mechanisms may work together to produce the variety of negative and positive effects observed in the literature—this possibility will be discussed later. One of the greatest difficulties for the retrieval-based processing account, however, has involved the perceived lack of a relationship between the contents of verbal descriptions and subsequent identification performance. In the next section we seek to provide the first quantitative review of this relationship by examining studies that have estimated this correlation. In our analysis we also consider various methodological variables (relating to those described earlier) that might mediate the variance across studies.

THE DESCRIPTION-IDENTIFICATION RELATIONSHIP IN MEMORY FOR FACES

It seems quite intuitive that witnesses who are better at describing a perpetrator should also be better at identifying him/her. The nature of this relationship is inherent in the arguments posed in many eyewitness cases where inconsistencies between a witness's initial description of a perpetrator and the appearance of the suspect are highlighted to undermine the credibility of the identification. Both the US Supreme Court (*Neil v. Biggers, 1972*) and the German Supreme Court (for reviews, see Meurer, Sporer, & Rennig, 1990; Odenthal, 1999) have used the quality of person descriptions as indicators of the accuracy of person identifications in criminal trials (see Sporer & Cutler, 2003). Unfortunately, at the time of these rulings little empirical research had been conducted from which the Courts might have based their decisions.

Despite the appeal of the belief that a strong relationship should exist between face description quality and identification accuracy, estimates of this relationship appear to vary considerably across studies. A few circumstances have been identified under which a significant relationship has been observed. For example, studies that have compared the relative ease with which different faces can be described versus recognised (e.g., multiple face, recognition paradigms) have noted significant description-identification correlations. Wells (1985) showed participants multiple faces and then examined both their ability to describe and recognise each face. He found that distinctive faces tended to be both easier to describe and easier to recognise than less distinctive faces, thereby leading to a modest relationship between recognition accuracy and description quality ($r = .27$) across faces. Along similar lines, Wickham and Swift (2006) have demonstrated that typical faces tend to produce verbal overshadowing effects, whereas easier-to-describe distinctive faces were unaffected by a verbalisation task.

A second condition under which a relationship between description quality and recognition performance has been observed involves studies in which participants were forced to generate rather elaborate descriptions of faces and were later asked to identify these individuals in a lineup identification task (Finger & Pezdek, 1999; Meissner, 2002; Meissner et al., 2001). In these studies, it appears that the elicitation of elaborate verbal descriptions may lead participants to generate inaccurate details, producing a self-generated misinformation effect that subsequently impairs recognition performance (Meissner, 2002; Meissner et al., 2001; Sauerland et al., 2008 this issue). As noted previously, studies that have varied response output on the description task also reduce the likelihood of range restriction on estimates of description quality, and thereby maximise their opportunity to estimate the description-identification relationship.

Interestingly, reviews of description and identification performance in memory for faces have noted many conditions that influence both recall and recognition measures in the same manner (either positively or negatively; see Meissner, Sporer, & Schooler, 2007; Sporer, 1996; Tredoux et al., 2004). These include a variety of encoding manipulations (e.g., opportunity to view the target face, stress or anxiety, alcohol intoxication at the time of encoding, and weapon focus), testing conditions (e.g., context reinstatement instructions), and the retention interval between encoding and retrieval (e.g., length of the retention interval, misinformation effects, and cowitness effects). Furthermore, studies have suggested that factors such as the age of the witness can influence both description quality and identification accuracy (e.g., Haas & Sporer, 1989). In fact, finding conditions under which the two measures become dissociated may prove quite valuable to understanding the constraints of the relationship between the two processes. One notable example has involved the cross-race effect in memory for faces (for reviews, see Meissner & Brigham, 2001b; Sporer, 2001). While studies have consistently demonstrated the cross-race effect in face identification, only a handful of studies have examined the quality of descriptions generated for same- and other-race target faces, producing rather mixed results (Dore,

Brigham, Moussallie, Bennett, & Butz, 2005; Ellis, Deregowski, & Shepherd, 1975; McQuiston-Surrett & Topp, 2004; Mitchell, Meissner, & MacLin, in press; Shepherd & Deregowski, 1981).

In short, despite the intuition that witnesses who are better at describing a target should also be better at recognising him/her, this relationship has often proven quite difficult to demonstrate empirically. It may be that while verbal and perceptual tasks overlap to a certain degree in the processes demanded at encoding and retrieval (cf. Cabeza & Kato, 2000; Wickham & Swift, 2006), description tasks may encourage somewhat more featural processing (e.g., Sporer, 1989; Wells & Turtle, 1988), and make difficult the expression of less verbalisable, configural information regarding a face (e.g., Diamond & Carey, 1986). This minimal degree of covariance for featural information across description and identification tasks may well explain the modest correlations between description and identification performance frequently observed across studies (Meissner et al., 2007; Sporer, 1996), as well as the stimulus-based effects noted by other researchers (Wells, 1985; Wickham & Swift, 2006).

Given the variability of findings across studies and the frequency with which Courts often rely upon witness descriptions as indicators of identification accuracy, we sought to conduct the first meta-analysis of the description-identification relationship in memory for faces. As will be described later, we assessed this relationship across a variety of description quality measures (including accuracy, quantity, correct details, and incorrect details) and examined a number of methodological variables that might moderate the relationship. After presenting the results of this meta-analysis, we return to a brief discussion of its impact on the theoretical underpinnings of the relationship between description quality and identification accuracy and address the practical implications this relationship for eyewitness memory.

META-ANALYSIS OF THE DESCRIPTION-IDENTIFICATION RELATIONSHIP IN MEMORY FOR FACES

Method

Studies

Research papers were obtained via several methods, including: (a) searches of the *PsycINFO*, *Dissertation Abstracts*, *Social Sciences Citation Index*, and *First Search* databases using the key words “face identification”, “face description”, “verbal overshadowing”, “eyewitness memory/recall/recognition”, and “facial memory/recall/recognition”; (b) a search of selected conference programs (e.g., American Psychological Association,

American Psychology–Law Society, Association for Psychological Science, Psychonomic Society, and Society for Applied Research in Memory and Cognition) over the past 5 years; and (c) contact with colleagues in the field who may have had knowledge of research studies that had neither been published nor presented at a conference.

Inclusion versus exclusion criteria. A total of 33 research papers were identified for inclusion in the meta-analysis, representing the responses of 4278 participants. Six of these manuscripts represented unpublished data, while three additional manuscripts had recently been accepted for publication. To be included in the primary analysis, studies must have required participants to both verbally describe and perceptually identify one or more faces, and must have provided an estimate of the relationship between some measure of description quality (or quantity) and identification accuracy. Studies may have employed either a single face or a multiple face paradigm, and could utilise either a lineup identification task or a recognition paradigm at test. Studies were generally excluded from the analyses if they failed to provide an estimate of the relationship between description quality and identification accuracy.

When there was reason to assume that an experimental condition (e.g., presence of a weapon in studies on weapon focus, or rereading one's prior description before identification) would lead to different correlations that would not be considered representative of the associations normally found between the description variables and identification accuracy, we used only those correlations for our analyses that were not likely to have changed from experimental manipulations along with their respective sample sizes. Thus, we used only the no-weapon control group condition for a study on weapon focus (Bothwell, Trahan, & Newsome, 1991), and the description-only condition in studies that also had a description rereading group (Davids et al., 2006; Sauerland et al., 2008 this issue; Sporer, 2007). These instances are documented in the notes to Appendix A.

Estimates of effect size. Most studies included in our meta-analyses reported point-biserial correlations between identification accuracy and the description variables. As correlations reported in the original studies should not be used for meta-analytic purposes (Lipsey & Wilson, 2001; Rosenthal, 1991), we first converted the respective *r*s using Fisher's *Zr* transformation. All analyses were conducted with these *Zr* values; however, for better understanding, all reports of effect sizes and confidence intervals were back-transformed using the inverse of Fisher's *Zr* transformation.

Some authors simply reported that a specific correlation was "not significant". In cases where we could not obtain the exact values by writing to the authors, these correlations were set to $r = .00$. This was only necessary for a few correlations (overall 8 of the 119 correlations analysed), and such instances are documented in the results (Table 1) as well as in Appendix A. Some studies reported separate correlations for different experimental conditions (e.g., target-present vs. target-absent lineups), or for subgroups of participants (e.g., children vs. adults, choosers vs. nonchoosers). In most of these cases we used the values of each condition as independent estimates of the associations of interest, coding the respective conditions as potential moderator variables.

Measures of description quality. Five measures of description quality were examined in the current meta-analysis. First, the relationship between identification accuracy and *description accuracy* (generally calculated as the proportion of correct details divided by the total number of details provided) was calculated and presented in 21 of the research papers and resulting in $k = 32$ hypothesis tests of this relationship across a total of 2973 participants. Second, we identified 18 research papers that estimated the relationship between identification accuracy and *description quantity* (generally calculated as the total number of facial descriptors, not including subjective or personality aspects, generated by a participant), representing $k = 33$ hypothesis tests of the relationship across 2578 participants. Third, 13 research papers assessed the relationship between identification accuracy and the *number of correct descriptors* generated for a given face, representing

TABLE 1
Meta-analytic summary of correlations between measures of description quality and identification accuracy

Summary statistics	*Accuracy*	*Quantity*	*Correct descriptors*	*Incorrect descriptors*	*Congruence*
k	32	33	22	16	5
k (est. = .00)	4	1	1	2	0
N	2973	2578	1932	1640	279
Min r	−.22	−.61	−.33	−.46	−.25
Max r	.39	.69	.31	.11	.25
Unweighted mean r	.12	.02	.01	−.16	.07
Weighted mean r	.14	−.04	−.02	−.18	.12
p	.000	.065	.335	.000	.046
95% CI—low	.11	−.08	−.07	−.23	.00
95% CI—high	.18	.00	.02	−.13	.24
N_{FS}	440	−32	−22	217	1
Homogeneity Q	66.52	102.16	43.05	41.89	6.51
$df(Q)$	31	32	21	15	4
$p(Q)$	.000	.000	.003	.000	.164

k = number of significance tests; k (est. = .00) = number of "*ns*" results set to $r = .00$; N_{FS} = failsafe N.

$k = 22$ tests of the hypothesis across 1932 participants. Fourth, the relationship between identification accuracy and the *number of incorrect descriptors* generated for a given face was estimated in nine research papers, resulting in $k = 16$ tests of the hypothesis across 1640 participants. Finally, four research papers assessed the relationship between description accuracy and the *congruence* (or degree of similarity) between the description provided and the face that was identified from the photo array, representing $k = 5$ tests of the hypothesis across 279 participants.

Coding of study characteristics as moderator variables. Two independent raters coded a host of study characteristics that served not only to document the type of studies reviewed but also to allow us (and future researchers) to analyse for systematic differences across studies. The following study characteristics were recorded for each study: (a) degree of realism at encoding (i.e., slide or photo vs. video vs. live event), (b) type of description task (i.e., rating scales vs. checklist vs. cued recall vs. free recall), (c) time permitted to encode each target face, (d) number of faces encoded at study, (e) delay between encoding and the description task, (f) delay between generating the description and subsequent identification, and (g) publication status (i.e., unpublished vs. published). We also coded a host of other study characteristics. Although moderator analyses with these variables were also conducted, they are somewhat redundant with those reported here, but are available from the authors upon request. Few disagreements occurred in the coding, and these differences were resolved by the first and second authors. Appendix B provides the codings of study characteristics across the sample of studies.

Results and discussion

Effect size analyses

In this section, we present the results of separate meta-analyses involving various relationships between description quality and identification accuracy in memory for faces. For each of these meta-analytic integrations we (1) calculate the mean relationship across studies, along with 95% confidence levels (CI); (2) assess whether the results can be considered homogeneous; and (3) in case of heterogeneity search for relevant moderator variables that may account for differences across studies. The meta-analytic procedures used followed recommendations by Lipsey and Wilson (2001), as well as Rosenthal (1991), and the respective chapters in Cooper and Hedges (1994). To assess computational accuracy, we used different software algorithms developed by Lipsey and Wilson, as well as adaptations of the examples provided by Becker (1994) and Hedges and Olkin (1985) that were programmed by the second author.

Primary analyses are reported as weighted means calculated by using the inverse variance weights for each coefficient (which is based on the sample size of the respective studies); however, unweighted means are also provided as an additional measure of central tendency. Appendix A provides the point-biserial correlations of the various description-identification relationships that were used as the basis for our meta-analyses. In most cases, the units of analyses are identical with individual experiments; however, in some experiments, different conditions were likely to lead to different correlations between description quality and identification accuracy. Whenever available, we recorded separate correlations for subgroups of experiments. Therefore, the unit of analysis for any meta-analysis conducted is the number of hypothesis tests, k, available for the particular association. Appendix B provides a description of all the variables coded from the respective method sections of the reports and/or from consulting with the authors. The primary results of our meta-analyses are summarised in Table 1. As we discuss the significance and magnitude of each relationship, we base our interpretations within the context of effect size conventions proposed by Cohen (1988). Specifically, a point-biserial correlation of .10 is considered a small effect size, .24 a medium effect size, and .37 a large effect size. Table 1 also contains fail-safe numbers (N_{FS}) based on unweighted integrations involving p-values using the Stouffer method (see Rosenthal, 1991). Figure 1 displays the distributions of relationships investigated (median, quartiles, and deciles of the Zr values).

Practically all of the relationships examined were highly heterogeneous (see Table 1). One way to address this problem is to identify potential outliers that may have obscured meaningful patterns in the relationships studied. We utilised both graphical methods (stem-and-leaf plots and line plots that involved rank ordered individual study effect sizes with 95% confidence intervals; see Begg, 1994), as well as more formal meta-analytic techniques such as those suggested by Hedges and Olkin (1985).[1] As such, we provide an assessment of the impact of such outliers for each effect size

[1] Hedges and Olkin (1985) have suggested the use of standardised residuals as well as homogeneity statistics to search for outliers. Unfortunately, they only provide formulae for the effect size d. We have adjusted these procedures to Zr as effect size, calculating the residuals and homogeneity statistics for Zr analogous to the procedure adopted by Hedges and Olkin for d. The basic rationale of this procedure is to calculate adjusted mean effect sizes after removing the effect size in question and then examine the standardised residual of this particular effect size, as well as the homogeneity Q after removal of this study. Residuals larger than 2 are considered as potential outliers. Removal of one, or several, outliers should reduce the observed heterogeneity indicated by a failure to reject the null hypothesis of homogeneity for the reduced number of studies. However, removal of these studies may inadvertently lead to a drop of important "exceptions" of the general observed pattern which (through the conduct of moderator analyses) could be particularly interesting in understanding the underlying theoretical mechanisms.

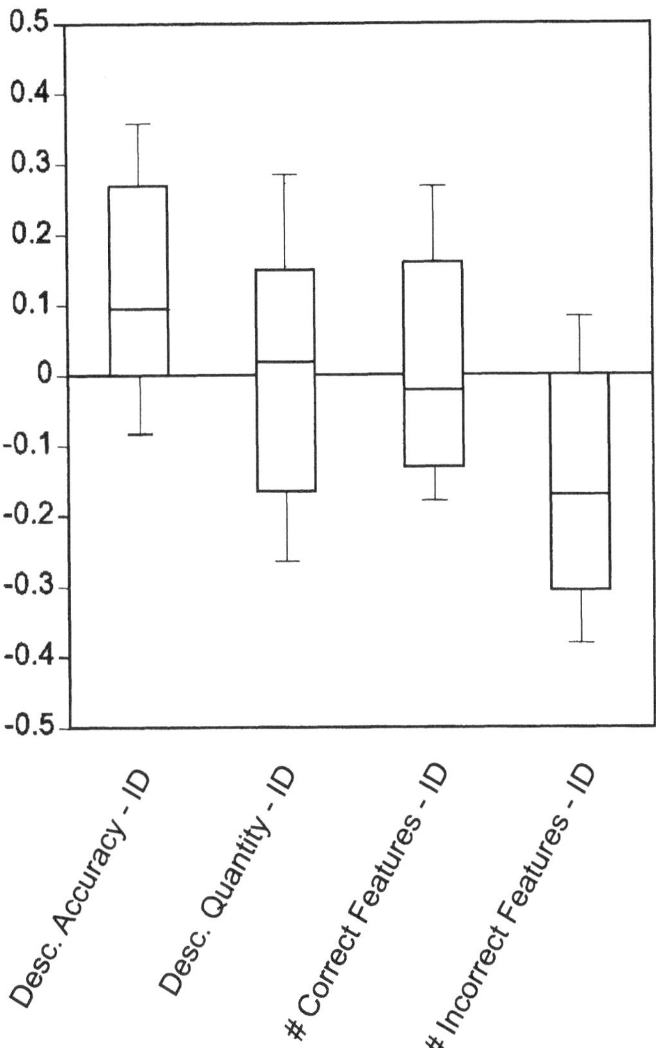

Figure 1. Box plots of correlations between measures of description quality and identification accuracy.

calculated. Box plots of all relationships were also examined here (Figure 1; see also Light, Singer, & Willett, 1994).[2]

Relationship between description accuracy and identification accuracy. Most of the studies reviewed reported point-biserial correlations

[2] Additional figures displaying these relationships are available from the second author.

between description accuracy and identification accuracy, leading to a $k = 32$ hypothesis tests of this relationship with $N = 2973$. The weighted mean effects size was $r = .14$, a small yet significant effect, $p < .001$, with CIs of .11 and .18, $N_{FS} = 440$. Results were heterogeneous, $Q(31) = 66.52$, $p < .001$. Analysis of the data for outliers suggested that studies by Bothwell et al. (1991, Exp. 2) and Pigott, Brigham, and Bothwell (1990) had shown the two most negative relationships, while studies by Meissner (2002, Exp. 1) and Meissner et al. (2001, Exp. 1) had observed significant positive relationships with fairly large samples. These four studies all had standardised residuals larger than 2.0 when compared with the weighted mean effect size after removal of the respective studies. Although dropping none of the studies individually would make the results homogeneous, removing all four as outliers led to a nonsignificant $Q(27) = 36.53$, $p > .10$. The removal of these studies, however, did not significantly alter the mean weighted effect size, $r = .12$, $p < .001$, CIs of .08 and .16, now based upon $k = 28$ hypothesis tests with $N = 2244$. Nonetheless, the variability across studies is still large enough to take a closer look at potential moderators.

Relationship between the description quantity and identification accuracy. In actual criminal cases, the accuracy of person descriptions cannot be ascertained as this requires knowledge of the true perpetrator; however, description quantity can be assessed. A total of $k = 33$ tests of the hypothesis involving $N = 2578$ resulted in a nonsignificant weighted mean of $r = -.04$, $p = .07$, with CIs of $-.08$ and .00. The results were highly heterogeneous, $Q(32) = 102.16$, $p < .001$, with *r*s ranging from $-.61$ to .69. Outlier analyses revealed 11 studies with standardised residuals above 2.0 (including Studies 34, 39, 23, 29, 38 with negative, and 51, 45, 28, 19, 32, and 31 with positive values; see Appendix A). Although the heterogeneity is extreme, we decided not to remove these outliers, but rather to search for moderators that might explain these differences.

Relationship between the number of correct descriptors and identification accuracy. Besides description accuracy, some studies have also reported the number of correct and/or the number of incorrect descriptors and their relationship to identification accuracy. For $k = 22$ tests of the hypothesis involving $N = 1932$, there was no significant relationship between the number of correct descriptors and identification accuracy, weighted mean $r = -.02$, with CIs of $-.07$ and .02. Results were also heterogeneous, $Q(21) = 43.05$, $p < .01$. Analysis of outliers suggested that studies by Memon, Rose, Searcy, and Bartlett (1999, Exp. 2), Finger (2002, Exp. 1), Gwyer and Clifford (1997, target-present lineups), Geiselman, Schroppel, Tubridy, Konisi, and Rodriguez (2000, Exp. 2, target-absent lineups), and Hosch and Bothwell (1990) had standardised residuals over 2.0. The study by Memon et al. (1999), with an effect size of $r = -.33$, appears particularly out of the range of most other values. Removal of three studies (Studies 26, 22, and 28) with more extreme standardised residuals (one with a negative, two with positive effect sizes) resulted in a homogeneous distribution, $Q(18) = 25.42$, $p > .10$; however, the overall conclusion that there is no relationship between number of correct descriptors and identification accuracy does not change when these more extreme values are removed, weighted mean $r = -.03$, CIs $-.08$ and .01 based upon $k = 19$ hypothesis tests with $N = 1741$.

Relationship between the number of incorrect features and identification accuracy. For the $k = 16$ hypothesis tests with $N = 1640$ investigating incorrect details, a significant effect was observed, with mean weighted $r = -.18$, $p < .001$, CIs of $-.23$ and $-.13$, $Nfs = 217$. Results of this relationship were also heterogeneous, $Q(15) = 41.89$, $p < .001$. Analysis of outliers suggested that the study by Geiselman et al. (2000, Exp. 2, target-present lineups) had a standardised residual close to 3.0, while studies by Sauerland et al. (2008 this issue), Meissner (2002, Exp. 2), Kitagami et al. (2002), and Geiselman et al. (2000, Exp. 2, target-absent lineup) showed standardised residuals slightly above 2.0. Removal of these studies rendered the distribution homogeneous, $Q(10) = 15.13$, $p > .10$, though the relationship between incorrect descriptors and identification accuracy remained significant, with a mean weighted $r = -.21$, $p < .001$, CIs of $-.26$ and $-.15$, based upon $k = 11$ tests of the hypothesis with $N = 1214$ participants.

Relationship between congruence and identification accuracy. Finally, only five studies with a total of 279 participants investigated the relationship between congruence and identification accuracy. The weighted mean $r = .12$, $p < .05$, with CIs of .00 and .24, $N_{FS} = 1$. The results appear to be homogeneous, $Q(4) = 6.51$, $p = .16$, with *r*s ranging from $-.25$ to .25. It should be noted, however, that the Wells (1985) study used the number of faces as the unit of analysis, which led to an $r = .19$.

Relationships among the description quality measures. Though ancillary to our primary analyses, some studies provided estimates of the correlation between various measures of description quality. We focus briefly on two of these relationships. First, $k = 9$ studies ($N = 1098$) examined the relationship between the number of descriptors and description accuracy. A significant correlation was observed across studies, with a mean weighted $r = -.26$, $p < .001$, and CIs of $-.32$ and $-.21$, $N_{FS} = 79$. The results were heterogeneous, $Q(8) = 63.22$, $p < .001$, with *r*s ranging from $-.48$ to .34. The two extreme values were observed in studies by Meissner (2002), $N = 432$) and Davids et al. (2006), $N = 48$), both of which could be considered outliers.

When removed from the analysis, the results become homogeneous, $Q(6) = 7.22$, $p = .301$, though the significance of the relationship remains with a mean weighted $r = -.13$, $p < .001$, with CIs of $-.21$ and $-.05$, $N_{FS} = 12$. Second, as only two studies investigated the relationship between description accuracy and congruence, no detailed meta-analytic analyses were performed; however, we include these studies here to note the rather high correlations observed by both Wells (1985), $r(125) = .87$, and Pigott et al. (1990), $r(24) = .67$. The weighted mean effect size across the two studies was $r = .85$, with CIs of .80 and .89, $N_{FS} = 103$.

Moderator analyses

As noted previously, practically all of the effect size relationships examined were highly heterogeneous, suggesting that a search for study characteristics may help us to understand the differences across studies. In the current analyses we examine the association between effect sizes across studies and the study characteristics recorded. Unfortunately, the number of studies is too small to conduct more complex blocking or multiple regression analyses due to mutual dependencies (collinearity) among predictors. Hence, we focus only on a few moderators that were likely to have affected these relationships. Tables 2, 3, 4, and 5 display the results of moderator analyses of effect sizes as a function of study characteristics. For each analysis, the Q_{BET} indicates whether the subgroups differed as a function of this moderator. Q_{WIT} indicates whether the remaining variance is homogeneous. When no studies or only a single study was available for a certain subgroup, subgroups were collapsed. Next we discuss the significant patterns observed in these analyses and present the mean weighted *r*s for each condition where applicable. Given the small and nonsignificant nature of the relationships observed in the earlier effect size analyses, we further restrict our discussion

TABLE 2
Moderator analysis of the relationship between description accuracy and identification accuracy

Predictor variable	Q_{BET}	*df*	*p*	Q_{WIT}	*df*	*p*
Encoding realism	32.07	2	.00	34.45	29	.22
Description task	3.08	3	.38	63.43	28	.00
Encoding time	3.93	2	.14	62.59	29	.00
Encoding load	3.96	1	.05	62.56	30	.00
Encoding-description delay	6.40	2	.04	60.12	29	.00
Description-identification delay	22.20	2	.00	44.32	29	.03
Publication status	0.00	1	.95	66.51	30	.00

TABLE 3
Moderator analysis of the relationship between description quantity and identification accuracy

Predictor variable	Q_{BET}	*df*	*p*	Q_{WIT}	*df*	*p*
Encoding realism	14.82	2	.00	87.34	30	.00
Description task	2.86	2	.24	99.29	30	.00
Encoding time	15.02	2	.00	87.14	30	.00
Encoding load	2.77	2	.25	99.38	30	.00
Encoding-description delay	24.77	2	.00	77.39	30	.00
Description-identification delay	9.38	2	.01	92.77	30	.00
Publication status	0.00	1	.98	102.16	31	.00

to those moderators that produced patterns yielding significant relationships between description measures and identification accuracy.

Relationship between description accuracy and identification accuracy. Table 2 displays the results of moderator analyses conducted on the relationship between description accuracy and identification accuracy. A few notable findings merit discussion. First, this correlation appears to decrease when realism increases at encoding such that the strongest correlation is observed in studies that employed photographic stimuli, $r = .26$, $p < .001$, $k = 9$, followed by studies that utilised video stimuli, $r = .12$, $p < .001$, $k = 12$. In contrast, studies that employed a live event showed no significant relationship between description accuracy and identification accuracy, $r = .04$, *ns*, $k = 11$. Second, face recognition paradigms that employed more than one target face generally showed larger relationships, $r = .27$, $p < .001$, $k = 5$, when compared with lineup identification studies that utilised only a single target face, $r = .13$, $p < .001$, $k = 27$.

Finally, the delay between encoding, description, and identification phases across experiments appears to have moderated the relationship

TABLE 4
Moderator analysis of the relationship between number of correct details and identification accuracy

Predictor variable	Q_{BET}	*df*	*p*	Q_{WIT}	*df*	*p*
Encoding realism	7.10	2	.03	35.95	19	.01
Description task	3.61	1	.06	39.43	20	.01
Encoding time	0.41	2	.82	42.64	19	.00
Encoding load	3.42	1	.06	39.63	20	.01
Encoding-description delay	6.37	1	.01	36.68	20	.01
Description-identification delay	2.31	2	.31	40.73	19	.00
Publication status	4.89	1	.03	38.16	20	.01

TABLE 5
Moderator analysis of the relationship between number of incorrect details and identification accuracy

Predictor variable	Q_{BET}	*df*	*p*	Q_{WIT}	*df*	*p*
Encoding realism	11.67	2	.00	30.22	13	.00
Description task	0.77	1	.38	41.12	14	.00
Encoding time	0.96	2	.62	40.93	13	.00
Encoding load	0.22	1	.64	41.67	14	.00
Encoding-description delay	5.03	1	.02	36.86	14	.00
Description-identification delay	20.17	2	.00	21.72	13	.06
Publication status	0.77	1	.38	41.12	14	.00

between description accuracy and identification accuracy. In particular, shorter delays between encoding and generation of a description produced stronger effects when compared with delays longer than 1 day: no delay, $r = .11$, $p < .001$, $k = 14$; 5 min to 1 day delay, $r = .19$, $p < .001$, $k = 16$; more than 1 day delay, $r = .09$, $p < .05$, $k = 2$. In contrast, the presence of a delay between the description and identification phases yielded stronger correlations between description accuracy and identification accuracy: no delay, $r = .06$, $p < .05$, $k = 17$; 5 min to 1 day delay, $r = .23$, $p < .001$, $k = 10$; more than 1 day delay, $r = .23$, $p < .001$, $k = 5$.

Relationship between the description quantity and identification accuracy. The moderator analyses for the relationship between description quantity and identification accuracy are shown in Table 3. Consistent with the prior analyses, studies that employed photographic stimuli showed a small, but significant, negative association, $r = -.11, p < .001, k = 11$, while studies utilising video stimuli, $r = .03$, *ns*, $k = 11$, and live interactions, $r = .07$, *ns*, $k = 11$, produced nonsignificant, though positive, effects. Studies that employed shorter encoding times for each target face also produced significant negative effects: 1 to 5 s, $r = -.10, p < .001, k = 9$; 5 to 60 s, $r = -.07, p \leq .06$, $k = 12$, while those that permitted longer encoding times produced significant positive effects: greater than 60 s, $r = .09, p < .05, k = 12$.

The delays between encoding, description, and identification phases across studies appears to moderate the relationship between description quantity and identification accuracy as well. With regard to the encoding to description phase delay, it appears that a modest amount of delay leads to the significant negative association between quantity and identification accuracy: 5 min to 1 day delay, $r = -.12, p < .001, k = 13$. In contrast, studies that employed either no delay, $r = .06$, $p \leq .06$, $k = 14$, or lengthy delays, $r = .12$, $p \leq .08$, $k = 6$, produced only marginally significant, but positive, relationships. Delays between the description and identification phases also yielded stronger negative correlations between description quantity and identification accuracy: no delay, $r = .04$, *ns*, $k = 18$; 5 min to 1 day delay, $r = -.08$, $p < .001$, $k = 10$; more than 1 day delay, $r = -.11$, $p \leq .07$, $k = 5$.

Relationship between the number of correct descriptors and identification accuracy. Moderator analyses for the relationship between the number of correct descriptors and identification accuracy were much less successful in shedding light on the diverse findings (see Table 4). In fact, only two of the moderator analyses produced conditions under which a significant relationship appears to exist. In particular, and consistent with prior analyses, studies utilising photographic stimuli showed a small, but significant, negative association, $r = -.07$, $p < .05$, $k = 9$, while studies utilising video stimuli, $r = .02$, *ns*, $k = 9$, and live interactions, $r = .11$, $p \leq .09$, $k = 4$, produced nonsignificant positive effects. Furthermore, the encoding-description delay also affected this relationship. When giving descriptions immediately, the relationship tended to be positive, $r = .11$, $p \leq .06$, $k = 6$, while studies with delays of 5 min up to several days showed a small but significantly negative relationship, $r = -.05$, $p \leq .06$, $k = 16$.

Relationship between the number of incorrect descriptors and identification accuracy. A small to medium relationship appears to exist between the number of incorrect descriptors mentioned and identification accuracy. Although there were only 16 hypothesis tests of this relationship, some of the moderator variables further illuminate the observed relationship (see Table 5). Once again, studies utilising photographic stimuli showed the strongest negative association, $r = -.23$, $p < .001$, $k = 9$, while studies utilising video stimuli, $r = -.06$, *ns*, $k = 5$, and live interactions, $r = .00$, *ns*, $k = 2$, produced nonsignificant effects. The effects of delay were also evident here. Longer delays between encoding and generation of a description produced stronger effects: 5 min to 1 day delay, $r = -.21$, $p < .001$, $k = 11$, while studies employing no delay showed nonsignificant effects, $r = -.06$, *ns*, $k = 5$. (It should be noted that no studies using this dependent measure included delays longer than 1 day.) In contrast, the presence of a delay between the description and identification phases yielded a stronger negative correlation when compared with the absence of a delay: no delay, $r = -.01$, *ns*, $k = 6$; 5 min to 1 day delay, $r = -.23$, $p < .001$, $k = 6$; more than 1 day delay, $r = -.30$, $p < .001$, $k = 4$.

Multiple regression analyses with encoding time, encoding-description delay, and description-identification delay

The results regarding encoding time, encoding-description delay, and description-identification delay were puzzling. One of the reasons may have

TABLE 6
Regression-based moderator analysis of the relationship between description accuracy and identification accuracy

Predictor variable	*B*	*SE*	*CI low*	*CI high*	*Z*	*p*	*Beta*
Encoding time	−.06	.04	−.14	.01	−1.58	.11	−.19
Encoding-description delay	.00	.02	−.05	.05	0.09	.93	.01
Description-identification delay	.06	.02	.02	.10	3.13	.00	.41

been that the categorical coding we used may not adequately reflect the large variations in encoding and delay times across studies. There is also the possibility that the respective encoding and delay times may have been confounded in the studies reviewed, which cannot be detected when only one variable is investigated at a time. Therefore, we conducted (multiple) regression analyses to postdict the description-identification associations from the actual times in seconds (as opposed to the categorisations reported earlier) used for encoding and for delay intervals. As the distributions of these times were heavily skewed, we employed a logarithmic transformation of these values, adding the constant 1 as many studies used no delay intervals (i.e., encoding time = log10(s + 1); delay = log10(min + 1)). These analyses were carried out for measures of description accuracy and description quantity. For the other description measures, there was not a sufficient number of studies as a prerequisite for these types of analyses. The multiple regression model involving the description accuracy measure yielded a significant $Q(3) = 13.39$, $p < .01$. Table 6 displays the results of this meta-regression analysis following the procedures by Lipsey and Wilson (2001). Only the description-identification delay reliably predicted the size of the association; however, the residual variance remained significant, $Q(28) = 53.12$, $p < .001$. An analogous multiple regression analysis was carried out for the measure of description quantity (see Table 7). The model was significant, $Q(3) = 23.30$, $p < .001$. Encoding time showed a significant positive association such that the longer participants had time to encode the target face, the stronger the relationship between description quantity and identification accuracy. In addition, description-identification delay showed

TABLE 7
Regression-based moderator analysis of the relationship between description quantity and identification accuracy

Predictor variable	*B*	*SE*	*CI low*	*CI high*	*Z*	*p*	*Beta*
Encoding time	.11	.03	.06	.16	4.17	.00	.42
Encoding-description delay	−.02	.02	−.06	.01	−1.15	.25	−.12
Description-identification delay	−.05	.02	−.09	−.02	−2.75	.01	−.28

a significant negative association such that increasing the description-identification delay produced a smaller relationship between description quantity and identification accuracy. However, as the residual variance remained highly significant, $Q(29) = 78.86$, $p < .001$, other factors may also be responsible for these associations.

Summary of findings

Across 33 research papers and a total of 4278 participants, the current meta-analysis found some support for the relationship between description quality and identification accuracy in memory for faces. More specifically, three of the five relationships examined demonstrated significant small-to-moderate effect sizes (see Table 1) such that: (a) More accurate descriptions were significantly associated with greater accuracy in identification; (b) descriptions that contained more incorrect details were associated with greater inaccuracy in identification; and (c) greater congruence between the description and the person identified was associated with greater accuracy in identification.

As is typically the situation, however, it is important to consider the boundary conditions that moderate these effects. Our analyses on this front suggest that the strongest relationships were produced in studies that employed photographic stimuli (e.g., face recognition paradigms), whereas studies that utilised more realistic stimuli such as video or live events (e.g., eyewitness identification paradigms) produced smaller and often nonsignificant effects. On a similar basis, face recognition paradigms that employed more than one target face generally showed larger relationships between description accuracy and identification accuracy when compared with lineup identification studies that utilised only a single target face.

Another important factor appeared to involve delays between the encoding, description, and identification phases of the experiment. With regard to the delay between encoding and the description phase, shorter delays produced stronger effects for the measure of description accuracy, while longer delays produced stronger effects for the number of incorrect descriptors generated. Given the effect of delay on the likely accuracy of a description, the variability of this moderator across the description measures appears reasonable and further supports the role of retrieval-based processes. Finally, across the description measures of accuracy, quantity, and number of incorrect details, a delay between the description and identification tasks produced stronger effects when compared with studies that presented the identification task immediately thereafter.

GENERAL DISCUSSION

In the present paper we have reviewed the empirical and theoretical literatures that have addressed the description-identification relationship in memory for faces. As noted previously, descriptions can sometimes impair (or "overshadow") and other times facilitate subsequent attempts at perceptual identification; however, understanding the relationship between these two tasks and the theoretical mechanisms that bridge this relationship has proven difficult. Furthermore, given the Court's assumptions regarding the usefulness of examining a witness's description when assessing the likely accuracy of his/her identification (*Neil v. Biggers*, 1972), we felt it was important to further examine this relationship across studies spanning four decades of empirical analysis. Taken together, the results of our meta-analysis suggest that a significant relationship does exist between the description measures of description accuracy, number of incorrect descriptors, and congruence with subsequent identification accuracy. Furthermore, certain conditions appear to exacerbate the magnitude of this relationship, including the use of face recognition versus eyewitness identification paradigms, and the length of delays between relevant tasks. Next we discuss both the theoretical, methodological, and practical implications of our findings, and suggest future directions for research in this area.

Theoretical implications

As reviewed previously, descriptions can render both positive and negative effects on subsequent identification performance, leading to either verbal facilitation or verbal overshadowing, respectively. Several theoretical accounts have been proposed to explain these effects, including retrieval-based processing, transfer inappropriate processing, and levels of processing theories. Each of these theories can account for a variety of findings in this literature. For example, retrieval processes can explain the effects of instructional bias and facial typicality, and are generally consistent with the effects of self-generated misinformation and repeated testing (cf. Meissner et al., 2001; Roediger, Wheeler, & Rajaram, 1993). Similarly, a levels of processing framework can account for the influence of description generation on subsequent identification performance, including verbal facilitation (Brown & Lloyd-Jones, 2005, 2006), and the role of output encoding on secondary task performance (Hintzman & Hatry, 1990). In contrast, transfer inappropriate processing can justify the effects of perceptual tasks that "release" the overshadowing of verbal descriptions and the effects of featural tasks (such as describing a different stimulus from that of the target face) that can lead to overshadowing on subsequent identification (for a review see

Schooler, 2002). Transfer inappropriate processing is also consistent with a variety of models that have proposed separable memory systems responsible for verbal versus visual processing (e.g., Tulving, 1985; Tulving & Schacter, 1990) and those suggesting independent coding of verbal vs. visual information in the cognitive system (Paivio, 1971; Woodhead & Baddeley, 1981).

One difficulty for a retrieval-based processing account has involved the often variable association between the contents of verbal descriptions and later attempts at identification. To address this issue, we sought to conduct the first meta-analysis of the description-identification relationship in memory for faces. As summarised previously, the results of this analysis provide a basis for supporting a significant weak-to-moderate relationship between the description measures of accuracy and number of incorrect descriptors on subsequent identification that is consistent with a retrieval-based (or output encoding) mechanism. However, the modest nature of this correlation may also be used to support the relative independence of verbal and visual processing that is consistent with a transfer inappropriate processing account (Schooler, 2002; see also Flexser & Tulving, 1978; Kahana, Hirsuto, & Schneider, 2005). Furthermore, the vast majority of studies exclude subjective descriptors for which it is difficult to determine accuracy, including such aspects as personality or comparative judgements (e.g., his chin is similar to that of Dick Cheney) that might be considered more "holistic" aspects. A transfer inappropriate processing account would propose that a focus on such holistic information would lead to less accurate identifications. Though we were unable to assess this prediction using the current database of studies, it is noteworthy that several recent studies conducted by Brown and Lloyd-Jones (2005, 2006) failed to find any significant correlations between the production of holistic features in a face description and subsequent recognition performance—though the authors were able to confirm the transfer inappropriate processing prediction when participants were explicitly instructed to generate holistic versus featural descriptions (but only when the analysis was conducted across items; Brown & Lloyd-Jones, 2005, Exp. 4).

While the current analysis appears to provide some support for the role of retrieval-based processing in the description-identification relationship, should this be interpreted to preclude any possibility that transfer inappropriate processing might account for some of the effects of verbal description on perceptual identification? That is, should these two accounts be considered mutually exclusive? The simple answer, we believe, is "no". Just as the effects of retrieval processes and repeated testing have been shown throughout the study of human memory, so too have the effects of encoding specificity and transfer appropriate processing. As such, we believe that most models of cognitive processing would readily accommodate the two perspectives as situationally determined effects—that is, conditions arise whereby one or both of the processes may come to influence subsequent attempts at identification. It is this line of future research, namely to determine the parameters under which the two theories might independently versus conjointly account for the effects of verbal overshadowing versus verbal facilitation, that we believe will prove fruitful to our understanding of the relationship between verbal and perceptual processes in memory for faces.

For example, one manner in which to account for a modest description-identification relationship may involve the extent to which certain processes are invoked by both recall and recognition tasks. For example, dual-process theories of memory propose that while *familiarity-based processes* support performance on recognition and implicit memory tasks, *recollection-based processes* can be applied to both recognition and recall tasks (see Yonelinas, 2002). Thus, to the extent that recollection may be employed at the time of identification, overlap may be seen in performance on description and identification tasks. For example, Brown and Lloyd-Jones (2006) found evidence of an increase in recollection-based judgements for previously verbalised faces (though an increase in familiarity-based judgements was also seen), and this recollection increase was associated with the verbal facilitation effect observed in their study. To the extent that verbalisation might invoke recollection-based processes that can subsequently be applied in an identification task, we would expect a greater relationship between performance across the two tasks—including both verbal facilitation and verbal overshadowing depending upon the veracity of the description output. This role of recollection in facilitating performance across tasks is also consistent with levels of processing manipulations within the dual-process memory literature (e.g., Gardiner, 1988).

Several moderator variables were found to exacerbate the magnitude of the description-identification relationship, including the use of facial recognition paradigms and various delays between the encoding, description, and identification phases of an experiment. We believe that theoretical accounts of memory for faces and the effect of verbal overshadowing versus verbal facilitation must take into consideration these conditions. First, studies employing facial recognition paradigms generally demonstrated stronger correlations between description and identification performance based upon study characteristics such as the use of more than one target face (as opposed to a single target face) and a shorter delay between encoding of the face and generation of a description. Although we did not code the specific nature of the identification task (i.e., recognition vs. lineup identification), this may also be an important variable to consider. Our sense is that the vast majority of such studies incorporated the description task within the context of encoding and thereby created a stronger (and more precise) representation that could be applied on the subsequent identification task. This is consistent with the predictions of both a levels of processing framework and retrieval-based mechanisms. In addition, Wells (1985) has noted that the description-identification relationship may be driven not by the ability of the participant to describe and identify faces, but rather by the variation across faces that renders some faces more easily described and identified than others. As such, facial recognition paradigms that employ a diversity of target faces provide a stronger basis upon which to estimate the description-identification relationship across target faces.

Delays between the description and identification phases also produced stronger effects. Longer delays (of several days) may facilitate memories for described faces in yet little understood ways. Some authors have recently argued that verbal facilitation effects will be more likely when the memory trace is poor, be it for a lack of encoding or an increased retention interval (Itoh, 2005). Distinctive targets may be encoded by labelling these distinctive aspects in ways that serve as retrieval cues (Sporer, 1989, 2007) or as a means of rehearsal (Read, 1979; Sporer, 1988), consistent with the notion of output encoding. Alternatively, the vagueness of descriptions may make participants aware that their memory is apparently rather poor, leading to a cautious shift in target-absent lineups (Brown & Lloyd-Jones, 2005; Sauerland et al., 2008 this issue).

Methodological implications

Our attempts to provide a meta-analytic synthesis of previous findings was hampered by some difficulties we encountered when comparing and coding the studies. While we are very grateful to many authors who have provided us with additional information on request, we believe that to be able to draw firm conclusions about the role of verbal processes and their relationship to identification several standards of reporting should be followed. As both encoding times and the delays between encoding, description, and identification seem to be quite important for the relationships observed, exact times for presentation of the stimulus and the two delays should be routinely reported. To the extent that forensic implications are sought, there is also a clear need for longer retention intervals (the longest ones we found in this literature were 2 days and 1 week, respectively, while the majority of studies used recognition tests in the same session). Researchers should also be mindful of the types of descriptions asked from their participants (see Appendix B). Estimating somebody's height and weight is unlikely to be related to a recognition task where only faces are shown, and defining accuracy simply by agreement may be an unreliable estimate of measuring description accuracy. While counting the number of features mentioned is unlikely to pose a problem when measuring description quantity, pilot testing and training of coders to assess description accuracy should lead to a better estimate of the construct of description accuracy. Although not included in Tables 2, 3, 4, and 5, additional analyses showed that effect sizes were stronger for studies that reported interrater reliabilities than for those that had either reported no reliability data or had simply indicated that accuracy was merely coded "by agreement". As is evident from the studies by Meissner et al. (2001), exact instructions regarding the amount of information requested from witnesses may also be crucial as they are likely to change the decision criterion for reporting (incorrect) details. Given the lack of methodological detail provided in the vast majority of studies, this variable could not be appropriately coded across studies. Indirectly, this problem may also be inherent in the use of checklists, which may foster featural processing by isolating individual aspects of a face to be described. Requesting many details or ratings may also induce perceivers to mark responses they may not really remember at all (Sporer, 2007; Wogalter, 1991, 1996).

We were stunned by the large variations across studies in the number of features provided and the accuracy rates obtained. Obviously, these differences are not only likely to reflect differences in description tasks (e.g., instructions to participants about the reporting criterion), but also differences in scoring and operationalisations of "accuracy". Some studies involved only physical descriptions of faces (for which our vocabulary appears to be rather limited), while others contained descriptions of body and clothing characteristics, as well as estimates of height, weight, and age. While these aspects of descriptions may add to the quantity of the numbers of features mentioned, they may also obscure the correlations between description accuracy and a face identification task (see Davids et al., 2006; Sauerland et al., 2008 this issue; Sporer, 1996). Furthermore, person descriptions frequently contain subjective impressions of the targets described (e.g., "attractive", "aggressive") that refer to inferred (personality) characteristics for which accuracy cannot be scored (see Sporer, 1996), and most studies appear to have omitted such aspects from their feature calculations. Researchers should be careful to report what proportions of the descriptions provided refer to such characteristics and how these were considered/eliminated in the description measures used for reporting description-identification correlations.

In general, we cannot expect to find substantive correlations between two variables if one, or both, of the variables is ill-defined and not measured with objectivity. Similarly, such correlations are likely to be attenuated if one of the variables refers to various aspects of a person (e.g., body and character descriptions) while identification is only measured via a photospread or a facial recognition task. Future studies should clearly specify the instructions given to participants and carefully operationalise the various aspects of person descriptions measured. For each characteristic of a description, evidence of high interrater reliability needs to be established. To the extent that previous studies have not followed these guidelines they may have underestimated the true relationships between these variables.

Practical implications

In *Neil v. Biggers* (1972), the US Supreme Court rendered the assertion that a witness's description could be used as a basis from which to evaluate the veracity of his/her memory and subsequent identification of the suspect. The current paper has provided the first opportunity to evaluate the Court's ruling regarding the description-identification relationship via a meta-analysis of the available literature. Across 33 research papers and a total of 4278 participants, our analysis found support for a significant relationship between description accuracy and identification accuracy, as well as a relationship between the number of incorrect descriptors recalled and identification (in)accuracy. While this would seem to provide support for the Court's assertions, these relationships were somewhat small and it is important to consider the conditions under which the strongest effects were identified.

In particular, results of a moderator analysis suggested that the relationship between description accuracy and identification accuracy was *strongest* in studies that employed facial recognition paradigms involving the presentation of multiple target faces in the context of photographic materials and involving a short delay between encoding and description, and *weakest* in studies that utilised eyewitness identification paradigms that focused encoding and identification on a single target face presented in a more realistic manner (via a videotaped or live event). As noted earlier, one interpretation of this effect is that descriptions generated in multiple-face paradigms help to preserve memory against interference effects and provide individuals an opportunity to generate elaborate, individuated encodings regarding each stimulus face. In fact, this is quite consistent with studies of verbal facilitation reviewed earlier (e.g., Brown & Lloyd-Jones, 2005, 2006) and the "trial effect" observed in studies of verbal overshadowing (see Schooler et al., 1996). Alternatively, it may be that multiple faces and/or trials are required to vary description quality and thereby supersede the effects of range restriction inherent in description performance or, as Wells (1985) has suggested previously, that stimulus variability in the distinctiveness of faces serves to increase this variance in description quality and is associated with both ease/difficulty of description and identification (see also Sporer, 1989). Regardless of one's interpretation of this effect, however, it is clear that the courts may have considerable difficulty attempting to utilise a witness's single description of the perpetrator as a basis to judge the likely veracity of his/her identification.

Of course, the central issue of concern in transferring these research findings from the laboratory to the field involves that of determining *ground truth* with respect to accuracy. That is, how do we determine in practice that a witness has accurately described the perpetrator of the crime without assuming (sometimes falsely) that the suspect identified by the witness is, in fact, the perpetrator? As Wells (1985) has noted, what the courts mistakenly refer to as accuracy is rather the *congruence* between a witness's description and the individual they identified from the lineup. While only a handful of studies have examined this measure of description quality, the results suggest that it demonstrates a small, but significant, relationship with identification accuracy; and, more importantly, two of these studies suggest that measures of congruence show a rather strong correlation with that of description accuracy (of the actual target face). This relationship between description accuracy, congruence, and identification accuracy merits further research in our estimation—particularly given its relevance to the court's desire to evaluate the description quality of witnesses at trial. Ideally, these studies should examine targets differing in distinctiveness (and race), as well as vary encoding times and ecologically valid retention intervals (weeks or months).

One measure of a description that the courts could directly rely upon involves that of *description quantity*. Unfortunately, the current meta-analysis suggested that only a small, marginally significant, relationship existed between description quantity and identification accuracy, and this effect is likely counter to the court's assumptions regarding what constitutes description quality—as more complete descriptions were associated with a greater likelihood of *inaccurate* identification. Furthermore, certain conditions only exacerbated this negative relationship, including the use of more contrived face recognition paradigms, shorter encoding times, and lengthier delays between description and identification tasks. Finally, quantity of the description was significantly associated with description accuracy across studies, but again this relationship is likely counter to the court's assumption regarding description quality as more complete descriptions tended to *less accurately* describe the target face. Taken together, the court should be careful of how it uses description quantity as an estimate of the quality of a witness's memory for the perpetrator.

CONCLUSIONS

Verbal descriptions can lead to both negative (verbal overshadowing) and positive (verbal facilitation) effects on subsequent identification accuracy. Understanding the relationship between verbal description and perceptual identification processes is important to appreciating the factors that lead to these two effects. The current meta-analysis of the description-identification relationship in memory for faces suggests that performance on these two tasks is related to a certain degree, particularly in measures of description accuracy and number of incorrect details recalled. Furthermore, moderator analyses suggested that this effect is strongest in facial recognition studies that employ larger stimulus sets and provide more opportunities for assessing the relationship within and across both participants and faces. Delays between the encoding, description, and identification phases also appeared to moderate this relationship. Taken together, the findings provide some support for a retrieval-based account of the effects of verbal description on subsequent identification performance, though they do not preclude the role of featural versus configural processing (transfer inappropriate processing). The courts have suggested that a witness's description may be used to assess the veracity of his/her identification of the suspect (*Neil v. Biggers*, 1972); however, the current review questions the application of this assumption and suggests future research that might lead to the use of measures of *congruence* in applied settings.

(*Note*: Studies denoted with an asterisk were included in the meta-analysis.)

REFERENCES

Anderson, J. R., & Reder, L. M. (1979). An elaborative processing explanation of depth of processing. In L. Cermak & F. Craik (Eds.), *Levels of processing in human memory* (pp. 385–403). Hillsdale, NJ: Lawrence Erlbaum Associates, Inc.

Becker, B. J. (1994). Combining significance levels. In H. Cooper & L. V. Hedges (Eds.), *The handbook of research synthesis* (pp. 215–230). New York: Russell Sage Foundation.

Begg, C. B. (1994). Publication bias. In H. Cooper & L. V. Hedges (Eds.), *The handbook of research synthesis* (pp. 399–409). New York: Russell Sage Foundation.

*Bothwell, R. K. (1985). *The effects of gender and arousal on facial recognition and recall.* Unpublished doctoral dissertation, Florida State University, Tallahassee, FL.

Bothwell, R. K., Deffenbacher, K. A., & Brigham, J. C. (1987). Correlation of eyewitness accuracy and confidence: Optimality hypothesis revisited. *Journal of Applied Psychology, 72*, 691–695.

*Bothwell, R. K., Trahan, M. A., & Newsome, S. R. (1991). *Eyewitness description accuracy as a function of weapon presence and delay.* Paper presented at the annual meeting of the Southeastern Psychological Association, New Orleans, LA.

Brandimonte, M. A., Hitch, G. J., & Bishop, D. V. M. (1992). Influence of short-term memory codes on visual image processing: Evidence from image transformation tasks. *Journal of Experimental Psychology: Learning, Memory, and Cognition, 18*, 157–165.

Brewer, N., & Burke, A. (2002). Effects of testimonial inconsistencies and eyewitness confidence on mock-juror judgments. *Law and Human Behavior, 26*, 353–364.

*Brigham, J. C., & Pigott, M. (1983). *The relationship between accuracy of prior description and facial recognition.* Paper presented at the American Psychological Association, Anaheim, CA.

Brown, C., & Lloyd-Jones, T. J. (2002). Verbal overshadowing in a multiple face presentation paradigm: Effects of description instruction. *Applied Cognitive Psychology, 16*, 873–885.

Brown, C., & Lloyd-Jones, T. J. (2003). Verbal overshadowing of multiple face and car recognition: Effects of within- versus across-category verbal descriptions. *Applied Cognitive Psychology, 17*, 183–201.

*Brown, C., & Lloyd-Jones, T. J. (2005). Verbal facilitation of face recognition. *Memory and Cognition, 33*, 1442–1456.

*Brown, C., & Lloyd-Jones, T. J. (2006). Beneficial effects of verbalization and visual distinctiveness on remembering and knowing faces. *Memory and Cognition, 34*, 277–286.

Cabeza, R., & Kato, T. (2000). Features are also important: Contributions of featural and configural processing to face recognition. *Psychological Science, 11*, 429–433.

Chance, J., & Goldstein, A. G. (1976). Recognition of faces and verbal labels. *Bulletin of the Psychonomic Society, 7*, 384–386.

Clare, J., & Lewandowsky, S. (2004). Verbalizing facial memory: Criterion effects in verbal overshadowing. *Journal of Experimental Psychology: Learning, Memory, and Cognition, 30*, 739–755.

Cohen, J. (1988). *Statistical power analysis for the behavioral sciences* (2nd ed.). Hillsdale, NJ: Lawrence Erlbaum Associates, Inc.

Cooper, H., & Hedges, L. V. (1994). *The handbook of research synthesis.* New York: Russell Sage Foundation.

Craik, F. I. M., & Lockhart, R. S. (1972). Levels of processing: A framework for memory research. *Journal of Verbal Learning and Verbal Behavior, 11*, 671–684.

Cutler, B. L., Penrod, S. D., & Martens, T. K. (1987). The reliability of eyewitness identification: The role of system and estimator variables. *Law and Human Behavior, 11*, 233–258.

*Davids, M. S. C., Sporer, S. L., & McQuiston-Surrett, D. (2006). *The verbal facilitation effect: Person descriptions as a means to improve identification performance.* Manuscript submitted for publication.

Deffenbacher, K. A. (1983). The influence of arousal on reliability of testimony. In S. M. A. Lloyd-Bostock & B. R. Clifford (Eds.), *Evaluating witness evidence* (pp. 235–251). Chichester, UK: Wiley.

Deffenbacher, K. A., Bornstein, B. H., Penrod, S. D., & McGorty, E. K. (2004). A meta-analytic review of the effects of high stress on eyewitness memory. *Law and Human Behavior, 28*, 687–706.

Diamond, R., & Carey, S. (1986). Why faces are and are not special: An effect of expertise. *Journal of Experimental Psychology: General, 115*, 107–117.

Dodson, C. S., Johnson, M. K., & Schooler, J. W. (1997). The verbal overshadowing effect: Why descriptions impair face recognition. *Memory and Cognition, 25*, 129–139.

Dore, H. S., Brigham, J. C., Moussallie, N. M., Bennett, L. B., & Butz, D. A. (2005). *What did he look like? Is there an "other-race effect" in description accuracy?* Unpublished manuscript.

Ellis, H. D., Deregowski, J. B., & Shepherd, J. W. (1975). Descriptions of white and black faces by white and black subjects. *International Journal of Psychology, 10*, 119–123.

Fallshore, M., & Schooler, J. W. (1995). The verbal vulnerability of perceptual expertise. *Journal of Experimental Psychology: Learning, Memory, and Cognition, 21*, 1608–1623.

*Finger, K. (2002). Mazes and music: Using perceptual processing to release verbal overshadowing. *Applied Cognitive Psychology, 16*, 887–896.

*Finger, K., & Pezdek, K. (1999). The effect of verbal description on face identification accuracy: "Release from verbal overshadowing". *Journal of Applied Psychology, 84*, 340–348.

Fiore, S. M., & Schooler, J. W. (2002). How did you get here from there? Verbal overshadowing of spatial mental models. *Applied Cognitive Psychology, 16*, 897–909.

Flexser, A., & Tulving, E. (1978). Retrieval independence in recognition and recall. *Psychological Review, 85*(3), 153–171.

Gardiner, J. M. (1988). Functional aspects of recollective experience. *Memory and Cognition, 16*, 309–313.

*Geiselman, R. E., Schroppel, T., Tubridy, A., Konisi, T., & Rodriguez, V. (2000). Objectivity bias in eyewitness performance. *Applied Cognitive Psychology, 14*, 323–332.

*Goldstein, A. G., Johnson, K. S., & Chance, J. E. (1979). Does fluency of face description imply superior face recognition? *Bulletin of the Psychonomic Society, 13*, 15–18.

*Grass, E., & Sporer, S. L. (1991, March). *Richtig oder falsch? Zur Vorhersage von Identifizierungsleistungen durch weitere Aussagen von Zeugen* [Correct or false? Post-dicting eyewitness identification accuracy from verbal statements]. Paper presented at the 33rd Tagung experimentell arbeitender Psychologen, Giessen, Germany.

*Gwyer, P., & Clifford, B. R. (1997). The effects of the cognitive interview on recall, identification, confidence and the confidence/accuracy relationship. *Applied Cognitive Psychology, 11*, 121–145.

Haas, S., & Sporer, S. L. (1989, April). *Zur Entwicklung von Enkodierungsstrategien beim Wiedererkennen von Gesichtern* [On the development of encoding strategies in the recognition of human faces]. Paper presented at the 31st Tagung experimentell arbeitender Psychologen, Bamberg, Germany.

Hedges, L. V., & Olkin, I. (1985). *Statistical methods for meta-analysis*. Orlando, FL: Academic Press.

Hintzman, D., & Hatry, A. L. (1990). Item effects in recognition and fragment completion: Contingency relations vary for different subsets of words. *Journal of Experimental Psychology: Learning, Memory, and Cognition, 16*, 965–969.

*Hosch, H. M., & Bothwell, R. K. (1990). Arousal, description and identification accuracy of victims and bystanders. *Journal of Social Behavior and Personality, 5*, 481–488.

Humphreys, M. S., & Bowyer, P. A. (1980). Sequential testing effects and the relation between recognition and recognition failure. *Memory and Cognition, 8*, 271–277.

Itoh, Y. (2005). The facilitating effect of verbalization on the recognition memory of incidentally learned faces. *Applied Cognitive Psychology, 19*, 421–433.

*Jenkins, F., & Davies, G. (1985). Contamination of facial memory through exposure to misleading composite pictures. *Journal of Applied Psychology, 70*, 164–176.

Kahana, M. J., Hirsuto, D. S., & Schneider, A. R. (2005). Theoretical correlations and measured correlations: Relating recognition and recall in four distributed memory models. *Journal of Experimental Psychology: Learning, Memory, and Cognition, 31*, 933–953.

*Kitagami, S., Sato, W., & Yoshikawa, S. (2002). The influence of test-set similarity in verbal overshadowing. *Applied Cognitive Psychology, 16*, 963–972.

Light, R. J., Singer, J. D., & Willett, J. B. (1994). The visual presentation and interpretation of meta-analyses. In H. Cooper & L. V. Hedges (Eds.), *The handbook of research synthesis* (pp. 439–453). New York: Russell Sage Foundation.

Lindsay, D., Read, J., & Sharma, K. (1998). Accuracy and confidence in person identification: The relationship is strong when witnessing conditions vary widely. *Psychological Science, 9*(3), 215–218.

Lipsey, M. W., & Wilson, D. B. (2001). *Practical meta-analysis*. Thousand Oaks, CA: Sage.

Lovett, S. B., Small, M. Y., & Engstrom, S. A. (1992, November). *The verbal overshadowing effect: Now you see it, now you don't*. Paper presented at the annual meeting of the Psychonomic Society, St Louis, MO.

Mauldin, M. A., & Laughery, K. R. (1981). Composite production effects on subsequent facial recognition. *Journal of Applied Psychology, 66*, 351–357.

McKelvie, S. J. (1976). The effects of verbal labeling on recognition memory for schematic faces. *Quarterly Journal of Experimental Psychology, 28*, 459–474.

McQuiston-Surrett, D., & Topp, L. D. (2004, March). *Cross-race face recall: Assessing perceptual expertise in a description and facial composite task*. Paper presented at the annual conference of the American Psychology–Law Society, Scottsdale, AZ.

*Meissner, C. A. (2002). Applied aspects of the instructional bias effect in verbal overshadowing. *Applied Cognitive Psychology, 16*, 911–928.

Meissner, C. A., & Brigham, J. C. (2001a). A meta-analysis of the verbal overshadowing effect in face identification. *Applied Cognitive Psychology, 15*, 603–616.

Meissner, C. A., & Brigham, J. C. (2001b). Thirty years of investigating the own-race bias in memory for faces: A meta-analytic review. *Psychology, Public Policy, and Law, 7*, 3–35.

*Meissner, C. A., Brigham, J. C., & Kelley, C. M. (2001). The influence of retrieval processes in verbal overshadowing. *Memory and Cognition, 29*, 176–186.

Meissner, C. A., Sporer, S. L., & Schooler, J. W. (2007). Person descriptions as eyewitness evidence. In R. Lindsay, D. Ross, J. Read, & M. Toglia (Eds.), *Handbook of eyewitness psychology: Memory for people* (pp. 3–34). Hillsdale, NJ: Lawrence Erlbaum Associates, Inc.

Melcher, J. M., & Schooler, J. W. (1996). The misremembrance of wines past: Verbal and perceptual expertise differentially mediate verbal overshadowing of taste memory. *Journal of Memory and Language, 35*, 231–245.

*Memon, A., & Bartlett, J. (2002). The effects of verbalization on face recognition in young and older adults. *Applied Cognitive Psychology, 16*, 635–650.

*Memon, A., & Rose, R. (2002). Identification abilities of children: Does a verbal description hurt face recognition? *Psychology, Crime, and Law, 8*, 229–242.

*Memon, A., Rose, R., Searcy, J., & Bartlett, J. C. (1999). *The verbal overshadowing effect and eyewitness identification: A developmental and aging perspective.* Unpublished manuscript.

Meurer, D., Sporer, S. L., & Rennig, C. (1990). Der Beweiswert von Personenidentifizierungen: Auf dem Weg von alltagspsychologischen Erfahrungssaetzen zu empirisch ueberpruefbaren Fragestellungen [The probative value of eyewitness identifications: From common sense psychology to empirically testable hypotheses]. In D. Meurer & S. L. Sporer (Eds.), *Zum Beweiswert von Personenidentifizierungen* (pp. 1–18). Marburg, Germany: N. G. Elwert.

Mitchell, T. L., Meissner, C. A., & MacLin, O. H. (2006). *The influence of the cross-race effect on lineup construction and fairness.* Manuscript submitted for publication.

Neil v. Biggers, 409 US 188 (1972).

Odenthal, H. J. (1999). *Die Gegenüberstellung im Strafverfahren* [The lineup in criminal procedure] (3rd ed.). Stuttgart, Germany: Boorberg.

Paivio, A. (1971). *Imagery and verbal processes.* New York: Holt.

*Pigott, M. A., & Brigham, J. C. (1985). Relationship between accuracy of prior description and facial recognition. *Journal of Applied Psychology, 70*, 547–555.

*Pigott, M. A., Brigham, J. C., & Bothwell, R. K. (1990). A field study on the relationship between quality of eyewitnesses' descriptions and identification accuracy. *Journal of Police Science and Administration, 17*, 84–88.

*Pozzulo, J. D., & Warren, K. L. (2003). Descriptions and identification of strangers by youth and adult eyewitnesses. *Journal of Applied Psychology, 88*, 315–323.

Read, J. D. (1979). Rehearsal and recognition of human faces. *American Journal of Psychology, 92*, 71–85.

Roediger, H. L., & Guynn, M. J. (1996). Retrieval processes. In E. L. Bjork & R. A. Bjork (Eds.), *Memory* (pp. 197–231). San Diego, CA: Academic Press.

Roediger, H. L., Wheeler, M. A., & Rajaram, S. (1993). Remembering, knowing, and reconstructing the past. In D. L. Medin (Ed.), *Advances in research and theory: Vol. 37. The psychology of learning and motivation* (pp. 97–134). San Diego, CA: Academic Press.

Rosenthal, R. (1991). *Meta-analytic procedures for social research.* Newbury Park, CA: Sage.

Ryan, R. S., & Schooler, J. W. (1998). Whom do words hurt? Individual differences in susceptibility to verbal overshadowing. *Applied Cognitive Psychology, 12*, 105–126.

*Sauerland, M., Holub, F. E., & Sporer, S. L. (2008). Person descriptions and person identifications: Verbal overshadowing or recognition criterion shift? *European Journal of Cognitive Psychology, 20*, 496–528.

Schooler, J. W. (2002). Verbalization produces a transfer inappropriate processing shift. *Applied Cognitive Psychology, 16*, 989–997.

*Schooler, J. W., & Engstler-Schooler, T. Y. (1990). Verbal overshadowing of visual memories: Some things are better left unsaid. *Cognitive Psychology, 22*, 36–71.

Schooler, J. W., Fiore, S. M., & Brandimonte, M. A. (1997). At a loss from words: Verbal overshadowing of perceptual memories. In D. Medin (Ed.), *Handbook of learning and motivation* (Vol. 37, pp. 291–340). Orlando, FL: Academic Press.

Schooler, J. W., Ryan, R. S., & Reder, L. M. (1996). The costs and benefits of verbalization. In D. Herrmann, M. Johnson, C. McEvoy, C. Hertzog, & P. Hertel (Eds.), *Basic and applied memory: New findings* (pp. 51–65). Hillsdale, NJ: Lawrence Erlbaum Associates, Inc.

*Searcy, J. H., Bartlett, J. C., Memon, A., & Swanson, K. (2001). Aging and lineup performance at long retention intervals: Effects of metamemory and context reinstatement. *Journal of Applied Psychology, 86*, 207–214.

Shepherd, J. W., & Deregowski, J. B. (1981). Races and faces: A comparison of the responses of Africans and Europeans to faces of the same and different races. *British Journal of Social Psychology, 20*, 125–133.

Smith, S. M. (1988). Environmental context-dependent memory. In G. Davies & D. Thomson (Eds.), *Memory in context: Context in memory* (pp. 13–34). Chichester, UK: Wiley.

Sporer, S. L. (1988). Long-term improvement of facial recognition through visual rehearsal. In M. M. Gruneberg, P. E. Morris, & R. N. Sykes (Eds.), *Practical aspects of memory* (pp. 182–188). London: Wiley.

Sporer, S. L. (1989). Verbal and visual processes in person identification. In H. Wegener, F. Loesel, & J. Haisch (Eds.), *Criminal behavior and the justice system: Psychological perspectives* (pp. 303–324). New York: Springer.

Sporer, S. L. (1991). Deep—deeper—deepest? Encoding strategies and the recognition of human faces. *Journal of Experimental Psychology, Learning, Memory, and Cognition, 17*, 323–333.

*Sporer, S. L. (1992). Postdicting eyewitness identification accuracy: Confidence, decision-times and person descriptions among choosers and non-choosers. *European Journal of Social Psychology, 22*, 157–180.

Sporer, S. L. (1996). Describing others: Psychological issues. In S. L. Sporer, R. S. Malpass, & G. Koehnken (Eds.), *Psychological issues in eyewitness identification* (pp. 53–86). Hillsdale, NJ: Lawrence Erlbaum Associates, Inc.

Sporer, S. (2001). Recognizing faces of other ethnic groups: An integration of theories. *Psychology, Public Policy and Law, 7*, 36–97.

*Sporer, S. L. (2007). Person descriptions as retrieval cues: Do they really help? *Psychology, Crime, and Law, 13*, 591–609.

Sporer, S. L., & Cutler, B. L. (2003). Identification evidence in Germany: Common sense assumptions, empirical evidence, guidelines, and judicial practices. In P. J. van Koppen & S. D. Penrod (Eds.), *Adversarial vs. inquisitorial justice: Psychological perspectives on criminal justice systems* (pp. 191–208). New York: Plenum.

Sporer, S. L., Penrod, S., Read, D., & Cutler, B. (1995). Choosing, confidence, and accuracy: A meta-analysis of the confidence-accuracy relation in eyewitness identification studies. *Psychological Bulletin, 118*, 315–327.

Tredoux, C. G., Meissner, C. A., Malpass, R. S., & Zimmerman, L. A. (2004). Eyewitness identification. In C. Spielberger (Ed.), *Encyclopedia of applied psychology* (pp. 875–887). San Diego, CA: Academic Press.

Tulving, E. (1985). How many memory systems are there? *The American Psychologist, 40*, 385–398.

Tulving, E., & Schacter, D. L. (1990). Priming and human memory systems. *Science, 247*, 301–306.

*Wegener, H. (1966). *Experimentelle Untersuchungen ueber die Personenbeschreibung und identifizierung 10- bis 12-jaehriger Kinder* [Experimental investigations on person descriptions and identifications of 10- to 12-year-old children]. In J. Gerchow (Ed.), *An den Grenzen von Medizin und Recht* (pp. 115–125). Stuttgart, Germany: Enke.

Wells, G., & Hryciw, B. (1984). Memory for faces: Encoding and retrieval operations. *Memory and Cognition*, *12*(4), 338–344.

*Wells, G. L. (1985). Verbal descriptions of faces from memory: Are they diagnostic of identification accuracy. *Journal of Applied Psychology*, *70*, 619–626.

Wells, G. L., & Olson, E. A. (2003). Eyewitness testimony. *Annual Review of Psychology*, *54*, 277–295.

Wells, G. L., & Turtle, J. W. (1988). What is the best way to encode faces? In M. M. Gruneberg, P. E. Morris, & R. N. Sykes (Eds.), *Practical aspects of memory: Current research and issues* (pp. 163–168). New York: Wiley.

Westerman, D. L., & Larson, J. D. (1997). Verbal overshadowing effect: Evidence for a general shift in processing. *American Journal of Psychology*, *110*, 417–428.

Wickham, L. H. V., & Swift, H. (2006). Articulatory suppression attenuates the verbal overshadowing effect: A role for verbal encoding in face identification. *Applied Cognitive Psychology*, *20*, 157–169.

Winograd, E. (1981). Elaboration and distinctiveness in memory for faces. *Journal of Experimental Psychology: Human Learning and Memory*, *7*, 181–190.

Wogalter, M. S. (1991). Effects of post-exposure description and imaging on subsequent face recognition performance. *Proceedings of the Human Factors Society*, *35*, 575–579.

*Wogalter, M. S. (1996). Describing faces from memory: Accuracy and effects on subsequent recognition performance. *Proceedings of the Human Factors and Ergonomics Society*, *40*, 536–540.

Woodhead, M., & Baddeley, A. (1981). Individual differences and memory for faces, pictures, and words. *Memory and Cognition*, *9*(4), 368–370.

*Yarmey, A. D. (1986). Verbal, visual, and voice identification of a rape suspect under different levels of illumination. *Journal of Applied Psychology*, *71*, 363–370.

*Yarmey, A. D. (2004). Eyewitness recall and photo identification: A field experiment. *Psychology, Crime and Law*, *10*, 53–68.

Yonelinas, A. P. (2002). The nature of recollection and familiarity: A review of 30 years of research. *Journal of Memory and Language*, *46*, 441–517.

Yu, C. J., & Geiselman, R. E. (1993). Effects of constructing identi-kit composites on photospread identification performance. *Criminal Justice and Behavior*, *20*, 280–292.

APPENDICES

TABLE A1

Correlations (effect size *r*) between measures of description quality and identification accuracy across studies

Study ID	*Authors*	*Year*	*Experiment*	*N*	*Accuracy*	*Quantity*	*Correct descriptors*	*Incorrect descriptors*	*Congruence*
1	Wegener	1966	Boys	63	.03	na	na	na	na
2	Wegener	1966	Girls	32	.12	na	na	na	na
3	Goldstein et al.	1979		22	.15	na	na	na	na
4	Brigham & Pigott	1983	Lineup A	32	na	na	na	na	.01
5	Brigham & Pigott	1983	Lineup B	36	na	na	na	na	−.25
6	Bothwell	1985		128	.08	na	na	na	na
7	Pigott & Brigham	1985		120	.00[a]	na	na	na	.16[b]
8	Jenkins & Davies	1985	2—Control	29	−.16	na	na	na	na
9	Wells	1985	Choosers	127	.27	.05	na	na	.19
10	Yarmey	1986		128	.00[c]	na	na	na	na
11	Hosch & Bothwell	1990	2	42	na	na	.31	na	na
12	Schooler & Engstler-Schooler	1990	1	35	−.01	.11	−.01	na	na
13	Schooler & Engstler-Schooler	1990	2	40	.23	−.14	−.15	na	na
14	Schooler & Engstler-Schooler	1990	4	36	.23	−.26	.04	na	na
15	Pigott et al.	1990		47	−.16	.09	na	na	.25[d]
16	Bothwell et al	1991	1	31	.02[f]	na	na	na	na
17	Bothwell et al	1991	2	70	−.22[f]	na	na	na	na
18	Grass & Sporer	1991		79	na	−.06	−.05	na	na
19	Sporer	1992		49	na	.28	na	na	na

Table A1 (*Continued*)

Study ID	*Authors*	*Year*	*Experiment*	*N*	*Accuracy*	*Quantity*	*Correct descriptors*	*Incorrect descriptors*	*Congruence*
20	Wogalter	1996		48	.38	na	na	na	na
21	Wogalter	1996		48	.35	na	na	na	na
22	Gwyer & Clifford	1997	TP	70	.00[c]	.00[c]	.26	.00[c]	na
23	Gwyer & Clifford	1997	TA	70	.00[c]	−.28	.00[c]	.00[c]	na
24	Finger & Pezdek	1999	1	75	na	na	−.22	−.32	na
25	Finger & Pezdek	1999	2	69	na	na	.16	.00	na
26	Memon et al.	1999	2	60	.19	na	−.33	na	na
27	Geiselman et al.	2000	2—TP	99	−.05	.02	−.03	.11	na
28	Geiselman et al.	2000	2—TA	61	.06	.27	.29	.09	na
29	Meissner et al.	2001	1	180	.34	−.23	−.15	−.29	na
30	Meissner et al.	2001	2	60	.38	−.08	−.03	−.38	na
31	Searcy et al.	2001	Young—TP	23	na	.69	na	na	na
32	Searcy et al.	2001	Old—TP	25	na	.48	na	na	na
33	Searcy et al.	2001	Young—TA	22	na	.15	na	na	na
34	Searcy et al.	2001	Old—TA	24	na	−.61	na	na	na
35	Finger	2002	1	89	na	.07	.19	−.18	na
36	Finger	2002	2	73	na	−.23	−.13	−.16	na
37	Kitagami et al.	2002		110	na	.04	−.03	.02	na
38	Meissner	2002	1	432	.27	−.18	−.07	−.25	na
39	Meissner	2002	2	108	.27	−.30	−.16	−.37	na
40	Memon & Bartlett	2002	Young	34	.00	na	na	na	na
41	Memon & Bartlett	2002	Senior	36	.14	na	na	na	na
42	Memon & Rose	2002		25	−.02	na	na	na	na
43	Pozzulo & Warren	2003	1—TP	76	na	−.07	na	na	na
44	Pozzulo & Warren	2003	1—TA	74	na	.15	na	na	na
45	Pozzulo & Warren	2003	2—TP	85	na	.24	na	na	na
46	Pozzulo & Warren	2003	2—TA	86	na	.08	na	na	na

(*Continued overleaf*)

Table A1 (*Continued*)

Study ID	*Authors*	*Year*	*Experiment*	*N*	*Accuracy*	*Quantity*	*Correct descriptors*	*Incorrect descriptors*	*Congruence*
47	Yarmey	2004		590	.09	na	na	na	na
48	Sauerland et al.	2008 this issue	Description	48	.39	−.18	.07	−.46	na
49	Brown & Lloyd-Jones	in press-a		84	na	.02	na	na	na
50	Brown & Lloyd-Jones	in press-b	1	56	na	−.16	na	na	na
51	Brown & Lloyd-Jones	in press-b	4	89	na	.21	na	na	na
52	Sporer	in press	Description	25	na	.31	na	na	na
53	Davids et al.	2006	Description, Target 1	48	.10	−.02	.08	−.09	na
54	Davids et al.	2006	Description, Target 2	48	.30	.12	.25	−.18	na

Correlations with identification accuracy are point-biserial correlations. All other correlations are Pearson product-moment correlations.

[a]Averaged across choosers and nonchoosers as well as other conditions. [b]Based on $N = 37$ only. [c]Estimated as .00 from report of being "*ns*". [d]Based on $N = 25$ only. [e]Based on $N = 24$ only. [f]No weapon condition only. [g]Rereading condition was not considered here.

TABLE A2
Coding of study characteristics

Study ID	*Realism of encoding event*	*Description task*	*Encoding time (s)*	*No. of faces encoded*	*Encoding-description delay (min)*	*Description-identification delay (min)*	*Publication status*
1	Live event	Recall & checklist	30	1	0	5	Journal article
2	Live event	Recall & checklist	30	1	0	5	Journal article
3	Photograph	Checklist	2.5	10	0	0	Journal article
4	Live event	Checklist	15	1	0	5	Unpublished
5	Live event	Checklist	15	1	0	5	Unpublished
6	Live event	Cued recall	15	1	0	20	Journal article

Table A2 (*Continued*)

Study ID	*Realism of encoding event*	*Description task*	*Encoding time (s)*	*No. of faces encoded*	*Encoding-description delay (min)*	*Description-identification delay (min)*	*Publication status*
7	Live event	Checklist	15	1	0	5	Journal article
8	Video	Checklist	50	1	15	20, 2880, & 10,080	Journal article
9	Photograph	Recall	240	1	10	10	Journal article
10	Photograph	Recall	120	1	0	0	Journal article
11	Live event	Recall	20	1	10	0	Conference Presentation
12	Video	Recall	30	1	20	0	Journal article
13	Video	Recall	30	1	20	0	Journal article
14	Video	Recall	30	1	0	10	Journal article
15	Live event	Recall	90	1	270	0	Journal article
16	Live event	Recall	15	1	20	0	Journal article
17	Live event	Recall	15	1	20	0	Journal article
18	Live event	Recall	70	1	10,080	0	Conference Presentation
19	Live event	Recall	20	1	10,080	0	Journal article
20	Photograph	Recall & checklist	5	6	0	5	Journal article
21	Photograph	Recall	5	6	0	5	Journal article
22	Live event	Recall	3	1	30	0	Journal article
23	Live event	Recall	3	1	30	0	Journal article
24	Photograph	Recall	240	1	10	10	Journal article
25	Photograph	Recall	240	1	10	60	Journal article
26	Video	Recall	90	1	30	0	Journal article
27	Video	Recall	5	1	0	0	Journal article
28	Video	Recall	5	1	0	0	Journal article
29	Photograph	Recall	10	1	5	0 & 30	Journal article
30	Photograph	Recall	10	1	5	0	Journal article
31	Live event	Recall	1200	1	43,200	0	Journal article
32	Live event	Recall	1200	1	43,200	0	Journal article
33	Live event	Recall	1200	1	43,200	0	Journal article

(*Continued overleaf*)

Table A2 (*Continued*)

Study ID	*Realism of encoding event*	*Description task*	*Encoding time (s)*	*No. of faces encoded*	*Encoding-description delay (min)*	*Description-identification delay (min)*	*Publication status*
34	Live event	Recall	1200	1	43,200	0	Journal article
35	Photograph	Recall	30	1	5	5	Journal article
36	Photograph	Recall	30	1	5	5	Journal article
37	Photograph	Recall	10	1	5	0	Journal article
38	Photograph	Recall	5	1	15	5	Journal article
39	Photograph	Recall	5	1	15	5 & 10,080	Journal article
40	Video	Recall	60	1	45	2	Journal article
41	Video	Recall	60	1	45	2	Journal article
42	Live event	Recall	480	1	1440	0	Journal article
43	Video	Recall	500	1	0	5	Journal article
44	Video	Recall	500	1	0	5	Journal article
45	Live event	Recall	500	1	0	5	Journal article
46	Live event	Recall	500	1	0	5	Journal article
47	Live event	Cued recall	15	1	2240	0	Journal article
48	Video	Recall & cued recall	18	1	0	2880	Conference Presentation
49	Photograph	Recall	5	24	0	0	Journal article
50	Photograph	Recall	2	23	0	0	Journal article
51	Photograph	Recall	2	23	0	0	Journal article
52	Video	Recall & checklist	18	1	0	10,080	Journal article
53	Video	Recall & cued recall	42	2	0	2880	Unpublished
54	Video	Recall & cued recall	70	2	0	2880	Unpublished

EUROPEAN JOURNAL OF COGNITIVE PSYCHOLOGY
2008, 20 (3), 456–477

Verbal overshadowing of multiple face recognition: Effects on remembering and knowing over time

Toby J. Lloyd-Jones
Swansea University, UK

Charity Brown
Leeds University, UK

"Verbal overshadowing", the phenomenon whereby the verbal reporting of a visual memory of a face interferes with subsequent recognition of that face, arises for the presentation of multiple faces following a single face description. We examined the time course of verbal overshadowing in the multiple face paradigm, and its influence on recollection and familiarity-based recognition judgements. Participants were presented with a series of faces and then described a further face (or not, in the control condition). Study faces were subsequently discriminated from distractors at either a short or long lag after initial presentation, in a yes/no recognition task using the remember/know procedure. Verbal overshadowing was most apparent at the short lag, for discrimination and false "know" judgements. We discuss these findings in terms of the nature of verbal interference in this paradigm.

How may language shape our thoughts? "Verbal overshadowing" refers to the phenomenon whereby verbally describing a visual memory of a face can interfere with subsequent visual recognition of that face (for reviews, see Schooler, Fiore, & Brandimonte, 1997; Schooler, 2002; and a special issue of *Applied Cognitive Psychology*, 2002).

In a seminal study, Schooler and Engstler-Schooler (1990) presented participants with a 30 s video of a bank robbery, after which participants were assigned to either a description or no description control condition. Those in the description condition were instructed to use the next 5 min to describe the facial features of the bank robber, whilst control participants were given an unrelated filler task. Description condition participants were less able to

Correspondence should be addressed to Toby J. Lloyd-Jones, Department of Psychology, Swansea University, Singleton Park, Swansea, SA2 8PP, Wales, UK.
E-mail: T.J. Lloyd-Jones@swansea.ac.uk

This research was supported by ESRC research grant RES000-23-0057 to Toby J. Lloyd-Jones.

http://www.psypress.com/ecp DOI: 10.1080/09541440701728425

subsequently identify the robber, as compared with the control group, when given a lineup comprising the robber and several potential suspects.

Two accounts of verbal overshadowing are predominant: (1) Schooler and colleagues have suggested a "transfer-inappropriate retrieval" account. According to this account, performance is impaired because: (a) Participants fail to apply the same nonverbal processing operations at retrieval that were used at encoding, where a good match between encoding and retrieval processes normally benefits memory performance (cf. the transfer-appropriate processing view; Roediger, Weldon, & Challis, 1989); and (b) engaging in one kind of retrieval operation (e.g., verbal) may inhibit the subsequent operation of another kind of retrieval operation (e.g., nonverbal). However, as Schooler (2002) notes, retrieval inhibition may not be a component of verbal overshadowing; and (2) Meissner, Brigham, and Kelley (2001) have proposed a "misinformation" account. They found that forcing participants to generate an elaborate description of the target face, thereby producing details of which they were unsure, impaired later recognition of that face, whereas warning participants to generate only correct descriptors benefited face recognition. They proposed that nonveridical information elicited by the description may have an unfavourable influence upon memory.

DIFFERENT TYPES OF VERBAL INTERFERENCE?

Studies of verbal overshadowing have almost exclusively used a single stimulus exposure and tested recognition using a lineup procedure. However, in a paradigm developed by Brown and Lloyd-Jones (2002, 2003), participants were exposed to a series of to-be-remembered stimuli (12 faces or cars) and then described (or not) an additional stimulus (e.g., a 13th face). Description of a single face impaired subsequent old/new recognition of both faces and cars (see also Dodson, Johnson, & Schooler, 1997; Westerman & Larsen, 1997). They argued that verbalisation encouraged a relatively long-lasting shift (over a number of trials) towards greater visual processing of individual facial features, at the expense of more global visual processing which is particularly useful for the recognition of highly visually similar objects such as faces and cars.

Brown and Lloyd-Jones (2002) also contrasted "piecemeal" description instructions, encouraging the veridical recall of particular features of the face, with "elaborative" instructions used by Meissner et al. (2001) and which did not explicitly focus on particular facial features but rather encouraged erroneous recall of the face. Verbal overshadowing was apparent only for piecemeal instructions. Brown and Lloyd-Jones suggested that a key difference between their paradigm and that used by Meissner and colleagues was that description of a single face impaired recognition of *a number of different faces*, whereas Meissner and colleagues elicited erroneous descriptors of a face which later impaired recognition of *the same face*. Thus, they suggested that verbalisation may reflect either a change in "processing style" or an alteration to a particular memory representation of a face, depending on the nature of the paradigm.

In fact, the paradigm of Brown and Lloyd-Jones (2002, 2003) differs in a number of ways from the original paradigm of Schooler and Engstler-Schooler (1990): (1) Participants describe a single face, which is not subsequently presented for recognition (although see Dodson et al., 1997); (2) performance is assessed over a series of study and test trials; and (3) perceptual memory is assessed in an old/new recognition task rather than identification using a lineup procedure (see also Clare & Lewandowsky, 2004). These differences may be responsible for a different form of interference from that observed in the traditional paradigm, or a form of interference that can contribute to the verbal overshadowing effect.

THE PRESENT STUDY

The aim of the present study was to place some parameters on verbal overshadowing observed in the Brown and Lloyd-Jones (2002, 2003) paradigm. First, traditional studies have shown that verbal overshadowing can persist for up to 2 days (Schooler & Engstler-Schooler, 1990) and possibly 2 weeks (Read & Schooler, 1994). We therefore examined whether verbal overshadowing in the multiple face paradigm was apparent at relatively short (across 0–46 intervening items) and long (across 47–70 intervening items) lags after initial presentation. Note, the short lag here is comprised of more trials than used previously (which was on average across 0–34 intervening items) and we also used a new set of "morphed" faces (i.e., head models newly constructed from real faces through synthesis by morphing). If verbal interference here is comparable to that observed in the traditional paradigm we may expect it to be evident at both short and long lags.

We should note however that, as in previous studies using the multiple face paradigm, exposure to multiple faces can lead to both proactive (i.e., encoding of faces is impaired by prior exposure to earlier faces) and retroactive (i.e., where the retrieval of faces is impaired by prior exposure to earlier recognition tests) interference (e.g., Davies, Shepherd, & Ellis, 1979; Deffenbacher, Carr, & Leu, 1981). This raises the concern that recognition performance may be too low to observe any effects of verbalisation, particularly at the long lag. Nevertheless, in the original paradigm verbal overshadowing was observed over and above any influence of these factors, and on the basis of previous studies we predict that recognition performance, even at the longer lag, will be sufficient for verbal overshadowing to be observed here.

Second, we examined the influence of verbal overshadowing on different aspects of recognition memory. Models of recognition memory may be classified broadly as comprised of one or two processes (for reviews, see Rugg & Yonelinas, 2003; Yonelinas, 2002). Single-process models assume that recognition judgements are based on the target items familiarity or its total similarity to the contents of memory. Dual-process accounts propose that a second, slower, recall-like process operates as well, which is more accurate for fine discriminations between items. Familiarity is thought to reflect a purely quantitative "strength-like" memory signal, whereas recollection yields qualitative information about the previous study event (such as when or where an item was studied). One method used to measure recollection and familiarity is the remember/know procedure (Tulving, 1985). This requires participants to introspect about the basis of their recognition memory judgements and report whether they recognise items on the basis of remembering qualitative information about the study event ("remember" responses) or knowing the item is familiar in the absence of recollection ("know" responses).

Although many researchers consider the remember/know procedure valuable (e.g., Gardiner, 1988; Gardiner, Ramponi, & Richardson-Klavehn, 2002; Kishayami & Yonelinas, 2003; Parkin, Gardiner, & Rosser, 1995; Yonelinas, 2002; Yonelinas & Jacoby, 1995), others have recently questioned its usefulness (e.g., Wixted & Stretch, 2004). However, the focus here is primarily on how dissociations between remember and know judgements may inform our understanding of verbal overshadowing. We make no strong claims concerning the relationship between remember and know judgements and the underlying processes of recollection and familiarity, respectively.

The effect of verbal overshadowing on remember and know judgements has not been studied previously. However, an unpublished study by Schooler, Fiore, Melcher, and Ambadar (1996, cited in Schooler et al., 1997) examined the influence of verbal overshadowing on just know/reason judgements in the traditional paradigm. After the recognition task, participants decided whether recognition was based on "specific reasons" or "just based on a 'gut' reaction without any specific reasons". Verbal overshadowing was observed only for just know judgements. This suggests that verbalisation may influence a particular aspect of recognition memory, namely the process of familiarity rather than recollection, and may also be a useful variable in dissociating behaviourally different aspects of recognition memory performance.

Finally, we should note an added complication to the present study. In Brown and Lloyd-Jones (2002, 2003) effects of verbal overshadowing were moderated by task-specific carryover effects arising in their repeated measures design. In particular, verbal overshadowing only arose when the verbalisation task followed the control condition. They argued that carryover effects from the description onto the control condition attenuated the observation of verbal overshadowing: When participants initially verbally described the stimulus they were then more likely to covertly describe the stimulus in the control condition. Verbal overshadowing is fragile, and a number of laboratories have failed to replicate Schooler and colleagues findings (e.g., Clifford, 2003; Davies & Thasen, 2000; Yu & Geiselman, 1993). Furthermore, verbal overshadowing is attenuated in the standard paradigm when participants are asked to repeatedly view, describe, and identify a series of faces (Fallshore & Schooler, 1995; Schooler, Ryan, & Reder, 1996). Nevertheless, power in the Brown and Lloyd-Jones paradigm compares very favourably with studies included in the meta-analysis of Meissner and Brigham (2001; in Brown & Lloyd-Jones, 2003, p. 198, Fisher's $Z_r = -.40$ was significantly greater than the meta-analysis value of $Z_r = -.12$). We therefore decided to remain with the original design, and carefully examine the influence of any carryover effects on verbal overshadowing.

The following experiment examined verbal overshadowing at short and long lags after initial presentation on face recognition using the remember/know procedure.

METHOD

Participants

Sixty-four undergraduate students (49 females, 15 males) from the University of Kent participated as partial fulfilment of a course requirement. All were native English speakers, with normal or corrected to normal vision.

Materials and apparatus

The study and test stimuli were greyscale head and shoulder images of 96 male faces. To ensure that the recognition task involved face recognition rather than image recognition, two views of each face were used (cf. Baddeley & Woodhead, 1983; Sporer, 1991). For each face, a full frontal view was presented during the study phase whilst a three-quarters view (facing left) was presented at test.

Face stimuli were provided by the Max Planck Institute for Biological Cybernetics in Tübingen, Germany. These were head models that had been newly constructed from real faces through synthesis by morphing. None of the faces had any distinctive marks or attributes and hair cues had been removed. The stimuli therefore differ to some extent from those used by Brown and Lloyd-Jones (2002, 2003) where hair cues were present. The description stimuli were the full frontal images of two faces from the same database, different from those appearing as study and test materials.

Stimuli were presented on a PC using E-prime presentation software (Version 1.1, Psychology Software Tools, Inc.) and appeared in the centre of the computer screen. The faces images were approximately 8.5 × 6.5 cm in size. Each face was centrally mounted on a black background measuring 9.5 × 9.5 cm.

Design and procedure

A 2 × 2 × 2 mixed factorial design was employed with both description (description vs. no description) and lag (short vs. long) as within-participants factors and condition order (description condition first vs. description condition second) as a between-participants factor. The dependent variables were taken from signal detection theory, and were discrimination (d'), and response bias (C). In addition, remember and know responses were recorded for hits and false alarms. Accuracy in the recognition test was measured by a keypress response.

Each participant received both description and no description conditions. Thus, participants viewed two separate experimental blocks during the experiment. Each experimental block comprised a study phase of 24 target faces, and a test phase consisting of two separate stimulus blocks (note, blocks were presented continuously to the participants). The first short lag test block consisted of three-quarter views of 12 previously seen target faces mixed randomly with 12 new distractor faces. The second long lag test block consisted of three-quarter views of the remaining 12 previously seen target faces mixed randomly with 12 new distractor faces. To achieve this, the 96 faces were divided into eight sets of 12 faces. These were rotated across both description and no description conditions as: (a) target faces presented at the short lag (i.e., faces that appeared in the study phase and were presented within trials 25–48 of the experimental block); (b) target faces presented at the long lag (i.e., faces that appeared in the study phase and were presented within trials 49–72 of the experimental block); and (c) distractors (i.e., new faces in the experimental block). The eight face sets were rotated across conditions so that every set appeared equally often as target faces presented at the short lag, target faces presented at the long lag, and distractors for an equal number of participants (i.e., eight participants within each description condition). No face was repeated for any participant.

At study, two of the eight face sets were paired together so that 12 faces to be presented subsequently as targets at the short lag were mixed with 12 faces to be presented as targets at the long lag. To carefully control for possible effects of presentation order at study there were eight different pairings of particular face sets in the study phase. Four sequence templates (i.e., orders of stimulus presentation) were constructed for the 24 study faces. These comprised two random (forward) sequences plus the reverse of these two random sequences (reverse sequences were used to ensure that faces presented late and early in the study phase were rotated). The four sequence templates were rotated across the eight face-set pairings so that equal numbers of participants viewed each sequence template within each face-set pairing (i.e., four participants within each face-set pairing). In addition, the four sequence templates were rotated so that equal numbers of participants viewed each sequence template in both the description and no description conditions (i.e., 16 participants in each condition).

In addition, two description stimuli (D_1 and D_2) were rotated so that each appeared as the last item in both the description and no description condition, for an equal number of participants. Thus, half of the participants described D_1 in the description condition whilst viewing D_2 in the no description condition and half described D_2 in the description condition whilst viewing D_1 in the no description condition. Furthermore, the two description stimuli were rotated across face-set pairings and sequence templates. For four of the eight face-set pairings presentation of D_1 followed faces presented in the two random (forward) sequences, whilst presentation of D_2 followed faces presented in the two corresponding reverse sequences. For the remaining four face-set pairings, presentation of D_2 followed faces presented in the two random (forward) sequences, whilst presentation of D_1 followed faces presented in the two corresponding reverse sequences. The description stimulus appeared as the last item in the study phase, whether or not it was to be described, and did not reappear in the recognition test.

The order in which participants undertook the description and no description conditions was counterbalanced, with half the 64 participants undertaking the description condition as the first experimental block and half the no description condition as the first experimental block.

Each participant was tested individually. During the study phase (for both description and no description conditions) participants viewed a series of 25 faces. Faces were presented sequentially. Each face remained on the screen for 5 s and was preceded by a fixation cross presented for 1 s. Prior to viewing the faces, participants were instructed to study each face for the whole time that it appeared on the screen. In addition, participants were informed that they would later be asked to recognise the items they were about to see but that each of these items would be presented in a different view from how they were to appear in the study phase.

Following the study phase participants were provided with instructions concerning the experimental manipulation. These instructions were taken from Brown and Lloyd-Jones (2003). During a 5 min period, description condition participants were asked to write a detailed description of the last face they had viewed in the study phase. The following general instructions were provided: "Please try to write down a description of the last face you saw in the study phase. Try to be as complete as possible so that another person seeing only your description could get as accurate an idea as possible of what the face is like." Participants were then provided with a series of specific questions directing them to consider six specific aspects of the face (forehead, eyes and eyebrows, nose, mouth, chin, ears; cf. Finger & Pezdek, 1999). Participants were told that it was important for them to concentrate on the task of describing the face for the entire 5 min period. No description condition participants engaged in a filler activity for a period of 5 min. A series of 10 numbers was presented upon the computer screen and following the presentation of each number participants were given 30 s in which to count backwards from that number in intervals of three. When the computer sounded, participants were to stop counting and press the spacebar on the keyboard to view the next number.

Immediately following the experimental manipulation, face recognition was tested in a yes/no recognition task in which the 24 previously seen target faces were mixed with 24 new distractor faces (at either the short or long lag). Participants were instructed to respond "yes" if the face had appeared in the study phase and "no" if it had not. The recognition decision was indicated by pressing one of two keys ("Z" or "M") on the computer keyboard. Decision-key mapping and hand dominance were counter-balanced. Each face remained in view until the participant responded as quickly and accurately as possible.

Participants were also asked to make a further "remember" or "know" judgement to those faces they responded "yes" to in the recognition test. Following a "yes" response the face was replaced by a prompt to press either "R" for "remember" or "K" for "know" on the keyboard. Following an "R" or a "K" response (or a "no" recognition decision) a prompt appeared instructing the participant to rest their fingers on the recognition decision keys ("Z" and "M") and to press the spacebar to view the next face. Prior to completing the recognition test, participants were provided with instructions concerning the definitions of remember/know judgements. These definitions were adapted from Dewhurst and Conway (1994) and were as follows:

> When you see a face in this test that you recognize, you may be able to remember specific details about seeing the face in the earlier study phase. You may, for example, recollect the thoughts or feelings that the face evoked when you saw it earlier, or some aspect of the face's physical appearance. In short, any detail that supports your belief that the face appeared in the earlier study phase. For other faces, you simply know that they appeared earlier. These faces may feel familiar, but you cannot recall their actual occurrence in the earlier list. Therefore, every time you recognize a face press either R for remember if you can remember specific

details of the face's earlier occurrence, or K for know if you recognize the face from the earlier study phase but you cannot recollect its actual occurrence.

Following completion of the recognition test for the first experimental condition, participants immediately began the second experimental condition. They were informed that the second part of the experiment contained completely new items and that the task in between the study and test phases would be different.

RESULTS

Analyses of accuracy were carried out to assess whether verbalisation, lag, and condition order influenced discrimination (d') or response bias (C). Statistical analyses of discrimination and response bias were calculated according to the prescriptions set out by Snodgrass and Corwin (1988). That is, difficulties arise for the signal detection theory model at hit or false alarm rates of 1 or 0. Therefore, we transformed accuracy data by adding .5 to each frequency and dividing by $N+1$, where N is the number of old or new trials/stimuli. For d', larger values indicate a greater ability to discriminate between old and new items in the recognition test. For C, values above 0 indicate a conservative bias (i.e., a tendency to say "no") and values below 0 a liberal bias in the recognition test.

In addition, we examined whether verbalisation and lag influenced participants' sense of recollection and familiarity in face recognition. There is some disagreement concerning the appropriateness of different measurement methods. For instance, two contrasting models are the exclusivity (e.g., Gardiner & Java, 1990; Gardiner & Parkin, 1990; Gardiner et al., 2002) and independence models (Yonelinas, 2002; Yonelinas & Jacoby, 1995). The exclusivity view assumes that remember and know judgements provide measures of two subjective states of awareness associated with memory performance. Remember judgements reflect conscious recollection, whilst know responses reflect conscious memorial states of familiarity. These two states are assumed to be mutually exclusive and map directly onto the absolute proportions of remember and know responses (e.g., Gardiner, 1988; Parkin et al., 1995). Critics argue however, that the exclusivity approach makes the implicit assumption that processes underlying recollection and familiarity-based recognition are also mutually exclusive (Yonelinas, 2002; Yonelinas & Jacoby, 1995; although see Richardson-Klavehn, Gardiner, & Java, 1996). A contrasting view is that the processes underlying recollection and familiarity-based recognition judgements are independent (Yonelinas, 2002; Yonelinas & Jacoby, 1995). In this approach, remember and know responses are used as a basis for estimating the relative contributions of these independent processes to recognition memory. As participants are instructed to respond "remember" whenever an item is recollected, the proportion of remember responses can be taken as a relatively unbiased measure of recollection. However, the proportion of know responses will underestimate the probability that a given item is familiar. This is because participants are instructed to give a "know" response whenever an item is familiar, but not recollected, whereas under the independence assumption there will be some proportion of items that are both recollected and familiar. Therefore, estimates of familiarity are derived by dividing the proportion of know responses by one minus the proportion of remember responses (Yonelinas & Jacoby, 1995).

We therefore examine know responses, and we also use know responses as a basis for estimating the underlying process of familiarity as defined by Yonelinas and Jacoby (1995).

Table 1 shows discrimination, response bias, hits, and false alarms as a function of description condition, lag, condition order, and response type (i.e., remember or know). Analyses consisted of three-way mixed design analyses of variance (ANOVA) with description (description vs. no description) and lag (short vs. long) as within-participant factors and condition order (description condition first vs. description condition second) as a between-participants factor.[1] The data were analysed in four ways: (1) We calculated d' from signal detection theory as a measure of discrimination; (2) the proportion of hits and false alarms were analysed separately for remember and know judgements (i.e., the number of old (new) remember or know responses was divided by the total number of old (new) items); (3) we computed separate familiarity estimates for hits and false alarms, as suggested by Yonelinas (2002). Note, that the proportion of remember responses already provides a direct estimate of recollection under this procedure; and (4) we further measured participant accuracy by calculating separate d' scores for remember responses, know responses, and familiarity estimates. We report only significant ($p < .05$) or marginally nonsignificant ($p \leq .06$) findings.

Finally, as noted in the introduction, we were concerned that recognition performance should not be too low for effects of verbalisation to be observed, particularly at the long lag. To test this, we conducted pairwise

[1] An alternative but less powerful analysis is to compare description versus no description conditions between groups, when both groups received these conditions as either the first or second experimental block. When we do this, there was some evidence of a trend towards overshadowing when the description and no description condition was each presented first to participants: For familiarity estimates derived for correct recognition decisions, there was a trend towards a Description × Lag interaction, $F(1, 92) = 3.34$, $p = .07$, $MSE = 0.012$. The largest mean difference indicated lower familiarity estimates associated with the description as compared with the no description, at the short lag (.34 vs. .39, respectively). No other findings approached significance.

TABLE 1
Means (standard deviations in brackets) for discrimination, response bias, hits, and false alarms as a function of description, lag, condition order, and remember/know judgements

	Description		*No description*	
	Short	*Long*	*Short*	*Long*
Description first				
d′	.50 (.51)	.30 (.61)	.41 (.48)	.47 (.60)
C	.20 (.31)	.32 (.42)	.12 (.37)	.33 (.35)
Remember				
Hits	.29 (.16)	.19 (.14)	.27 (.16)	.24 (.12)
FA	.13 (.12)	.12 (.13)	.15 (.13)	.14 (.15)
d′	.57 (.60)	.26 (.54)	.42 (.64)	.44 (.64)
Know				
Hits	.23 (.11)	.25 (.16)	.26 (.11)	.22 (.16)
FA	.19 (.10)	.19 (.15)	.22 (.15)	.15 (.12)
d′	.12 (.44)	.16 (.66)	.15 (.44)	.24 (.62)
Familiarity estimates				
Hits	.34 (.15)	.32 (.21)	.36 (.15)	.29 (.20)
FA	.22 (.12)	.21 (.15)	.26 (.18)	.17 (.13)
d′	.33 (.51)	.29 (.73)	.31 (.50)	.38 (.66)
Description second				
d′	.39 (.58)	.34 (.48)	.70 (.67)	.20 (.52)
C	−.01 (.28)	.28 (.33)	.11 (.32)	.26 (.37)
Remember				
Hits	.29 (.15)	.23 (.14)	.33 (.13)	.21 (.14)
FA	.16 (.16)	.11 (.12)	.13 (.12)	.12 (.12)
d′	.47 (.70)	.48 (.50)	.64 (.50)	.33 (.60)
Know				
Hits	.29 (.15)	.22 (.15)	.26 (.15)	.23 (.15)
FA	.26 (.14)	.21 (.15)	.19 (.13)	.23 (.14)
d′	.07 (.46)	.03 (.67)	.22 (.74)	−.02 (.57)
Familiarity estimates				
Hits	.41 (.19)	.28 (.18)	.39 (.21)	.29 (.17)
FA	.31 (.15)	.23 (.16)	.23 (.16)	.27 (.16)
d′	.27 (.56)	.16 (.71)	.49 (.85)	.06 (.61)

For *d′* larger values indicate a greater ability to discriminate between old and new items. For C, values above 0 indicate a conservative bias and values below 0 a liberal bias. Familiarity estimates are derived by dividing the proportions of know responses by one minus the proportion of remember responses (Yonelinas & Jacoby, 1995), whereas remember responses are a direct estimate of recollection.

comparisons of each condition with zero, for the overall d' measure, using a multistage Bonferroni procedure (Holm, 1979). T-values ranged from 2.15 (for the no description, description second, long lag condition) to 5.88 (for the no description, description second, short lag condition) and all comparisons were significant (alpha = .05). We therefore do not regard floor effects as a serious concern.

Overall discrimination

There was a main effect of lag, d' $F(1, 62) = 5.51$, $p < .05$, $MSE = 0.34$, with discrimination significantly better at the short lag (mean discrimination scores of .50 and .33, for the short and long lag, respectively). There was also a significant Description × Lag × Condition order interaction, d' $F(1, 62) = 8.11$, $p < .01$, $MSE = 0.25$.

The interaction was analysed further by carrying out separate ANOVAs for short and long lag conditions. For the short lag, there was a significant Description × Condition order interaction, d' $F(1, 62) = 4.78$, $p < .05$, $MSE = 0.25$. Discrimination was significantly poorer in the description than no description condition, for participants undertaking the description condition second (a description–no description difference of $-.31$), $t(31) = -2.34$, $p < .05$.

Response bias

There was a main effect of lag, C $F(1, 62) = 67.90$, $p < .001$, $MSE = 0.04$, with more liberal responding at the short lag (a mean response bias of .10 and .30, for the short and long lag, respectively). There was also marginally nonsignificant Description × Lag × Condition order interaction, C $F(1, 62) = 3.94$, $p = .05$, $MSE = 0.05$. The means indicate a similar pattern to that observed for discrimination at the short lag, with more liberal responding in the description than no description condition, for participants undertaking the description condition second (a description–no description difference of $-.12$).

Remember judgements

Correct responses. There was a main effect of lag, $F(1, 62) = 33.05$, $p < .001$, $MSE = 0.01$, with more remember responses at the short lag (mean responses of .29 and .22, for the short and long lag, respectively). There was also a significant Description × Lag × Condition order interaction, $F(1, 62) = 5.48$, $p < .05$, $MSE = 0.01$. The interaction was analysed further by carrying out separate ANOVAs for the short and long lag. For the short lag there were no significant findings. However, for the long lag there was a significant Description × Condition order interaction, $F(1, 62) = 5.41$, $p < .05$, $MSE = 0.01$. There were fewer remember responses in the description than no description condition for participants undertaking the description condition first (a description–no description difference of −.05), $t(31) = -2.69$, $p < .05$. (There were no significant findings for participants undertaking the description condition second.)

Incorrect responses. There was a marginally nonsignificant main effect of lag, $F(1, 62) = 3.67$, $p = .06$, $MSE = 0.01$. The means indicate that more remember responses accompanied false alarms at the short lag (mean remember responses of .14 and .12, for short and long lag conditions, respectively).

Discrimination. There was a main effect of lag, d' $F(1, 62) = 5.46$, $p < .05$, $MSE = 0.24$, with more remember responses for the short lag (mean discrimination scores of .52 and .38, for short and long lags, respectively). There was also a Description × Lag × Condition order interaction, d' $F(1, 62) = 6.93$, $p = .01$, $MSE = 0.24$.

The interaction was analysed further by carrying out separate ANOVAs for the short and long lag. For the short lag, there was a marginally nonsignificant Description × Condition order interaction, d' $F(1, 62) = 3.66$, $p = .06$, $MSE = 0.22$. The means indicated that discrimination for remember judgements was poorer in the description than no description condition, for participants undertaking the description condition second (a description–no description difference of −.17). Although we should note that there was also evidence for poorer discrimination for remember judgements in the no description than description condition for participants undertaking the description condition first (a description–no description difference of .15).

KNOW JUDGEMENTS

Correct responses. There was a main effect of lag, $F(1, 62) = 4.42$, $p < .05$, $MSE = 0.01$, with more know responses at the short lag (mean know responses of .26 and .23, for short and long lag conditions, respectively).

Incorrect responses. There was a significant Description × Lag × Condition order interaction, $F(1, 62) = 9.75$, $p < .01$, $MSE = 0.01$.

The interaction was analysed further by carrying out separate ANOVAs for the short and long lag. For the short lag, there was a description × condition order interaction, $F(1, 62) = 8.56$, $p < .01$, $MSE = 0.01$. There were more know responses to incorrect recognition decisions in the description than no description condition, for participants undertaking the description condition second (a description–no description difference of .07), $t(31) = 2.65$, $p < .05$.

Discrimination. There were no significant findings.

Familiarity estimates

Correct responses. There was a main effect of lag, $F(1, 62) = 18.30$, $p < .001$, $MSE = 0.02$, with higher familiarity estimates at the short lag (mean familiarity estimates of .37 and .29, for short and long lag conditions, respectively). There was also a Lag × Condition order interaction, $F(1, 62) = 4.19$, $p < .05$, $MSE = 0.02$. Familiarity estimates were higher for the short than the long lag, for both condition orders, with a greater difference when the description condition was second: a difference of .04, $t(31) = 2.05$, $p < .05$, when the description was first, and a difference of .11, $t(31) = 3.76$, $p < .005$, when the description condition was second.

Incorrect responses. There was a main effect of lag, $F(1, 62) = 5.81$, $p < .05$, $MSE = 0.01$, with higher familiarity estimates at the short lag (mean familiarity estimates of .25 and .22, for short and long lags, respectively). There was also a Description × Lag × Condition order interaction, $F(1, 62) = 10.99$, $p < .01$, $MSE = 0.01$.

The interaction was analysed further by carrying out separate ANOVAs for the two lag conditions. For the short lag, there was a significant Description × Condition order interaction, $F(1, 62) = 9.13$, $p < .005$, $MSE = 0.01$. There were higher familiarity estimates associated with false alarms in the description than no description condition, for participants undertaking the description condition second (a description–no description difference of .08), $t(31) = 2.67$, $p < .05$. For the long lag, there was a marginally nonsignificant Description × Condition order interaction, $F(1, 62) = 3.79$, $p = .06$, $MSE = 0.01$. The means indicate no difference between the description and no description conditions for either condition order (a description–no description difference of .04 and −.04, when the description condition is undertaken first and second, respectively). The interaction is best explained by higher familiarity estimates to incorrect recognition decisions for those participants undertaking the no description condition first as compared with second (a no description first–no description second difference of −.10).

Discrimination. There were no significant findings.

DISCUSSION

The present experiment has produced a number of novel findings. First, we have replicated and extended the findings of Brown and Lloyd-Jones (2002, 2003) with a greater number of items intervening between initial study and test, and a new set of morphed faces. Verbal overshadowing influenced discrimination performance with a lag ranging from 0 to 46 intervening items between initial presentation and test (designated the short lag condition, here). This extends verbal overshadowing from a lag of 0–34 intervening items observed in previous studies. However, as with Brown and Lloyd-Jones (2002, 2003) verbal overshadowing was only evident when the verbal description followed the control task. A concern therefore, is that the effects on performance observed here may not be the result of verbal overshadowing, but rather the fact that performance decreases generally over time, due to the build-up of proactive and retroactive interference through exposure and testing on multiple faces (e.g., Davies et al., 1979; Deffenbacher et al., 1981). In fact, two pieces of evidence argue against such an interpretation.

First, if the effects observed here were solely due to a build-up of proactive and retroactive interference, performance should have been statistically significantly poorer in the control condition when it followed the verbal description. Generally, this was not the case (although an exception was discrimination performance on remember responses).

Second, we suggest that the pattern of findings observed here at the short lag is due to carryover effects from the description onto the control condition which attenuate the observation of verbal overshadowing. If verbalisation depresses accuracy, and if the effects of verbalisation carry-over to the subsequent no description control task, then accuracy should be reduced in three conditions in the present paradigm: In the description condition when it is first and second, and in the no description condition when it is second. An inspection of the mean accuracy scores in Table 1 confirms this assertion. For the short lag, mean accuracy is much higher in the no description condition when it is presented first ($d' = .70$, $SD = 0.67$) as compared with the description condition when it is first ($d' = 50$, $SD = 0.51$) or second ($d' = .39$, $SD = 0.58$) and as compared with the no description condition when it is presented second ($d' = .41$, $SD = 0.48$). Furthermore, a direct comparison of no description control conditions shows that performance was poorer in the no description condition when it followed the description condition as compared with when it preceded the description condition, $t(62) = -1.96$, $p = .05$.

How might we explain this carryover effect theoretically? One possibility is that when participants verbally describe the final face in the study phase of the description condition they are then more likely to covertly describe the final face in the study phase of the subsequent no description control condition. This is because there is no reason for participants to change their "mental set". A concern with this suggestion, however, is that we might expect the demanding control task of counting backwards in threes to suppress any effects of describing the final face on subsequent recognition performance. Nevertheless, the filler task of counting backwards is very different from learning, describing, and recognising faces, and we would expect participants to differentiate easily between tasks involving faces and numbers and so prevent one contaminating the other (cf. Brown & Lloyd-Jones, 2005; Westerman & Greene, 1998, p. 385). A second possibility is that the carryover effect is more general. For instance, Brown and Lloyd-Jones (2002, 2003) have argued that describing the final face in the study phase of the description condition may lead to a shift in processing "style" or strategy towards greater processing of individual facial features during the recognition test, at the expense of more global visual processing which normally benefits recognition. It follows that the carryover effect observed here may reflect the continuation of an emphasis on processing individual features, at least on some trials, during the study phase of the subsequent no description condition. If this is the case and faces have not been encoded optimally in this control condition, then we may expect poorer recognition as compared with a control condition where faces have been encoded using a more efficient global visual processing style. Moreover, this suggestion is also consistent with the notion of transfer-inappropriate processing, as suggested by Schooler (2002). When the control condition is presented first, for both study and test phases, participants may be presumed to invoke an optimal global visual processing style. However, when the control condition follows the description condition, participants may have been encouraged to shift towards a nonoptimal featural processing style during encoding before the carryover effect dissipates and they return to an optimal global processing style at recognition. Thus, for this control condition there is both: (a) a mismatch between participants' processing style at encoding and test; and (b) the use of nonoptimal encoding processes. On the basis of this, we would expect recognition to be poorer in this control condition as compared to when the control condition is encountered first during the experiment.

The second main finding was that verbal overshadowing was most apparent at the short lag. It was evident on overall discrimination, know responses to incorrect recognition decisions (i.e., know false alarms), familiarity estimates associated with false alarms, and response bias. (We note there was also some evidence for verbal overshadowing of remember judgements at the short lag, although in this case the finding could be solely a reflection of the build-up of interference from other faces that had been encountered.) Importantly, verbal overshadowing was not apparent on these measures at the long lag (i.e., across 47–70 intervening items). Together, these findings suggest that verbal overshadowing is limited in this paradigm. This limitation may be due either to the passage of time or to the build-up of retroactive interference. We note here that some of the present lag effects (e.g., on response bias, and on remember responses) are similar to those observed in the Norman (2002) study of retroactive interference.

Third, it is of further interest that at the short lag verbally describing a single face encouraged an increase in false alarms, and in familiarity estimates associated with false alarms, for a series of faces not encountered previously.

Finally, we note that there was evidence of verbal overshadowing at the long lag reducing the number of correct remember responses (although in this case, unlike at the short lag, there was no evidence of an effect of verbal overshadowing on overall discrimination performance when combining remember and know judgements together). This was only the case when participants first described a face and then completed the control task, and therefore it cannot be explained by a build-up of proactive and retroactive interference. This finding suggests the intriguing (but tentative) possibility, under a dual-process approach to recognition memory, that verbalisation may influence familiarity-based processes initially but later on its effects are seen more strongly on recollection, perhaps when discrimination between items becomes more difficult. This notion is only partly consistent however with studies showing that familiarity decreases rapidly across intermediate delays, whereas recollection is generally unaffected (for a review, see Yonelinas, 2002).

Let us turn now to the two main issues relating to this study, namely how we may explain verbal overshadowing in the multiple presentation paradigm, and how the interference observed here compares with that observed in the more traditional paradigm.

The nature of verbal interference

Brown and Lloyd-Jones (2002, 2003) proposed that verbal overshadowing in the multiple face paradigm involves a shift in processing "style". They argued that verbalisation encouraged a relatively long-lasting shift (over a number of trials) towards greater visual processing of individual facial features, at the expense of more global visual processing which is particularly useful for the recognition of highly visually similar objects (such as faces and cars; see also Dodson et al., 1997, who invoked this idea as part of their account of verbal overshadowing). Of the two dominant accounts outlined in the introduction, it is consistent with the view of verbal overshadowing as a shift in processing rather than the acquisition of misinformation (cf. Meissner et al., 2001; Schooler, 2002).

The fact that verbal overshadowing was evident at the short lag, and most evident for know judgements appears, on initial inspection, to be consistent with this account. First, we can argue that the emphasis on verbalisation was strong enough to encourage an initial shift in visual processing. However, after a period of time and intervening trials the requirements of the recognition task became more evident, encouraging a further shift towards a processing style more efficient for recognition. Consequently, effects of verbal overshadowing diminished. Second, a number of theorists have proposed that knowing/familiarity is primarily sensitive to perceptual properties of stimuli, whereas remembering/recollection is most sensitive to conceptual processing (e.g., Gardiner & Java, 1993; Rajaram, 1993; Roediger, 1990; Rugg & Yonelinas, 2003).

Consistent with this account, there are studies using the traditional paradigm that have shown effects of a postdescription delay on identification which correspond to the findings presented here. The meta-analysis of verbal overshadowing studies by Meissner and Brigham (2001) found that verbal overshadowing was evident when identification followed the description task either immediately or shortly thereafter (≤ 10 min). In contrast, there was no verbal overshadowing with a longer delay (≥ 30 min). Indeed, at the longer delay, participants in the control condition exhibited a significant degree of forgetting, whereas there was no change in performance for the verbalisation condition. We observed a similar pattern of findings in the present study (discrimination in the control task fell from .70 at the short lag to .20 at the long lag, whereas discrimination in the verbalisation task remained similar at short and long lags, at .39 and .34, respectively). This suggests the possibility that in both kinds of paradigm the influence of verbalisation may change over time from being initially disruptive to becoming an aid to memory (see also Ryan & Schooler, 1998).

However, a simple perceptual/conceptual distinction mediating remembering and knowing is more problematic (e.g., Dewhurst & Anderson, 1999; Mäntylä, 1997; Rajaram & Geraci, 2000). Thus, Rajaram and colleagues (Rajaram 1993, 1996; Rajaram & Geraci, 2000) have proposed that whereas remembering is influenced by processing the distinctive features of events, knowing is influenced by the fluency of processing which can be modulated either by perceptual or conceptual factors. On this account, verbal overshadowing arising from a shift from global to local visual processing disrupted perceptual processing fluency. However, we found that verbalisation produced: (1) an increase in know false alarms; (2) an increase in familiarity estimates associated with false alarms; and also (3) a shift towards a liberal response bias driven by an increase in false alarms. In contrast, most manipulations of processing fluency have found an increase, rather than a decrease, in processing fluency to be associated with an increase in both hits and false alarms (for a review, see Yonelinas, 2002). Thus, our findings are not consistent with a decrease in processing fluency produced by a shift in visual processing style.

An alternative approach that maintains the notion of a processing shift can be described as follows. If we assume, in line with current similarity-based theories of false recognition, that similarity between targets and distractors makes the distractors familiar and this in turn can lead to false recognition, then it follows that a shift in processing style resulting from a verbal description may have increased this similarity in some way (for a review, see Roediger & Gallo, 2005; see also, e.g., Arndt & Hirshman, 1998; Brainerd, Wright, Reyna, & Mojardin, 2001; Schooler, 1998). Consistent with this suggestion, the vast majority of participants provided a generic face description which could apply equally well to a number of different faces that were subsequently encountered. For instance, different participant descriptions of the eyes included: "dark eyes, fairly big", "dark eyes, quite wide-set", "eyes were dark, but not particularly deep-set". Thus, the verbal description likely heightened familiarity for faces not previously encountered, which in turn reduced performance efficiency, for instance through increased interference at retrieval.

To take one particular account, fuzzy trace theory proposes that remember judgements usually result from the retrieval of verbatim traces (or representations) of detailed item-specific information, whereas know responses result from gist traces consisting of more general thematic, semantic, or elaborative characteristics of items (e.g., Brainerd, Reyna, & Kneer, 1995; Reyna & Brainerd, 1995). On this account, verbalisation encouraged a shift towards a greater reliance on the gist trace, and faces consistent with the gist of faces presented at study were then highly familiar and hence falsely recognised.

Finally, it is of interest that findings here were similar to those observed by Schooler et al. (1996, cited in Schooler et al., 1997). In both studies verbal overshadowing was apparent on familiarity-based recognition judgements. Schooler and colleagues report that verbalisation reduced successful recognition, whereas here it increased false alarms. However, they report correct responses assessed using a lineup procedure which we assume did not have a "not present" option. If this is the case, then verbalisation must have also increased false alarms. Thus, verbal overshadowing influenced familiarity-based recognition judgements in similar ways across the yes/no multiple forced-choice recognition procedure used here and the single target lineup procedure.

In conclusion, the findings presented here show some similarities with those observed in previous studies. Nevertheless, additional factors, such as proactive and retroactive interference over multiple items, or interference from similar distractors in a multiple-item forced two-choice recognition task, may come into play depending on the nature of the paradigm.

REFERENCES

Arndt, J., & Hirshman, E. (1998). True and false recognition in MINERVA2: Explanations from a global matching perspective. *Journal of Memory and Language, 39*, 371–391.

Baddeley, A. D., & Woodhead, M. (1983). Improving face recognition ability. In S. M. A. Lloyd-Bostock & B. R. Clifford (Eds.), *Evaluating witness evidence* (pp. 125–136). Chichester, UK: Wiley.

Brainerd, C. J., Reyna, V. F., & Kneer, R. (1995). False recognition reversal: When similarity is distinctive. *Journal of Memory and Language, 34*, 157–185.

Brainerd, C. J., Wright, R., Reyna, V. F., & Mojardin, A. H. (2001). Conjoint recognition and phantom recollection. *Journal of Experimental Psychology: Learning, Memory, and Cognition, 27*, 307–327.

Brown, C., & Lloyd-Jones, T. J. (2002). Verbal overshadowing in a multiple face presentation paradigm: Effects of description instruction. *Applied Cognitive Psychology, 16*, 873–885.

Brown, C., & Lloyd-Jones, T. J. (2003). Verbal overshadowing of multiple face and car recognition: Effects of within- versus across-category verbal descriptions. *Applied Cognitive Psychology, 17*, 183–201.

Brown, C., & Lloyd-Jones, T.J. (2005). Verbal facilitation of face recognition. *Memory and Cognition, 33*, 1442–1456.

Clare, J., & Lewandowsky, S. (2004). Verbalizing facial memory: Criterion effects in verbal overshadowing. *Journal of Experimental Psychology: Learning, Memory, and Cognition, 30*, 739–755.

Clifford, B. R. (2003). The verbal overshadowing effect: In search of a chimera. In G. Vervaeke (Ed.), *Much ado about crime* (pp. 151–161). Leuven, The Netherlands: de Gruyter.

Davies, G., Shepherd, J., & Ellis, H. (1979). Effects of interpolated mugshot exposure on accuracy of eyewitness identification. *Journal of Applied Psychology, 64*, 96–101.

Davies, G., & Thasen, S. (2000). Closed-circuit television: How effective an identification aid? *British Journal of Psychology, 91*, 411–426.

Deffenbacher, K. A., Carr, T. H., & Leu, J. R. (1981). Memory for words, pictures, and faces: Retroactive interference, forgetting and reminiscence. *Journal of Experimental Psychology: Human Learning and Memory, 7*, 299–305.

Dewhurst, S. A., & Anderson, S. J. (1999). Effects of exact and category repetition in true and false recognition memory. *Memory and Cognition, 27*, 664–673.

Dewhurst, S. A., & Conway, M. A. (1994). Pictures, images, and recollective experience. *Journal of Experimental Psychology: Learning, Memory, and Cognition, 20*, 1088–1098.

Dodson, C. S., Johnson, M. K., & Schooler, J. W. (1997). The verbal overshadowing effect: Why descriptions impair facial recognition. *Memory and Cognition, 25*, 129–139.

Fallshore, M., & Schooler, J. W. (1995). The verbal vulnerability of perceptual expertise. *Journal of Experimental Psychology: Learning, Memory, and Cognition, 21*, 1608–1623.

Finger, K., & Pezdek, K. (1999). The effect of verbal description on face identification accuracy: "Release from verbal overshadowing". *Journal of Applied Psychology, 84*, 340–348.

Gardiner, J. M. (1988). Functional aspects of recollective experience. *Memory and Cognition, 16*, 309–313.

Gardiner, J. M., & Java, R. I. (1990). Recollective experience in word and nonword recognition. *Memory and Cognition, 18*, 23–30.

Gardiner, J. M., & Java, R. I. (1993). Recognising and remembering. In S. E. Gathercole & A.F. Collins (Eds.), *Theories of memory* (pp. 163–188). Hillsdale, NJ: Lawrence Erlbaum Associates, Inc.

Gardiner, J. M., & Parkin, A. J. (1990). Attention and recollective experience in recognition memory. *Memory and Cognition, 18*, 579–583.

Gardiner, J. M., Ramponi, C., & Richardson-Klavehn, A. (2002). Recognition memory and decision processes: A meta-analysis of remember, know, and guess responses. *Memory, 10*, 83–98.

Holm, S. (1979). A simple sequentially rejective multiple test procedure. *Scandinavian Journal of Statistics, 6*, 65–70.

Kishiyama, M. M., & Yonelinas, A. P. (2003). Novelty effects on recollection and familiarity in recognition memory. *Memory and Cognition, 31*, 1045–1051.

Mäntylä, T. (1997). Recollections of faces: Remembering differences and knowing similarities. *Journal of Experimental Psychology: Learning, Memory, and Cognition, 23*, 1203–1216.

Meissner, C. A., & Brigham, J. C. (2001). A meta-analysis of the verbal overshadowing effect in face identification. *Applied Cognitive Psychology, 15*, 603–616.

Meissner, C. A., Brigham, J. C., & Kelley, C. M. (2001). The influence of retrieval processes in verbal overshadowing. *Memory and Cognition, 29*, 176–186.

Norman, K. A. (2002). Differential effects of list strength on recollection and familiarity. *Journal of Experimental Psychology: Learning, Memory, and Cognition, 6*, 1083–1094.

Parkin, A. J., Gardiner, J. M., & Rosser, R. (1995). Functional aspects of recollective experience in face recognition. *Consciousness and Cognition: An International Journal, 4*, 387–398.

Rajaram, S. (1993). Remembering and knowing: Two means of access to the personal past. *Memory and Cognition, 21*, 89–102.

Rajaram, S. (1996). Perceptual effects on remembering: Recollective processes in picture recognition memory. *Journal of Experimental Psychology: Learning, Memory, and Cognition, 22*, 365–377.

Rajaram, S., & Geraci, L. (2000). Conceptual fluency selectively influences knowing. *Journal of Experimental Psychology: Learning, Memory, and Cognition, 26*, 1070–1074.

Read, J. D., & Schooler, J. W. (1994). *Verbalization decrements in long-term person identification.* Paper presented at the third Practical Aspects of Memory conference, College Park, MD.

Reyna, V. F., & Brainerd, C. J. (1995). Fuzzy-trace theory: An interim synthesis. *Learning and Individual Differences, 7*, 1–75.

Richardson-Klavehn, A., Gardiner, J. M., & Java, R. I. (1996). Memory: Task dissociations, process dissociations and dissociations of consciousness. In G. Underwood (Ed.), *Implicit cognition* (pp. 85–158). Oxford, UK: Oxford University Press.

Roediger, H. L. (1990). Implicit memory: Retention without remembering. *The American Psychologist, 45*, 1043–1056.

Roediger, H. L., & Gallo, D. A. (2005). Associative memory illusions. In R. F. Pohl (Ed.), *Cognitive illusions: A handbook on fallacies and biases in thinking, judgement and memory* (pp. 309–326). New York: Psychology Press.

Roediger, H. L., Weldon, M. S., & Challis, B. H. (1989). Explaining dissociations between implicit and explicit measures of retention: A processing account. In H. L. Roediger & F. I. M. Craik (Eds.), *Varieties of memory and consciousness: Essays in honour of Endel Tulving* (pp. 3–14). Hillsdale, NJ: Lawrence Erlbaum Associates, Inc.

Rugg, M. D., & Yonelinas, A. P. (2003). Human recognition memory: A cognitive neuroscience perspective. *Trends in Cognitive Sciences, 7*, 313–319.

Ryan, R. S., & Schooler, J. W. (1998). Whom do words hurt? Individual differences in susceptibility to verbal overshadowing. *Applied Cognitive Psychology, 12*, S105–S125.

Schooler, J. W. (1998). The distinctions of false and fuzzy memories. *Journal of Experimental Child Psychology, 71*, 130–143.

Schooler, J. W. (2002). Verbalization produces a transfer inappropriate processing shift. *Applied Cognitive Psychology, 16*, 989–997.

Schooler, J. W., & Engstler-Schooler, T. Y. (1990). Verbal overshadowing of visual memories: Some things are better left unsaid. *Cognitive Psychology, 22*, 36–71.

Schooler, J. W., Fiore, S. M., & Brandimonte, M. A. (1997). At loss from words: Verbal overshadowing of perceptual memories. In D. L. Medin (Ed.), *The psychology of learning and motivation* (Vol. 37, pp. 291–340). San Diego, CA: Academic Press.

Schooler, J. W., Ryan, R. S., & Reder, L. (1996). The costs and benefits of verbally rehearsing memory for faces. In D. Hermann, M. Johnson, C. McEvoy, C. Hertzog, & P. Hertel (Eds.), *Basic and applied memory: New findings* (pp. 51–65). Hillsdale, NJ: Lawrence Erlbaum Associates, Inc.

Snodgrass, J. G., & Corwin, J. (1988). Pragmatics of measuring recognition memory: Applications to dementia and amnesia. *Journal of Experimental Psychology: General, 117*, 34–50.

Sporer, S. K. (1991). Deep—deeper—deepest? Encoding strategies and the recognition of human faces. *Journal of Experimental Psychology: Learning, Memory, and Cognition, 17*, 323–333.

Tulving, E. (1985). Memory and consciousness. *Canadian Journal of Psychology, 26*, 1–12.

Westerman, D. L., & Greene, R. L. (1998). The revelation that the revelation effect is not due to revelation. *Journal of Experimental Psychology: Learning, Memory, and Cognition, 24*, 377–386.

Westerman, D. L., & Larsen, J. D. (1997). Verbal-overshadowing effect: Evidence for a general shift in processing. *American Journal of Psychology, 110*, 417–428.

Wixted, J. T., & Stretch, V. (2004). In defence of the signal detection interpretation of remember/know judgements. *Psychonomic Bulletin and Review, 11*, 616–641.

Yonelinas, A. P. (2002). The nature of recollection and familiarity: A review of 30 years of research. *Journal of Memory and Language, 46*, 441–517.

Yonelinas, A. P., & Jacoby, L. L. (1995). The relation between remembering and knowing as bases for recognition: Effects of size congruency. *Journal of Memory and Language, 34*, 622–643.

Yu, C. J., & Geiselman, R. E. (1993). Effects of constructing identikit composites on photo-spread identification performance. *Criminal Justice and Behaviour, 20*, 280–292.

EUROPEAN JOURNAL OF COGNITIVE PSYCHOLOGY
2008, 20 (3), 478–496

The role of verbal processing at different stages of recognition memory for faces

Kazuyo Nakabayashi and A. Mike Burton
University of Glasgow, Glasgow, UK

Four experiments examined the role of verbal processing at different stages of face recognition memory. In Experiment 1 participants learned faces with or without articulatory suppression, then engaged in an old/new recognition task. Using the same procedure, Experiment 2 examined performance under single and dual encoding conditions, using articulatory suppression and face verbalisation. In Experiment 3 performance deriving from these conditions was compared with a tapping control. The results were consistent; articulatory suppression impaired performance in comparison to the other conditions, which themselves did not differ. Experiment 4 examined the effects of postencoding verbalisation on performance, and showed some evidence for a standard verbal overshadowing effect. These results suggest that the role of verbal processing in face memory is complex, depending on the time when such processes occur. The results are discussed with reference to theories of verbal overshadowing.

This paper is concerned with the role of verbal processing at different stages of face recognition memory. The aim of this research was to address whether or not the effects of verbal processing on face recognition would differ depending on the time of verbalisation. In doing so, we introduced a face verbalisation task both at encoding and postencoding. Moreover, in order to address the applicability of dual coding theory to face recognition we devised single and dual encoding conditions, and examined recognition performance deriving from these conditions. Findings from these experiments will help provide a comprehensive view of the role of verbal processing in recognition memory for faces.

Correspondence should be addressed to Kazuyo Nakabayashi, Department of Psychology, School of Social Sciences & Law, University of Teeside, Middlesborough, Tees Valley, TS1 3BA, UK. E-mail: k.nakabayashi@tees.ac.uk

This research was supported by a doctorial studentship from the EPSRC to Kazuyo Nakabayashi. We wish to thank Jonathan Schooler for his helpful comments and suggestions on an earlier version of the paper.

http://www.psypress.com/ecp DOI: 10.1080/09541440801946174

DUAL CODING THEORY

Dual coding theory posits that there are two types of representation in memory, one visual and the other verbal (Paivio, 1971). The former is said to capture perceptual experience, whereas the latter is said to represent a more abstract mode of experience. These representations are independent of each other, but are partially interconnected for encoding, storage, organisation, and retrieval of information. Thus, information can be transferred from one to the other. In addition, the two types of representations function in an additive manner so that dual coding of information can lead to better subsequent memory performance than mono coding (see Paivio, 1986, for a review). Research in this paradigm often involves intentional learning of a stimulus either visually, verbally, or both (e.g., Paivio, 1971; Paivio & Csapo, 1973). Participants are given specific learning instructions, and the consequences of these for memory are examined. For example, Paivio and Csapo (1973) found that words were recalled better when they were encoded both visually (e.g., draw a picture of the word) and verbally (e.g., say the word) than when they were encoded only verbally. Subsequent studies also found beneficial effects of verbal rehearsal and elaboration on memory performance for both verbal (e.g., Craik & Tulving, 1975; Maki & Schuler, 1980) and visual stimuli (e.g., Bartlett, Till, & Levy, 1980; Daniel & Ellis, 1972). However, there appears to be little work examining the possibility of dual coding of faces.

VERBAL PROCESS AT ENCODING AND MEMORY PERFORMANCE

More recent research in the memory literature has demonstrated that dual coding of visual materials does not necessarily facilitate subsequent memory performance (Brandimonte, Hitch, & Bishop, 1992a, 1992b; Hitch, Brandimonte, & Walker, 1992; Pellizzon, Brandimonte, & Favretto, 1999). Different stimuli give rise to inherently different emphases on visual and verbal codes during learning (see, e.g., Bahrick & Boucher, 1968; Schooler & Engstler-Schooler, 1990). So, for example, in studies by Brandimonte and colleagues (Brandimonte et al., 1992a,1992b; Hitch et al., 1992; Pelizzon et al., 1999), articulatory suppression was used to examine the role of *spontaneous* verbal encoding in image transformation tasks. The technique is said to prevent phonological encoding of a stimulus without attentional costs (cf. Baddeley, 1986). In one study, Brandimonte et al. (1992b) examined the effects of articulatory suppression on subsequent mental imagery performance. Participants were first asked to remember a set of composite pictures (either easy-to-name or difficult-to-name pictures) with or without articulatory suppression. In a subsequent mental imagery task, the participants were shown one part of a picture and asked to identify the other part of the picture using mental imagery. The authors found that imagery performance for the easy-to-name stimuli was significantly improved when verbal encoding was prevented, indicating that the verbal representations of those pictures have little value in performing the imagery task. However, articulatory suppression had no effect on imagery performance when stimuli were difficult to name. These findings were attributed to the fact that people tend spontaneously to name and describe stimuli when this is possible, whether this is relevant to the task at hand or not. Furthermore, success of memory-based imagery performance, depended on whether the initial encoding condition inhibited or encouraged verbal processing. Pelizzon et al. (1999) also reported the beneficial effect of articulatory suppression on imagery performance while demonstrating the opposite effect on picture recognition performance when either the imagery or picture recognition task was performed alone. However, when participants performed both tasks, an overall benefit of articulatory suppression on imagery performance disappeared (though the benefit of articulatory suppression was still observed for the first trial) while the detrimental effect on recognition performance remained. From these findings the authors suggested that different tasks involve different proportions of visual and verbal processing, and that imagery tasks rely more on perceptual/visual processing while picture recognition tasks place more emphasis on featural/verbal processing. Hence, performing both tasks caused contamination, diminishing the beneficial effect of articulatory suppression on imagery performance.

In the domain of face recognition, Wichkam and Swift (2006) showed the importance of spontaneous verbal encoding for line-up identification, in that when face learning was accompanied by articulatory suppression, subsequent identification suffered significantly, in comparison to control where no articulatory suppression was involved. From the results, the authors suggested that spontaneous verbal processes are involved in face encoding, and that these are important for subsequent face identification. However, in order to fully understand the role of verbal processing in face encoding, it is important to examine the effects of verbalisation during encoding. If spontaneous verbal encoding were really involved in face learning, then it is possible that asking participants to describe a face during learning has no effect. In other words, the only difference between control and verbalisation conditions would be whether verbalisation is subvocal (in the control condition) or articulated (in the verbalisation condition). This would provide stronger evidence suggesting the involvement of dual coding in face memory processing. In this paper we attempt to address this in a single experiment that would provide better understanding of the role of verbal processing in face encoding.

VERBAL PROCESS AT POSTENCODING AND MEMORY PERFORMANCE

A key study demonstrating the detrimental effect of postencoding verbalisation on face recognition is reported by Schooler and Engstler-Schooler (1990). The authors demonstrated that describing a previously seen face impaired subsequent recognition of that face (the verbal overshadowing effect). The effect is said to depend on the verbalisability of a stimulus, and is likely to be seen in memory for difficult-to-describe stimuli, such as faces and colours (Schooler & Engstler-Schooler, 1990). Originally, the authors suggested that verbalisation of nonverbal memory might produce a verbally biased memory representation that can interfere with the application of the original visual memory at test, and this could be the cause of recognition impairment (the recoding interference hypothesis). However, more recently, Schooler and his colleagues (Schooler, 2002; Schooler, Fiore, & Brandimonte, 1997) suggested that the verbal overshadowing effect arises when there is a mismatch between encoding and retrieval processes (i.e., transfer inappropriate processing shift hypotheses). The term was borrowed from 'the transfer appropriate processing principle' in that memory performance is a function of overlap between the type of processing used during learning and test (e.g., Morris, Bransford, & Franks, 1977). In the context of the verbal overshadowing literature, visual processing is often associated with the notion of configural perception: a global or holistic processing style that is held to be important in face recognition (see Farah, Tanaka, & Drain, 1995; Farah, Wilson, Drain, & Tanaka, 1998). This is contrasted with verbally based processing, emphasising feature-by-feature description, which is held to be suboptimal for face recognition. Engaging in verbalisation of nonverbal memory provokes this suboptimal processing, which dampens the activation of configural processing at test, impairing performance. This processing shift affects not only the recognition of the described face, but also the recognition of other faces, whether they were described or not (see Brown & Lloyd-Jones, 2002, 2003; Dodson, Johnson, & Schooler, 1997). However, the notion of the processing shift account can be challenged by evidence reporting verbal facilitation of face recognition (Brown & Lloyd-Jones, 2005). The authors found that face recognition performance was better when participants described the target immediately after exposure than when they did not. This was true for both holistic- and feature-based descriptions.

What emerges from the studies described so far is that visual memory performance can be affected by verbal processing occurring at encoding (e.g., the studies by Brandimonte and her colleagues described earlier on imagery tasks), and also postencoding (e.g., the verbal overshadowing studies). However, these studies used very different methodologies (i.e., articulatory suppression at encoding, but active memory verbalisation at postencoding), making it difficult to establish whether similar processes might underlie these various effects. Moreover, although there has been much work examining the effects of postencoding verbalisation, little attention has been paid to understanding the effects of verbalisation during encoding. It is possible that the effects of verbalisation may vary depending on the time when verbalisation takes place. In the experiments here, we manipulate both encoding and postencoding stages in a face memory task in the same experimental context, and attempt to provide, for the first time, a coherent account of the effects of verbal processing on memory for faces.

EXPERIMENT 1

Explanations for the verbal overshadowing effect, described earlier, rely on the notion that faces are very difficult to put into words (Schooler & Engstler-Schooler, 1990). If this is true, then it would seem unlikely that verbal processes would be engaged in face learning, and so preventing verbal encoding during learning should not affect subsequent recognition performance. In this first experiment, we examine the effect of articulatory suppression on recognition performance. Articulatory suppression is assumed to disrupt verbal rehearsal of to-be-learned materials, and forces a reliance on visual processing of the stimuli (Baddeley, 1986, 1992). The detrimental effects of articulatory suppression have been demonstrated for line-up identification where faces are presented simultaneously at test (Wickham & Swift, 2006). However, this is the only available evidence demonstrating the detrimental effect of articulatory suppression on face memory performance. Therefore, we attempted to replicate the finding by using an old/new face recognition task where faces are presented one at a time sequentially. If verbal processing is not involved in face learning, we expect articulatory suppression to have little or no effect on performance. If, however, there is normally subvocal processing during face learning, then we predict that articulatory suppression would impair subsequent recognition of these faces.

Method

Participants. Twenty undergraduate students from University of Glasgow took part in this experiment for course credit. There were 6 males and 14 females, all of whom had normal or corrected-to-normal vision.

Stimuli/apparatus. An Apple Macintosh computer was used to present stimuli and record responses, using Superlab 1.75. Stimuli consisted of greyscale head and shoulder pictures of 60 young Caucasian men, taken from the United Kingdom Home Office Police Information Technology Organisation database (the same source as that in Bruce et al., 1999). These men were clean shaven, had short hair, and wore no accessories or spectacles. These images varied in expression, lighting conditions, and viewing angles. For half these men (those to be used as targets), there were two images differing in pose and expression. For the other half, a single image was used as a distractor face at test. Clothing and background of all pictures were removed by using Photoshop 5.5. The picture size was approximately 3.5 cm × 4.5 cm.

Design/procedure. Learning conditions (control/suppression) were manipulated within subjects, and blocked, such that the experiment followed the format: learning phase 1, filler task, test phase 1, rest, learning phase 2, filler task, test phase 2. In each of the learning phases participants were shown 15 target faces, each for 7 s. Each target was preceded by a cross for 2.5 s. Participants were instructed that their task was to remember the faces for subsequent testing. During one of the learning phases (the control condition), participants were given no secondary task. During the other learning phase (the suppression condition), they were instructed to say *da, da, da* aloud while learning each face. The rate of articulatory suppression (3 to 4 *da*'s per s) was similar to previous studies (e.g., Brandimonte et al., 1992b), and care was taken to maintain this rate. The participants remained silent while a cross was on the screen for 2.5 s. The order of condition was counterbalanced across participants. Furthermore, the facial stimuli were counterbalanced across the experiment such that each target face occurred equally often in the control and suppression conditions.

Test phases were identical in each condition. Participants were shown 30 faces, half of which were (new pictures of) the people they had seen in the preceding learning phase; the other half were new distractor faces (i.e., pictures of new people). Images of the targets between learning and test phases were always different to ensure that the task tapped onto face recognition performance, and not image recognition performance. Participants made a speeded keypress response as to whether each of these people was old (i.e., had been seen during the learning phase) or new (i.e., had not been seen). Stimuli remained on the screen until a response had been made, and the next stimulus appeared after a 2 s interstimulus interval (ISI). Across the experiment, the two photographs of target stimuli were counterbalanced, such that each image occurred equally often as a learning and a test item. In addition, the distractor faces were counterbalanced between the conditions so that each image was used equally frequently in each condition.

To summarise, participants took part in two learning and test phases, each with completely different face stimuli for any individual participant. Filler tasks between learning and tests phases comprised writing lists from memory for 10 min, for example lists of school subjects, hobbies, countries, and movies. There was a rest period of 5 min following the first test phase. In total, the experiment took approximately 45 min to run.

Results

Table 1 shows performance across conditions. As well as d', we also present hits and false positives (FPs). A t-test on d' revealed that participants performed better in the control condition than in the suppression condition, $t(19) = 3.02$, $p < .01$. Separate t-tests on hits and FPs, revealed no significant difference between conditions for hits, $t(19) = 1.75$, $p > .05$, but a significantly higher FP rate in the suppression condition, $t(19) = 2.43$, $p < .05$. RTs were relatively long (overall mean 990 ms) and showed no reliable effects.

Discussion

The results showed that articulatory suppression significantly impaired face recognition performance, suggesting the involvement of subvocal rehearsal in face encoding that seems to be beneficial to subsequent recognition. This is in agreement with the findings of Wickham and Swift (2006), and indicates that verbal representations of faces have important values in performing a face recognition task, whether it is sequential or simultaneous recognition. These results suggest that faces may be one class of stimuli that can be readily verbalised. As demonstrated in the mental imagery study by Brandimonte et al. (1992b), articulatory suppression had an effect only on easy-to-name pictures, but not on difficult-to-name-pictures, reflecting participants' tendency to name stimuli spontaneously when it was easy to do so. Similarly, it is possible that the current participants engaged in subvocal processing of faces because it was easy to do so. Moreover, as shown in Pelizzon et al. (1999) picture recognition performance, assumed to rely more on verbal/featural processing, also suffered significantly following articulatory suppression. What all these studies seem to indicate is that

TABLE 1
Performance in Experiment 1 as a function of learning condition

	Control *Mean (SD)*	*Suppression* *Mean (SD)*
d'	1.06 (0.6)	0.7 (0.51)
Hits	66%	61%
False positives	30%	39%

neither imagery nor recognition task is purely visual or verbal, but that they may involve different proportions of visual and verbal processing.

This calls into question the idea that faces are inherently nonverbal stimuli (Schooler & Engstler-Schooler, 1990), and may suggest that the current explanations for the verbal overshadowing effect may not be wholly accurate. It is clearly demonstrated by various verbal overshadowing studies (e.g., Brown & Lloyd-Jones, 2002, 2003; Dodson et al., 1997; Fallshore & Schooler, 1995; Ryan & Schooler, 1998; Schooler & Engstler-Schooler, 1990) that engaging in verbal processing of a face at postencoding can have detrimental effects on subsequent memory performance. However, this is held to occur because faces are nonverbal stimuli that rely on configural processing, and the subsequent description phase engages a mode of featural processing that is suboptimal for face recognition (Schooler, 2002). Nonetheless, the results of our experiment seem to suggest that face encoding does involve some verbal processes, and that these may actually be beneficial to subsequent recognition.

Despite this initial conclusion, it is important to note that the present results demonstrated only that performance under articulatory suppression was worse than that under a control. We have no direct evidence that this is due to spontaneous subvocal processes in the control condition (we are uncertain how participants actually encoded faces). Alternatively, it is possible that the negative effect of articulatory suppression could have simply been due to the fact that articulatory suppression functioned as a concurrent task, interfering with a primary task of learning faces. Although articulatory suppression is thought not to demand attention (cf. Baddeley, 1986), this possibility cannot be completely discarded. In Experiment 2 we manipulate learning processing in both conditions by using articulatory suppression (encouraging single visual encoding) and face verbalisation (ensuring verbal encoding).

EXPERIMENT 2

In this experiment we make an explicit comparison between single (verbal processing suppressed) and dual coding of faces (verbal processing enforced). The results from Experiment 1 demonstrated the negative effect of articulatory suppression on face recognition. However, it remains uncertain whether the results were due to spontaneous verbal encoding in the control condition or due to the learning disruption caused by articulatory suppression. In order to clarify this, a control condition was replaced with a verbalisation condition where participants are asked to describe each face aloud during learning. Thus, face learning in both conditions was accompanied by *a verbally based* secondary task (i.e., articulatory suppression and face description respectively). From the results of Experiment 1 we expect worse performance under articulatory suppression than under verbalisation.

Method

Participants. Twenty new volunteers participated in this experiment from the same source as Experiment 1. There were 5 males and 15 females, all of whom had normal or corrected-to-normal vision.

Stimuli/apparatus. The stimuli and apparatus were the same as those in Experiment 1.

Design/procedure. The design and procedure were identical to those in Experiment 1, with the exception that the control condition was replaced with a verbalisation condition in which participants described each face aloud during learning. They were asked to describe the appearance of the face in as much detail as possible, starting when the face appeared, and stopping when it disappeared 7 s later. As with Experiment 1, a learning phase was followed by a 10 min filler task, and then a test phase. Face stimuli were counterbalanced across the experiment in the same way as Experiment 1.

Results

Table 2 shows performance across conditions. A *t*-test on d' revealed better performance in the verbalisation condition than in the suppression condition, $t(19) = 2.95$, $p < .01$. Separate *t*-tests on hits and FPs revealed a significant difference between conditions for hits, $t(19) = 3.25$, $p < .01$, but no significant difference for FPs, $t(19) = 1.88$, $p > .05$. RTs were relatively long (overall mean 1065 ms) and showed no reliable effects.

Discussion

The negative effect of articulatory suppression on performance was, once more, observed in the current experiment, in comparison to the verbalisation condition, which ensured the use of verbal resources. This is direct evidence supporting a dual coding account of face memory performance. It appears then, that participants who actively describe a face (Experiment 2) or who are given no instructions as to what to do with it (Experiment 1) perform consistently better in recognition memory than participants whose articulation is disrupted with a standard suppression technique.

TABLE 2
Performance in Experiment 2 as a function of learning condition

	Suppression *Mean (SD)*	*Verbalisation* *Mean (SD)*
d′	0.67 (0.53)	1.17 (0.59)
Hits	62%	72%
False positives	35%	31%

If faces were a class of stimuli that are difficult-to-put-into-words, then requiring participants to describe them aloud should have prevented successful encoding (i.e., one was forced to do a difficult task, "face verbalisation" while attempting to learn the faces), leading to performance impairment. However, this was not the case for the current experiment. Instead, we suggest that in *both* Experiments 1 and 2, a certain amount of verbal processing during learning was occurring, and this seems to be the same whether it was articulated or subvocal. This suggests that even under a control condition (in which participants were given no instructions about how to encode the face) they may spontaneously invoke verbal descriptions.

However, Experiment 1 and 2 do not give a direct comparison between control and forced verbalisation conditions. In order to investigate the relationship between these further, Experiment 3 directly compares participants' performance when given instructions to describe a face, when given no instructions or when required to carry out articulatory suppression. We also introduce a further component to the control ("no instructions") condition. It is possible that the costs of articulatory suppression, above, arise because this secondary task simply adds to participants' overall load. In Experiment 3 a tapping task was introduced into the control condition to ensure that participants engaged in a concurrent task across all conditions. Tapping (e.g., Emerson & Miyake, 2003; Wickham & Swift, 2006) is often used as a control in studies examining the effect of articulatory suppression, and so it is introduced in Experiment 3 to provide a more stringent test.

EXPERIMENT 3

If spontaneous verbal encoding is involved in face learning, then we expect little or no difference in performance between control and verbalisation conditions. Further, we expect both to differ from an articulatory suppression condition. What we are assuming here is that the key determiner of performance is whether or not participants are able to engage in verbal processing during learning. We provide a direct test of this hypothesis across all three conditions. This is not straightforward, since we prefer to retain a within-subjects design. However, by reducing the number of trials in each condition, it is possible to provide a single experiment that combines the tests so far examined in Experiment 1 and 2. To summarise, in this experiment participants performed a recognition memory task in each of the three conditions: In the control condition the participants learned faces while tapping a desk; in the suppression condition they learned faces with articulatory suppression; in the verbalisation condition they learned faces while describing each face aloud.

Method

Participants. Twenty-four new volunteers participated in this experiment from the same source as the previous experiments. There were 6 males and 18 females, all of whom had normal or correct-to-normal vision.

Stimuli/apparatus. The stimuli and apparatus were the same as those in the previous experiments.

Design/procedure. The design and procedure were similar to those in the previous experiments. Participants carried out learning/filler/test phases for each of the three conditions: control, suppression, and verbalisation. Each learning phase comprised the presentation of 10 target faces, and each test phase comprised the same 10 identities (different pictures) mixed with 10 new distractor faces. In the control condition, participants tapped a table at a rate of 3 or 4 taps per s while learning each face (i.e., the same rate as repetitions in the suppression condition). Care was taken to maintain this rate. Participants started tapping the table when each face appeared, and stopped when it disappeared from the screen. They did not engage in desk tapping between trials, during which a cross was on the screen for 2.5 s. The order of condition was systematically varied. As with the previous experiments, stimuli were fully counterbalanced across the experiment, and no face appeared in more than a single condition for a given participant. It took approximately 1 hour to complete the experiment.

Results

Table 3 shows performance across conditions. ANOVA on d' revealed a significant effect of condition, $F(2, 46) = 5.47$, $p < .01$. Tukey HSD showed significantly poorer performance in the suppression than in the verbalisation condition, $p < .01$. The similar trend between the control and suppression conditions just failed to reach significance, $p = .053$. ANOVA on hits showed a significant effect of condition, $F(2, 46) = 4.57$, $p < .05$, with Tukey HSD

TABLE 3
Performance in Experiment 3 as a function of learning condition

	Control *Mean (SD)*	*Suppression* *Mean (SD)*	*Verbalisation* *Mean (SD)*
d′	1.18 (0.75)	0.79 (0.47)	1.33 (0.59)
Hits	70%	61%	69%
False positives	29%	36%	24%

revealing significantly worse performance following articulatory suppression than following control or verbalisation, $p < .05$. ANOVA on FPs showed a significant effect of condition, $F(2, 46) = 3.89$, $p < .05$, with Tukey HSD revealing significantly worse performance in the suppression condition than the verbalisation condition, $p < .05$. RTs were relatively long (overall mean 1097 ms) and showed no reliable effects.

Discussion

This experiment is consistent with the results from the earlier studies. When verbal encoding during learning was prevented, subsequent recognition performance suffered, in comparison both to the tapping control (reaching significance) and verbalisation conditions, which themselves did not differ. It appears that any general effect of a secondary task cannot account for the results from Experiments 1 and 2, but rather that the key determiner of performance across the three experiments is participants' ability to verbalise during encoding. Once more, these results seem to indicate that face encoding entails some sort of verbal processing, and that this occurs spontaneously. Since this is a strong conclusion, we should qualify it, recognising that further research will be necessary to fully understand these effects. We should point out that the time given for participants to describe faces was rather short. In a multi-item experiment, one is forced to see stimuli for rather a short time, and it is possible that under more realistic viewing conditions, one could detect a difference between the effects of forced and spontaneous verbalisation. However, under the conditions in our experiments, we were unable to do so.

To summarise, the results so far seem to suggest that verbal processing of faces is not necessarily harmful to recognition memory. We found recognition impairment resulting from the prevention of subvocal processing, but a null effect of forced verbalisation. These findings hint at the possibility that the effects of verbalisation on face recognition may vary depending on the time of verbalisation. This tentative hypothesis will be examined in the final experiment where we try to relate the data so far to the verbal overshadowing effect.

EXPERIMENT 4

So far, we have examined the role of verbal encoding in face recognition by manipulating verbal processing during learning. However, this does not have direct relevance to the verbal overshadowing literature as the phenomenon refers to recognition impairment caused by verbalisation at postencoding. Therefore, this final experiment examined the effect of verbal processing occurring at postencoding by adopting the multiple recognition paradigm used by Brown and Lloyd-Jones (2002). In the present study we will manipulate the *time* of verbalisation. The results reported so far strongly suggest the involvement and importance of subvocal processing during learning on subsequent recognition. If a standard verbal overshadowing effect is replicated in the same experimental context, it would support the tentative suggestion that the effects of verbalisation vary depending on the time when it is executed. In this experiment participants carried out learning/filler/test sequences under conditions in which they were sometimes asked to describe a face during the filler phase. In the verbalisation condition they described a single face from the learning set, a manipulation that has been shown to elicit the verbal overshadowing effect (Brown & Lloyd-Jones, 2002).

Method

Participants. Twenty new volunteers participated in this experiment from the same source as the previous experiments. There were 6 males and 14 females, all of whom had normal or correct-to-normal vision.

Stimuli/apparatus. The stimuli and apparatus were the same as those in the previous experiments.

Design/procedure. The design and procedure were similar to Experiments 1 and 2. The experiment followed the format: learning phase 1, filler task 1, test phase 1, rest, learning phase 2, filler task, test phase 2. In each of the learning phases, participants were shown 15 target faces, each for 7 s. Each target was preceded by a cross for 2.5 s. Participants were given no secondary task in either learning phase.

The only difference between the two conditions was in the nature of the postencoding task. In the control condition, there were two filler tasks, each lasting for 5 min, and both requiring participants to write lists (e.g., school subjects, movies, or hobbies). In the verbalisation condition, participants first carried out a 5 min filler task, following which they described one of the faces recently seen, in as much details as possible. Participants were allowed to describe the face from the most recent learning session that they remembered best. They wrote down a description of this face for 5 min.

Test phases were identical across conditions. Participants were shown 30 faces, half of which were (new pictures of) the people they had seen in the preceding learning phase; the other half were distractor faces (i.e., pictures of new people). Participants made speeded keypress responses as to whether each of these people was old (i.e., seen during learning) or new (not seen during learning). Stimuli remained on the screen until a response had been made, and the next stimulus appeared after 2 s ISI. As with the previous experiments, the stimuli were counterbalanced across the experiment, such that target faces appeared equally often in each condition. Furthermore, the order of conditions was counterbalanced across participants.

Results

Table 4 shows performance across conditions. A *t*-test on d' showed no significant difference between control and verbalisation conditions, $t(19) = 1.49$, $p > .05$. However, there was a reliable effect for hits, with poorer performance following verbalisation, $t(19) = 2.46$, $p < .05$, but no significant difference for FPs, $t(19) = 1.03$, $p > .05$. RTs were relatively long (overall mean 1286 ms) and showed no reliable effects or interactions.

Discussion

If we consider first the hit rate data, the results demonstrate a classical verbal overshadowing effect in that describing a previously seen face impaired recognition performance, compared to not describing a face. A similar trend was observed, though not significantly, for FPs and d', in that postencoding verbalisation damaged performance. It has previously been reported that verbalisation does not seem simply to affect participants'

TABLE 4
Performance in Experiment 4 as a function of postencoding condition

	Control *Mean (SD)*	*Verbalisation* *Mean (SD)*
d'	1.08 (0.68)	0.91 (0.42)
Hits	71%	63%
False positives	33%	36%

willingness to select the target in that the proportions of misses and misidentifications do not differ between control and verbalisation groups (Schooler & Engstler-Schooler, 1990). Therefore, it seems possible to find a reliable, but small, effect of verbal overshadowing for hits, but not for FPs or d'. Overall, we take these results to indicate a (relatively weak) detriment to performance, consistent with the verbal overshadowing effect. Certainly, there is no hint at all of the *benefits* of verbal processing, observed in Experiments 1–3, where such processing occurred at encoding. Taken together with the findings from Experiments 1–3, we suggest that the detrimental effect of verbalisation in this experiment was unlikely to be due to the change in processing styles between learning and test, from visual processing to verbal processing, and we will return to this in the General Discussion.

GENERAL DISCUSSION

In this series of experiments we examined the role of verbal processing at different stages of a face recognition memory task. Experiments 1–3 demonstrated that articulatory suppression damaged subsequent memory performance, in comparison both to forced verbalisation and no-instruction control. Our suggestion is that verbal processes are engaged during face encoding, whether or not participants are instructed to do so. Disrupting this verbal encoding can lead to poorer memory performance, highlighting the importance of verbal processing in face recognition and dual coding of faces. In Experiment 4, we showed that providing a face description can harm face recognition, but only when participants were asked to describe a face after having seen it.

Our results have a number of theoretical implications. First, it seems clear that further research is needed on verbal processes during face learning and its effect on memory performance. This area has been underresearched, since the task seems naturally to involve mostly visual processing. In fact, some early research addressed the type of information that helps participants to remember faces (Kerr & Winograd, 1982; Winograd, 1976). These studies showed that encouraging participants to encode faces semantically (i.e., in terms of their apparent personality, likely occupation, etc.) produced better subsequent memory performance than encouraging a description of their physical characteristics (e.g., nose length). These experiments were typically interpreted as showing the standard levels of processing advantage for materials processed deeply (Craik & Lockhart, 1972; Craik & Tulving, 1975). In our experiments, we have not manipulated the level at which participants describe faces, instead encouraging physical descriptions.

Whether or not these results generalise to different levels of descriptions remains to be seen.

A second implication of the present results is that they appear to challenge some of the underlying assumptions for the verbal overshadowing effect. We certainly agree that faces are visual stimuli, and that some aspects of facial information (e.g., information about spatial layout among facial features) may not adequately be captured in words. However, this does not necessarily eliminate the possibility of the involvement of verbal processing during encoding nor its contribution to subsequent memory performance. Indeed, consistent with an earlier study (Wickham & Swift, 2006), our results demonstrate that verbal processes are active during the encoding stage. Wickham and Swift suggest that verbal overshadowing of line-up identification in their study may have been due to interference between verbal representations formed during and after learning, rather than interference between the original visual representation and the subsequent verbal representation. However, this is unlikely to account for our findings in Experiment 4. In their study participants described every face from memory, whereas participants in our experiment described only a single face from memory. In other words, it cannot be the interference between the contents of verbal descriptions formed at different stages of memory processing led to the recognition impairment.

Our suggestion is that the verbal overshadowing effect may not primarily be due to the difficulty with articulating the visual percept into words at the initial encoding stage, at least in the case of faces. Rather, the phenomenon could be due to the *act of elaborate recall of one's memory* per se. Indeed, Meissner, Brigham, and Kelley (2001) report that postencoding verbalisation can have no effect, improve, or impair later identification, depending on response criterion (providing participants with different recall instructions aimed at manipulating participants' quality of memory recall). The authors found that forcing participants to provide a more elaborate description of the target impaired face recognition, while warning instructions (report only that you are confident and certain you remember) improved performance. They suggest that the elaborateness of recall influences the quality of descriptions, affecting the effects of verbalisation. Our conclusion is that the detrimental effect seen in Experiment 4 was likely to be due to retrieval-based interference, rather than interference between verbal representations formed at different stages of memory processing.

Although we certainly have not provided sufficient evidence to determine between these two accounts, we suggest that the verbal interference account is worth exploring further. In our previous research, we have demonstrated very large differences in participants' ability to match familiar and unfamiliar faces (Bruce et al., 1999; Burton, Wilson, Cowan, & Bruce, 1999). We have suggested that this reflects a fundamental difference in the representations underlying familiar and unfamiliar faces (Burton, Bruce, & Hancock, 1999; Hancock, Bruce, & Burton, 2000). In short, unfamiliar faces are represented as *images* rather than as persons, and superficial descriptions of changeable features (e.g., hairstyle, weight, and expression) are the only descriptions available to the perceiver. All these superficial characteristics are discarded in the representations of familiar faces, since they are not diagnostic of a person's identify. Now recall that our experimental procedure in this paper has been to recognise a *person* and not an image: The image was changed between learning and test in all four experiments presented here. This presumably means that verbal descriptions of one image do not transfer completely to a different image of the same person, and hence one might expect interference between them. Our view is that face memory is almost always best studied by changing the image between learning and test. With regard to forensic identification, image memory is rarely interesting in identification studies. However, in this case, we might predict that the verbal overshadowing effect would be moderated by repeating the same image at learning and test. Although the phenomenon can arise even when there is no relationship between the contents of the description and subsequent recognition (e.g., describing a completely different face can lead to the verbal overshadowing effect; Dodson et al., 1997), it is worth exploring the issue in the future.

In summary, we hope to have demonstrated systematic effects of verbal processes in face recognition memory, a task that seems superficially to rely almost wholly on visual processes. We have demonstrated differential effects of verbal processing on recognition memory for faces, depending on when this is carried out. It seems that the role of verbal processing in face recognition is rather complex, and will require careful examination in future experiments.

REFERENCES

Baddeley, A. D. (1986). *Working memory.* Oxford, UK: Clarendon Press.

Baddeley, A. D. (1992). Is working memory working? The fifth Bartlett lecture. *Quarterly Journal of Experimental Psychology, 44A*, 1–31.

Bahrick, H. P., & Boucher, P. (1968). Retention of visual and verbal codes of the same stimuli. *Journal of Experimental Psychology, 78*, 417–422.

Bartlett, J. C., Till, R. E., & Levy, J. C. (1980). Retrieval characteristics of complex pictures: effects of verbal encoding. *Journal of Verbal Learning and Verbal Behavior, 19*, 430–449.

Brandimonte, M. A., Hitch, G. J., & Bishop, D. V. M. (1992a). Influence of short-term memory codes on visual image processing: Evidence from image transformation tasks. *Journal of Experiment Psychology: Learning, Memory, and Cognition, 18*, 157–165.

Brandimonte, M. A., Hitch, G. J., & Bishop, D. V. M. (1992b). Verbal recoding of visual stimuli impairs mental image transformations. *Memory and Cognition, 20*, 449–455.

Brown, C., & Lloyd-Jones, T. J. (2002). Verbal overshadowing in a multiple face presentation paradigm: Effects of description instruction. *Applied Cognitive Psychology, 16*, 873–885.

Brown, C., & Lloyd-Jones, T. J. (2003). Verbal overshadowing of multiple face and car recognition: Effects of within- versus across- category verbal descriptions. *Applied Cognitive Psychology, 17*, 183–201.

Brown, C., & Lloyd-Jones, T. J. (2005). Verbal facilitation of face recognition. *Memory and Cognition, 33*, 1442–1456.

Bruce, V., Henderson, Z., Greenwood, K., Hancock, P., Burton, A. M., & Miller, P. (1999). Verification of face identities from images captured on video. *Journal of Experimental Psychology: Applied, 5*, 339–360.

Burton, A. M., Bruce, V., & Hancock, P. J. B. (1999). From pixels to people: A mode of familiar face recognition. *Cognitive Science, 23*, 1–31.

Burton, A. M., Wilson, S., Cowan, M., & Bruce, V. (1999). Face recognition in poor quality video: Evidence from security surveillance. *Psychological Science, 10*, 243–248.

Craik, F. I. M., & Lockhart, R. S. (1972). Levels of processing: A framework for memory research. *Journal of Verbal Leaning and Verbal Behavior, 11*, 671–684.

Craik, F. I. M., & Tulving, E. (1975). Depth of processing and the retention of words in episodic memory. *Journal of Experimental Psychology: General, 104*, 268–294.

Daniel, T. C., & Ellis, H. C. (1972). Stimulus codability and long-term recognition memory for visual form. *Journal of Experimental Psychology, 93*, 83–89.

Dodson, C. S., Johnson, M. K., & Schooler, J. W. (1997). The verbal overshadowing effect: Why descriptions impair face recognition. *Memory and Cognition, 25*, 129–139.

Emerson, M. J., & Miyake, A. (2003). The role of inner speech in task switching: A dual-task investigation. *Journal of Memory and Language, 48*, 148–168.

Fallshore, M., & Schooler, J. W. (1995). Verbal vulnerability of perceptual expertise. *Journal of Experimental Psychology: Learning, Memory and Cognition, 21*, 1608–1623.

Farah, M. J., Tanaka, J. W., & Drain, H. M. (1995). What causes the face inversion effect? *Journal of Experimental Psychology: Human Perception and Performance, 21*, 628–634.

Farah, M. J., Wilson, K. D., Drain, M., & Tanaka, J. N. (1998). What is special about face perception? *Psychological Review, 105*, 482–498.

Hancock, P. J. B., Bruce, V., & Burton, A. M. (2000). Recognition of unfamiliar faces. *Trends in Cognitive Science, 4*, 330–337.

Hitch, G. J., Brandimonte, M. A., & Walker, P. (1995). Two types of representation in visual memory: Evidence from the effects of stimulus contrast on image combination. *Memory and Cognition, 23*, 147–154.

Kerr, N. H., & Winograd, E. (1982). Effects of contextual elaboration on face recognition. *Memory and Cognition, 10*, 603–609.

Maki, R. H., & Schuler, J. (1980). Effects of rehearsal duration and levels of processing on memory for words. *Journal of Verbal Learning and Verbal Behavior, 19*, 36–45.

Meissner, C. A., Brigham, J. C., & Kelley, C. M. (2001). The influence of retrieval processes in verbal overshadowing. *Memory and Cognition, 29*, 176–186.

Morris, C. D., Bransford, J. D., & Franks, J. J. (1977). Levels of processing versus transfer appropriate processing. *Journal of Verbal Learning and Verbal Behavior, 16*, 519–533.

Paivio, A. (1971). *Imagery and verbal processes*. New York: Holt, Rinehart & Winston.

Paivio, A. (1986). *Mental representations: A dual coding approach*. New York: Oxford University Press.

Paivio, A., & Csapo, K. (1973). Picture superiority in free recall: Imagery or dual coding? *Cognitive Psychology, 5*, 176–206.

Pellizzon, L., Brandimonte, M. A., & Favretto, A. (1999). Imagery and recognition: Dissociable measures of memory? *European Journal of Cognitive Psychology, 11*, 429–443.

Ryan, R. S., & Schooler, J. W. (1998). Whom do words hurt? Individual differences in susceptibility to verbal overshadowing. *Applied Cognitive Psychology, 12*, 105–125.

Schooler, J. W. (2002). Verbalization produces a transfer inappropriate processing shift. *Applied Cognitive Psychology, 16*, 989–997.

Schooler, J. W., & Engstler-Schooler, T. Y. (1990). Verbal overshadowing of visual memories: Some things are better left unsaid. *Cognitive Psychology, 22*, 36–71.

Schooler, J. W., Fiore, S. M., & Brandimonte, M. A. (1997). At a loss from words: Verbal overshadowing of perceptual memories. In D. L. Medin (Ed.), *The psychology of learning and motivation: Advances in research and theory* (Vol. 37, pp. 293–334). San Diego, CA: Academic Press.

Wickham, L. H. V., & Swift, H. (2006). Articulatory suppression attenuates the verbal overshadowing effect: A role for verbal encoding in face identification. *Applied Cognitive Psychology, 20*, 157–169.

Winograd, E. (1976). Recognition memory for faces following nine different judgements. *Bulletin of the Psychonomic Society, 8*, 419–421.

EUROPEAN JOURNAL OF COGNITIVE PSYCHOLOGY
2008, 20 (3), 497–528

Person descriptions and person identifications: Verbal overshadowing or recognition criterion shift?

Melanie Sauerland
University of Giessen, Giessen, Germany

Franziska E. Holub
Free University of Berlin, Berlin, Germany

Siegfried L. Sporer
University of Giessen, Giessen, Germany

In order to test rival theoretical accounts of the verbal overshadowing effect, participants ($N = 144$) either gave no description or provided written descriptions after viewing a crime on video. Half of the describers reread their target descriptions prior to attempting to identify the thief either in a target-absent or target-present lineup 1 week later. Rereaders showed a criterion shift, that is, they less frequently chose somebody from the lineup than the other two groups. Within rereaders, description accuracy and choosing were positively correlated whereas number of incorrect details reported were negatively correlated with choosing. For describers that did not reread their description, there was a significant positive correlation between description accuracy and identification accuracy, and a negative correlation between number of incorrect descriptors and identification accuracy. The results lend support to the decision criterion shift approach (Clare & Lewandowsky, 2004) and shed light on the decision processes underlying target description and identification.

Any eyewitness identification task such as a live lineup or a photospread is usually preceded by a description of the perpetrator provided by an eyewitness.

Correspondence should be addressed to Melanie Sauerland, Department of Psychology and Sports Science, University of Giessen, Otto-Behaghel-Str. 10F, 35394 Giessen, Germany. E-mail: melanie.sauerland@psychol.uni-giessen.de or sporer@psychol.uni-giessen.de

We wish to thank Miriam Kirschner, Christina Almera, and Norman Koch for their help in data collection. This paper is part of Melanie Sauerland's doctoral dissertation conducted at Giessen University and part of it was presented at the annual meeting of the American Psychology-Law Society in March 2006.

This paper was supported by a grant from the Deutsche Forschungsgemeinschaft (German Science Foundation) to the second author.

http://www.psypress.com/ecp DOI: 10.1080/09541440701728417

However, numerous studies have shown that the very process of describing a target face can have negative effects on identification performance, that is, a *verbal overshadowing effect* (VOE) can occur (see the meta-analysis by Meissner & Brigham, 2001; Meissner, Sporer, & Schooler, 2007; Chin & Schooler, this issue). Different theoretical explanations have been proposed to account for this phenomenon. The present study examines the mental processes involved. In particular, we investigated the influence that describing a target freely and with open-ended questions can have on identification performance, and also how a witness's *rereading* of his or her own description prior to the identification task affects identification performance.

VERBAL OVERSHADOWING

The VOE, that is, decreased recognition performance in persons describing a face compared to nondescribers was investigated in a series of six experiments by Schooler and Engstler-Schooler (1990). Since this initial set of experiments the body of research on the VOE has grown vastly (see Meissner & Brigham, 2001; Meissner, Sporer, & Susa, 2008 this issue). While some researchers succeeded in replicating the VOE in face recognition experiments (e.g., Dodson, Johnson, & Schooler, 1997; Fallshore & Schooler, 1995; Ryan & Schooler, 1998; Schooler, Ryan, & Reder, 1996), others failed to replicate the VOE (e.g., Clifford, 2003; Meissner, Brigham, & Kelley, 2001; Memon & Bartlett, 2002; Tunnicliff & Clark, 1999; Yu & Geiselman, 1993) or even reported verbal facilitation effects (Cutler, Penrod, & Martens, 1987; Krafka & Penrod, 1985). In these studies, however, verbal and visual context reinstatement variables were manipulated together so that it remained unclear, which manipulation the positive effects have to be ascribed to. In a meta-analysis across 15 research papers with a total of 29 effect size comparisons ($N = 2018$), Meissner and Brigham (2001) found a small, yet significant, verbal overshadowing effect ($Z_r = -0.12$), demonstrating that participants who described a target face were 1.27 times more likely to later make an identification error when compared to nondescribers. Furthermore, postdescription delay and type of description instruction were found to moderate this relationship (Meissner & Brigham, 2001). Specifically, overshadowing effects were more likely to occur when the identification task immediately followed the description task, and when participants were given an elaborative description instruction, as opposed to a standard (free recall) description instruction. A comparison of studies using immediate or short delays (< 10 min) with those using long delays (> 30 min) revealed that the long delay influenced only participants in the no-description control condition. These participants showed a significant degree of forgetting compared to a short delay, whereas participants who had previously described the target face showed no change in performance across the delay conditions. As an explanation for these findings, the authors suggest that a preservation of the memory trace across the extended postdescription delay occurs due to verbalisation.

However, an exception to these findings are those of Finger and Pezdek (1999, Exp. 3), where the description condition showed better identification performance after a retention interval of 24 min compared to an immediate testing description group. When compared to an immediate testing control group, there was no difference. As an explanation for release from verbal overshadowing, Meissner and Brigham (2001) suggested that differences in performance resulted from memory decay across the delay for the control condition. Unfortunately, as Finger and Pezdek did not include a postdescription delay for the control group, this hypothesis cannot be investigated with their data (Meissner & Brigham, 2001). Another exception to the effect of postdescription delay, as postulated by Meissner and Brigham, are the findings by Schooler and Engstler-Schooler (1990, Exp. 5) where a significant VOE was observed even after a retention interval of 2 days.

There are three major theoretical explanations of the VOE. The first approach, originally termed *transfer-inappropriate retrieval* (Schooler, Fiore, & Brandimonte, 1997), but subsequently renamed *transfer-inappropriate processing shift* (TIPS; Schooler, 2002), suggests that the activation of *verbal* processes, involved in providing a face description inhibits subsequent *nonverbal* processes considered primarily responsible for face recognition. However, these verbal processes are not assumed to alter the original memory of the face. Schooler et al. (1997) hypothesised that in verbal processing of faces the emphasis lies on the featural information, whereas in visual processing configural information is crucial. Hence, after describing a face, participants are involved in a verbal (featural) mode of processing faces, and attempt to recognise a face by referring to the verbal instead of the visual memory trace. According to TIPS, VOE is not attributed to excessive reliance on a memory representation corresponding to verbalisation. Rather, verbal recall is hypothesised to disrupt the successful application of nonreportable processes omitted in the initial verbal retrieval. Further support for the TIPS was provided by Dodson et al. (1997) and Brown and Lloyd-Jones (2002, 2003).

Another assumption made by the TIPS account is that the original memory only *temporarily* becomes *inaccessible* instead of being *permanently altered* by verbalisation. Support for this assumption was found in several studies reporting *release from verbal overshadowing*. For example, Finger and Pezdek (1999, Exp. 3) found even an increase in identification accuracy after a retention interval between description and identification task of only 24 min (see also Finger, 2002).

Whether the VOE constitutes a temporal or a permanent interference with an eyewitness's memory of a face is of utmost practical importance in criminal investigations. While it is a standard procedure for police officials to interview eyewitnesses after a crime was committed and ask for a description of the perpetrator the probability of an *immediately* following identification task with a photospread or live lineup is highly unlikely. Even a time interval of 2 days between the witness's statement and an identification task as in Schooler and Engstler-Schooler (1990, Exp. 5) appears to be the exception rather than everyday practice (see Behrman & Richards, 2005; Valentine, Pickering, & Darling, 2003). Thus, a nonpermanent effect of verbalising visual memories would have little practical relevance for identification procedures in police investigations in real cases.

Another theoretical explanation of the VOE, known as *retrieval-based interference* (RBI), suggests that the VOE arises from an alteration of the original memory trace caused by verbalisation. The RBI was first introduced by Meissner et al. (2001) following a study in which they manipulated the amount and elaboration of people's verbalisation. In an earlier study, Finger and Pezdek (1999, Exp. 1) had already compared the VOE after an elaborate verbalisation (using the *cognitive interview*) and a standard verbalisation of a previously seen photograph. In the elaborate interview participants recalled significantly more correct, incorrect, and subjective details and also performed significantly less accurate in the identification task than participants in the standard interview condition. Meissner et al. partly replicated these results. By using three different instruction types they altered people's response criterion for descriptions. Specifically, when participants were explicitly instructed to provide a detailed and extensive description of the perpetrator and were even encouraged to guess (forced recall), subsequent identification accuracy significantly decreased both immediately and 30 min after the verbalisation. Thus, unlike Finger and Pezdek (1999, Exp. 3), no release from verbal overshadowing was found after a similar retention interval. However, note that Meissner et al. used forced recall instructions in this condition. In contrast, when participants were discouraged from guessing and asked to only tell what they were sure they remembered correctly (warning condition) no VOE occurred. In this condition, identification performance improved in both immediate and delay conditions, relative to the control and forced recall conditions (Meissner et al., 2001). In another condition in which participants were given standard description instructions (free recall), identification accuracy did not differ significantly from the control condition, that is, no VOE occurred. This instructional bias effect was replicated in several studies (MacLin, Tapscott, & Malpass, 2002; Meissner, 2002) and has been found to be persistent after delays of 30 min or 1 week. As guessing also evokes more inaccurate details, Meissner et al. argued that these inaccuracies interfere with the original memory of the face, thus causing a higher error rate in the identification task. These results obviously challenge the TIPS account and strongly suggest that the visual memory trace is permanently altered by erroneous verbalisation.

A novel account of the VOE, first introduced by Clare and Lewandowsky (2004), could possibly explain the results of those studies in which no apparent negative effect of verbalisation was found. Clare and Lewandowsky pointed out that previous research has left open two major issues involving (a) the types of responses witnesses can make during identification and (b) the nature of the lineup. Obviously it should make a difference if participants merely have the option to choose from a lineup (*forced-choice procedure*) or can also reject a lineup (*optional-choice procedure*). Furthermore, only presenting target-present (TP) lineups in an experiment does not create a realistic scenario of the situation in a crime investigation because it does not allow to adequately assess the rate of false identifications.

Therefore, for the sake of ecological validity any experiment should also include target-absent (TA) lineups, along with optional-choice instructions. Consequently, participants need to decide not only who the perpetrator is but also whether the lineup must be rejected entirely (Clare & Lewandowsky, 2004). This decision requires a response criterion, such that witnesses say "not present" when no lineup member matches their memory or make an identification if a particular face in the lineup meets the response criterion. The placement of that response criterion is likely to influence identification performance: With a conservative criterion, people might prefer not to choose anyone from the lineup, whereas with a liberal criterion, identification attempts might increase (Clare & Lewandowsky, 2004). Criterion effects are pervasive and have frequently been observed in other memory paradigms that permit optional choice, especially when there is a tradeoff between quantity and accuracy (Koriat & Goldsmith, 1994; Koriat, Goldsmith, & Pansky, 2000).[1] Therefore, criterion shifts may also be a contributing factor to the VOE if verbalisation raises people's response criterion. As one possible explanation for a criterion shift following verbalisation, Clare and Lewandowsky (2004) proposed that people monitor their descriptive ability the same way they monitor their performance during other memory tasks (Brigham & Pressley, 1988; Koriat & Goldsmith, 1996; Schraw, 1998).

In the identification context with a previous description task, people's inexperience with providing descriptions of faces implies that they might find the task rather difficult and that they are unlikely to have an appropriate reference against which they can compare their own description (Clare & Lewandowsky, 2004). Clare and Lewandowsky (2004) hypothesised that those two factors combined may make people unsure about the quality of their provided description, which in turn might lower their tendency to

[1] Note, however, that identification decisions are binary and therefore no such tradeoff is possible.

choose someone from a lineup. According to this assumption, the criterion shift to be expected after verbalisation is a *cautious shift* as people become more cautious in their actions after experiencing their lacking ability to satisfyingly describe the perpetrator. Thus, Clare and Lewandowsky reasoned that in an experimental design including both TA and TP lineups the rate of correct identification decisions for describers should decrease in TP lineups (increase of false rejections) but increase in TA lineups (decrease of false alarms). Accordingly, no VOE should occur in forced-choice methodologies in which the decision of choosing or not choosing is reduced to one of choosing among alternatives (Clare & Lewandowsky, 2004). These assumptions clearly differentiate the criterion shift account from the competing TIPS and RBI accounts, as it focuses on choosing rates rather than considering only accuracy rates (TIPS) or suggesting that most errors should consist of false identifications (RBI).

As the distinction between optional-choice and forced-choice, and in consequence the use of TA lineups, has largely been ignored in previous research on the VOE (note that all studies included in the meta-analysis by Meissner & Brigham, 2001, used TP lineups only), Clare and Lewandowsky (2004) assumed that people's response criterion may have contributed in unknown ways to existing experimental outcomes. However, it should be noted that in the initial set of experiments by Schooler and Engstler-Schooler (1990) the optional-choice methodology (yet, no TA lineups) was used and no criterion effect was found. Furthermore, Meissner (2002, Exp. 1) used TA and TP lineups but did not find a criterion shift in any of the description conditions.

In a series of experiments accounting for the factors of optional-choice and TA lineups, Clare and Lewandowsky (2004) reexamined the possibility of criterion effects in verbal overshadowing. The results of Experiment 1 clearly supported the criterion shift account: In an optional-choice identification task participants who had previously described the target significantly less often chose someone from a lineup, which in turn lead to a decrease of decision accuracy in the TP condition, but also to increased identification accuracy in the TA condition (i.e., correct rejections), relative to nondescribers.

In order to further test their response criterion shift interpretation of Experiment 1, Clare and Lewandowsky (2004) applied the forced-choice methodology with TP lineups only in Experiment 2. They argued that, with the option of lineup rejection no longer available, participants in the verbalisation condition should no longer make more errors than the control group if a response criterion shift was actually taking place. Supporting the criterion shift account, it turned out that describers did not perform less accurately than nondescribers in the identification task when they were forced to choose someone from a lineup. Based on the findings in their study, the authors argued, that unlike the TIPS and RBI accounts, the criterion shift explanation can simultaneously account for (a) the results of those experiments in which standard description instructions and forced-choice identifications were used and no VOE occurred, (b) a large VOE in optional-choice TP lineups, and (c) the beneficial effect of verbalisation with optional-choice TA lineups.

In summary, the results of both the meta-analysis (Meissner & Brigham, 2001) and the more recent study by Clare and Lewandowsky (2004) suggest that more than one process may be responsible for the observed variations in the VOE (see also Chin & Schooler, this issue). The effect observed after standard verbalisation may be based on a response criterion shift, while the impact of an elaborative description on identification performance appears to be due to either a change in processing style or an alteration of the original memory trace.

In the present study, three description groups were assessed: nondescribers, describers only (describers *without* rereading the description prior to the identification task), and rereaders (describers *with* rereading of the description immediately before the identification task). A rereading group was included in order to put some participants back into a verbal mode. If this leads to inappropriate processing, then the VOE should be particularly high in this group.[2] In any realistic case where a witness describes the target, it is very unlikely that a suspect is found and that a lineup is constructed within less than 24 hours (see Behrman & Richards, 2005; Valentine et al., 2003). To ensure ecological validity, we therefore allowed for a 1 week delay between the description of the target and the identification task. In order to analyse the data with regard to the discussed decision criterion shift due to target descriptions (Clare & Lewandowsky, 2004), we included both TA and TP lineups. As standard description instructions (see Meissner & Brigham, 2001) were used, no VOE as caused by a change in processing style (TIPS) or an alteration of the original memory trace (RBI) was expected. Instead, we expected a response criterion shift (Clare & Lewandowsky, 2004). Specifically, we expected that describers shift their criterion towards a more conservative direction leading to a higher rate of lineup rejections in the identification task relative to the control group. As no results or theories regarding the duration of this cautious shift existed to date, there were two possible outcomes: (1) If the response criterion shift is permanent, all describers should reject the lineup equally often; (2) however, if the criterion

[2] Note, however, describing and rereading are not the same; describing a person is the effort to verbally *retrieve* a visually encoded stimulus, whereas rereading the description merely reactivates the previously encoded verbal memory trace. One assumption is that both processes have a similar effect due to the VOE. Yet, the possibility that rereading has an associative effect in terms of context reinstatement should not be ignored.

shift is temporary, the description only group should choose equally often as nondescribers and only rereaders should show a larger degree of lineup rejections. Furthermore, as both TA and TP lineups were included, the tendency of rereaders (respectively describers in general) to not choose a person from a lineup (as expected in the hypothesis above) should lead to less correct identifications (hits) in TP lineups but also to an increase of correct rejections in TA lineups.

CONTEXT REINSTATEMENT

Verbalisation apparently can have negative implications for identification accuracy by "overshadowing" the original memory trace, altering it, or producing a cautious shift in people's response criterion. However, contrary to the verbal overshadowing accounts, the use of person descriptions as a means of context reinstatement prior to the identification task may also lead to *memory facilitation* (e.g., Cutler et al., 1987; Cutler, Penrod, O'Rourke, & Martens, 1986). Cutler et al. (1987) provided context reinstatement cues by conducting an *interview* using the mnemonic instructions of the cognitive interview (see Geiselman, Fisher, MacKinnon, & Holland, 1985), providing snapshots of the crime scene, the victim, and another person involved, and by having the participants reread their written description of the incident and the perpetrator. Additionally, the target's disguise and presence of a weapon were manipulated. A significant interaction between disguise and context reinstatement was observed. That is, only when the target's face was difficult to see in the encoding situation was subsequent identification performance improved by the context reinstatement cues.

Cutler et al. (1986) conducted an extensive study in order to determine which of different context reinstatement methods was the most effective and under which circumstances. They found that only the rereading of a description about the incident had a significant effect on the identification decision, however, only in interaction with other factors. The first interaction found was between rereading and the retention interval: Those participants who did not reread their descriptions showed impairment of identification performance after a retention interval of 1 month compared to a retention interval of 1 week, whereas those participants who reread their own description performed almost equally well after both retention intervals. The second interaction was found between rereading and target presence in the lineup. In the TA condition, rereading was associated with better identification performance, while in the TP condition, rereading was associated with decreased identification performance. However, this effect only occurred when the offender was disguised and thus the encoding situation was nonoptimal for the observer. While these results have been interpreted primarily on the basis of a possibly facilitative effect of context reinstatement it should be noted that they can also be explained with Clare and Lewandowsky's (2004) criterion shift account: While the memory preserving effect due to rereading across the 1 month retention interval only occurred in the target-disguise condition also a general tendency of rereaders to not choose (55%) when compared to nonrereaders (40%) was observed. Sporer (2007) compared describers only to describers with rereading and found a nonsignificant tendency toward a facilitative effect of rereading (51.7% vs. 36.0% accuracy in the description only condition) in the expected direction. However, Sporer's experiment may have lacked statistical power to detect a context reinstatement effect.

Thus, while several lines of research have tried to produce a memory facilitating effect by including the rereading of the target description, the results suggest the effect to be unstable. Possibly, other effects of describing the to be identified person and rereading the description prior the identification task, such as verbal overshadowing or response criterion shifts may counteract the impact context reinstatement may have under the given circumstances. Therefore, in the present study we included the rereading of one's own target description prior to the identification task to examine these rival views. According to the principle of context reinstatement, rereaders were expected to experience memory facilitation due to context reinstatement cues provided in their own person descriptions relative to the control group and the description only group. Therefore, rereaders should perform better in the identification task than the other groups.

Relationship between quantity and quality of descriptions and identification accuracy

The significance of person descriptions for assessing eyewitness identification accuracy became apparent when the US Supreme Court specified the accuracy of a witness' description of the criminal as one of five factors to be considered in the evaluation of identification evidence (*Neil v. Biggers, 1972*). The practical importance of person descriptions is evident from the discussion on their utility to assess ("postdict") the accuracy of a given identification (Sporer, 1992b, 1996; Wells, 1985; for a recent meta-analytic review, see Meissner et al., 2008 this issue). Two aspects of person descriptions can be distinguished: description accuracy (usually defined as the number of correct descriptors divided by the number of correct plus incorrect descriptors), and description quantity (the total number of descriptors, irrespective of accuracy). In actual criminal cases, the accuracy of person descriptions cannot be established as this requires knowledge of the true perpetrator. Description quantity, however, can be ascertained by the number of descriptors or features mentioned which may or may not be related to identification accuracy (see Sporer, 1996). Quantity, and indirectly also accuracy of descriptions, is likely to be influenced by the type of instruction given, i.e., standard instructions vs. elaborative description instructions, which have been an important moderator of the VOE (Meissner & Brigham, 2001).

Correlations between description accuracy and identification accuracy

While some studies observed positive correlations between description accuracy and identification accuracy (e.g., Meissner et al., 2001; Wogalter, 1996), other studies did not find an association between the two variables (Goldstein, Johnson, & Chance, 1979; Grass & Sporer, 1991; Pigott & Brigham, 1985; Pigott, Brigham, & Bothwell, 1990; see Sporer, 1996). In a recent meta-analysis, Meissner et al. (2008 this issue) synthesised the reported point-biserial correlations between various aspects of description quality and quantity and identification accuracy. Across $k = 32$ hypothesis tests of the relationship between description accuracy and identification accuracy with $N = 2973$ participants, the weighted mean effect size was $r = .14$ ($p < .001$), with CIs of .11 and .18.

Sporer (2007) found a significant interaction between identification accuracy and choosing with accurate nonchoosers ($M = 5.5$) reporting more correct descriptors than inaccurate nonchoosers ($M = 3.3$). No effect was found for choosers ($M = 4.2$ vs. 4.6). Additionally, a series of experiments conducted by Meissner and colleagues (Meissner, 2002; Meissner et al., 2001) consistently demonstrated a significant negative association between the number of incorrect descriptors provided and identification accuracy while no such association was found for the number of correct descriptors given. Finger and Pezdek (1999) found that inaccurate identifiers reported more incorrect description details ($M = 4.0$) than accurate identifiers ($M = 2.1$) when only a 10 min delay between description and identification task was inserted (Exp. 1). However, no such differences were found when longer delays between description and identification were used (Exp. 2: 1 hour; Exp. 3: 24 min).

Number of features mentioned and identification accuracy

Among other studies, Sporer (1992b) observed a positive correlation between the number of descriptors and identification accuracy ($r = .28$). However, other studies failed to find such an association (Franzen & Sporer, 1994b; Pigott et al., 1990; Wells, 1985; see Sporer, 1996). The meta-analysis by Meissner et al. (2008 this issue) analysed 33 studies with $N = 2578$ participants that examined the relationship between the number of features mentioned (description quantity) and identification accuracy. A weighted mean $r = -.04$, *ns*, with CIs of $-.08$ and .00, was found. Thus, the number of features mentioned seems to be unrelated to identification accuracy.

As Meissner et al. (2008 this issue) noted, the results of studies on description accuracy and quantity are difficult to compare as the various authors used different operationalisations of description accuracy (e.g., some analysed only facial descriptors while others included bodily descriptors or estimates of height and weight). Also, studies varied considerably with respect to the methodological rigor with which descriptions were assessed. For example, some analyses were carried out by establishing clear criteria for scoring and reporting high interrater agreement using Pearson's *r*, while others used single raters or established agreement simply by consensus of raters. Finally, some studies reported only few descriptive elements with little variation across participants while others contained lengthy descriptions that varied considerably. Of course, to the extent that description quantity and accuracy are not precisely measured or show very little variation across participants we cannot expect substantial correlations between these measures and identification accuracy.

The relationship between description quantity and identification accuracy will again be tested in the present study, using an elaborate coding scheme for description accuracy and quantity. Participants who gave more elaborate person descriptions in terms of quantity of details could be expected to experience a VOE in form of a change in processing style (TIPS; Schooler, 2002) or an alteration of the original memory trace (RBI; Meissner et al., 2001). If an alteration of the original memory trace (RBI) takes place, then both description groups should be equally affected by description elaborateness and accuracy. Specifically, elaborate describers of both description groups would be expected to show lower identification accuracy due to a form of VOE. Furthermore, a negative relation between description accuracy and identification accuracy would be expected for both groups.

On the other hand, if a change in processing style (TIPS) takes place, one would expect no effect of description accuracy or elaborateness on identification accuracy for describers only, as it would not be expected to last over an interval of 1 week. However, a change in processing style might be reactivated by rereading. Therefore, according to TIPS, elaborately describing rereaders would be expected to show lower identification accuracy rates than less elaborately describing rereaders. Additionally, rereaders who make an incorrect identification decision should have reported more incorrect descriptors. Consequently, description accuracy was expected to be positively correlated with identification accuracy for rereaders.

METHOD

Participants

One hundred and forty four individuals (72 males and 72 females; age 16–53, Mdn = 23 years) completed this experiment. Most participants were psychology majors (59%) who received course credit for their participation. Other participants were students with other areas of study (26%) and persons of various occupations (15%). They were randomly assigned to the conditions and tested individually. Half of the participants were tested at the Free University Berlin and half at the Justus Liebig University Giessen, Germany.

Design

A 3 (description: no description vs. description only vs. description with rereading) × 2 (target presence: TP vs. TA) between-subjects design was used. Dependent variables were identification accuracy and choosing rate. For the two description groups we measured description quantity and quality and their association with identification accuracy.

Stimulus film

The stimulus film was taken from an earlier study by Franzen and Sporer (1994a). The film showed the theft of an expensive pair of sunglasses in an optometrist's store. Altogether, five amateur actors (one woman and four men) participated in the film, which lasted 6 min and 30 s. The target person could be seen for 18 s. A close-up showing the target's head and shoulders in half-profile lasted for about 2 s. For the remaining time the target was filmed from a distance of several metres, where his head and whole torso could be seen. The actual theft took about 30 s (looking at the sunglasses on the rack, taking a pair and putting it in the pocket). The content of the film can be described as follows:

> A young female (optician) is standing behind the counter, polishing glasses. One after another, three male customers enter the store. When a fourth customer comes in, the optician asks him to wait for a moment until she has served the other customers. While she is taking care of the other customers, the fourth customer walks up to a rack, takes a pair of sunglasses from the shelve and puts it in his pocket. At that time he can be seen in the background while the third customer stands in the foreground at the counter waiting for the optician. He then leaves the store with the words: "This is taking too long, I'll come back later." After the third customer has paid and is about to leave the shop, the optician discovers the theft.

Photo lineup

Each lineup consisted of six frontal 6 × 9 cm photographs simultaneously displayed on the computer screen at a colour depth of 16.7 million colours, that is, 32 bit and a resolution of 1024 × 768 pixels, depicting six male individuals who all fit the general description of the target person as determined by a pilot study (effective size = 4.7). The men all wore the same sweater (different from clothing in the film) and each picture had been taken in the same windowless room with the same illumination and in front of the same wall.

The photos were arranged in two rows of three pictures each. For half of the participants, the target photograph was present (TP), for the other half it was replaced with an innocent foil (TA). Target position as well as distractor position were completely balanced to appear at any of the six positions an equal number of times.

Procedure

In the present experiment, an effort was made to achieve a high ecological validity by (a) inserting a retention interval of 1 week between description and identification task, and (b) including TA lineups equally often as TP lineups as well as a "not present" option following unbiased lineup instructions. In line with common police practice, we collected person descriptions first via free report followed by open-ended questions.

Before and between the separate parts of the experiment the participants were given thorough instructions on the computer screen how to respond to the questions and which keys to use. All instructions and lineup presentation were programmed with SuperLab 1.75 (www.cedrus.com).

Participants were informed that they were taking part in an experiment concerned with witness statements. The advertisement for the experiment displayed the question "Are You A Good Witness?", in order to appeal to people's ambition and curiosity but did not explicitly mention the topic of person identification. Participants were tested individually. Before viewing the video they were asked to watch the film closely and pay attention to every detail. Afterwards, participants completed a 30 min filler task consisting of 40 general knowledge questions. In the following, participants of the experimental groups were instructed to give a detailed written description of the crime they had witnessed earlier in the film. Participants were asked to imagine they were making a witness statement for a real police investigation. This description was to be a free report consisting only of the information the participants remembered by themselves. Subsequently, participants were asked to answer eight open-ended questions concerning the crime on another sheet. The same procedure was followed for the description of the culprit. First, participants were asked to describe the target with their own words and as detailed as possible ("the description should be precise enough for another person to be able to recognise the culprit in a crowd"). Then, 12 open questions concerning the target's appearance followed (see Appendix). The description instructions were in line with the standard description instructions as used in previous studies (e.g., Finger & Pezdek, 1999; Meissner & Brigham, 2001).

The identification task was scheduled exactly 1 week later. Half of those participants who had provided a target description a week earlier were given the opportunity to reread their free description of the perpetrator as well as their answers to the specific questions concerning the physical appearance of the thief which they had provided. Before the identification task, participants indicated their predecision confidence regarding the accuracy of their identification decision on an 11-point scale ranging from 0% to 100% (with intervals marked in 10% steps: 0%, 10%, ... , 100%). Subsequently, participants were asked to identify the culprit on the computer screen. Participants were advised that the culprit might or might not be present in the lineup. Decision time was measured automatically via SuperLab. After giving a rating of recollective experience, postdecision confidence ratings concerning the identification decision were assessed on an 11-point scale ranging from 0% to 100% for all participants.

Coding of the person description details

Two raters received training in which they individually rated all details named in ten cases and discussed the discrepancies with each other and the trainer. Subsequently, all descriptions were coded for correct, incorrect or subjective details (cf. Finger & Pezdek, 1999). *Subjective details* contained descriptors of personality traits or impressions the three raters could not objectively agree on as correct or incorrect (e.g., "looked tired", "unfriendly face") and were excluded from further analyses. Interrater correlations were computed for clothing, body, facial, and other (e.g., posture, nationality) details separately for free report and the open questions. Due to the nonambiguity of the coding system the mean interrater correlations after Fisher's Z-transformation of free descriptions and specific questions was equally high for body, facial, and other details, $rs = .99$. The mean interrater correlation after Fisher's Z-transformation for clothing details was $r = .86$ for free reports and $r = .99$ for open-ended questions. Estimates of age, height, and weight of the target were excluded from analysis due to a lack of standard for coding "accuracy" (e.g., is a response of "20–25 years" to be considered accurate when a person is 25 years old?).

For data analysis, description scores combining free descriptions and specific questions were formed in addition to the four categories listed above. When a participant named the same detail in the free report and the following questions, this repetition was excluded from computations. The subsequent analyses were carried out with the total number of details (correct + incorrect details = *description quantity*). Additionally, *description accuracy* scores[3] were computed (description accuracy = correct details/[correct + incorrect details]). We chose this rather time-consuming method to evaluate description accuracy and quantity because this allowed us to analyse data differently than in most other VOE studies. Specifically, we wanted to analyse data not only according to the description condition participants were allocated to but also with regard to the actual descriptive features of the descriptions. Although participants in the description conditions all received the same instructions, individual differences may lead to differences in description elaborateness (quantity) and description accuracy which in turn may have an influence on the processes believed to underlie the VOE.

RESULTS

An alpha level of .05 was used for all inferential analyses. Cohen's (1988) d and f, are reported as measures of effect size for ANOVAs, and Cramer's V and phi are reported for nonparametric analyses of 3×2 and 2×2 contingency tables, respectively.

In the following, we first report descriptive results for the whole sample. Subsequently, we look at the influence of the description conditions on identification accuracy and choosing behaviour, followed by analyses of the relationship between description accuracy and quantity and identification outcomes.

Identification accuracy

Table 1 displays the distribution of identification decisions for TA and TP lineups in the three experimental conditions. Altogether, 47.2% of the 144

[3] Using description accuracy as a predictor for identification accuracy has been criticised in previous research (Sporer, 1996; Wells, 1985) because the accuracy coefficient does not differentiate between more and less detailed descriptions. A description consisting of only one correct detail will obviously have a higher accuracy score (100%) than a description consisting of 10 details with 2 of them wrong (80%). However, the minimum of total descriptors provided by participants in our experiment was 7 (M = 16.8; SD = 4.1), which made analyses with description accuracy appropriate and justifiable.

TABLE 1
Distribution of identification decisions (in %) in target-absent and target-present lineups

	Target-absent ($n = 72$)		Target-present ($n = 72$)			Total sample ($N = 144$)	
	Choosers	*Nonchoosers*	*Choosers*		*Nonchoosers*		
Condition	*False alarm*	*Correct rejection*	*Hit*	*Foil identification*	*False rejection*	*Mean accuracy*	*Mean choosing rates*
No description ($n = 48$)	33.3	66.7	29.2	25.0	45.8	47.9	43.8
	(8)	(16)	(7)	(6)	(11)	(23)	(21)
Description only ($n = 48$)	37.5	62.5	33.3	33.3	33.3	47.9	52.1
	(9)	(15)	(8)	(8)	(8)	(23)	(25)
Rereading ($n = 48$)	29.2	70.8	20.8	8.3	70.8	45.8	29.2
	(7)	(17)	(5)	(2)	(17)	(22)	(14)
Total sample ($N = 144$)	33.3	66.7	27.8	22.2	50.0	47.2	41.7
	(24)	(48)	(20)	(16)	(36)	(68)	(60)

Figures enclosed in parentheses represent absolute frequencies.

participants made a correct decision. Identification accuracy differed significantly for the 60 choosers (33.3%) from the 84 nonchoosers (57.1%), $chi^2(1, N = 144) = 7.96$, $p = .007$, phi = −0.24. Identification accuracy for TA lineups (66.7%) was higher than for TP lineups (27.8%), $chi^2(1, N = 144) = 21.85$, $p < .001$, phi = −0.39.

Target descriptions

Table 2 displays the means and standard deviations of accuracy rates and the number of descriptors separately for free reports, and for free reports and open-ended questions combined. The mean number of descriptors in the free report was $M = 10.40$ ($SD = 3.75$, Min = 4, Max = 20) and $M = 14.05$ for the open-ended questions ($SD = 3.49$, Min = 6, Max = 23). On average, open-ended questions increased the number of details reported by $M = 6.38$ ($SD = 2.33$), after eliminating descriptors mentioned in both. There were no differences in description accuracy for free report ($M = 70.12\%$, $SD = 17.51$) and open-ended questions ($M = 69.28\%$, $SD = 11.75$), $t(95) = 0.66$, $p = .512$, $d = -0.07$. The mean description accuracy for free report and open-ended questions together, after eliminating duplicates, was $M = 69.68\%$ ($SD = 11.64$).

For descriptors concerning the face only (holistic facial descriptors, hair, eyes, nose, skin, and other features) the mean number descriptors named across both free report and open-ended questions was $M = 7.01$ ($SD = 2.01$). Of these, a mean of $M = 4.52$ ($SD = 2.05$) descriptors had already been named in the free report. Thus, on average, 41.78% of the descriptors referred to the face of the perpetrator, most of which concerned hair style and colour (59.63%).

Additionally, descriptors of age, weight, and height occurred with a mean of $M = 2.25$ ($SD = 0.52$), and subjective details with a mean of $M = 1.27$ ($SD = 1.16$), across both free report and open-ended questions. However, for the reasons explained earlier these latter details were not included in any of the following analyses.

Effects of describing and rereading

Effects on identification accuracy. Our main hypotheses were based on the question of whether identification performance was affected by the different description conditions. Identification accuracy did not differ as a function of the three conditions (no description: 47.9%; description only: 47.9%; rereading: 45.8%), $chi^2(2, N = 144) = 0.06$, $p = .973$, Cramer's $V = .02$, that is, no VOE in the traditional sense was found, nor did the results confirm our expectations concerning a context reinstatement effect, or an effect of memory preservation due to describing the target (see Table 1).

TABLE 2
Means and Standard Deviations of Total Descriptors and Proportion Correct in Free Reports and in Free Reports and Open-Ended Questions Combined ($N = 96$).

	Free report				*Free report and open-ended questions*			
	Total number descriptors		*Proportion correct*		*Total number descriptors*		*Proportion correct*	
	M	*SD*	*M*	*SD*	*M*	*SD*	*M*	*SD*
Face total	4.52	2.05	.72	.23	7.01	2.01	.67	.17
Hair	2.77	1.10	.69	.25	4.18	1.15	.67	.17
Face holistic	.35	.58	.55	.47	1.11	.69	.55	.44
Eyes	.56	.68	.80	.38	.58	.69	.77	.39
Nose	.15	.48	.87	.32	.19	.53	.78	.38
Skin	.25	.44	.92	.28	.28	.45	.89	.32
Face other	.44	.69	.86	.33	.66	.86	.84	.33
Body	.59	.61	.35	.47	1.54	.91	.39	.40
Clothes	5.28	2.97	.74	.24	8.23	2.95	.78	.15
Total	10.40	3.75	.70	.18	16.78	4.06	.70	.12

Effects on choosing rates. Table 1 above also displays the distribution of choosers and nonchoosers in the three conditions. First, comparing describers (describers only and rereaders; 39.6%) to nondescribers (43.8%), showed no effect on choosing rates, $chi^2(1, N = 144) = 0.13$, $p = .724$, phi = -0.03. Second, comparing rereaders to nonrereaders showed that rereaders significantly less often chose a person from the lineup (29.2%) than nonrereaders (47.9%), $chi^2(1, N = 144) = 4.63$, $p = .033$, phi = -0.18. Choosing rates in the rereading condition (29.2%) also differed from those in the description only condition (52.1%), $chi^2(1, N = 96) = 5.23$, $p = .037$, phi = -0.23. These results indicate a cautious shift in the rereading condition.

Quality and quantity of descriptions and their relationships to identification accuracy

Analyses of variance and correlational analyses were conducted to examine the associations between different aspects of person descriptions with identification accuracy and choosing behaviour.

Three $2 \times 2 \times 2$ unweighted means ANOVAs with choice (choosers vs. nonchoosers), description condition (description only vs. rereading), and decision outcome (correct vs. incorrect) as classification variables and description accuracy, total number of descriptors, and number of false descriptors as dependent variables were computed. The main effect for choosing became significant for description accuracy, $F(1, 88) = 4.60$, $p = .035$, $d = 0.11$, and number of false descriptors, $F(1, 88) = 5.08$, $p = .027$, $d = 0.12$, but not for total number of descriptors, $F(1, 88) = 0.88$, $p = .352$, $d = 0.05$. Specifically, choosers gave more accurate descriptions ($M = 70.06\%$) and less false descriptors ($M = 4.81$) than nonchoosers ($M = 65.27\%$; $M = 6.08$). The main effects of decision outcome and description condition were nonsignificant for the three ANOVAs, $Fs \leq 2.62$, $ds \leq .09$. All three ANOVAs revealed significant interactions of decision outcome and description condition: description accuracy, $F(1, 88) = 5.29$, $p = .024$, $f = .25$; total number of descriptors, $F(1, 88) = 3.99$, $p = .049$, $f = .21$; number of false descriptors, $F(1, 88) = 9.14$, $p = .003$, $f = .32$.

Figures 1 and 2 display the interactions of description condition with identification accuracy for description accuracy and number of false descriptors. There was a simple main effect of identification accuracy within describers only for description accuracy, $F(1, 88) = 7.56$, $p = .007$, $d = 0.14$, and for number of false descriptors, $F(1, 88) = 8.33$, $p = .005$, $d = 0.15$. That is, within describers only, inaccurate identifiers gave less accurate descriptions ($M = 65.86\%$) than correct identifiers ($M = 74.89\%$). Likewise, within describers only, inaccurate identifiers reported more incorrect descriptors

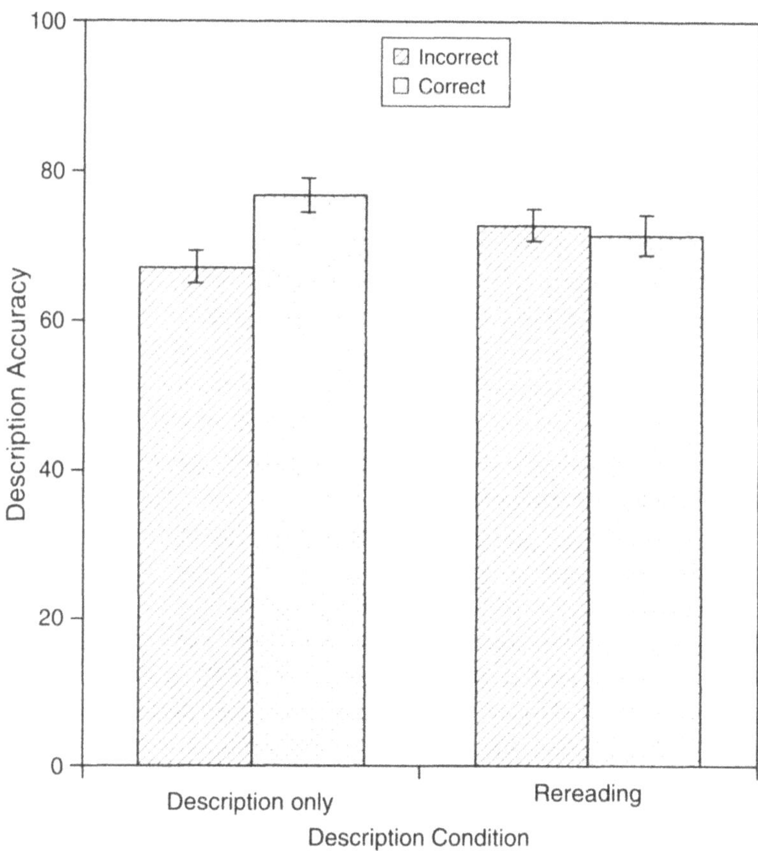

Figure 1. Description accuracy (%) of correct and incorrect lineup decisions with or without rereading.

($M = 5.76$) than accurate identifiers ($M = 3.91$). Within rereaders, no significant differences were found for description accuracy, $F(1, 88) = 0.03$, $p = .855$, $d = 0.00$, or number of false details reported, $F(1, 88) = 0.38$, $p = .541$, $d = 0.03$. The simple main effects of identification accuracy for total number of descriptors were nonsignificant for describers only, $F(1, 88) = 1.38$, $p = .244$, $d = 0.06$, and rereaders, $F(1, 88) = 1.15$, $p = .286$, $d = 0.06$.

Analogous ANOVAs with description accuracy of *facial* descriptions, total number of *facial* descriptors, and number of false *facial* descriptors as classification variables were carried out. No significant main effects for choice, decision outcome, and description condition were found, $Fs \leq 2.06$, $ds \leq .08$. The only significant interaction was between decision outcome and description condition for number of incorrect facial descriptors, $F(1, 88) = 6.25$, $p = .014$, $f = .27$. That is, within describers only, incorrect identifiers

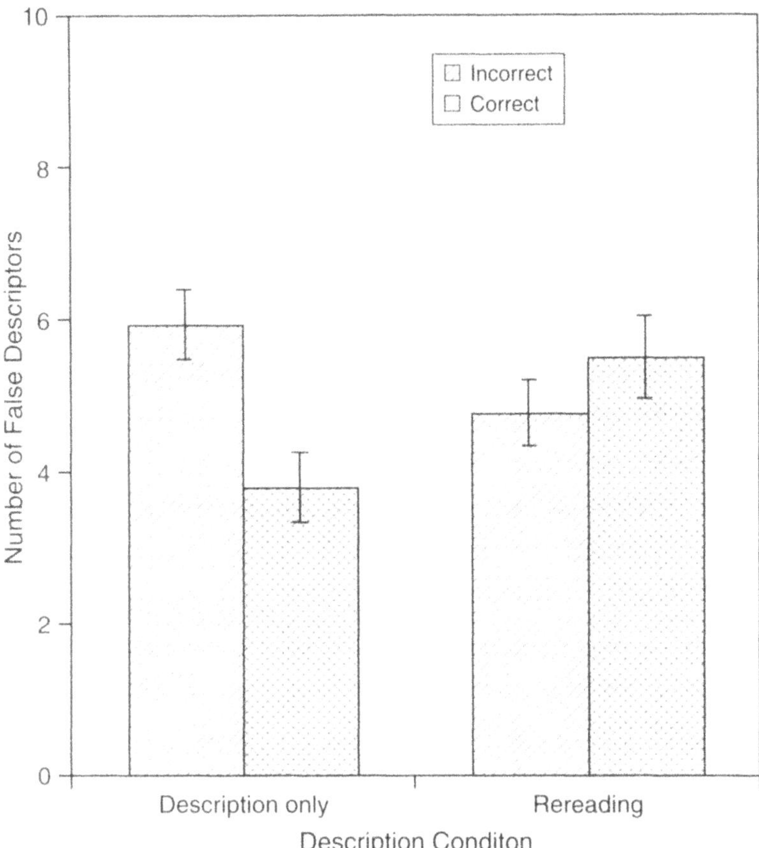

Figure 2. Number of false descriptors in correct and incorrect lineup decisions with or without rereading.

($M = 2.48$) reported more incorrect facial descriptors than correct identifiers ($M = 1.74$), $F(1, 88) = 4.33$, $p = .040$, $d = 0.11$. No significant difference was found within rereaders, $F(1, 88) = .55$, $p = .461$, $d = 0.04$. These interactions between decision outcome and description condition were nonsignificant for accuracy of facial descriptors, $F(1, 88) = 2.74$, $p = .101$, $f = .18$, and total number of facial descriptors, $F(1, 88) = 2.44$, $p = .122$, $f = .17$.

Correlational analyses of description accuracy and identification accuracy

Overall description accuracy (i.e., referring to all descriptors, not just facial descriptors) and description quantity did not correlate significantly,

$r(94) = -.16$, $p = .877$. Table 3 displays the correlations of description accuracy, description quantity, as well as number of correct and incorrect details with identification accuracy for all describers and separately for describers only and rereaders. Additionally, associations are reported not only for all descriptors but also for facial descriptors. In the following, we will concentrate on the different result patterns of describers only and rereaders with regard to all descriptors named. Results for facial descriptors and the whole sample can be obtained from the table.

Positive associations between description accuracy and identification accuracy were found for the description only group for open-ended questions, $r(46) = .41$, $p = .004$, and the combination of free report and open-ended questions, $r(46) = .39$, $p = .006$. No significant results emerged for the rereading group, all $|r|\text{s} \leq .04$, *ns*.

Correlational analyses of description quantity, correct and incorrect details, and identification accuracy

No significant associations between identification accuracy and description quantity were found, $|r|\text{s} \leq .28$, *ns*, with correlations for describers only tending to be negative, correlations for rereaders tending to be positive. Likewise, no significant associations between identification accuracy and number of correct details were found, $|r|\text{s} \leq .26$, *ns*. However, for describers only, significant negative associations between number of incorrect details named and identification accuracy emerged for free report, $r(46) = -.30$, $p = .038$, open-ended questions, $r(46) = -.49$, $p < .001$, as well as the combination of both, $r(46) = -.46$, $p = .001$. No such associations were found for rereaders, $|r|\text{s} \leq .12$, *ns*.

Correlational analyses of description accuracy and choosing

Table 4 displays the correlations of description accuracy, description quantity as well as number of correct and incorrect details named with choosing for all describers and separately for describers only and rereaders. Additionally, associations are reported not only for all descriptors but also for facial descriptors. As for identification accuracy, we will concentrate on the different result patterns of describers only and rereaders with regard to all descriptors named. Results for facial descriptors and the whole sample can be obtained from the table.

For rereaders, choosing and description accuracy were positively associated for free report, $r(46) = .41$, $p = .004$, open-ended questions, $r(46) = .29$, $p = .047$, and the combination of both, $r(46) = .37$, $p = .011$. That is, witnesses who reread their low accuracy descriptions tended to not choose,

TABLE 3
Correlations of Identification Accuracy with Description Accuracy, Description Quantity, Number of Correct Details, and Number of Incorrect Details

	All describers (N = 96)	*Description only (n = 48)*	*Rereading (n = 48)*
Description accuracy			
Free report			
All descriptors	.14	.25°	.04
Facial descriptors	.14	.23	.08
Open questions			
All descriptors	.22*	.41**	.02
Facial descriptors	.19°	.30*	.07
Free report and open questions[a]			
All descriptors	.18°	.39**	−.03
Facial descriptors	.12	.29*	−.06
Description quantity (correct and incorrect details)			
Free report			
All descriptors	.11	−.08	.28°
Facial descriptors	.08	−.08	.22
Open questions			
All descriptors	−.08	−.20	.04
Facial descriptors	.00	−.00	.00
Free report and open questions[a]			
All descriptors	−.01	−.18	.16
Facial descriptors	−.01	−.12	.10
Number correct details			
Free report			
All descriptors	.17	.07	.26°
Facial descriptors	.12	.04	.19
Open questions			
All descriptors	.06	.06	.05
Facial descriptors	.13	.21	.04
Free report and open questions[a]			
All descriptors	.10	.07	.14
Facial descriptors	.06	.08	.03
Number incorrect details			
Free report			
All descriptors	−.07	−.30*	.12
Facial descriptors	−.05	−.26°	.10
Open questions			
All descriptors	−.23*	−.49**	−.01
Facial descriptors	−.18°	−.30*	−.05
Free report and open questions[a]			
All descriptors	−.16	−.46**	.09
Facial descriptors	−.10	−.35*	.11

°$p \leq .10$; *$p \leq .05$; **$p \leq .01$.
[a]Features mentioned in both free report and open-ended questions were only coded once.

TABLE 4
Correlations of Choosing with Description Accuracy, Description Quantity, Number of Correct Details, and Number of Incorrect Details

	All describers *(N = 96)*	*Description only (n = 48)*	*Rereading* *(n = 48)*
Description accuracy			
Free report			
All descriptors	.22*	−.01	.41**
Facial descriptors	.11	−.17	.28°
Open questions			
All descriptors	.09	−.07	.29*
Facial descriptors	.10	−.06	.21
Free report and open questions[a]			
All descriptors	.16	−.05	.37*
Facial descriptors	.11	−.03	.25°
Description quantity (correct and incorrect details)			
Free report			
All descriptors	−.11	−.20	.02
Facial descriptors	−.00	−.10	.00
Open questions			
All descriptors	−.19°	−.15	−.24°
Facial descriptors	−.20°	−.35*	−.03
Free report and open questions[a]			
All descriptors	−.10	−.13	−.05
Facial descriptors	−.05	−.19	.14
Number correct details			
Free report			
All descriptors	.02	−.17	.22
Facial Descriptors	.07	−.12	.24°
Open questions			
All descriptors	−.12	−.18	−.05
Facial descriptors	−.10	−.30*	.09
Free report and open questions[a]			
All descriptors	.00	−.14	.17
Facial descriptors	.04	−.14	.26°
Number incorrect details			
Free report			
All descriptors	−.23*	−.09	−.31*
Facial descriptors	−.12	.02	−.18
Open questions			
All descriptors	−.17	.02	−.35*
Facial descriptors	−.16	−.12	−.15
Free report and open questions[a]			
All descriptors	−.19	−.02	−.31*
Facial descriptors	−.14	−.08	−.13

°$p \leq .10$; *$p \leq .05$; **$p \leq .01$.
[a]Features mentioned in both free reports and open-ended questions were only coded once.

while accurately describing rereaders tended to choose. No associations between choosing and description accuracy were found for describers only, $|r|$s $\leq .07$, *ns*, with all the correlations tending to be negative.

Correlational analyses of description quantity, correct and incorrect details, and choosing

No significant associations between choosing and description quantity with regard to all descriptors were found, $|r|$s $\leq .24$, *ns*. Likewise, no significant associations between identification accuracy and number of correct details were found, $|r|$s $\leq .22$, *ns*. However, for rereaders, significant negative associations between number of incorrect details and choosing emerged for free report, $r(46) = -.31$, $p = .032$, open-ended questions, $r(46) = -.35$, $p = .016$, and the combination of both for rereaders, $r(46) = -.31$, $p = .035$. No significant results were obtained for describers only, $|r|$s $\leq .09$, *ns*.

DISCUSSION

The major aim of this study was to investigate the influence of describing a target-thief seen in a film and the influence of rereading one's description prior to a lineup on identification performance and choosing rates. We considered a number of possible theoretical approaches with partly opposing predictions. Extensive care was taken to ensure ecological validity. First, the identification task was postponed until a week after both seeing the film and providing a written description of the target. Second, both TP and TA lineups were used. Third, the description instructions used were similar to the ones used in real criminal proceedings (free recall followed by a few open-ended questions to elicit additional details). The results of our experiment emphasise the need to reconsider the effect that person descriptions can have on eyewitness identification performance.

We found no impact of person descriptions and rereading on identification performance but only on choosing rates under certain conditions. No VOE as postulated by a change in processing style (TIPS; Schooler, 2002; Schooler et al., 1997) or by an alteration of the original memory trace (RBI; Meissner et al., 2001) was found. This was in line with previous research that used standard description instructions (Meissner & Brigham, 2001). Apparently, only the inclusion of a forced recall condition allows for a more direct test of RBI and TIPS (Meissner et al., 2001).

Also, our results yielded no support for a memory facilitation effect through context reinstatement by rereading of one's target description as found in some earlier studies (Cutler et al., 1986, 1987). Instead, consistent with our hypothesis, our results support the recognition criterion shift approach as suggested by Clare and Lewandowsky (2004). The fact that control and experimental conditions did not differ in identification accuracy supports the assumption that the standard description instruction (or *free recall*) is a reasonably "safe" way to obtain a person description with regard to the VOE (cf. Meissner & Brigham, 2001), without reducing the description quantity to a minimum as observed with *warning recall* instructions (e.g., Meissner, 2002).

Our results are in line with other studies that also did not find a VOE after postdescription delays of 24 hours or longer (e.g., Clifford, 2003; Memon & Rose, 2002; Yu & Geiselman, 1993) and the meta-analysis by Meissner and Brigham (2001), which detected a VOE only for elaborate description instructions. To our knowledge, the only exception is Schooler and Engstler-Schooler (1990, Exp. 5), who used a retention interval of 48 hours and found a VOE. Yet, most studies examining the VOE used only short postdescription delays of less than 24 hours (cf. Meissner & Brigham, 2001). Therefore, there is a clear need of studies with longer postdescription delays in order to address the questions of the durability and permanence that target descriptions can have on identification performance. Also, we need to pay closer attention to the type of description instructions and the way description quantity and accuracy are measured. After all, the probability that a lineup is carried out immediately after the description is very low as documented in archival analyses of real criminal cases (Behrman & Richards, 2005; Sporer, 1992a; Valentine et al., 2003; van Koppen & Lochun, 1997). Hence, the ecological validity of previously reported findings is arguable.

With regard to the criterion shift, our results differed for rereaders and nonrereaders. Specifically, there were more nonchoosers within rereaders than within nonrereaders (description only and control conditions). As no such effect was found for describers in general, we have to assume that the recognition criterion shift only occurs if (a) the identification task immediately follows the description task, as assessed in the study by Clare and Lewandowsky (2004), or (b) the description is reactivated before the identification task, for example by rereading it, as it was the case in the present study. Our results in this regard are in line with the underlying processes proposed by Clare and Lewandowsky. According to Clare and Lewandowsky, a criterion shift occurs due to the perceived difficulty of the description task combined with the presumed inadequacy of the description itself. Especially the latter of these factors is not confined to the situation immediately after the description task but can also be applied to the situation when participants reread their own descriptions. Concerning the duration of the criterion shift, our results indicate the effect to only prevail temporarily, for less than a week, as it appeared for rereaders only.

Similar to the present study, Sporer (in press) had applied a 1 week delay and used the same stimulus materials. He found a nonsignificant tendency of rereaders to be more accurate in their identification on TA and TP lineups than describers only but no effect of the experimental manipulations on choosing. Note, however, that Sporer did not include a no-description control group, against which identification accuracy usually is contrasted in VOE studies.

The second aim of our study concerned the relationship of different aspects of person descriptions with identification accuracy and choosing behaviour. The lack of a relationship between description accuracy and quantity suggests that these two aspects need to be considered separately. Differences in description quantity can also be interpreted as differences in elaboration, not evoked by varying instructions but most likely by the participants' individual differences in their description criterion or ability. Participants in the present study provided rather detailed target descriptions (descriptive details: $M = 16.8$; $SD = 4.1$) when compared to the findings in archival analyses (Sporer, 1992a, $M = 9.7$; van Koppen & Lochun, 1997, Mdn = 8) or staged event studies (e.g., Lindsay et al., 1994, $M = 7.6$; Sporer, 1992b, $M = 5.5$). Also, the rate of descriptors referring to the perpetrator's face was higher (42%) than the rate found in the archival analysis by Sporer (1992a; 30%). Different from the findings by van Koppen and Lochun (1997), the majority of the facial descriptors in our study were correct (67%). Yet, again in concordance with the findings of the archival analysis by Sporer (1992a), most of the facial descriptors referred to hair style and colour (60%). Although description accuracy coefficients have been criticised in the past (Sporer, 1996; Wells, 1985) because they do not differentiate between more and less complete descriptions, we believe that the minimum number of total descriptors provided by our participants was sufficiently large (Min = 7) to make analyses with description accuracy appropriate.

Even though the accuracy of a person description cannot be assessed in actual cases (see Wells, 1985) it has been listed as one of the criteria to be considered in the evaluation of identification evidence by the US Supreme Court (*Neil v. Biggers, 1972*). Yet, analyses of description accuracy can be useful in order to find out more about the decision processes underlying identification decisions with regard to target descriptions. In line with previous studies (e.g., Meissner, 2002; Meissner et al., 2001; see also the meta-analysis by Meissner et al., 2008 this issue), we found a positive association between description accuracy and identification accuracy along with a negative association between the number of false details and identification accuracy. However, here this effect was limited to the description only condition. These results are neither in line with the RBI approach nor with the TIPS approach. According to the RBI approach, associations for both description groups, not just for one, would have been expected. According to the TIPS approach, one would expect the observed relationships for rereaders but not describers only. At first sight it seems puzzling that descriptions that are reread prior to the identification task should have less impact on identification performance than descriptions that are not reread. However, within rereaders, description accuracy was positively associated with choosing, supporting the idea that lineup rejections might be due to the perceived inadequacy of the description (Clare & Lewandowsky, 2004). Apparently, rereaders somehow became aware of the accuracy or inaccuracy of their descriptions. Comparing the observed associations with rereaders and with describers only, it seems that the positive association between description accuracy and identification accuracy within describers only changed to an association with choosing behaviour for rereaders. Possibly, the inclusion of two repeated descriptions—once shortly after observing the target, and again before the identification after the 1 week delay—may have resulted in a correlation between identification accuracy and number of descriptors as reported by Meissner (2002, Exp. 2).

When we consider the description-only group by itself, the present study showed higher correlations between various measures of description accuracy and identification accuracy than previous studies, thus questioning findings that have reported null-findings. We attribute these higher correlations to our careful attempts to operationalise and measure face and person descriptions. In Meissner et al.'s (2008 this issue) meta-analysis, higher correlations were also observed when substantial effort was invested into measuring description quality more rigorously. Correlations were also found to be higher when there were longer description-identification delays than when the recognition test was conducted shortly after the description phase.

Although much care was taken to ensure ecological validity in the present study in form of a complex filmed scenario of 6 min length, a 1 week delay, the use of TP and TA lineups, and the description procedure, generalisability of the findings may be limited as we used only a single target. Stimulus sampling through the use of multiple targets is desirable for two reasons: First, to ensure stimulus generalisability and to allow for internal replication (Wells & Windschitl, 1999). Second, previous research discussed the role of facial distinctiveness/typicality not only regarding face recognition performance (e.g., Shapiro & Penrod, 1986) but also concerning the relationship between target descriptions and identification (Wells, 1985). This issue should be addressed in future research.

In summary, our results help to understand the decision processes underlying eyewitness identifications in connection with person descriptions. First, a retention interval of 1 week between description and identification appears to be sufficient to eliminate the negative effects of person descriptions on identification accuracy as observed in other studies (Dodson et al., 1997; Fallshore & Schooler, 1995; Ryan & Schooler, 1998; Schooler & Engstler-Schooler, 1990; Schooler et al., 1996). For police practice, this means that no change in proceedings is necessary in most cases as the presentation of a lineup rarely happens within less than 1 week after the description (Behrman & Richards, 2005; Valentine et al., 2003). Second, a rereading task did not lead to a VOE, but to a criterion shift (Clare & Lewandowsky, 2004), however without affecting identification accuracy. Furthermore, an association between description accuracy and choosing emerged for rereaders. Interestingly, rereaders seemed to be aware of the quality of their descriptions and this affected their choosing behaviour. In contrast, an association between description accuracy and identification accuracy materialised for describers only. Apparently, when describers reread their own descriptions, the memory effect of the description which lead bad describers to be bad identifiers shifts to a decision criterion effect which lead bad describers to become nonchoosers. Whether one or which of these two effects is (more) desirable is left for further studies to investigate. Specifically, the (non-)existence of an effect of rereading on identification (in-)accuracy needs to be reexamined before further conclusions can be drawn.

REFERENCES

Behrman, B. W., & Richards, R. E. (2005). Suspect/foil identification in actual crimes and in the laboratory: A reality monitoring analysis. *Law and Human Behavior, 29*, 279–301.

Brigham, J. C., & Pressley, M. (1988). Cognitive monitoring and strategy choice in younger and older adults. *Psychology and Aging, 3*, 249–257.

Brown, C., & Lloyd-Jones, T. J. (2002). Verbal overshadowing in a multiple face presentation paradigm: Effects of description instruction. *Applied Cognitive Psychology, 16*, 873–885.

Brown, C., & Lloyd-Jones, T. J. (2003). Verbal overshadowing of multiple face and car recognition: Effects of within- versus across-category verbal descriptions. *Applied Cognitive Psychology, 17*, 183–201.

Clare, J., & Lewandowsky, S. (2004). Verbalizing facial memory: Criterion effects in verbal overshadowing. *Journal of Experimental Psychology: Learning, Memory, and Cognition, 30*, 739–755.

Clifford, B. R. (2003). The verbal overshadowing effect: In search of a chimera. In M. Vanderhallen, G. Verwaeke, P. J. van Koppen, & J. Goethals (Eds.), *Much ado about crime: Chapters on psychology and law* (pp. 151–162). Brussels: Politeia.

Cohen, J. (1988). *Statistical power analysis for the behavioral sciences*. Hillsdale, NJ: Lawrence Erlbaum Associates, Inc.

Cutler, B. L., Penrod, S. D., & Martens, T. K. (1987). Improving the reliability of eyewitness identification: Putting context into context. *Journal of Applied Psychology, 72*, 629–637.

Cutler, B. L., Penrod, S. D., O'Rourke, T. E., & Martens, T. K. (1986). Unconfounding the effects of contextual cues on eyewitness identification accuracy. *Social Behaviour, 1*, 113–134.

Dodson, C. S., Johnson, M. K., & Schooler, J. W. (1997). The verbal overshadowing effect: Why descriptions impair face recognition. *Memory and Cognition*, *25*, 129–139.

Fallshore, M., & Schooler, J. W. (1995). The verbal vulnerability of perceptual expertise. *Journal of Experimental Psychology: Learning, Memory, and Cognition*, *21*, 1608–1623.

Finger, K. (2002). Mazes and music: Using perceptual processing to release verbal overshadowing. *Applied Cognitive Psychology*, *16*, 887–896.

Finger, K., & Pezdek, K. (1999). The effect of the cognitive interview on face recognition accuracy: Release from verbal overshadowing. *Journal of Applied Psychology*, *84*, 340–348.

Franzen, S., & Sporer, S. L. (1994a). Personenverwechslungen durch irreführende Rekonstruktionsbilder: Zum Einfluss nachträglicher Informationen und der Wiederherstellung des Wahrnehmungskontextes [Person mixups as a function of misleading composites: On the influence of postevent information and context reinstatement]. In S. L. Sporer & D. Meurer (Eds.), *Die Beeinflussbarkeit von Zeugenaussagen* (pp. 207–236). Marburg, Germany: N. G. Elwert.

Franzen, S., & Sporer, S. L. (1994b). Personenverwechslungen und Möglichkeiten ihrer Vermeidung: Können Augenzeugen durch Visualisierung gegen den Einfluss von irreführenden Rekonstruktionsbildern immunisiert werden? [Person mixups and possible countermeasures: Can eyewitnesses be inoculated against misleading composites through visualisation?]. In S. L. Sporer & D. Meurer (Eds.), *Die Beeinflussbarkeit von Zeugenaussagen* (pp. 237–283). Marburg, Germany: N. G. Elwert.

Geiselman, R. E., Fisher, R. P., MacKinnon, D. P., & Holland, H. L. (1985). Eyewitness memory enhancement and the police interview: Cognitive retrieval mnemonics versus hypnosis. *Journal of Applied Psychology*, *70*, 401–412.

Goldstein, A. G., Johnson, K. S., & Chance, J. (1979). Does fluency of face description imply superior face recognition? *Bulletin of the Psychonomic Society*, *13*, 15–18.

Grass, E. & Sporer, S. L. (1991, March). *Zur Vorhersage von Identifizierungsleistungen durch weitere Aussagen von Zeugen* [*Correct or false? Post-dicting eyewitness identification accuracy from verbal statements*]. Paper presented at the 33rd annual meeting of Experimental Psychologists, Giessen.

Koriat, A., & Goldsmith, M. (1994). Memory in naturalistic and laboratory contexts: Distinguishing the accuracy-oriented and quantity-oriented approaches to memory assessment. *Journal of Experimental Psychology: General*, *123*, 297–315.

Koriat, A., & Goldsmith, M. (1996). Monitoring and control processes in the strategic regulation of memory accuracy. *Psychological Review*, *103*, 490–517.

Koriat, A., Goldsmith, M., & Pansky, A. (2000). Toward a psychology of memory accuracy. *Annual Review of Psychology*, *51*, 481–537.

Krafka, C., & Penrod, S. D. (1985). Reinstatement of context in a field experiment on eyewitness identification. *Journal of Personality and Social Psychology*, *49*, 58–69.

Lindsay, R. C. L., Martin, R., & Webber, L. (1994). Default values in eyewitness descriptions: A problem for the match-to-description lineup foil selection strategy. *Law & Human Behavior*, *18*, 527–541.

MacLin, O. H., Tapscott, R. L., & Malpass, R. S. (2002). The development of a computer system to collect descriptions of culprits. *Applied Cognitive Psychology*, *16*, 937–945.

Meissner, C. A. (2002). Applied aspects of the instructional bias effect in verbal overshadowing. *Applied Cognitive Psychology*, *16*, 911–928.

Meissner, C. A., & Brigham, J. C. (2001). A meta-analysis of the verbal overshadowing effect in face identification. *Applied Cognitive Psychology*, *15*, 603–616.

Meissner, C. A., Brigham, J. C., & Kelley, C. M. (2001). The influence of retrieval processes in verbal overshadowing. *Memory and Cognition*, *29*, 176–186.

Meissner, C. A., Sporer, S. L., & Schooler, J. W. (2007). Person descriptions as eyewitness evidence. In R. C. L. Lindsay, D. F. Ross, J. D. Read, & M. P. Toglia (Eds.), *Handbook of eyewitness psychology* (Vol. 2, pp. 3–34). Mahwah, NJ: Lawrence Erlbaum Associates.

Meissner, C. A., Sporer, S. L., & Susa, K. J. (2008). A theoretical review and meta-analysis of the description-identification relationship in memory for faces. *European Journal of Cognitive Psychology, 20*, 414–455.

Memon, A., & Bartlett, J. (2002). The effects of verbalisation on face recognition in young and older adults. *Applied Cognitive Psychology, 16*, 635–650.

Memon, A., & Rose, R. (2002). Identification abilities of children: Does a verbal description hurt face recognition? *Psychology, Crime, and Law, 8*, 229–242.

Neil v. Biggers, No. 409 US 188 (1972).

Pigott, M., & Brigham, J. C. (1985). Relationship between accuracy of prior description and facial recognition. *Journal of Applied Psychology, 70*, 547–555.

Pigott, M. A., Brigham, J. C., & Bothwell, R. K. (1990). A field study of the relationship between quality of eyewitnesses' descriptions and identification accuracy. *Journal of Police Science and Administration, 17*, 84–88.

Ryan, R. S., & Schooler, J. W. (1998). Whom do words hurt? Individual differences in susceptibility to verbal overshadowing. *Applied Cognitive Psychology, 12*, 105–125.

Schooler, J. W. (2002). Verbalisation produces a transfer inappropriate processing shift. *Applied Cognitive Psychology, 16*, 989–997.

Schooler, J. W., & Engstler-Schooler, T. Y. (1990). Verbal overshadowing of visual memories: Some things are better left unsaid. *Cognitive Psychology, 22*, 36–71.

Schooler, J. W., Fiore, S. M., & Brandimonte, M. A. (1997). At a loss from words: Verbal overshadowing of perceptual memories. In D. L. Medin (Ed.), *The psychology of learning and motivation* (pp. 293–334). San Diego, CA: Academic Press.

Schooler, J. W., Ryan, R. S., & Reder, L. (1996). The costs and benefits of verbally rehearsing memory for faces. In D. Herrmann, M. Johnson, C. McEvoy, C. Hertzog, & P. Hertel (Eds.), *Basic and applied memory: New findings* (pp. 51–65). Hillsdale, NJ: Lawrence Erlbaum Associates, Inc.

Schraw, G. (1998). Promoting general metacognitive awareness. *Instructional Science, 26*, 113–125.

Shapiro, P. N., & Penrod, S. (1986). Meta-analysis of facial identification studies. *Psychological Bulletin, 100*, 139–156.

Sporer, S. L. (1992a, March). *An archival analysis of person descriptions.* Paper presented at the biennial meeting of the American Psychology-Law Society, San Diego, CA.

Sporer, S. L. (1992b). Post-dicting eyewitness accuracy: Confidence, decision-times and person descriptions of choosers and non-choosers. *European Journal of Social Psychology, 22*, 157–180.

Sporer, S. L. (1996). Psychological aspects of person descriptions. In S. L. Sporer, R. S. Malpass, & G. Koehnken (Eds.), *Psychological issues in eyewitness identification* (pp. 53–86). Mahwah, NJ: Lawrence Erlbaum Associates, Inc.

Sporer, S. L. (2007). Person descriptions as retrieval cues: Do they really help? *Psychology, Crime, and Law, 13*, 591–609.

Tunnicliff, J. L., & Clark, S. E. (1999). Unpublished raw data. Cited in C. A. Meissner & J. C. Brigham (2001). A meta-analysis of the verbal overshadowing effect in face identification. *Applied Cognitive Psychology, 15*, 603–616.

Valentine, T., Pickering, A., & Darling, S. (2003). Characteristics of eyewitness identification that predict the outcome of real lineups. *Applied Cognitive Psychology, 17*, 969–993.

Van Koppen, P. J., & Lochun, S. K. (1997). Portraying perpetrators: The validity of offender descriptions by witnesses. *Law and Human Behavior, 21*, 661–685.

Wells, G. (1985). Verbal descriptions of faces from memory: Are they diagnostic of identification accuracy? *Journal of Applied Psychology, 70*, 619–626.

Wells, G. L., & Windschitl, P. D. (1999). Stimulus sampling and social psychology experimentation. *Personality and Social Psychology Bulletin*, *25*, 1115–1125.

Wogalter, M. S. (1996). Describing faces from memory: Accuracy and effects on subsequent recognition performance. *Proceedings of the Human Factors Society*, *40*, 536–540.

Yu, C. J., & Geiselman, R. E. (1993). Effects of constructing identi-kit composites on photospread identification performance. *Criminal Justice and Behavior*, *20*, 280–292.

APPENDIX

Open-ended questions asked after free report was given

1. How old do you think the culprit was?
2. How tall was the culprit in cm?
3. Describe the culprit's build!
4. Describe the culprit's clothing!
5. Describe the culprit's hair color!
6. Describe the culprit's hairdo!
7. Describe the culprit's face shape!
8. Which of the culprit's special features caught your eye?
9. Did the culprit wear headgear? If yes, what kind?
10. Did the culprit wear glasses? If yes, what did they look like?
11. Did the culprit have a beard? If yes, what did it look like?
12. Did the culprit speak in a dialect or did he have an accent? If yes, which?

EUROPEAN JOURNAL OF COGNITIVE PSYCHOLOGY
2008, 20 (3), 529–560

Eliciting person descriptions from eyewitnesses: A survey of police perceptions of eyewitness performance and reported use of interview techniques

Charity Brown
Institute of Psychological Sciences, University of Leeds, Leeds, UK

Toby J. Lloyd-Jones
Department of Psychology, Swansea University, Swansea, UK

Mark Robinson
Kent Police College, Coverdale Avenue, Maidstone, UK

Techniques such as the cognitive interview (CI) have the potential to improve witness recall. Nevertheless, there is also laboratory evidence of "verbal overshadowing"; the phenomenon whereby verbally describing aspects of an event (such as the face of a perpetrator) can have negative consequences for eyewitness memory. Seventy-two UK police officers were surveyed regarding their perceptions of eyewitness performance and the methods they use to elicit person descriptions from witnesses. Factors commonly believed to influence description quality were the viewing conditions of the event, the characteristics of the witness, and their mental distress. When eliciting person descriptions there was a consensus that some components of the CI were more frequently used and believed to be more useful than others. Witnesses were generally believed to provide accurate, but incomplete person descriptions. Nevertheless, there were instances where officers reported requesting elaborative face descriptions. We propose that verbal overshadowing is unlikely to be a major concern for most police officers; however, under some circumstances its potential impact should be considered. It is also clear that it would be of benefit for future research on verbal overshadowing to examine a number of variables relevant to the forensic setting.

The assumption that eyewitnesses are important to police investigations has given rise to a great deal of research aimed at identifying the factors that influence eyewitness performance. This research has largely focused either upon variables which are inherent to the witnessed event (see Kebbell &

Correspondence should be addressed to Charity Brown, Institute of Psychological Sciences, University of Leeds, Leeds LS2 9JT, UK. E-mail: psccbr@leeds.ac.uk

http://www.psypress.com/ecp DOI: 10.1080/09541440701728474

Wagstaff, 1999, for a review) or upon the procedural aspects of eliciting witness testimony (e.g., Fisher & Geiselman, 1992). In contrast, less attention has been given to evaluating: (1) police officers' perceptions of eyewitness performance; and (2) the methods officers report using when eliciting witness testimony in the field.

Police officers generally value the information witnesses provide in criminal investigations. Kebbell and Milne's (1998) survey of 159 UK police officers showed most respondents to believe that witnesses usually or almost always provide the major leads to an investigation. In addition, most officers believed that the information witnesses provide is rarely incorrect (see also Brigham & WolfsKeil, 1983). This suggests that police officers may at times place a great deal of emphasis upon witness testimony. A prominent issue, however, appears to be the completeness of that testimony. One type of information for which this was reported to be a particular issue was person information:76% of officers reported that witnesses never or rarely remember as many specific details about persons as they would like.

Person descriptions can be important in the initial search for an unknown suspect. Witnesses can also be asked throughout a criminal investigation to provide detailed descriptions to help create a composite of the suspect or prior to being shown mugshots (Memon & Bartlett, 2002). Importantly, a witness's first description of a perpetrator is used by identification officers' as a basis for selecting fillers when constructing a live or video identity parade (Kebbell, 2000). The importance of person descriptions to criminal investigations has led researchers to examine the variables that affect the quality of witnesses' recollections of person details. Research has identified many variables that can influence the accuracy and completeness of person descriptions. These can be divided into estimator and system variables (Wells, 1978). Estimator variables are those over which the legal system has little or no control such as witness characteristics (e.g., age, race), encoding variables (e.g., lighting, proximity, alcohol, weapon presence, and stress), and the delay between witnessing an event and providing a person description. In contrast, systems variables are those variables relating to the procedures used by the police to elicit witness testimony, such as the way in which the witness is questioned and the providing of repeated descriptions (see Meissner, Sporer, & Schooler, 2007, for a review). To date, however, little attention has been given to officers' perceptions of the quality of the person descriptions given by witnesses and the variables that affect those descriptions. It may be that police perceptions regarding witness performance shape the way in which witness descriptions are elicited.

As far as we are aware, only two published studies have examined police officers' knowledge of factors that affect eyewitness performance (Benton, Ross, Bradshaw, Thomas, & Bradshaw, 2006; Brigham & WolfsKeil, 1983). In these studies, the particular emphasis has been upon person identification and general eyewitness recall. Both studies survey US officers' and highlight significant limitations in aspects of their knowledge relating to eyewitness issues. Most recently, Benton et al. (2006) compared the knowledge of US police officers to that of eyewitness memory experts previously surveyed by Kassin and colleagues (Kassin, Tubb, Hosch, & Memon, 2001). Officers disagreed with experts on 60% of the presented issues. In particular, officers (as well as judges and jurors also surveyed) were more aware of the potential role of systems, compared with estimator, variables in influencing the quality of witness testimony.

Much research concerning the system variables which influence person identification and general witness recall has been incorporated into police practice, although little specific attention has been given to evaluating the procedures the police use for eliciting person descriptions. Of relevance here is research that has focused upon developing techniques which enhance the completeness of witness recall. The Cognitive Interview (CI) is a well-established procedure that has been incorporated into police recruit training in England and Wales since 1992. The original CI devised by Geiselman, Fisher, and colleagues (e.g., Geiselman et al., 1984) comprised four retrieval mnemonics: (a) mentally reinstating the context of the witnessed event; (b) encouraging the witness to report everything; (c) recalling the event from a variety of different temporal orders; and (d) recalling the event from a different perspective. Subsequently, an enhanced version of the CI has been devised which includes social techniques aimed at improving interviewer-witness communication (e.g., rapport building, transfer of control, open-ended questions, and witness-compatible questioning) as well as additional cognitive techniques for activating and probing a witness's mental image of a specific part of an event (Fisher & Geiselman, 1992).

Officers trained in the CI perceive it as a useful procedure which elicits more information than a standard police interview (Kebbell, Milne, & Wagstaff, 1999). Nevertheless, some CI components are perceived as more useful than others and officers report using these components more frequently in the field (Kebbell et al., 1999). Researchers of eyewitness memory have long been aware that the way in which witnesses are questioned can influence the completeness and accuracy of their memory reports. Several field studies have identified common shortcomings in the way in which police officers interview witnesses. These include both the excessive use of closed questions (e.g., Clifford & George, 1996; Myklebust & Alison, 2000; Wright & Alison, 2004), and the use of leading or suggestive questions (e.g., Fisher, 1995; Wright & Alison, 2004). The adoption of such nonoptimal interview strategies by officers when eliciting elaborative face descriptions may lead witnesses to incorporate misinformation into their person descriptions (see Meissner et al., 2007, for a review).

In addition, officers' perceptions of witness performance may influence their willingness to use the CI. For instance, Wright and Holliday (2005) found that some officers believe it is inappropriate to use the CI with older witnesses (i.e., > 60 years) as it may be too time consuming, mentally demanding, or upsetting.

It seems likely that police perceptions concerning both witness performance and the efficacy of interview techniques will shape the assessments officers make concerning a witness's ability to provide accurate and complete person descriptions. As a consequence, it may be that in some circumstances officers are failing to use procedures that could effectively maximise witness retrieval. The present study aims to gain an understanding of the perceptions commonly held by police officers, which may influence how they elicit information from witnesses in the field.

Further, we examine the methods police officers report using when eliciting descriptions. Whilst interview techniques such as the CI have been developed with the aim of improving the completeness of witness recall, recent empirical work has shown that under some circumstances eliciting descriptions from witnesses may either help or hinder performance. We turn now to this line of research.

BENEFICIAL AND DETRIMENTAL EFFECTS OF PROVIDING VERBAL DESCRIPTIONS

Empirical studies have generally found the CI to elicit more correct information relative to a control interview, although some studies have not found an effect, and some studies have even reported a small increase in incorrect details (for reviews, see Fisher, Brennan, & McCauley, 2002; and a meta-analysis by Köhnken, Milne, Memon, & Bull, 1999). Nevertheless, beneficial effects of the CI have been found to extend beyond laboratory settings. In particular, two field studies have shown police officers to elicit improvements in witness recall following CI training (Clifford & George, 1996; Fisher, Geiselman, & Amador, 1989).

Importantly, however, there is also evidence from laboratory studies of "verbal overshadowing"; the phenomenon whereby verbally describing an event can have a detrimental influence on memory (for a recent review, see Schooler, 2002). For instance, in their seminal study, Schooler and Engstler-Schooler (1990) presented participants with a video of a bank robbery, after which participants had to describe (or not, in the control condition) the facial features of the bank robber from memory. Compared with the control group, those participants providing a description were subsequently less able to recognise the robber from a lineup comprising the robber and several potential suspects. More recently, a meta-analysis by Meissner and Brigham

(2001) of studies of the verbal overshadowing effect, including 29 effect size comparisons involving over 2000 participants, revealed a small but reliable negative effect of verbal overshadowing. Compared with those providing no description, participants describing the target face were found to be 1.27 times more likely to *misidentify* the face from a lineup including similar distractors. Nevertheless, we do note that a number of studies have failed to replicate the finding (e.g., Lovett, Small, & Engstrom, 1992; Yu & Geiselman, 1993).

The precise theoretical underpinnings of the verbal overshadowing phenomenon have remained somewhat elusive and a single unified account of verbal overshadowing has not yet been accepted. It is likely that multiple mechanisms are involved (Chin & Schooler, 2008 this issue; Meissner et al., 2007). Currently, three separate accounts have been proposed, each of which is supported by favourable evidence (see Chin & Schooler, 2008 this issue, for a review).

The "recoding interference" account proposes that verbal overshadowing arises due to the individual generating and later relying upon an inaccurate or imprecise verbal description of the contents of their original nonverbal memory of the face (Schooler & Engstler-Schooler, 1990; see also Meissner, Brigham, & Kelley, 2001). On this account effects of verbal overshadowing are restricted to the face that is initially described, and depend to some extent upon a newly formed memory representation corresponding to the verbal description. In contrast, the "transfer-inappropriate processing shift" account proposes that verbalisation gives rise to a more general form of interference (Schooler, 2002; Schooler, Fiore, & Brandimonte, 1997). Following encoding verbalisation encourages the application of verbal or featural processes at the expense of critical nonverbal or global processes that are necessary for successful face recognition. This account has been favoured when interference from verbalisation has been found to extend beyond the described face to other nondescribed faces (e.g., Brown & Lloyd-Jones, 2003; Dodson, Johnson, & Schooler, 1997). Finally, a "criterion shift" account has been proposed which relies upon neither memory content nor processing. Instead engaging in verbalisation induces a conservative bias in responding, whereby individuals become less willing to make a positive identification from a line-up (Clare & Lewandowsky, 2004). In this case, a conservative bias leads participants to more frequently reject lineups in which the target is present (i.e., to say "not present"), thereby increasing misses and reducing accuracy. This account is of direct relevance to forensic settings as the suspect involved in the identification procedure may not be the actual culprit. However, a number of findings cannot be easily reconciled with a criterion shift account. In particular, verbal overshadowing effects have been found to occur in paradigms where a "not present" option is unavailable to participants (e.g., Fallshore & Schooler, 1995).

One critical determinant of verbal overshadowing appears to be the nature of the description (e.g., Brown & Lloyd-Jones, 2002, Clare & Lewandowsky, 2004; Meissner & Brigham, 2001). Several studies have examined the importance of description accuracy (e.g., Finger & Pezdek, 1999; MacLin, Tapscott, & Malpass, 2002; Meissner, 2002; Meissner et al., 2001) and it seems clear that nonveridical information (i.e., misinformation) elicited by the description may impact unfavourably upon memory. Other studies have considered the nature of the descriptors that participants' generate, and found that directing participants to consider particular facial features (such as eyes, nose, ears, and so on) may invoke a strong shift in processing "style" towards featural visual processing at the expense of more global visual processing, which is normally more beneficial for face recognition (Brown & Lloyd-Jones, 2002).

In a similar vein, a number of studies have examined the influence of eliciting descriptions using the CI on subsequent face recognition accuracy. Two studies failed to find any difference in recognition accuracy following a CI as compared to unaided free recall (e.g., Fisher, Quigley, Brock, Chin, & Cutler, 1990; Gwyer & Clifford, 1997). However, in a study by Finger and Pezdek (1999) participants instructed in several components of the CI (i.e., to reinstate their thoughts and feelings when encountering the face, to report everything, and to visualise the face) were significantly less likely to recognise the target face when compared with those given a standard instruction (i.e., to describe the person's physical features). This may have been because the CI encouraged either an increase in misinformation or an inappropriate shift in processing style.

THE PRESENT STUDY

Verbal overshadowing is clearly an important phenomenon. Furthermore, verbal overshadowing has been reported to persist across delays of up to 30 min (Meissner et al., 2001), 2 days (Schooler & Engstler-Schooler, 1990), and possibly 2 weeks (Read & Schooler, 1994) between description and memory retrieval. This has led some researchers to suggest that verbal overshadowing has important practical implications for the way in which descriptions are elicited from real-world witnesses (e.g., Meissner, 2002). However, the apparent fragility of verbal overshadowing has led other researchers to question the extent to which verbal overshadowing is likely to be of applied importance (e.g., Finger & Pezdek, 1999; Memon & Bartlett, 2002). From an applied perspective it is important to assess whether verbal overshadowing effects are likely to extend beyond laboratory settings and be of concern to real-world police investigations. To date, however, little attention has been given to the methods police officers report using to gain person descriptions in the field.

The present study used a detailed questionnaire to gain information on: (1) officers' perceptions of eyewitness performance and the efficacy of witness interview techniques; (2) the circumstances under which person descriptions are elicited in the field; and (3) the techniques that officers report using to elicit descriptions. The information obtained here will be useful for understanding police practice, and it will also provide a basis for future laboratory-based work on the influence of verbal descriptions on eyewitness performance.

METHOD

Participants

Members of the UK Kent police force were either contacted through the Kent Police College when attending training courses or via a general e-mail shot, which potentially reached 2000 uniform and CID officers across the county. Out of the 90 questionnaires distributed via the police college, 52 were returned (a response rate of 57.7%). Response to the e-mail shot was poor with only an additional 26 questionnaires returned (a response rate of 1.3%). In total there were 78 respondents. Six respondents were excluded because they were either office clerks, or reported having less than 6 weeks of interviewing experience.

Materials

The questionnaire consisted of 65 items. Seven items requested demographic details including age, gender, length of service, rank, operational role, training, and years of interviewing experience. Participants were then asked to answer questions based on their experiences of eliciting person descriptions from witnesses/victims of crime. Items concerning officers' perceptions of eyewitness performance included the perceived importance of witness descriptions, and factors believed to influence both description quality and the time spent eliciting descriptions. Items concerning the methods used to elicit descriptions included the circumstances under which descriptions are elicited, the techniques used to elicit descriptions, and the reported use and perceived usefulness of a number of CI components. Forty-seven of the items required participants to respond using a rating scale. Eleven items were worded as open-ended questions to avoid suggesting or influencing respondents' answers. Note that for the 47 rating scales there were a small number of missing responses. This occurred in a minority of cases (0.88% of all responses). Therefore, we did not consider it necessary to drop such cases from the analysis.

To analyse responses to the open-ended questions, a series of response categories was derived. In the first instance, the first author developed a content dictionary for each open-ended question designed to reflect every possible response given by respondents. As each questionnaire was coded any response that was not already reflected in the content dictionary was added. Following the development of the content dictionary, the first author and a second coder identified common themes emerging across dictionary items. Dictionary items reflecting an agreed common theme were then combined into a single response category. The final number of categories for each open-ended question ranged between 7 and 23. Reliability was checked by having the first author and a third coder independently code a subsample of 16 (22.2%) responses for each question. Interrater reliability for categorising responses to each open-ended question ranged from $r = .71$ to $r = .91$ ($ps < .001$).

RESULTS

Respondents

Of the 72 respondents, 59.72% were male and 40.28% were female. Age ranged from 20 to 51 years ($M = 33.87$, $SD = 7.59$). Length of service ranged from 1 to 30 years ($M = 9.44$, $SD = 7.40$), with a mean of 8.18 ($SD = 7.32$) years of interviewing experience. Most respondents were police constables (63.9%), detective constables (20.8%), and sergeants or detective sergeants (12.5%). Of the 72 respondents, 19.44% were involved with front line uniform duties (e.g., attending initial calls, patrol work), 55.55% were involved with investigating reported crimes and dealing with arrested persons, and 11.11% were attached to special units including domestic and sexual violence and child protection. All respondents had received training in investigative interviewing. This was through the "National Interviewing Package" (Central Planning and Training Unit, 1992) which is also known as the "PEACE" approach (81.9%), and/or via specialised in-force PEACE courses in Kent (90.3%). National Interviewing Package courses are typically delivered during initial police training and normally last for 5 days, with up to 2 days spent on the CI for use with witnesses (see also Kebbell et al., 1999). The in-force PEACE courses were taught to a national model and were thought by the third author, an experienced police trainer at the Kent Police College, to typically reflect the national training picture at the time of this survey. PEACE courses train police officers in the four basic mnemonics of the cognitive interview and at advanced stages of PEACE training officers learn to apply these mnemonics in a number of contexts, including those with able, cooperative suspects. A quarter of officers (26.4%) reported receiving in-force enhanced CI training specifically relating to witness interviewing. This consisted of a 3 day course including 1 day's training with an academic outlining the theoretical rationale of the enhanced CI and 2 days practising to apply the enhanced CI in witness interview settings. Consequently, enhanced CI trained officers responses may not be entirely representative of officers receiving training elsewhere in the UK. However, the Kent Police College is involved in training police interview trainers for a number of forces in England and Wales, and thus similar police training practices are likely to be operating in other regions.

Officers perceptions of eyewitness performance

Importance of descriptions. Respondents answered a series of questions (adapted from Kebbell & Milne, 1998) concerning their perceptions of witness performance (see Table 1). Responses were indicated on a 5-point scale ranging from "never/not at all" (scored 1) to "always/extremely" (scored 5).

Over half the officers (59.7%) believed that person descriptions given by witnesses usually or almost always provide the major leads for an investigation, although 37.5% of officers thought this was rarely the case. Most officers (80.6%) reported that witnesses rarely provide as many person details as they would like; however, many officers (61.1%) believed witness descriptions to be quite accurate. Finally, most officers (68.1%) believed that they usually or almost always had enough time to elicit a good person description from a witness.

Completeness of descriptions. Officers were asked to rate 29 face and body characteristics according to the frequency with which they are mentioned by witnesses. The scale ranged from "rarely" (scored 1) to "always" (scored 5). Items with a mean above the mid-point of the 5-point scale were: sex (4.44), clothing (3.85), hair colour (3.64), age (3.30), race (3.24), height (3.11), and hair length (3.10). Those items with a mean below the mid-point of the scale were: build (2.99), hair style (2.62), facial hair (2.60), accessories (2.54), speech characteristics (2.49), eye colour (1.94), eye shape (1.86), skin complexion (1.86), weight (1.79), eyebrows (1.74), nose (1.55), teeth (1.55), ears (1.51), facial shape (1.48), hair parting (1.42), hair texture (1.35), forehead (1.35), chin (1.33), lips (1.30), posture (1.22), cheeks (1.22), and neck (1.16). A Kendall coefficient of concordance showed that officers were consistent in their rankings, $W(28) = .64$, $p < .001$.

TABLE 1
Police officers' perceptions of witness performance when reporting person descriptions

Question	*Percentage of responses*						
	Never or not at all	*Rarely or not very*	*Usually or quite*	*Almost always or very*	*Always or extremely*	*M*	*SD*
In your opinion, how often do person descriptions given by witnesses/victims provide major leads for an investigation?	0.00	37.50	51.40	8.30	1.40	2.73	0.67
How often do witnesses/victims remember as many person details as you want?	9.70	80.60	9.70	0.00	0.00	2.00	0.44
In your experience, how accurate are the descriptions of people given to you by witnesses/victims?	0.00	36.10	61.10	2.80	0.00	2.67	0.53
How often (if ever) do you have as much time as you believe is necessary to elicit a good person description?	1.40	18.10	43.10	25.00	11.10	3.27	0.94

Missing responses for each item ranged from 0 to 1.4%.

Factors which officers consider influence the quality of descriptions

Influence on quality. We asked officers (open-ended) what factors influenced the quality of person descriptions. Most frequently mentioned (50%) were the circumstances under which the event was viewed, including event duration and speed, time of day, visibility, number of offenders, witness's attention, and the time elapsed between witnessing the event and giving a description. Forty-nine per cent referred to witness characteristics. For instance, 12 respondents thought that age had a detrimental influence upon description quality, e.g., "elderly persons tend to struggle more with details". Cognitive ability was also thought to play a role, e.g., "generally the more intelligent the easier it is to obtain details", although one officer noted that "those who are less well educated often give a better (importantly) more detailed description including brand names of clothing, jewellery worn, make of training shoe etc.". The witness's ability to communicate information was also mentioned, e.g., "sometimes witnesses do not have the language skills to accurately describe a person and/or ethnicity may also play a role".

Forty-four per cent of officers stated that the mental distress suffered by a witness influences description quality. Fourteen officers explicitly stated that mental distress has a negative impact. Mental distress was thought to influence (1) the witness's encoding of the event, e.g., "victims may not want to look into [the] offender's face or appear to stare", and "the more violent, the less [the] witness will be able to describe the offender and the more they will focus on the violence of the incident or [the] weapon used"; and (2) the witness's ability to retrieve information, e.g., "circumstances could create mental blocks to unlocking the information". Interestingly, one officer noted that witnesses who were fearful at the time of the event "seem to recollect more accurately", whilst another noted that although mental distress can have a negative effect upon memory, "some traumatised witnesses give excellent recall".

Factors mentioned by less than 20% of respondents were: (1) the witness's level of involvement (19%), e.g., "a witness that has not been affected personally, i.e., a bystander, may be a better witness". Also mentioned was whether or not the witness had spoken to other witnesses prior to providing their description; (2) intoxication (i.e., drink or drugs) (18%); (3) witness stereotypes concerning the offender and crime, their attitude towards the crime, and their expectations concerning the type of information required by the police (17%). For example, a small number (five respondents) believed that people with some training in crime prevention (e.g., police staff, security officers, store detectives) made better witnesses as they possess experience of providing statements and are more likely to attend to crime-related event details; and (4) the effectiveness of the police interview (14%), including the training and professionalism of the interviewer and the quality of questioning.

Factors influencing the time spent eliciting descriptions. We asked officers (open-ended) what factors influenced the time spent eliciting person descriptions from witnesses. Overall, 49% of officers said that it depended upon how important the description was to the investigation. The value of a description depended upon (1) the severity of the crime, e.g., "when taking murder witnesses I do not have time pressures, when investigating lesser crimes time may be more of an issue"; and (2) the likelihood of charges or a court case. In addition, police officers reported spending less time eliciting person descriptions if the need for an identification is urgent, e.g., "if an incident has just occurred and [the] offender [is] probably in close proximity, [there is] only enough time to get basic details for [an] identification, and/or if evidence linking the suspect to the crime is already available".

Twenty-three per cent of officers reported the quality of the witness's description to be a factor, e.g., "if [the witness is] able to give more detail then I take longer over it", and another, "[it depends on] the witness's ability to recall descriptive detail unaided". Twenty-two per cent noted the influence of witness characteristics, including age, language difficulties, ability to communicate, cognitive ability, and memory. Twenty-two per cent referred to the circumstances under which the description is elicited. For instance, when taking the description at the location of the incident, factors such as availability of back-up, and the threat posed to officers and witnesses from hostile elements were perceived as important. Also mentioned were the number of witnesses to be interviewed, and whether the police officer planned to obtain a more detailed statement from the witness at a later time. In addition, 22% of officers referred to work and time pressures, including "external pressure from senior investigating officers", legal time constraints, and witness availability.

Other noted factors were the circumstances under which the event had been viewed (14%); the physical and mental state of the witness (17%); and the willingness of the witness to cooperate with enquiries, to attend court, and their attitude to the police (15%).

Methods used to elicit descriptions

Circumstances under which descriptions are elicited. Officers were asked (open-ended) to describe the circumstances under which they would first elicit a description of a perpetrator from a witness. Sixty-four per cent reported requesting a description shortly after the witness had reported the crime, either face-to-face or over the telephone. Thirty-four per cent said that this could be whilst attending the crime scene. Fifty per cent reported obtaining person descriptions at later stages of an investigation when interviewing a witness or taking a statement.

Officers were asked (open-ended) how much time on average they would spend eliciting a person description from a witness. A third (35%) reported spending up to 5 min. Others reported taking longer, with 28% spending 5–20 min and 18% up to half an hour with a witness. A small number (six respondents) reported that they can spend over an hour with a witness when obtaining a description.

Officers were asked (open-ended) how many times on average a witness is likely to provide a person description during the course of an investigation. The majority (82%) reported that a description would be requested more than once. Estimates ranged from 2 to 6 times. Officers reported that a description would be requested at the time of reporting the crime (e.g., during the initial 999 call) (47%), by the responding officer either at the scene or during the course of initial enquiries (67%), by the investigating officer assigned to collect evidence for the case (11.1%), and during an interview or when taking the witness's statement (73%). Eight officers further reported that the witness may be approached throughout the investigation to clarify details concerning the description. One officer noted that "it depends upon how many officers are involved and how thorough the investigation is; unfortunately there seems to be little officer continuity at times".

Officers were asked (open-ended) what the shortest time delay was between a witness providing a description of the perpetrator and attending an identification parade or video identification. The majority of respondents reported that the likely delay would range across weeks, rather than days or hours, with 29% estimating a delay of between 1–2 weeks and 32% estimating a delay of 2–6 weeks. A smaller proportion of respondents reported shorter delays, with 14% reporting delays of less than a week and 10% reporting that identification parades can be undertaken less than 24 hours following an incident; i.e., "several hours if an emergency for a serious arrestable offence".

Techniques used when eliciting person descriptions. Officers were asked (open-ended) how they generally attempt to elicit person descriptions from witnesses. Overall, 89% reported using an open question that encourages free recall. Twenty-six per cent reported that they would ask the witness to recall as much detail as possible.

Forty-seven per cent of respondents reported that they would follow free recall with specific probes to elicit more detail. Specific probes were used to elicit information about the person's physical characteristics (37%) (e.g., height, build, age, race, sex, gait, hairstyle, and colour), clothing, accessories (37%), distinguishing characteristics (19%), and accent (11%). Fifteen per cent of respondents reported explicitly directing the witness to describe the person's facial features. Other specific probes reported by <10% of respondents were (1) asking the witness if the target person reminded them of someone they knew (five respondents); (2) asking the witness to describe some aspect of the person in relation to a common reference point (eight respondents); e.g., "often people say medium build and I would usually use myself and them or people around to compare what they consider normal or medium"; and (3) encouraging the witness to recall nonvisual details about the person, such as smells, sound, and touch (seven respondents), e.g., "I would ask them to describe how fabrics would feel if they had touched them".

Seventeen per cent of respondents reported asking the witness to imagine or visualise the person they were describing, e.g., "I might ask them to imagine they had a video camera in their brain and could zoom in on the features of the suspect". A large proportion of respondents (48%) reported asking the witness to describe the person working down from the top of the person's head to their feet.

In addition, seven techniques for interviewing witnesses with examples were provided. Six of these techniques explicitly referred to components of the CI (and were adapted from Kebbell et al., 1999). The seventh technique, recall the person from different views, was included after informal conversations with police officers. Officers were asked to indicate how often they used each technique when eliciting person descriptions by circling a response on a 5-point scale from "never" (scored 1) to "always" (scored 5). Officers were also asked to indicate how useful they believed each technique to be from "not at all" (scored 1) to "extremely" (scored 5). The techniques were ranked according to how often police officers reported using them. Officers stated that they most frequently used report everything (e.g., "tell me everything you can remember, even details you think are trivial and information you can only partially remember") (ranked 1), followed by encourage concentration (e.g., "try to remember hard") (ranked 2), mental reinstatement (e.g., "try to think how you were feeling at the time" and "try to think of the physical environment where you witnessed the crime") (ranked 3) and mental imagery (e.g., "think of a mental image of the person you wish to remember") (ranked 4). Less frequently used were recall the person from different views (e.g., asking the witness to describe the person several times within the space of one interview, each time asking the witness to focus upon a different time point in the event and/or a different viewpoint of the person) (ranked 5), recall in different orders (e.g., "recall the event in a different order, for example start at the end and recall backwards from there") (ranked 6), and change perspectives (e.g., "try to remember the incident from the perspective of someone else who was involved or from a different physical location") (ranked 7). Table 2 displays the percentages of

TABLE 2
Officers' frequency of use and perceived usefulness of interview techniques

	Percentage of responses						
Question	*Never or not at all*	*Rarely or not very*	*Usually or quite*	*Almost always or very*	*Always or extremely*	*M*	*SD*
Mental reinstatement of context							
How often used	9.70	34.70	36.10	13.90	5.60	2.71	1.01
How useful	1.40	8.30	38.90	34.70	16.70	3.57	0.92
Report everything							
How often used	2.80	13.90	31.90	38.90	12.50	3.44	0.98
How useful	0.00	4.20	33.30	47.20	13.90	3.72	0.76
Recall in different orders							
How often used	37.50	47.20	11.10	4.20	0.00	1.82	0.79
How useful	6.90	36.10	37.50	15.30	2.80	2.70	0.92
Change perspectives							
How often used	63.90	29.20	5.60	0.00	0.00	1.41	0.60
How useful	8.30	48.60	30.60	1.40	4.20	2.40	0.85
Imagery							
How often used	18.10	29.20	25.00	22.20	4.20	2.65	1.15
How useful	5.60	9.70	38.90	31.90	9.70	3.32	0.99
Encourage concentration							
How often used	9.70	18.10	44.40	15.30	11.10	3.00	1.09
How useful	1.40	19.40	54.20	13.90	8.30	3.08	0.86
Recall the person from different views							
How often used	44.40	30.60	20.80	4.20	0.00	1.85	0.90
How useful	4.20	25.00	50.00	6.90	6.90	2.86	0.90

Missing responses for each item ranged from 0 to 7%.

responses for each category. A Kendall coefficient of concordance showed that officers were consistent in their use of these rankings, $W(6) = .49$, $p < .001$. However, it is noticeable that the majority of officers reported never or rarely using techniques such as recall in different orders (84.7%) and change perspectives (93.10%). In addition, whilst half the officers said that they usually or almost always used mental reinstatement of context (50%), a large proportion said that they never or rarely used this technique (44.4%).

Table 2 also shows officers' perceptions of the usefulness of these techniques. Each technique was ranked according to its perceived usefulness. Again, report everything was perceived to be most useful (ranked 1), followed by mental reinstatement (ranked 2), mental imagery (ranked 3), and encourage concentration (ranked 4). The techniques perceived to be less useful were recall the person from different views (ranked 5), recall in different orders (ranked 6), and change perspectives (ranked 7). A Kendall coefficient of concordance for these data also revealed a significant consensus, $W(6) = .34$, $p < .001$. It is of interest to note that the least frequently used techniques were also perceived by officers to be the least useful, with a substantial proportion of officers reporting recall in different orders (43%) and change perspectives (56.9%) to be "not at all" or "not very" useful. Furthermore, despite a large proportion of officers (44.4%) reporting that they never or rarely use mental reinstatement when eliciting person descriptions, 90.3% of officers did perceive this to be a useful technique.

Officers were asked whether they had ever elicited a person description during a CI. Twenty-one officers responded "yes", 49 responded "no", and 2 did not answer the question. Those who had used the CI were compared with those who had not in terms of the reported use and usefulness of the seven interview techniques, using a series of Wilcoxon tests. Means and standard deviations are displayed in Table 3. Officers who had used the CI were more likely to report that they used encourage concentration ($z = -2.48$, $p < .05$) and change perspectives ($z = -2.02$, $p < .05$). In addition, officers who had used the CI perceived encourage concentration ($z = -2.28$, $p < .05$) and recall the person from different views ($z = -2.311$, $p < .05$) as more useful techniques.

Those officers reporting that they had elicited a person description during the course of a CI were further asked to describe the techniques they used. Examples of the techniques described were:

1. "I would tend to ask them to picture the person initially when they first saw them. I often ask them to describe the person at the point they were nearest to them during the incident and the point they could see them but were farthest away as this will often give different bits of

TABLE 3
Reported frequency and perceived usefulness of interview techniques for officers who have used the CI versus those who have not

	CI use	
Technique	*Yes*	*No*
Mental reinstatement of context		
How often used	2.90 (1.04)	2.65 (1.01)
How useful	3.86 (0.73)	3.44 (0.94)
Report everything		
How often used	3.62 (1.07)	3.37 (0.95)
How useful	3.95 (0.80)	3.60 (0.71)
Recall in different orders		
How often used	2.00 (0.84)	1.75 (0.78)
How useful	2.95 (0.80)	2.60 (0.96)
Change perspectives		
How often used	1.62 (0.67)	1.31 (0.55)
How useful	2.55 (1.05)	2.29 (0.66)
Imagery		
How often used	2.52 (1.17)	2.64 (1.12)
How useful	3.25 (1.16)	3.32 (0.91)
Encourage concentration		
How often used	3.48 (0.98)	2.75 (1.06)
How useful	3.38 (0.80)	2.91 (0.83)
Recall the person from different views		
How often used	2.14 (0.85)	1.75 (0.90)
How useful	3.25 (0.91)	2.67 (0.80)

Standard deviations in brackets.

information like when nearest you can get more detail about their facial features, but when further away you can often get more on clothing, what they were holding or if they walked funny etc."

2. "Asked the witness to sit back, close her [his] eyes and to think of the time she [he] had the best view of the person. To hold that image and to describe what she [he] sees. Then go through each part of the description and probe each part i.e., hair, colour, texture etc."
3. "Asked witness to focus on that person, as if they were stood directly in front of them at that particular moment; to concentrate hard on everything about that person and describe them in as much detail as possible. Asked specific questions about all characteristics of that person i.e., hair, face, clothing, body size etc."

Results summary

Half of all respondents believe person descriptions provide important leads for investigations, although 37% thought this was rarely the case. Officers reported that descriptions tend to consist mostly of general characteristics (e.g., sex, age, race, height, hair colour, and length) and less often contain information concerning facial features.

The factors most commonly believed to influence description quality were the viewing conditions of the event (50%), witness characteristics (49%), and witness mental distress (44%). The time spent eliciting descriptions was commonly reported to depend upon the importance of the description to the police (50%), and how good the witness is in providing information (23%).

Most officers (64%) stated that a witness would provide a description shortly after a crime had been reported. Most officers would spend on average up to 5 (35%) or 20 min (28%) eliciting a description. In addition, most noted that a witness would provide a description to the police more than once (82%) and perhaps 2–6 times over the course of an investigation. In most officers' experience, the delay between a witness providing a description and attending an identification parade or video identification ranged from less than a week (14%), to 1–2 weeks (29%), to 2–6 weeks (32%).

When eliciting descriptions from witnesses, most officers (89%) reported using an open question to elicit free recall, with just under half (47%) using specific follow-up probes. Other commonly reported techniques were asking the witness to describe the person from head to toe (48%) and to visualise the person (17%). Of the seven interview techniques provided, officers most frequently used report everything, followed by encourage concentration, mental reinstatement, and imagery. There is a clear correspondence between officers' perceptions of the techniques that are most effective and the techniques that they report using.

DISCUSSION

The present study examined police officers' perceptions of witness variables and their reports of the methods they use to elicit descriptions. Before discussing these findings in detail we should first note that there are some limitations. First, a substantial number of respondents were recruited via the Kent Police College and therefore our sample may not be entirely representative of police officers in other parts of the UK. Potentially, this constrains the generalisability of our findings. In a similar fashion, several studies carrying out surveys with police officers have reported similar limitations with their sampling procedures (e.g., Benton et al., 2006; Kebbell & Milne, 1998; Kebbell et al., 1999). Second, it should be acknowledged that substantial differences may exist between what officers' report occurs in forensic investigations and what actually occurs (Kebbell & Milne, 1998; Robson, 1993). Nevertheless, it is important to note that despite these limitations, trends we observed in the present data are consistent with those found in previous surveys conducted with police officers in the UK and US (e.g., Benton et al., 2006; Brigham & WolfsKeil, 1983; Kebbell & Milne, 1998; Kebbell et al., 1999). The present findings therefore provide insight into police officers' perceptions of eyewitness performance, the quality of the descriptions they provide, and the efficacy of a number of CI components.

Many officers perceived person descriptions given by witnesses as providing important leads in police investigations. Kebbell and Milne (1998) similarly found eyewitnesses to usually or almost always play an important role in police investigations. However, of note is that over a third of officers surveyed here thought this was rarely the case. This may at least partly reflect the fact that the police do not always require detailed person information. For example, the perpetrator may be known to the witness/victim or police, or other evidence may link the perpetrator to the event.

Police officers commonly reported that description quality is likely to depend upon factors associated with how the event was viewed. Specifically, officers referred to factors such as visibility, time of day, event duration, the number of offenders, and the time elapsed between witnessing the event and giving a description. In an archival analysis of offender descriptions given by 2299 real-world witnesses in The Netherlands, van Koppen and Lochun (1997) found several event characteristics to be predictive of the completeness of descriptions, but not necessarily of description accuracy. In particular, less distance between the witness and the offender, better viewing positions relative to the offender, and a shorter delay between the witness viewing the crime and providing a description, were all associated with more complete descriptions. Interestingly, a relationship between event duration and description completeness was not observed. However, the survey by Kassin et al. (2001) of 64 experts on eyewitness testimony found experts to generally agree that the shorter the duration of the event the less well it will be remembered. In addition, the number of perpetrators described by a witness has been found to impact upon description quality. Newlands, George, Towell, Kemp, and Clifford (1999) found that as the number of perpetrators described increases, the information provided about each individual perpetrator decreases.

The quality of a witness's description was also reported by officers to depend upon the characteristics of the witness, including their age, cognitive ability, and ability to communicate information. Brigham and WolfsKeil (1983) also found a substantial number of police officers spontaneously reported witness characteristics, such as education/intelligence and emotional stability, to be important determinants of witness identification accuracy. In particular, in the present survey, 12 respondents thought that age impacted negatively on the quality of a witness's description. Similarly, Wright and Holliday (2005) found English police officers to perceive older witnesses as less reliable and less thorough than younger adult witnesses. They argue that such beliefs may create a self-fulfilling prophecy, as officers may expect less detailed descriptions from older adults and in turn may conduct less satisfactory interviews. In contrast, however, Pozzulo and Warren (2003) found youths (aged 10–14 years) report fewer person descriptors than adults, and provide less accurate descriptions of general characteristics such as height and weight, and of specific internal facial features.

The mental distress experienced by the witness during and/or after the event was also commonly reported as influencing description quality. Specifically, 14 officers stated that mental stress impacts negatively upon description quality. This view was also held by the majority of officers surveyed by Benton and colleagues (2006). Seventy-three per cent agreed that very high levels of stress impair the accuracy of eyewitness testimony. There is a general lack of consensus in psychological research concerning the relationship between emotional stress and subsequent memory performance (Christianson, 1992; Deffenbacher, Bornstein, Penrod, & McGorty, 2004; Kassin et al., 2001). Of relevance here is the fact that research on memory for real-life events consistently shows that details of emotional events appear to be well-retained (see Christianson, 1992, for a review). However, a recent meta-analysis of studies examining the effects of heightened stress on witness retrieval has found heightened stress to negatively impact on both eyewitness identification and the recall of crime related details (Deffenbacher et al., 2004).

Only a small number of officers made reference to systems variables, such as the effectiveness of the police interview, as having the potential to influence description quality (although we note that the way in which we phrased the question may have encouraged a bias towards the generation of estimator variables).[1] This contrasts with the Benton et al. (2006) survey where US officers provided more accurate responses to items relating to system compared to estimator variables. Previous studies, however, have found potential jurors to focus substantially more on the importance of estimator than system variables when asked to generate factors which

[1] We asked police officers "In your experience, what kinds of factors impact upon the quality of witnesses'/victims' person descriptions? For example, are there factors to do with the type of crime and the circumstances in which it was viewed or factors to do with the type of witness/victim you are interviewing that in your opinion influence the quality of person descriptions. Please mention any factors that you feel are important." We note that the phrasing of this question may have encouraged a bias towards generating estimator as opposed to systems variables.

influence witness performance (Shaw, Garcia, & McClure, 1999). Benton et al. suggest that although laypersons may not focus explicitly on systems variables, when given information about them they are able to effectively assess their significance.

Past questionnaire studies have found police officers to frequently cite having little time to conduct what they consider to be good witness interviews (see Kebbell & Milne, 1998; Wright & Holliday, 2005). In contrast, the majority of officers surveyed here (68%) felt that they usually or almost always have enough time to elicit a good person description. Almost a quarter of officers stated that the quality of information provided by the witness would determine how long they spent eliciting a description. Some officers reported that this would depend upon the amount of information the witness provided and their ability to recall details unaided. Interestingly, in a survey of South Australian police officers, Potter and Brewer (1999) found certain witness behaviours to be perceived as indicative of inaccurate testimony. One such behaviour was if the witness required a great deal of prompting when providing their statement.

Other factors reported to determine the time spent eliciting person descriptions were the importance of the description to the investigation and time pressures external to the event (e.g., caseloads, legal time constraints). Moreover, some officers reported that a "quick" interview would be undertaken if there was a need to urgently identify a perpetrator. It is clear that officers must make online decisions concerning the importance and immediate need of information given by witnesses. However, the importance of some details may not always be immediately obvious. Several field studies have found officers to commonly use nonoptimal interview strategies which may impair eyewitness performance, including interrupting the witness, excessive use of closed questions, and use of leading or suggestive questions (e.g., Fisher, 1995; Myklebust & Alison, 2000; Wright & Alison, 2004). Such strategies may reflect an attempt to curtail witness responses when an officer is time pressured or when they perceive that certain detail is not integral to their investigation (see also Kebbell & Milne, 1998). The present findings provide support for the need to develop rapid interview techniques which maximise the amount and accuracy of information elicited from witnesses under time critical conditions (cf., Davis, McMahon, & Greenwood, 2005).

Finally, in line with Kebbell et al. (1999), the present survey demonstrates a clear correspondence between officers' perceptions of the usefulness of CI components and their reported use in the field. Officers most frequently reported using the CI strategy of report everything, encourage concentration, mental reinstatement, and imagery. Those techniques least frequently used were recall in different orders and change perspectives. However, officers were more likely to report using encourage concentration and change perspective strategies if they had previously elicited a person description during a CI. It may be that officers are reluctant to use these instructions due to lack of training or a difficultly in communicating the instruction to the witness (Kebbell et al., 1999; Memon, Holley, Milne, Köhnken & Bull, 1994). Nevertheless, the present findings suggest that officers' perceptions concerning the forensic effectiveness of interview techniques are likely to drive the application of those techniques in the field.

Police procedures and verbal overshadowing

Laboratory research has shown that eliciting person descriptions can be detrimental for subsequent recognition performance (for a review, see Schooler, 2002). However, researchers have little knowledge of the methods police officers report using to elicit person descriptions in the field. The present findings therefore provide insight into the circumstances under which descriptions are elicited, the completeness of those descriptions, and the techniques officers use to obtain them. Let us now consider aspects of police procedure that are highlighted in the present survey and which relate to laboratory research on verbal overshadowing. In particular, we ask whether the conditions are necessary and sufficient for verbal overshadowing to occur. We also discuss the implications of these findings for current accounts of verbal overshadowing.

Circumstances under which descriptions are elicited. The extent to which witnesses have an opportunity to generate a person description may influence their susceptibility to verbal overshadowing. Officers estimated spending from 5 to 20 min eliciting a description. In the majority of verbal overshadowing studies participants spend approximately 5 min generating a description of a target face (e.g., Brown & Lloyd-Jones, 2002, 2003; Dodson et al., 1997; Fallshore & Schooler, 1995; Finger, 2002; MacLin, 2002; Meissner et al., 2001; Schooler & Engstler-Schooler, 1990). However, verbal overshadowing was not always observed following a 5 min description and the nature of the descriptors that are generated in that time may be a more important factor (e.g., Brown & Lloyd-Jones, 2002; Meissner et al., 2001). Interestingly, laboratory studies eliciting descriptions over shorter periods of time (e.g., ≤ 90 s) have found facilitative effects of verbal overshadowing, although these studies have asked participants to describe and recognise multiple faces (Brown & Lloyd-Jones, 2005, 2006; Wolgalter, 1991, 1996).

An issue of particular interest for applied settings is the role of retention factors in moderating susceptibility to verbal overshadowing effects. Most officers reported that they would ask a witness for a person description shortly after an incident has been reported. Verbal overshadowing has been observed with delays of 5 to 20 min between encoding and description tasks.

Moreover, Meissner (2002) has reported verbal overshadowing across a postencoding delay of 1 week. Nevertheless, in their meta-analysis, Meissner and Brigham (2001) found postencoding delay not to be a significant predictor of verbal overshadowing.

It is plausible that effects of postencoding delay on verbal overshadowing are mediated by the precise contents of the generated description. Laboratory research suggests that long delays can reduce both the completeness and accuracy of face descriptions (for a review, see Meissner et al., 2007). Under these conditions, a recoding interference account would propose that the increased likelihood of generating an imprecise description would make identification performance more susceptible to verbal interference over time. Alternatively, according to a criterion account, the generation of a less complete description may reduce participant's confidence in their ability to remember the target face. As a result they may apply a more conservative response criterion in the identification test leading to fewer correct identification decisions when the target is present (cf. Chin & Schooler, 2008 this issue; Clare & Lewandowsky, 2004).

We also asked officers on average what is the shortest time delay between a witness providing a person description and attending an identification parade or video identification. This was estimated by police officers to be 1–6 weeks. However, some officers stated that this delay could be less than a week and possibly less than 24 hours. It should be noted that some ambiguity may be evident in responses to this item. Some officers reported eliciting a description shortly after the event whilst others reported eliciting descriptions at later stages of an investigation. It may be that police officers are not always aware of subsequent descriptions elicited from witnesses. Thus, responses to this item may not necessarily always reflect the time between the last description given by the witness and viewing the identification parade. We address the issue of repeated descriptions later in this discussion.

The time course of verbal overshadowing is unclear. On the one hand, empirical data shows contrasting findings concerning the persistence of verbal overshadowing effects (e.g., Finger & Pezdek, 1999; Schooler & Engstler-Schooler, 1990). On the other hand, different theoretical accounts of verbal overshadowing predict that effects of verbalisation will persist over differing lengths of time (cf. Chin & Schooler, 2008 this issue). Let us develop these arguments more fully.

Several studies have shown that verbal overshadowing can persist for up to 30 min (Meissner et al., 2001), 2 days (Schooler & Engstler-Schooler, 1990), and possibly 2 weeks (Read & Schooler, 1994). In contrast, a study by Finger and Pezdek (1999) indicates that effects of verbal overshadowing can be relatively short lived. They found verbal overshadowing to be attenuated when a 24 min delay was inserted between the description and identification task. They termed this finding a "release from verbal overshadowing", as identification performance in the description condition was found to improve over the 24 min delay. Difficulty arises with interpreting this finding however, as the authors did not include an appropriate baseline condition with which to compare the delayed description condition (i.e., a no description condition at the 24 min delay was not included). Indeed, other studies have shown no description control participants to experience a significant degree of forgetting over time and this may confound interpretations concerning the attenuation of effects of verbal overshadowing. For instance, a meta-analysis of verbal overshadowing studies conducted by Meissner and Brigham (2001) indicates that whilst verbal overshadowing was only evident when the identification test shortly followed the description task ($\leq$ 10 min), the reduction in verbal overshadowing at long delays ($\geq$ 30 min) was due to control participants exhibiting a significant degree of forgetting across the delay. In contrast, identification performance in the description condition was found to remain unchanged over time (see also Lloyd-Jones & Brown, 2008 this issue). These findings suggest the possibility that the effects of verbalisation may well change over time.

To date, the empirical data concerning the time course of verbal overshadowing is mixed. Nevertheless, according to different theoretical accounts we may well expect verbal overshadowing to occur over different lengths of time depending upon the conditions under which it is elicited. According to a transfer-inappropriate processing shift account we may expect verbal overshadowing to be relatively short-lived: An emphasis on verbalisation may be strong enough to encourage an initial shift in processing, but time or task demands may result in processing reverting back to a form that is more efficient for face recognition. In these cases, effects of verbal overshadowing would diminish over time (cf. Chin & Schooler, 2008 this issue; Lloyd-Jones & Brown, 2008 this issue). In contrast, on a recoding interference account, where verbal interference arises due to participants generating and later relying upon an imprecise verbal representation of the contents of their memory, we may expect the source of interference to remain constant over time.

Finally, verbal overshadowing effects will further be determined by events the witness is exposed to during the retention interval. In particular, witnesses were reported to be likely to provide repeated descriptions during an investigation. To our knowledge only one study has examined the effects of providing repeated descriptions on verbal overshadowing. Meissner (2002) found verbal overshadowing to persist when participants provided repeated recall 1 week after the initial description, immediately prior to the identification test. Studies of eyewitness memory have reported beneficial and detrimental effects of eliciting repeated retrieval attempts. Some studies have found repeated retrieval attempts to elicit new information (e.g., Turtle

& Yuille, 1994). Others have found misinformation generated in the initial recall attempt to continue to be reported in subsequent recall attempts (e.g., Meissner, 2002). Further research should examine whether eliciting repeated descriptions influences the magnitude of verbal overshadowing. In particular, the pervasive nature of self-generated misinformation may contribute to the robustness of verbal overshadowing effects.

In sum, it is possible that verbal overshadowing may occur given the context in which descriptions are elicited. In particular, verbal overshadowing may be a matter of concern if witnesses are encouraged to generate an imprecise or inaccurate verbal memory representation, which they subsequently come to rely upon. This particular source of verbal interference may remain evident over longer retention intervals and repeated retrieval attempts. The present findings highlight the need to further examine the influence of postencoding delay, repeated description, and description-test delay.

The nature of person descriptors and techniques used to elicit person descriptions. Most officers believed witnesses to give generally incomplete but accurate person descriptions. Witnesses were reported to most often describe general person characteristics (e.g., sex, age, race, height) and details about the hair, and less often to provide information concerning individual facial features. This is consistent with a number of archival studies (Lindsay, Martin, & Webber, 1994; Tollestrup, Turtle, & Yuille, 1994; van Koppen & Lochun, 1997; Wagstaff et al., 2003). Thus, real-world witnesses rarely provide elaborative or detailed descriptions of facial features.

Furthermore, officers generally do not direct witnesses to provide elaborative descriptions of facial features. The vast majority of officers reported that when eliciting person descriptions they use an open question to encourage free recall. Moreover, although approximately half reported that they would follow up the witness's free recall with specific probes, on the whole they directed the witness to further consider the physical characteristics and clothing of the target person rather than requesting a detailed description of their facial features.

In contrast, laboratory studies of verbal overshadowing have normally directed participants to describe the target person's face, and studies that have instructed participants to provide elaborative face descriptions are more likely to demonstrate verbal overshadowing (and more robust effects) than studies employing standard free recall instructions (e.g., Brown & Lloyd-Jones, 2002; Meissner & Brigham, 2001).

Together this suggests that detrimental effects of verbalisation observed in the laboratory may not be a serious concern for the majority of police officers in the field. Nevertheless, the present findings also highlight some instances in which police officers report requesting more elaborative face descriptions from witnesses. For instance, a sizeable number of officers (15%) reported explicitly directing the witness to describe the facial characteristics of the target person. Thus, it seems likely that in a small number of cases the interview strategies adopted by police officers may run the risk of negatively influencing witness memory.

Accounts of verbal overshadowing provide differing explanations for why more robust effects of verbal overshadowing are evident following elaborative descriptions. A recoding interference account proposes that misinformation is more likely to be elicited under conditions requiring elaborative face recall. One way in which this might occur is if police officers make excessive use of closed and leading questions which can lead the witness to incorporate misinformation into their account (Fisher, 1995). This imprecise description is then later relied upon when viewing the identification test (Meissner et al., 2001). Alternatively, advocates of a transfer-inappropriate processing shift account propose that elaborative descriptions give rise to a more extensive shift from global to featural processing, which is subsequently less useful for identification (Brown & Lloyd-Jones, 2002; Schooler, 2002). As outlined previously, however, verbal overshadowing effects arising under conditions which encourage the generation of misinformation may be longer lasting and therefore of greater concern to applied settings where delays between encoding, description and test vary greatly.

We note also that the CI explicitly aims to elicit elaborative recall of an event. Thus, use of the CI, or its individual components, may leave witnesses vulnerable to effects of verbal overshadowing. In the present survey, the CI components that officers reported most frequently using were instructions to report everything and to encourage concentration. The former instruction, however, may encourage witnesses to lower their criterion for providing information (Memon, Wark, Bull, & Koehnken, 1997; Milne, Clare, & Bull, 1999; although see Fisher et al., 2002). For instance, Meissner et al. (2001) directly manipulated participants' criterion of responding when describing a target face. They demonstrated that "forcing" participants to generate a more elaborate description, thereby producing details of which they were unsure, impaired later face recognition. In contrast, warning participants to generate only correct descriptors and not to guess benefited later face recognition (see also Meissner, 2002). They suggest that in order to protect against effects of verbal overshadowing witnesses should be allowed to establish their own criterion of responding, which includes the option to withhold information of which they are uncertain. In a similar vein, Fisher and Geiselman (1992) have recommended that witnesses interviewed using the CI should be warned not to guess or fabricate information (see also Fisher et al., 2002). However, it is not known whether police officers exercise this instruction in the field. Indeed, only one officer in the present survey spontaneously mentioned warning a witness against guessing or fabricating information.

With regards to CI instructions to image the witnessed event, almost half the officers reported usually or almost always asking witnesses to think of a mental image of the person they were describing. In addition, a fifth of officers spontaneously reported asking the witness to imagine or visualise the person. The frequency with which officers report using imagery is perhaps surprising given that Kebbell et al. (1999) found officers rarely reported using instructions to image. Some researchers have found that instructing a witness to form an image and then probing the image with questions can increase the recall of both correct and incorrect information (Bekerian & Dennett, 1997; Memon et al., 1997). However, there is some concern that imaging may be detrimental to accurate memory recall (see Roberts, 1996; see also Memon & Higham, 1999, for a review). In particular, it has been suggested that errors in source monitoring may arise if there is repeated imagining, as the witness may confuse the original memory with subsequent images created during the course of the interview (Roberts, 1996; although see Fisher et al., 2002).

Finally, officers spontaneously mentioned two other interview strategies that may prove vulnerable to effects of verbal overshadowing. First, several officers reported asking the witness if the person in question reminds them of someone they know. This strategy has been found to produce effects of verbal overshadowing in a laboratory setting and therefore is likely to be a nonoptimal interview strategy for police officers to adopt (MacLin, 2002). Second, several officers also reported asking the witness to describe nonvisual details about the person, such as smells, sound, and touch. Such details may be of forensic relevance in that they can help to narrow down suspects, or identify clothing or locations. However, laboratory studies have shown that verbal overshadowing is not restricted to face recognition, but also extends to other nonverbal forms of memory including taste (Melcher & Schooler, 1996) and voice recognition (Perfect, Hunt, & Harris, 2002). Thus, witness memory for nonvisual details about the person may also be susceptible to verbal overshadowing.

CONCLUSIONS

Most police officers believed witnesses' person descriptions to play an important role in police investigations. Moreover, there was a clear correspondence between officers' perceptions of the usefulness of components of the CI and their reported use in the field.

For current police practice, the effects of verbal overshadowing on witness memory performance generally need not be a concern for many police officers. In the main, person descriptions elicited from real-world witnesses tend to be relatively general and broad-based, and from laboratory-based studies it appears that such descriptions do not appear to generate strong or robust verbal overshadowing. Nevertheless, there are times when police officers adopt more elaborative interview techniques. In these cases, officers should be aware that witnesses are likely to be vulnerable to effects of verbal overshadowing.

In particular, verbal overshadowing may become an issue in those circumstances where witnesses are strongly encouraged to provide elaborative person descriptions, and specifically in those situations in which they have been encouraged to lower their retrieval criterion to report information of which they are unsure. The introduction of misinformation into their newly formed verbal representation may well be consistently reported across repeated descriptions. Moreover, it has been suggested that verbal overshadowing effects arising from recoding interference are less likely to attenuate over time (Chin & Schooler, 2008 this issue). In contrast, effects of verbal overshadowing which arise due to a transfer-inappropriate shift in processing style may be particularly time sensitive and therefore less relevant to person descriptions elicited in real-world settings. The role of a criterion shift in eliciting verbal overshadowing effects is less clear cut. In particular, the precise source of such a criterion shift has not yet been investigated. However, as outlined previously, a criterion shift may be associated with the witnesses own assessment of the quality of their person description (Chin & Schooler, 2008 this issue; Clare & Lewandowsky, 2004). This could be influenced by a range of factors including the strength of the memory trace (Chin & Schooler, 2008 this issue) and confirming or disconfirming feedback from the interviewing officer (cf. Gudjonsson, 2003).

Finally, it is clear from the present survey that a number of variables that influence verbal overshadowing and which are also relevant to the forensic setting require further study. In particular, the postencoding retention interval, effects of repeated verbal description, and the delay between description and memory testing require further examination. In fact these variables may prove useful tools in distinguishing between the different theoretical accounts of verbal overshadowing. Moreover, in forensic settings these influences are unlikely to occur in isolation, and so research needs to investigate the combined influence of these variables on verbal overshadowing and memory performance.

REFERENCES

Bekerian, D. A., & Dennett, J. L. (1997). Imagery effects in spoken and written recall. In D. Payne & F. Conrad (Eds.), *Intersections in basic and applied memory research* (pp. 279–289). Mahwah, NJ: Lawrence Erlbaum Associates, Inc.

Benton, T. R., Ross, D. F, Bradshaw, E., Thomas, W. N., & Bradshaw, G. S. (2006). Eyewitness memory is still not common sense: Comparing jurors, judges and law enforcement to eyewitness experts. *Applied Cognitive Psychology, 20*, 115–129.

Brigham, J. C., & WolfsKeil, M. P. (1983). Opinions of attorneys and law enforcement personnel on the accuracy of eyewitness identifications. *Law and Human Behavior, 7*, 337–349.

Brown, C., & Lloyd-Jones, T. J. (2002). Verbal overshadowing in a multiple face presentation paradigm: Effects of description instruction. *Applied Cognitive Psychology, 16*, 873–885.

Brown, C., & Lloyd-Jones, T. J. (2003). Verbal overshadowing of multiple face and car recognition: Effects of within- versus across-category verbal descriptions. *Applied Cognitive Psychology, 17*, 183–201.

Brown, C., & Lloyd-Jones, T. J. (2005). Verbal facilitation of face recognition. *Memory and Cognition, 33*, 1442–1456.

Brown, C., & Lloyd-Jones, T. J. (2006). Beneficial effects of verbalization and visual distinctiveness on remembering and knowing faces. *Memory and Cognition, 34*, 277–286.

Central Planning and Training Unit. (1992). *Investigative interviewing: A guide to interviewing.* London: Home Office, Central Planning and Training Unit.

Chin, J. M., & Schooler, J. W. (2008). Why do words hurt? Content, process, and criterion shift accounts of verbal overshadowing. *European Journal of Cognitive Psychology, 20*, 396–413.

Christianson, S. (1992). Emotional stress and eyewitness memory: A critical review. *Psychological Bulletin, 112*, 284–309.

Clare, J., & Lewandowsky, S. (2004). Verbalizing facial memory: Criterion effects in verbal overshadowing. *Journal of Experimental Psychology: Learning, Memory, and Cognition, 30*, 739–755.

Clifford, B. R., & George, R. (1996). A field evaluation of training in three methods of witness/victim investigative interviewing. *Psychology, Crime and Law, 2*, 231–248.

Davis, M. R., McMahon, M., & Greenwood, K. M. (2005). The efficacy of mnemonic components of the cognitive interview: Towards a shortened variant for time- critical investigations. *Applied Cognitive Psychology, 19*, 75–93.

Deffenbacher, K. A., Bornstein, B. H., Penrod, S. D., & McGorty, E. K. (2004). A meta-analytic review of the effects of high stress on eyewitness memory. *Law and Human Behavior, 28*, 687–706.

Dodson, C. S., Johnson, M. K., & Schooler, J. W. (1997). The verbal overshadowing effect: Why descriptions impair facial recognition. *Memory and Cognition, 25*, 129–139.

Fallshore, M., & Schooler, J. W. (1995). The verbal vulnerability of perceptual expertise. *Journal of Experimental Psychology: Learning, Memory, and Cognition, 21*, 1608–1623.

Finger, K. (2002). Mazes and music: Using perceptual processing to release verbal overshadowing. *Applied Cognitive Psychology, 16*, 887–896.

Finger, K., & Pezdek, K. (1999). The effect of verbal description on face identification accuracy: "Release from verbal overshadowing". *Journal of Applied Psychology, 84*, 340–348.

Fisher, R. P. (1995). Interviewing victims and witnesses of crime. *Psychology, Public Policy and Law, 1*, 732–764

Fisher, R. P., Brennan H. K., & McCauley, M. R. (2002). The cognitive interview method to enhance eyewitness recall. In M. Eisen, G. Goodman, & J. Quas (Eds.), *Memory and suggestibility in the forensic interview* (pp. 265–286). Hillsdale, NJ: Lawrence Erlbaum Associates, Inc.

Fisher, R. P., & Geiselman, R. E. (1992). *Memory enhancing techniques for investigative interviewing*: The cognitive interview. Springfield, IL: Charles C. Thomas.

Fisher, R. P., Geiselman, R. E., & Amador, M. (1989). Field test of the cognitive interview: Enhancing the recollection of actual victims and witnesses of crime. *Journal of Applied Psychology, 74*, 722–727.

Fisher, R. P., Quigley, K. L., Brock, P., Chin, D., & Cutler, B. L. (1990). The effectiveness of the cognitive interview in description and identification tasks. Cited in D. Ross, J. Read., & M. Toglia (Eds.), *Adult eyewitness memory: Current trends and developments*. Cambridge, UK: Cambridge University Press.

Geiselman, R. E., Fisher, R. P., Firstenberg, I., Hutton, L. A., Sullivan, S., Avetissian, I., & Prosk, A. (1984). Enhancement of eyewitness memory: An empirical evaluation of the cognitive interview. *Journal of Police Science and Administration, 12*, 74–80.

Gudjonsson, G. H. (2003). *The psychology of interrogations and confessions*. Chichester, UK: Wiley.

Gwyer, P., & Clifford, B. R. (1997). The effects of the cognitive interview on recall, identification, confidence and the confidence/accuracy relationship. *Applied Cognitive Psychology, 11*, 121–145.

Kassin, S. M., Tubb, V. A., Hosch, H. M., & Memon, A. (2001). On the "general acceptance" of eyewitness testimony research: A new survey of the experts. *The American Psychologist, 56*, 405–416.

Kebbell, M. R. (2000). The law concerning the conduct of lineups in England and Wales: How well does it satisfy the recommendations of the American Psychology–Law Society? *Law and Human Behavior, 24*, 309–315.

Kebbell, M. R., & Milne, R. (1998). Police officers' perceptions of eyewitness performance in forensic investigations. *Journal of Social Psychology, 138*, 323–330.

Kebbell, M. R., Milne, R., & Wagstaff, G. F. (1999). The cognitive interview: A survey of its forensic effectiveness. *Psychology, Crime and Law, 5*, 101–115.

Kebbell, M. R., & Wagstaff, G. F. (1999). *Face value? Evaluating the accuracy of eyewitness information* (Police Research Paper No. 102). London: Home Office (UK) Policing and Reducing Crime Unit.

Köhnken, G., Milne, R., Memon, A., & Bull, R. (1999). The cognitive interview: A meta-analysis. *Psychology, Crime and Law, 5*, 3–27.

Lindsay, R. C. L., Martin, R., & Webber, L. (1994). Default values in eyewitness descriptions: A problem for the match-to-description lineup foil selection strategy. *Law and Human Behaviour, 18*, 527–541.

Lloyd-Jones, T. J., & Brown, C. (2008). Verbal overshadowing of multiple face recognition: Effects on remembering and knowing over time. *European Journal of Cognitive Psychology, 20*, 456–477.

Lovett, S. B., Small, M. Y., & Engstrom, S. A. (1992, November). *The verbal overshadowing effect: Now you see it, now you don't*. Paper presented at the annual meeting of the Psychonomic Society, St Louis, MO.

MacLin, M. K. (2002). The effects of exemplar and prototype descriptors on verbal overshadowing. *Applied Cognitive Psychology, 16*, 929–936.

MacLin, O. H., Tapscott, R. L., & Malpass, R. S. (2002). The development of a computer system to collect descriptions of culprits. *Applied Cognitive Psychology, 16*, 937–945.

Meissner, C. A. (2002). Applied aspects of the instructional bias effect in verbal overshadowing. *Applied Cognitive Psychology, 16*, 911–928.

Meissner, C. A., & Brigham, J. C. (2001). A meta-analysis of the verbal overshadowing effect in face identification. *Applied Cognitive Psychology, 15*, 603–616.

Meissner, C. A., Brigham, J. C., & Kelley, C. M. (2001). The influence of retrieval processes in verbal overshadowing. *Memory and Cognition, 29*(1), 176–186.

Meissner, C. A., Sporer, S. L., & Schooler, J. W. (2007). Person descriptions as eyewitness evidence. In R. C. L. Lindsay, D. F. Ross, J. D. Read, & M. P. Toglia (Eds.), *Handbook of eyewitness psychology, Vol. 2*. Mahwah, NJ: Lawrence Erlbaum Associates, Inc.

Melcher, J. M., & Schooler, J. W. (1996). The misremembrance of wines past: Verbal and perceptual expertise differentially mediate verbal overshadowing of taste memory. *Journal of Memory and Language, 35*, 231–245.

Memon, A., & Bartlett, J. (2002). The effects of verbalization on face recognition in young and older adults. *Applied Cognitive Psychology, 16*, 635–650.

Memon, A., & Higham, P. (1999). A review of the cognitive interview. *Psychology, Crime and Law, 5*, 177–196.

Memon, A., Holley, A., Milne, R., Köhnken, G., & Bull, R. (1994). Towards understanding the effects of interviewer training in evaluating the cognitive interview. *Applied Cognitive Psychology, 8*, 641–659.

Memon, A., Wark, L., Bull, R., & Koehnken, G. (1997). Isolating the effects of the cognitive interview techniques. *British Journal of Psychology, 88*, 179–197.

Milne, R., Clare, I. C. H., & Bull, R. (1999). Using the cognitive interview with adults with mild learning disabilities. *Psychology, Crime and Law, 5*, 81–99.

Myklebust, T., & Alison, L. (2000). The current state of police interviews with children in Norway: How discrepant are they from models based on current issues in memory and communication? *Psychology, Crime and Law, 6*, 331–351.

Newlands, P. J., George, R. C., Towell, N. A., Kemp, R. I., & Clifford, B. R. (1999). An investigation of description quality from real-life interviews. *Psychology, Crime and Law, 5*, 145–166.

Perfect, T. J., Hunt, L. J., & Harris, C. M. (2002). Verbal overshadowing in voice recognition. *Applied Cognitive Psychology, 16*, 973–980.

Potter, R., & Brewer, N. (1999). Perceptions of witness behaviour-accuracy relationships held by police, lawyers and mock-jurors. *Psychiatry, Psychology and Law, 6*, 97–103.

Pozzulo, J. D., & Warren, K. L. (2003). Descriptions and identifications of strangers by youth and adult eyewitnesses. *Journal of Applied Psychology, 88*, 315–323.

Read, J. D., & Schooler, J. W. (1994). *Verbalization decrements in long-term person identification*. Paper presented at the third Practical Aspects of Memory conference, College Park, MD.

Roberts, K. (1996). How research on source monitoring can inform cognitive interview techniques. *Psycoloquy, 7*(44).

Robson, C. (1993). *Real world research*. Oxford, UK: Blackwell.

Schooler, J. W. (2002). Verbalization produces a transfer inappropriate processing shift. *Applied Cognitive Psychology, 16*, 989–997.

Schooler, J. W., & Engstler-Schooler, T. Y. (1990). Verbal overshadowing of visual memories: Some things are better left unsaid. *Cognitive Psychology, 22*, 36–71.

Schooler, J. W., Fiore, S. M., & Brandimonte, M. A. (1997). At loss from words: Verbal overshadowing of perceptual memories. In D. L. Medin (Ed.), *The psychology of learning and motivation* (Vol. 37, pp. 291–340). San Diego, CA: Academic Press.

Shaw, J. S., Garcia, L. A., & McClure, K. A. (1999). A lay perspective on the accuracy of eyewitness testimony. *Journal of Applied Social Psychology, 29*, 52–71.

Tollestrup, P. A., Turtle, J. W., & Yuille, J. C. (1994). Actual victims and witnesses to robbery and fraud: An archival analysis. In D. F. Ross, J. D. Read, & M. P. Toglia (Eds.), *Adult eyewitness testimony: Current trends and developments* (pp. 144–160). Cambridge, UK: Cambridge University Press.

Turtle, J. W., & Yuille, J. C. (1994). Lost but not forgotten details: Repeated eyewitness recall leads to reminiscence but not hypermnesia. *Journal of Applied Psychology, 79*, 260–271.

Van Koppen, P. J., & Lochun, S. K. (1997). Portraying perpetrators: The validity of offender descriptions by witnesses. *Law and Human Behaviour, 21*, 661–685.

Wagstaff, G. F., MacVeigh, J., Boston, R., Scott, L., Brunas-Wagstaff, J., & Cole, J. (2003). Can laboratory findings on eyewitness testimony be generalized to the real world? An archival analysis of the influence of violence, weapon presence and age on eyewitness accuracy. *Journal of Psychology, 137*, 17–28.

Wells, G. L. (1978). Applied eyewitness-testimony research: System variables and estimator variables. *Journal of Personality and Social Psychology, 36*, 1546–1557.

Wolgalter, M. S. (1991). Effects of post-exposure description and imaging on subsequent face recognition performance. *Proceedings of the Human Factors Society, 35*, 575–579.

Wolgalter, M. S. (1996). Describing faces from memory: Accuracy and effects on subsequent recognition performance. *Proceedings of the Human Factors and Ergonomics Society, 40*, 536–540.

Wright, A. M., & Alison, L. (2004). Questioning sequences in Canadian police interviews: Constructing and confirming the course of events. *Psychology, Crime and Law, 10*, 137–154.

Wright, A. M., & Holliday, R. E. (2005). Police perceptions of older eyewitnesses. *Legal and Criminological Psychology, 10*, 211–233.

Yu, C. J., & Geiselman, R. E. (1993). Effects of constructing identi-kit composites on photospread identification performance. *Criminal Justice and Behavior, 20*, 280–292.

EUROPEAN JOURNAL OF COGNITIVE PSYCHOLOGY
2008, 20 (3), 561–576

Testing alternatives to Navon letters to induce a transfer-inappropriate processing shift in face recognition

Peter J. Hills and Michael B. Lewis
School of Psychology, Cardiff University, Cardiff, UK

Processing the local features of a Navon letter (a large global letter made up of small letters) causes a reduction in face identification accuracy (Macrae & Lewis, 2002). This is similar to the verbal overshadowing effect (where describing a face causes it to be less well recognised, see e.g., Schooler & Engstler-Schooler, 1990). Three experiments are presented that explore this Navon effect. Experiment 1 replicates the Navon effect using a new set of stimuli. Experiment 2 extends the effect using Navon shapes in a manner that removes verbal responses. Extending the logic of the proposed transfer-inappropriate processing shift explanation, Experiment 3 attempted to show the same effect using spatial-frequency filtered faces as an induction akin to Navon stimuli. The equivalent effect was not observed. We discuss whether the results indicate that the Navon effect is due to a different mechanism from the verbal overshadowing effect.

Processing the local features of Navon letters appears to cause a deficit in facial identification (e.g., Macrae & Lewis, 2002). A Navon letter (Navon, 1977) is a global figure made up of local features. An example is shown in Figure 1. After spending 10 min processing the local features of Navon letters, participants' performance on a lineup task was as low as 30%, whereas control participants had an accuracy of 63% and global processors performed at 83% accuracy (Macrae & Lewis, 2002). Perfect (2003) found similar results: Local processors had an accuracy of 43%, controls were at 70%, and global processors were at 80%, though the control-global difference was not significant.

Correspondence should be addressed to: Peter Hills, School of Psychology, Tower Building, Cardiff University, Park Place, Cardiff, CF10 3AT, UK. E-mail: HillsPJ@Cardiff.ac.uk

The authors would like to thank Michelle Cahill for collecting some of the data, ALS Industries for filming the football match, and Glyndwr's Army FC for being the models for the stimuli. The authors would also like to thank two anonymous reviewers and Christina Howard for comments on an earlier draft of this work. Moreover, the authors would like to offer special thanks to Toby Lloyd-Jones for careful reading and insightful comments on an earlier draft of this work. This research was supported by grant PTA-030-2003-00524 from the ESRC to PH.

http://www.psypress.com/ecp DOI: 10.1080/09541440701728524

```
NNNNNNNNNNNNN
NNNNNNNNNNNNNN
NNNNN    NNNNNN
NNNNN     NNNNN
NNNNN     NNNNN
NNNNN     NNNNN
NNNNN     NNNNN
NNNNN    NNNNN
NNNNNNNNNNNNN
NNNNNNNNNNNNNN
NNNNN    NNNNNN
NNNNN     NNNNN
NNNNN     NNNNN
NNNNN     NNNNN
NNNNN     NNNNN
NNNNN     NNNNN
NNNNN     NNNNN
```

Figure 1. A Navon letter: A global R made up of local Ns.

An explanation for the Navon effect was offered by Macrae and Lewis (2002) based upon verbal overshadowing. Verbal overshadowing is where describing a face impairs subsequent recognition of that and other faces (e.g., Brown & Lloyd-Jones, 2002, 2003; Dodson, Johnson, & Schooler, 1997; Schooler & Engstler-Schooler, 1990).

Two distinct explanations of verbal overshadowing have been offered. One is based on the idea of verbal and visual codes. Verbalising a face is said to induce the processing of faces using a verbal code rather than a visual code. As such, there is a mismatch between the originally visually coded face and the new verbal coding. This suggestion was put forward by Meissner, Brigham, and Kelley (2001). Nevertheless, it is incompatible with some findings showing an improvement of identification performance due to verbalisation (e.g., Brown & Lloyd-Jones, 2005, 2006). An alternative suggestion was that of a transfer-inappropriate processing shift.

Schooler and Engstler-Schooler's (1990) original transfer-inappropriate processing explanation suggests that verbalisation causes a shift in the style of processing faces to different but still visual codes. Rhodes (1993) distinguishes between configural and featural processing in face recognition (though, in the former case, she uses the term "second-order relational" to refer to configural processing). Face recognition primarily involves configural processing and faces will be processed configurally unless some extraneous variable affects this. Tanaka and Farah (1993), for example, demonstrated a shift to featural processing for scrambled faces and for inverted faces. Verbalisation, it is argued, causes featural processing to occur. As such, the act of verbalising a face causes a transfer-inappropriate processing shift away from configural processing. This explanation may also be able to explain the finding regarding the Navon effect described above (Macrae & Lewis, 2002). Nevertheless, what configural and featural (or global and local) processing are have not been clearly defined (see e.g., Lewis & Glenister, 2003). As such the processing shift is also not clearly defined.

According to Macrae and Lewis (2002) and Perfect (2003), the Navon effect causes the same transfer-inappropriate processing shift, but using a more perceptually based procedure. Focusing on the local features of a Navon letter leads to a greater emphasis on featural as compared with configural processing of the subsequent face. Since featural coding is not normally the most efficient kind of processing for face recognition, this leads to a reduction in subsequent face identification performance. This explanation can account for the reduction in performance observed by processing the local features of a Navon letter. Indeed, Perfect did not find a significant improvement. There are situations where global processing is not most appropriate for face recognition (e.g., inverted faces, Tanaka & Farah, 1993; simultaneous versus sequential lineup procedures, Steblay, Dysart, Fulero, & Lindsay, 2001). As such, some procedures may find a local advantage.

While the Navon effect appears replicable, some caveats must be noted with the published pieces of research on the topic. The video used by Macrae and Lewis (2002) and Perfect (2003)—the Schooler and Engstler-Schooler (1990) mock-up of a crime—creates accuracy rates of around 70% in the control condition. In applied settings, performance in lineups is rarely above 40% (Kemp, Towell, & Pike, 1997; Logie, Baddeley, & Woodhead, 1987). This suggests that the task used by Macrae and Lewis and Perfect may be so easy as to cause ceiling effects. Moreover, such ceiling effects may cloud any global advantage. Another aspect of validity is that many researchers are using copies of copies in their experiments. The video has been described as "grainy" (Perfect, personal communication). As such, new stimuli are developed here to ensure generalisability of the results.

Three experiments are presented here that were designed to add generalisability to the Navon effect. Experiment 1 was a baseline replication to ensure the reliability of the Navon effect using the newly created video stimuli. Experiment 2 used a novel kind of Navon stimuli and removed the vocalisation element of the task. Experiment 3 replaced the Navon letters with spatially filtered faces. This experiment was conducted to explore whether it is possible to produce a Navon-like effect by encouraging use of high or low spatial frequency information.

EXPERIMENT 1

The Navon Effect is not always borne out in research (see, e.g., Lawson, 2006; Ryan et al., 2006). As such, the first task was to replicate the basic

Navon effect and create a baseline to compare further findings. Moreover, this baseline will validate the new stimuli that are used here, and therefore increase the generalisability of the Navon effect.

Method

Participants. One hundred and twenty undergraduates from the School of Psychology at Cardiff University between 18 and 30 years old with normal vision, as defined by self-report, took part in this study for course credits. They were randomly divided into one of three conditions: local, control, and global.

Materials. A 30 s video clip was made of a football team scoring a goal. The football team was a five-a-side team based in a nearby town, such that participants were unlikely to know those in the video. Each of the football team had the same frontal view photograph, all wearing the same kit, presented in a lineup. There were 10 photographs in the lineup all photographed in the same team strip. The photographs were each 70 × 50 mm. The lineup and video were pretested to assess functional size (number of mock witnesses divided by correct guesses, see Lindsay, Smith, & Pryke, 1999) of the lineup: Four postgraduate students gave a short description of the goal scorer with the photograph in front of them. Subsequently, 36 undergraduate participants were given all four verbal descriptions of the goal scorer and asked to pick him out. The functional size was 8, giving an accuracy of 12.5%. The video was presented on a PC using Windows™ Media Player and the lineup was presented using QuickTime™ Image Viewer. The video was presented in 720 × 560 pixel dimensions and high resolution.

The set of 125 Navon letters produced by Brand (2005) were used.[1] The Navon stimuli were 91 × 47 mm. They have been used in several previous experiments and have been shown to produce reliable Navon effects. The Navon stimuli were presented on an RM PC using SuperlabPro 2™ Software.

Design. A three-level between-subjects design was employed, whereby participants were randomly divided into three groups and given the task of identifying the global Navon figure, the local Navon figure, or a control condition. The order of presentation of the Navon stimuli was randomised. The dependent measure was the accuracy (correct or incorrect) of the participants' response to the lineup of faces.

---

[1] The Navon stimuli were created by Andy Brand for his PhD thesis. They are available from the authors of this paper.

Procedure. The experiment had three phases: presentation, Navon, and identification. In the presentation phase, the participants were shown the video of the goal being scored. They were asked simply to watch the screen with no further instructions. This video lasted 30 s.

The participants were then introduced to Navon letters with three examples provided on screen. Participants were either instructed to identify the global Navon letter by saying it out loud, or instructed to identify the local letter, again by saying it out loud. In the control condition, participants were asked to read a book on cognitive psychology for the duration. After 5 min of processing either the local or global letters, participants in the experimental conditions swapped to the opposite Navon task and processed these critical letters for a further 5 min. The latter 5 min designated which condition the participants fell in. The first 5 min controlled for difficulty (see Perfect, 2003).

After 5 min of this Navon identification task, participants were asked to identify the person who scored the goal in the video by giving the number which corresponded to the face. All 10 were presented at the same time. After this phase, participants were debriefed and thanked.

Results

The raw frequency data was examined using a series of chi-square tests: an overall chi-square followed by pairwise comparisons between each condition. The only effect to approach significance was the difference between the global and local conditions, $\chi^2(1) = 3.737$, $p = .053$. No other differences were significant. The effect size for this result was $r = .2$. Figure 2 shows that

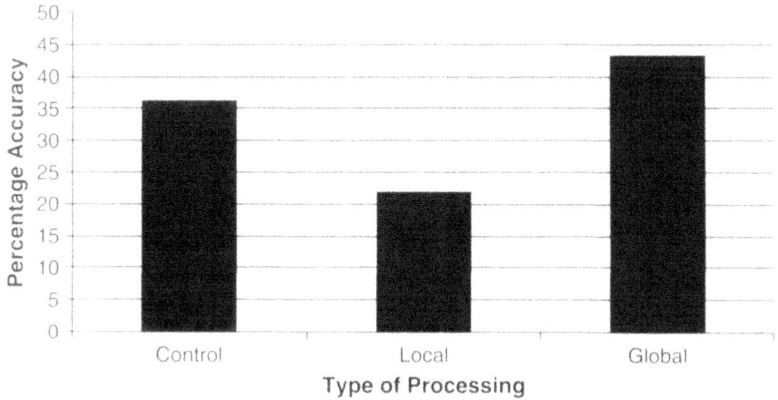

Figure 2. Accuracy in a lineup task depends on type of Navon processing undertaken.

local processing did indeed reduce performance, whereas global processing improved performance relative to the control condition.

Discussion

These results replicated the Navon effect, albeit only approaching significance using the standard two-tailed test. As the hypothesis is unambiguously one-tailed (as it is a replication) then the results can be seen as supportive of the standard effect. More importantly, however, the data allow comparison with other manipulations to explore the necessary properties of the intervening task required to produce this Navon effect.

Previous work has attempted to explain the Navon effect using verbal overshadowing (e.g., Perfect, 2003). Alternative explanations can be considered based on the perceptual properties of Navon stimuli; namely, their contrast and spatial frequency properties. The global figure within a Navon letter has lower contrast and lower spatial frequency than the local features.

Beyond this, the other observation that can be made from this study is that there is clearly no significant difference between global figure processors and control participants. On this basis we may conclude that the processing elicited by the global Navon task produces an optimal state for face processing.

EXPERIMENT 2

Experiment 1 established that the Navon effect observed on subsequent face processing can be elicited using new face stimuli. Thus far, the detrimental effect of verbalisation on subsequent face processing has been demonstrated using verbal descriptions of faces (e.g., Schooler & Engstler-Schooler, 1990) and Navon letters (e.g., Macrae & Lewis, 2002). It is possible to look for similarities between these disparate tasks. They both involve an element of verbalisation, and they both involve a lexical element. It is possible, therefore, that the act of making some kind of verbal response to fine detail is the cause for the observed alterations in performance. One explanation for the verbal overshadowing effect is that of a mismatch between verbal and visual codes. Though this explanation has not been widely suggested to explain the Navon effect observed here, it is possible since Navon letters contain a verbal component. By processing a series of Navon letters, a verbal code is induced which replaces the visual code. To explain why the local features cause a detriment, one could argue that since there are many more letters, the verbal code is exaggerated, whereas it would not be for the global figure.

Experiment 2, therefore, aims to test whether the verbal component of the Navon task is important for the observed detriment in performance. Instead of using Navon letters, Navon shapes are used. Navon shapes have the benefit that they can be responded to without a verbal component, and although they have associated semantic and lexical information, by pointing to pictures of the shapes rather than naming them the verbal component is most likely be removed.

A second aim of Experiment 2 is to further extend the generalisability of the Navon effect by using new Navon stimuli. As such, should the verbal overshadowing effect be based upon a transfer-inappropriate processing shift, and should Navon shapes successfully induce this shift, then we would expect to replicate Experiment 1 with shapes rather than letters. However, if the explanation based on verbal and visual codes is more accurate, then we predict that there would be either a smaller Navon effect, or none at all.

Method

Participants. One hundred and forty two participants from Cardiff University's School of Psychology served as the participants for this experiment. All had normal vision and were paid course credits for taking part. The participants were randomly divided into one of three conditions: local, control, and global.

Materials. The same lineup and video were used as in Experiment 1. A set of 25 Navon shapes were created using Adobe Photoshop™ software. Five basic shapes were used: triangle, star, square, circle, and diamond. Each basic shape was combined to form five large versions of the basic shapes. As such, 25 Navon shape stimuli were created. An example is shown in Figure 3. Images were presented at a size of 90 × 60 mm.

Design. The design was identical to Experiment 1 but with the different Navon stimuli.

Procedure. Participants were brought to the research laboratory in groups of three. As in Experiment 1, there were three phases: the presentation, Navon, and lineup. The presentation and lineup phases were identical to Experiment 1. In the Navon task, the participants were introduced to Navon shapes with three examples provided on screen. Participants were either instructed to identify the global Navon shape by pointing to a shape printed on the wall, or instructed to identify the local letter, again by pointing. The solid shapes were printed onto A4 paper, and were 150 × 150 mm positioned on the wall behind the computer screen 1 m back and 1 m higher than the computer screen. Participants processed either

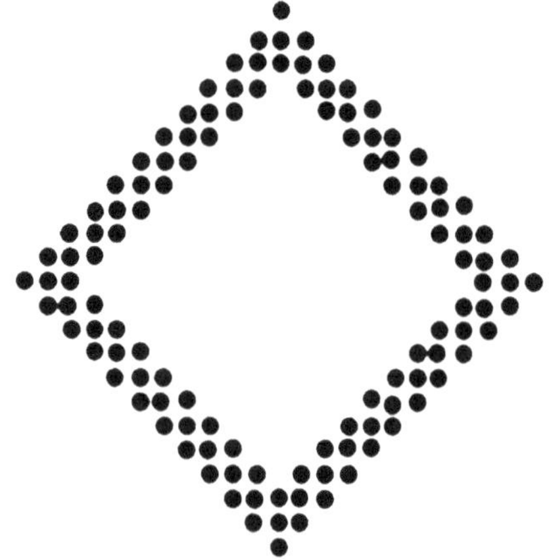

Figure 3. A Navon shape: a global diamond made up of local circles.

the local or global Navon shape for 5 min then swapped to the opposite Navon shape for a further 5 min, to replicate the Perfect (2003) design. In the control condition, participants were asked to read a book on cognitive psychology for the equivalent duration (10 min). All other aspects of the procedure were identical to Experiment 1.

Results

Percentage accuracy can be calculated and shown in Figure 4, but the raw frequency data was tested using a series of chi-square tests. The overall

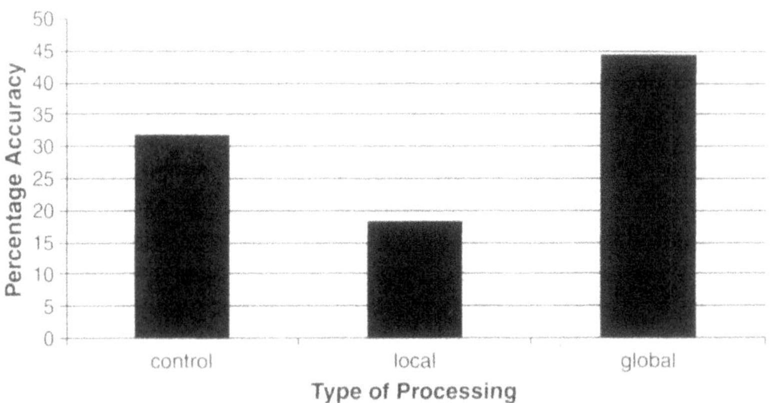

Figure 4. Accuracy in a lineup task depends on type of Navon processing undertaken in Experiment 2.

chi-square was significant, $\chi^2(2) = 7.645$, $p < .05$. The difference between global and local processing conditions was significant, $\chi^2(1) = 7.604$, $p < .05$, while the difference between control and local, and between control and global, was not found to be significant. The effect size for the global-local difference was $r = .28$.

A parallel analysis was conducted combining the data from Experiments 1 and 2. The overall chi-square was significant, $\chi^2(2) = 16.189$, $p < .05$, as was the difference between global and local, $\chi^2(1) = 11.231$, $p < .05$, and in this case the difference between control and local, $\chi^2(1) = 4.221$, $p < .05$. There was still no significant global advantage over control, however, $\chi^2(1) = 1.865$, $p > .1$, *ns*.

The data from Experiments 1 and 2 were combined and analysed using a logistic regression (computed using Statview 5™, SAS Institute Inc.™). The dichotomous dependent variable was accuracy of face recognition. The independent variables were: the Experiment (Navon letters or Navon shapes); and the Navon stimuli processing type. This analysis works in a similar manner to multiple regression except that sigmoidal functions are used to allow dichotomous data to be analysed. Comparing between local and global Navon stimuli processing revealed no significant effect of experiment, $\chi^2(1) = 0.064$, $p > .05$, and no significant experiment by condition interaction, $\chi^2(1) = 0.157$, $p > .05$. The same analyses were conducted for global-control and local-control comparisons. These all revealed no significant effect of experiment or interaction, all χ^2s < 0.1, all *p*s $> .5$.

Discussion

The observed Navon effect, whereby participants processing the local Navon features are less accurate in a face recognition task, was observed when using Navon shapes. Since it is most likely that the task did not involve a verbal component, as it did not require one, the explanation for this effect based on verbal and visual codes has not been supported. This result is consistent with the transfer-inappropriate processing shift explanation of verbal overshadowing rather than a verbal coding account. Since no previous researchers had posited a verbal account of the Navon effect on face processing, this is consistent with prior work on the topic.

Such results serve to generalise the Navon effect further. The logistic regression analysis demonstrates that these results are not significantly different from those in Experiment 1. We conclude, therefore, that the Navon effect is similar in magnitude for Navon shapes and Navon letters. This result implies that verbal codes are not incorporated in the Navon process.

The transfer-inappropriate processing shift explanation is consistent with the current data and they show that the shift in processing can be elicited by stimuli other than Navon letters. This finding, therefore, presents several possible developments. There may be alternative methods to induce the transfer-inappropriate processing shift on face processing using different stimuli which have a greater overlap in their properties, since Navon stimuli are very basic visual stimuli and faces are much more complex. Moreover, Navon stimuli are very artificial stimuli, whereas faces are natural stimuli, as such, using somewhat more natural stimuli to induce a transfer-inappropriate processing shift may be possible.

EXPERIMENT 3

Navon stimuli contain local features and a global figure. Faces can be processed through featural or configural processing. The previous studies and previous research indicate that the Navon stimuli cause a transfer-inappropriate processing shift away from configural processing to featural processing. It has been commented that featural information within faces is contained in the higher spatial frequencies, while configural (possibly global) information is contained in the lower spatial frequencies (Costen, Parker, & Craw, 1996). If this assumption is accurate, then it is plausible to suggest that the processing of such filtered faces would cause the same transfer-inappropriate processing shift. More specifically, if participants processed 5 min of faces that had low spatial frequencies filtered out, they would be forced to rely on featural processing. A subsequent lineup performance should, theoretically, be lower if the transfer-inappropriate processing shift explanation is accurate. Moreover, if the faces had the high spatial frequencies removed, the participants would have to rely on more on configural processes which should be akin to processing the global Navon figure.

By processing faces instead of Navon letters, participants will be exposed to many more faces within the experimental paradigm. The problem associated with this is the possibility of interference from the adjusted faces onto the test faces (see e.g., Davies, Shepherd, & Ellis, 1979; Deffenbacher, Carr, & Leu, 1981). This can be minimised by using different size stimuli in the test phase and the Navon phase. Nevertheless, since all participants will have faces to process in this paradigm, the interference will be the same across all conditions.

The same video and lineup procedure as Experiments 1 and 2 will be used. High spatial frequency filtered faces will contain only low spatial frequencies and should, therefore, induce global processing and enhance lineup performance. Low spatial frequency filtered faces will contain mostly high spatial frequencies and should, therefore, induce local processing and thereby impair lineup performance. To ensure that participants actively process the bandpass filtered faces, famous faces shall be used. The experiment explored whether the processing bias could be produced using these stimuli and hence affect subsequent lineup performance.

Method

Participants. One hundred Cardiff University Psychology undergraduates, all with self-reported normal vision, took part in this study as partial fulfilment of a course requirement.

Materials. The same video and lineup was used as in Experiments 1 and 2. Bandpass filtered faces were created using CorelDraw™ software. Two sets of 125 famous faces were created. One set was bandpass filtered images with all frequencies below 32 cycles per face removed, while the other set was filtered to have all spatial frequencies above 32 cycles per face removed using a method similar to Näsänen (1999). This value was chosen because it is the middle range of useable spatial frequencies for face recognition making the split roughly in the middle of the useful information. Eighty per cent of both high-pass- and low-pass-filtered faces were recognised during pretesting. Figure 5 shows an example of each. An additional set of unfiltered faces was also used. All faces were presented 100×100 mm. These faces were presented using Superlab™ on a PC.

Design. In this three-level between-subjects experiment, which follows the design of Experiments 1 and 2, the independent variable was the critical and final type of image that the participants were presented with during the intervening tasks The dependent variable for this experiment is accuracy of

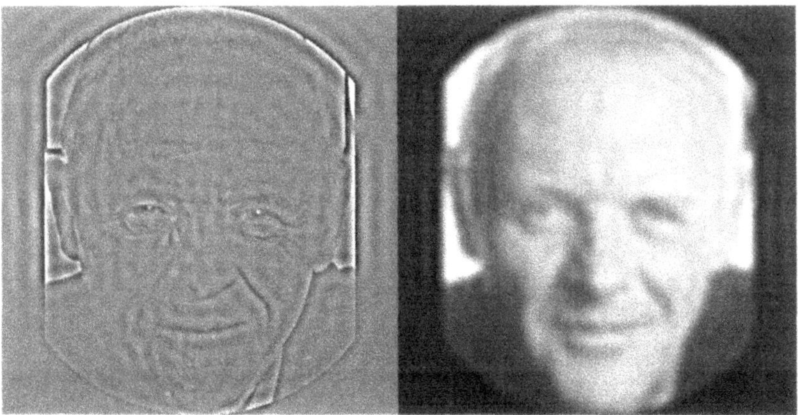

Figure 5. Anthony Hopkins containing only high spatial frequency information (left) and containing only low spatial frequency information (right).

face recognition at lineup. Participants were randomly selected to be in each group.

Procedure. As before, the video and lineup phases were identical to Experiment 1. Instead of the Navon task, participants were presented with one of the sets of bandpass filtered faces (faces containing mainly high or low spatial frequency), with 125 faces in all, and with each face viewed for 5 s. They were instructed to name the famous face. The instructions were the same for all three conditions (high spatial frequency filtered faces, low spatial frequency filtered faces, and unfiltered faces). After 5 min, the participants in both filtered conditions swapped to the other filtered condition, as a replication of the previous work. Instead of reading in the control task, participants were presented with the unfiltered faces shown at the same rate as the filtered faces for 10 min.

Results

The accuracy rate was 32% for participants in the low spatial frequency filtered faces condition (potentially featural processors), 35% for participants in the high spatial frequency filtered faces (potentially configural processors), and 38% for the control participants. Chi-square tests were carried out in the same sequence as Experiments 1 and 2: global, followed by pairwise comparisons. There were no significant differences between any conditions (all χ^2s < 1, all ps > 0.8, all effect sizes $r < .04$).

We compared identification of faces preceded by either global or local Navon letter conditions (Experiment 1) or high and low spatial frequency filtered faces (Experiment 3). The significant interaction, $\chi^2(1) = 4.085$, $p < .05$, reveals that the results in this experiment were significantly different from those in Experiment 1. That is the Navon-like effect was not just nonsignificant but it was significantly smaller than in another experiment where an effect was found.

Discussion

Costen et al. (1996) have suggested that featural or local aspects of faces are represented primarily by high spatial frequency information (albeit, the relative positions of the features remain in high-pass filtered faces). Conversely, configural or global information is primarily represented by low spatial frequency information. As such, processing high spatial frequencies for a considerable length of time (5 min in all) should induce featural processing, or at most processing first order relational information (cf. Rhodes, 1993), neither of which would be beneficial to face identification in this case. Furthermore, the control task used unfiltered faces, which we assume would induce a more expert, frequently used, and effective processing strategy (e.g., Tanaka & Farah, 1993). However, the results were statistically flat, indicating that this logic is flawed in some manner, and indeed the findings from this experiment were significantly different from the preceding experiments.

There are several possible reasons for the null results of Experiment 3. The first is that the Costen et al. (1996) paper is inaccurate in its assumption of spatial frequencies and their relation to types of processing. Even if their results are valid, it may be that studying faces is not able to induce configural or featural processing for other reasons, possibly due to the perceptual make-up of the stimuli set used. Each explanation will be elaborated on further.

Previous studies (e.g., Bruce, 1983) have suggested that there is a correlation between the nature of facial encoding and spatial frequency information available from the face. Fine detail is represented in high spatial frequencies (Costen et al., 1996). Nevertheless, being presented with a series of filtered faces might not be sufficient to evoke a particular type of processing. It can be suggested that faces convey much more detailed semantic information than Navon stimuli. Familiar faces are associated with biographical histories, names, occupations, and other semantic information (see, e.g., Bruce & Humphreys, 1994; Burton & Bruce, 1993). This semantic information is not associated with Navon stimuli that only have an identity (the letter). Subsequently, the fact that filtered famous faces did not cause the Navon effect may suggest that the additional semantic information somehow blocks the effect. Alternatively, to obtain the semantic information from the faces, participants must attend to the whole stimulus, whereas to identify a Navon stimulus, participants need only attend to a small portion of the stimuli. As such, it is possible that Navon stimuli direct attention to small components, rather than features of a whole. Further research could address this phenomenon.

A second possibility is that the spatial frequency information needs to be matched at the "Navon" processing stage and at the lineup stage. If this is the case, then it would imply that transfer-inappropriate processing shift does rely on the perceptual characteristics of the stimuli involved (namely spatial frequency). If global and local information is represented by different spatial frequencies then prolonged exposure to one type of processing should suffice in causing the Navon effect. Of course, this is based on the idea that configural information is represented only by low spatial frequencies. This is of course not entirely true. A low-pass filtered face still retains all the configurations of the features (two eyes next to each other and above a nose). Nevertheless, data from Lewis (2001) indicates that when talking about configural and featural information, researchers should talk about degrees rather than strictly one or the other (see also reviews by Schyns & Gosselin, 2003). As such, the adjustments conducted do adjust the degree of configural and featural information, but perhaps not significantly.

In relation to this, the relative and absolute spatial frequency of the stimuli in question may need to be matched. Spatial frequency in face recognition is usually measured in terms of cycles per face. Näsänen (1999) indicates that 32 cycles per face is the middle of the range of useful spatial frequencies in face recognition. Näsänen indicates that differences in absolute spatial frequencies will not affect the perception of the image unless they are by a factor of 4. In the present case, the absolute spatial frequency differences are of a factor of 2 and thus should not cause a problem.

It is also possible that semantic information has no influence on the Navon effect. The Navon effect on face processing may be much more low level, based biologically in the visual cortex and therefore a perceptual phenomena. In this case, the additional luminance and the sheer number of spatial frequencies within filtered faces outweigh those in the Navon stimuli. Without further evidence, it is difficult to establish which perceptual qualities of Navon stimuli contribute to the Navon effect. Indeed, manipulating attention to focus on certain spatial frequencies in filtered faces ignores the inhibition from other spatial frequencies. Further research needs to examine the relative contributions of perceptual size, spatial frequency and contrast of the Navon stimuli in producing the Navon effect on subsequent face processing.

GENERAL DISCUSSION

Three experiments were reported that explored the Navon effect on subsequent face recognition (Macrae & Lewis, 2002; Perfect, 2003). Importantly, we reproduced the Navon effect with letters, and also with a different kind of stimuli, namely Navon shapes (such as a square, circle, triangle, and so on). In a subsequent experiment, rather than using Navon stimuli we manipulated the spatial frequency information available in a set of face stimuli, in order to examine the influence of processing these stimuli on subsequent face identification of a different set of faces. In this case, we did not observe the decrement in performance that we had observed with the Navon stimuli in the preceding experiments.

The present findings confirm the importance of the Navon effect on subsequent face recognition. Furthermore, they raise a number of questions as to the locus of this effect. If one assumes that bandpass filtered faces are sufficient to induce featural or configural processing in this paradigm, then this change in processing was not sufficient to provide the detriment in performance that had been observed previously with Navon stimuli. This would tentatively suggest that the Navon effect may not be due to a shift from configural to featural processing. Nevertheless, it is difficult to argue from a null result, and we also acknowledge that there may not be a strong correlation between spatial frequency information and processing configural/global versus featural/local information in this paradigm. An alternative possibility is that such a shift may operate on lower level visual processes. We need to look more closely at the similarities and differences in processing Navon letters and shapes on the one hand, and faces on the other. Both faces and Navon stimuli have configural/global and featural/local and components, but there may also be some other similarities that are important in understanding both the Navon effect and the broader issue of effects of verbalisation on visual recognition.

REFERENCES

Brand, A. (2005). *Explaining the verbal overshadowing effect*. Unpublished PhD thesis, Cardiff University, Cardiff, UK.

Brown, C., & Lloyd-Jones, T. J. (2002). Verbal overshadowing in a multiple face presentation paradigm: Effects of description instruction. *Applied Cognitive Psychology, 16*, 873–885.

Brown, C., & Lloyd-Jones, T. J. (2003). Verbal overshadowing of multiple face and car recognition: Effects of within- versus across-category verbal descriptions. *Applied Cognitive Psychology, 17*, 183–201.

Brown, C., & Lloyd-Jones, T. J. (2005). Verbal facilitation of face recognition. *Memory and Cognition, 33*, 1442–1456.

Brown, C., & Lloyd-Jones, T. J. (2006). Beneficial effects of verbalization and visual distinctiveness on remembering and knowing faces. *Memory and Cognition, 34*, 277–286.

Bruce, V. (1983). Recognising faces. Philosophical Transactions of the Royal Society London. *Series B, 302*, 423–436.

Bruce, V., & Humphreys, G. W. (1994). Recognizing objects and faces. *Visual Cognition, 1*, 141–180.

Burton, A. M., & Bruce, V. (1993). Naming faces and naming names: Exploring an interactive activation model of person recognition. *Memory, 1*, 457–480.

Costen, N. P., Parker, D. M., & Craw, I. (1996). Effects of high-pass and low-pass spatial filtering on face identification. *Perception and Psychophysics, 58*, 602–612.

Davies, G. M., Shepherd, J. W., & Ellis, H. D. (1979). Effects of interpolated mugshot exposure on accuracy of eyewitness identification. *Journal of Applied Psychology, 64*, 232–237.

Deffenbacher, K. A., Carr, T. H., & Leu, J. R. (1981). Memory for words, pictures, and faces: Retroactive interferences, forgetting, and reminiscence. *Journal of Experimental Psychology: Human Learning and Memory, 7*, 299–305.

Dodson, C. S., Johnson, M. K., & Schooler, J. W. (1997). The verbal overshadowing effect: Why descriptions impair face recognition. *Memory and Cognition, 25*, 129–139.

Kemp, R., Towell, N., & Pike, G. (1997). When seeing should not be believing: Photographs, credit cards and fraud. *Applied Cognitive Psychology, 11*, 211–222.

Lawson, R. (2006, July). *Local and global processing biases fail to influence face, object and word recognition* [Abstract]. Poster presented at the meeting of the Experimental Psychology Society, Plymouth, UK.

Lewis, M. B. (2001). The lady's not for turning: Rotation of the Thatcher illusion. *Perception, 30*, 769–774.
Lewis, M. B., & Glenister, T. E. (2003). A sideways look at configural encoding: Two different effects of face rotation. *Perception, 32*, 7–14.
Lindsay, R. C. L., Smith, S. M., & Pryke, S. (1999). Measures of line-up fairness: Do they postdict identification accuracy? *Applied Cognitive Psychology, 13*, S93–S108.
Logie, R. H., Baddeley, A., & Woodhead, M. M. (1987). Face recognition, pose and ecological validity. *Applied Cognitive Psychology, 1*, 53–69.
Macrae, C. N., & Lewis, H. L. (2002). Do I know you? Processing orientation and face recognition. *Psychological Science, 13*, 194–196.
Meissner, C. A., Brigham, J. C., & Kelley, C. M. (2001). The influence of retrieval processes in verbal overshadowing. *Memory and Cognition, 29*, 176–186.
Navon, D. (1977). Forest before the trees: The precedence of global features in visual perception. *Cognitive Psychology, 9*, 353–383.
Näsänen, R. (1999). Spatial frequency bandwidth used in the recognition of facial images. *Vision Research, 39*, 3824–3833.
Perfect, T. J. (2003). Local processing bias impairs line-up performance. *Psychological Report, 93*, 393–394.
Rhodes, G. (1993). Configural coding, expertise, and the right-hemisphere advantage for face recognition. *Brain and Cognition, 22*, 19–41.
Ryan, R. S. Aulenbach, R. Becker, M. Johnson, T. Christman, J. Murray, K. & Bergmaier, J. (2006, May). *Global processing improves self-assessment of face recognition ability.* Poster presented at the 18th annual convention for the Association for Psychological Science, New York.
Schooler, J. W., & Engstler-Schooler, T. Y. (1990). Verbal overshadowing of visual memories: Some things are better left unsaid. *Cognitive Psychology, 22*, 36–71.
Schyns, P. G, & Gosselin, F. (2003). Diagnostic use of scale information for componential and holistic recognition. In M. A. Peterson & G. Rhodes (Eds.), *Perception of faces, objects, and scenes: Analytic and holistic processes.* Oxford, UK: Oxford University Press.
Steblay, N., Dysart, J., Fulero, S., & Lindsay, R. C. L. (2001). Eye-witness accuracy rates in sequential and simultaneous line-up presentations: A meta-analytic comparison. *Law and Human Behavior, 27*, 523–540.
Tanaka, J. W., & Farah, M. J. (1993). Parts and wholes in face recognition. *Quarterly Journal of Experimental Psychology, 46A*, 225–245.

EUROPEAN JOURNAL OF COGNITIVE PSYCHOLOGY
2008, 20 (3), 577–586

The effect of verbal description and processing type on face identification

Lee H. V. Wickham and Karen Lander

School of Psychological Sciences, University of Manchester, Manchester, UK

Research suggests that describing a face can have detrimental or beneficial effects upon its subsequent recognition (Brown & Lloyd-Jones, 2005; Schooler & Engstler-Schooler, 1990). This study manipulated the kind of description (holistic, featural, or no description) that participants engaged in, and also introduced a postdescription processing task (global or local letter identification; Navon, 1977). Identification of the faces across 10 trials was better for participants describing the faces holistically than in the no description or featural conditions, thus demonstrating verbal facilitation. Global processing tasks produced better identification than local processing tasks. We suggest that the effects of type of description and type of processing are independent, and the results are discussed in relation to Schooler's (2002) transfer inappropriate processing shift hypothesis.

There seems to be a class of memories that are very difficult to capture with words. These memories are for perceptual stimuli such as colours, voices, maps, music, faces, and wine. Furthermore, attempting to describe stimuli such as these can lead to a subsequent retrieval impairment, an effect termed the "verbal overshadowing effect" (Schooler & Engstler-Schooler, 1990). Although this effect can be difficult to replicate, a meta-analysis of verbal overshadowing research in face identification (Meissner & Brigham, 2001) found a small but reliable detrimental effect of verbalisation on identification accuracy. In contrast, a number of studies have reported beneficial effects of verbalisation on face recognition (Bloom & Mudd, 1991; Bower & Karlin, 1974; Brown & Lloyd-Jones, 2005; Mueller, Courtois, & Bailis, 1981).

The verbal overshadowing effect was originally explained in terms of interference: The act of description produces a verbally recoded representation of the stimulus that reduces access to the original memory (recoding

Correspondence should be addressed to Lee Wickham, School of Psychological Sciences, University of Manchester, Oxford Road, Manchester, M13 9PL, UK.
E-mail: lee.wickham@manchester.ac.uk

http://www.psypress.com/ecp DOI: 10.1080/09541440701728433

interference theory; Schooler & Engstler-Schooler, 1990). However, such an account fails to explain the lack of a reported correlation between identification accuracy and description quality (Schooler, Fiore, & Brandimonte, 1997; although see Meissner, Brigham, & Kelley, 2001). Furthermore, the detrimental effect of describing a nonverbal stimulus carries over to other items that were also studied, but that were not described (Brown & Lloyd-Jones, 2002; Dodson, Johnson, & Schooler, 1997). This suggests that rather than the verbal overshadowing effect being based on memory interference, it is due to a shift in the processing style adopted by participants (Schooler, 2002; Schooler et al., 1997). Basically, the Transfer Inappropriate Processing Shift hypothesis (Schooler, 2002) suggests that under normal conditions a face is encoded and stored in a predominantly holistic fashion. However, when a face is described, Schooler suggests that the mode of processing shifts from holistic to featural, which is not the optimum processing style for subsequent recognition of the face. Consequently, description produces detrimental recognition compared to a control task. This suggestion has received support from a study that investigated the effects of biasing processing style before completing a face recognition task (Macrae & Lewis, 2002). The idea here is that if the verbal overshadowing effect is a result of a shift in processing style, it should be possible to elicit the same pattern of results with an alternative task that involves the same kind of processing as the description task. Macrae and Lewis (2002) followed the same procedure and used the same stimuli as in the original Schooler and Engstler-Schooler (1990) study, but instead of asking participants to describe the faces, they engaged in a letter identification task (Navon, 1977). Here, large letters were presented that were made up of smaller letters (for example a large "T" made up of smaller "h"s). Participants were required to either identify the large letter (global processing) or the small letters (local processing). The rate of identification by these two groups was compared to a control group, and the results showed a beneficial effect of engaging in global processing compared to the control group, and a detrimental effect of engaging in local processing compared to the control group. Macrae and Lewis argue that global processing improves subsequent face recognition by increasing the level of holistic processing of the faces, whereas local processing reduces holistic processing. This idea that prior processing can change the level of holistic processing at test has received support from Weston and Perfect (2005) who found that local processing of Navon letters improved performance on a face-half recognition test (Young, Hellawell, & Hay, 1987), where holistic information has to be ignored in order to successfully identify the face-halves.

It seems reasonable to suggest, then, that it is possible to bias processing before a recognition or identification task. However, as Schooler (2002) acknowledges, this does not mean that this processing shift necessarily underlies the verbal overshadowing effect. Additional evidence that the verbal overshadowing effect results from a processing shift comes from research demonstrating that the effects of verbalisation can be reversed if a nonverbal task is introduced after verbalisation. Finger (2002) showed that participants who completed a verbal task after description showed the usual impairment in recognition accuracy, whereas participants completing a maze task or a tone-counting music task after description performed as well as controls. However, it is not clear how these verbal and nonverbal tasks relate to the kinds of processing discussed in Schooler's transfer inappropriate processing account. In his account, Schooler refers to the retrieval processes involved in describing a face as "verbal" or "featural", and those involved in recognising a face as "nonverbal" or "configural". However, it is not clear whether the crucial factor is the switching from a *verbal* task to a *nonverbal* task (as in Finger's 2002 study) or the switching from a *featural* task to a *configural* task (as in Macrae & Lewis's 2002 study). The present study follows a similar approach to Finger, and investigates whether postdescription tasks can produce a release from verbal overshadowing, but uses global/local processing tasks rather than verbal/non-verbal tasks.

The question of how verbalisation affects subsequent retrieval is complicated by research showing that under some circumstances verbalisation can have a facilitatory effect on face recognition (Bloom & Mudd, 1991; Bower & Karlin, 1974; Brown & Lloyd-Jones, 2005; Mueller et al., 1981). Brown and Lloyd-Jones (2005) found that description facilitated recognition of faces under a range of conditions, including descriptions focusing on featural aspects of the faces, and descriptions focusing on holistic aspects. They also found that the facilitation was tied to the face described. These results contrast with those of MacLin (2002) who found that asking participants to describe faces on the basis of their features produced the standard verbal overshadowing effect, whereas more holistic descriptions ("what does the person look like"—termed prototype descriptions) produced a level of identification comparable with controls (no description). As with most verbal overshadowing research, there is a lack of consensus over what the effects of different kinds of description are on face identification, and the paradigms used differ widely from one study to another. However, it does seem that featural descriptions do impair identification compared to holistic descriptions. The discrepancy is simply where the control (no description) participants are in comparison. Semantic processing accounts argue that processing faces with reference to semantic associations improves recognition (e.g., Anderson & Reder, 1979) and it is likely that this occurs more often when participants engage in holistic rather than featural descriptions. This study aims to compare different kinds of description (featural vs. holistic) to try to establish whether it is *verbalising* faces that causes impairment/facilitation, or whether the crucial factor is whether this description is based on featural or holistic processing.

This paper aims to explore, in a single experiment, the effects of different kinds of descriptions on identification, and whether these effects are mediated by subsequent processing operations. This allows us to detect the presence of an interaction between these two factors. The letter identification tasks used in Macrae and Lewis (2002) were used as these clearly involve global or local processing. Participants in the present study were instructed to view a face, and then either describe it holistically, describe it featurally, or engage in a filler activity (no description). After the description or filler task, participants engaged in either a global processing task (identifying large Navon letters) or a local processing task (identifying small Navon letters). Finally, participants performed an identification task. This procedure was repeated for 10 trials. Following Schooler's (2002) model, we would expect that (1) participants engaging in featural descriptions will demonstrate impaired identification performance compared to controls, and (2) impairment caused by featural descriptions will be reversed if participants carry out global processing just before identification, whereas local processing will have no effect when following featural descriptions. Based on Brown and Lloyd-Jones's (2005) results, we would predict that holistic descriptions may actually facilitate identification. We would also predict, based on the processing shift theory, that any beneficial effect of holistic descriptions will be reversed by subsequent local processing, whereas global processing should have no effect.

METHOD

Participants

Forty-five British undergraduates (38 female) took part for course credit. Their mean age was 19.5 years.

Materials

All the faces used in this experiment were monochrome prints of Scottish policemen supplied by the Home Office (see Bruce, Henderson, Newman, & Burton, 2001, for more details of these materials). Images included head and shoulders, and faces were shown with a neutral expression. The target face shown at presentation (75 × 95 mm) was a freeze frame taken from a video, and thus was different to the picture of the target shown at test. The recognition test consisted of a lineup of 10 unfamiliar faces, numbered 1 to 10, including the target and 9 distractor faces. In order to select the distractor faces, a matrix of similarity was constructed for two sets of 60 faces. Forty participants viewed each set of faces, and were asked to put them into piles based on their similarity. The similarity judgements were based on the participants' own judgements of what constitutes similarity, and therefore are likely to be based on similarity in terms of both global and local aspects of the faces. The matrices of similarity plotted the frequency with which any two faces were paired together. The nine faces paired most frequently with the target were selected as the distractor faces. The 10 prints in the array were of the same size (45 × 55 mm) and were arranged in two horizontal lines of 5 prints. There were 10 different targets and lineups, plus one practice trial. The position of the target face in the array was randomly decided, but the same arrays were presented to each participant. The Navon letters were printed on A4 paper, in landscape, in sets of 5 (25 × 45 mm each large letter). A mean of 25 small letters were used to make up each large letter.

Design

A 3 × 2 mixed factorial design was employed. Participants were randomly allocated to one of the description conditions (between factor: control, featural, or holistic). The other factor was processing type (within factor: global or local processing), with five trials each. The dependent variable was the number of target faces correctly identified out of five.

Procedure

Participants were tested individually. All participants read standardised instructions. Participants were shown a printed picture of a target face and asked to "please study this face carefully". All participants were shown each target face for 10 s, after which time it was removed from view. Immediately following presentation, participants in the description condition were given 2 min to "write a description of the face you have just seen in as much detail as possible" on the response sheet. Participants were instructed to continue describing for the full 2 min, and received further prompts if they failed to do so. Participants in the holistic condition were asked to describe the target face by giving details about the kind of person they looked like, for example personality, occupation, etc. Participants in the featural condition were asked to describe the target face in terms of its face features, for example eyes, nose, etc. Participants in the no description condition were instructed to complete a word-search as a distractor task.

After providing a description of the target face (holistic or featural) or completing a filler task (no description), participants were asked to perform a letter identification task (Kimchi, 1992; Navon, 1977). The stimuli used in this task were large letters, the constituents of which were several smaller mismatching letters (e.g., a "T" made up of "r"s). The task was to report the identity of the large letter (global processing task) or the small letters (local processing task). In total, 50 mismatching letters were created and printed on A4 paper in sets of 5. The experimenter cycled through the letters for a period of 1 min on each trial.

Following the letter identification (Navon) task, all participants were shown a printed copy of an array of 10 faces, including the target, and instructed to pick out the target face. They were asked to record on the response sheet which face in the array they believed corresponded to the target face; participants were not given a target-absent option. There was no time limit for the identification task. This procedure was repeated for the 10 target faces in a random order. To ensure all participants were familiar with the procedure, a practice trial was first conducted.

RESULTS

The total number of faces correctly identified out of 10 (from the 5 global trials and the 5 local trials) was calculated for each participant. The overall mean score was 6.2 (62.0% correct) with a standard deviation of 1.34. These scores were converted into proportion correct. The data were also analysed by items, whereby the total number of participants who correctly identified each face was calculated, giving a score out of 15. These scores were also converted to proportions correct. The overall mean score was 9.2 (61.33% correct) with a standard deviation of 2.06. An alpha level of .05 was adopted throughout this paper. See Table 1 for mean and standard deviations in each condition.

A 3 (description condition) × 2 (processing type) analysis of variance was performed with both the participant and the face (by items) as units of analysis. A significant main effect of description condition was demon-

TABLE 1
Percentage correct recognition and standard deviations (*SD*) for each condition in the reported experiment

	Processing type	
Description condition	*Global*	*Local*
Holistic	85.33 (14.07)	68.09 (23.66)
Featural	64.00 (28.48)	41.33 (24.46)
No description	64.00 (25.30)	49.33 (22.51)

strated: by participants, $F(2, 42) = 8.29$, $p < .001$, partial $\eta^2 = .28$; by-items, $F(2, 18) = 13.43$, $p < .001$, partial $\eta^2 = .58$. Further post hoc comparisons of the by-participants data using Scheffé tests revealed that the holistic description group (mean 76.67%) performed significantly better than the control (mean 56.67%, $p = .01$) or featural (mean 52.67%, $p = .002$) description groups. The difference between the control and featural groups failed to reach significance ($p = .82$).

There was also a significant main effect of processing type: by participants, $F(1, 42) = 14.75$, $p < .001$, partial $\eta^2 = .26$; by items, $F(1, 9) = 12.98$, $p < .001$, partial $\eta^2 = .59$. Global processing led to significantly higher performance (mean 71.11%) compared with local processing (mean 52.88%). Finally, there was no significant interaction between description condition and processing type: by participants, $F(2, 42) < 1$, $p > .05$, partial $\eta^2 = .12$; by items, $F(2, 18) < 1$, $p > .05$, partial $\eta^2 = .38$. The global processing task increased performance in all description conditions. Overall performance was best following holistic description and a global processing task (mean 85.34%) and worst following featural description and a local processing task (mean 41.34%). Post hoc comparisons using Scheffé tests revealed that this difference was significant ($p < .001$).

The only other difference to reach significance was between holistic description/global processing and no description/local processing ($p < .01$).

Further investigation examined the proportion of featural and holistic descriptors (i.e., total number of each type of descriptor divided by the total number of descriptors) produced by participants in the featural and holistic description conditions. Featural descriptors comprised of judgements about particular facial features: size/shape of chin, nose, eyes, forehead, eyebrows; distance between features; hair length and texture (see Brown & Lloyd-Jones, 2005). Holistic descriptors were classified as judgements concerning personality, height, weight, age, global face structure, and occupation. A small number of descriptors that did not fit into either of these categories were classified as "other descriptors". As expected, in the featural description condition 98.80% of the descriptors provided were featural, and in the holistic description condition 99.40% concerned holistic properties.

DISCUSSION

The experiment reported here aimed to test the hypothesis that the beneficial or detrimental effects of describing faces upon later identification can be reversed by introducing a processing task after description. Additionally, we introduced different kinds of description (holistic or featural). The results showed that providing featural descriptions did not worsen identification performance compared to controls, whereas providing holistic descriptions benefited identification. Rather than demonstrating the verbal overshadowing effect, this study has shown that describing faces can facilitate identification. Brown and Lloyd-Jones (2005) found verbal facilitation when participants engaged in either holistic or featural descriptions for 15 s, using a multitrial face recognition paradigm, whereas MacLin (2002) found verbal overshadowing for participants engaging in featural (attribute) description for 5 min, using a one-trial eyewitness procedure. The results of the present study fall somewhere between these two: We used a multitrial procedure, an identification task, and faces were described for 2 min, and we found facilitation for only holistic descriptions. It seems that there are circumstances under which describing a face is beneficial to recognition, and these seem to be where there are multiple faces that are described for short periods of time, possibly with reference to holistic attributes. It is not clear how a processing shift hypothesis (Schooler, 2002) can account for this. It is entirely possible, of course, that verbal overshadowing and verbal facilitation result from different processes.

Additionally, this study investigated whether performing global and local processing tasks after describing a face can affect identification. Specifically, we predicted that performing a global processing task (identifying large Navon letters) should reverse the verbal overshadowing effect, and performing a local processing task (identifying small Navon letters) should reverse any facilitative effects of verbalisation. Results showed that, as expected, global processing significantly improved identification compared to local processing. The optimum performance occurred on the holistic description/global processing trials, and the worst performance was on the featural description/local processing trials. As we did not find verbal overshadowing, the question becomes: Can the beneficial effects of describing a face holistically be reversed by introducing a local processing task after description? Although the processing shift hypothesis does not discuss verbal facilitation, we would expect that if the facilitation is the result of a processing shift, it should be reversed with a local processing task. In the present experiment, holistic description/global processing produced a marked improvement in identification (85.33%) compared to other conditions, whereas when a holistic description was followed by a local processing task, performance dropped to 68.09%. Although this difference is not significant, it is in the predicted direction. However, these results do differ somewhat from Finger (2002). Finger found that performing a perceptual task after description improved performance to the same level as controls, who showed no difference in performance after completing verbal and perceptual postdescription tasks. However, the present study found that all groups (holistic, featural, and no description) benefited from global processing compared to local processing to about the same degree. In other words, the effects of processing task and type of description seem to be independent and additive. Rather than local processing reversing the beneficial effects of holistic descriptions, it seems that it has a general detrimental effect across all three description conditions. Perhaps the critical factor is the *kind* of processing in the postdescription tasks. Finger's study found that a perceptual (maze or music) task reversed the verbal overshadowing effect compared to a verbal task, whereas the present study compared global and local processing tasks. If the verbal overshadowing effect arises from a shift from *nonverbal* to *verbal* processing, this could explain the difference in the findings from Finger's study to the present study. However, it is difficult to explore whether the shift is from nonverbal to verbal or global to local processing, as these are almost certainly confounded. Finger's maze and music tasks probably involve global processing, and the Navon task is also likely to involve verbal and nonverbal processing. Furthermore, it could be that the beneficial effect of holistic description could be a result of something else, such as semantic processing (Brown & Lloyd-Jones, 2005). On the face of it, these results seem to suggest that the effects of verbal facilitation are not based on a shift from holistic/global to featural/local processing. However, as is often the case in verbal overshadowing studies, a larger sample size would determine whether the interaction would appear with more experimental power.

The results of this experiment have raised a number of issues that require further investigation. First, is the processing "shift" a shift from nonverbal to verbal processing or a shift from configural to featural processing? Second, what are the circumstances under which verbalising a face facilitates recognition? Is it simply task difficulty? Also, do verbal facilitation and verbal overshadowing reflect the same processes? An account of the verbal overshadowing effect needs to be able to explain why description can sometimes aid recognition and sometimes hinder it.

REFERENCES

Anderson, J. R., & Reder, L. M. (1979). An elaborative processing explanation of depth of processing. In L. S. Cermak & F. I. M. Craik (Eds.), *Levels of processing in human memory.* (pp. 385–395) Hillsdale, NJ: Lawrence Erlbaum Associates, Inc.

Bloom, L. C., & Mudd, S. A. (1991). Depth of processing approach to face recognition—A test of 2 theories. *Journal of Experimental Psychology: Learning, Memory, and Cognition*, *17*, 556–565.

Bower, G. H., & Karlin, M. B. (1974). Depth of processing pictures of faces and recognition memory. *Journal of Experimental Psychology*, *103*, 751–757.

Brown, C., & Lloyd-Jones, T. J. (2002). Verbal overshadowing in a multiple face presentation paradigm: Effects of description instruction. *Applied Cognitive Psychology*, *16*, 873–885.

Brown, C., & Lloyd-Jones, T. (2005). Verbal facilitation of face recognition. *Memory and Cognition*, *33*, 1442–1456.

Bruce, V., Henderson, Z., Newman, C., & Burton, A. M. (2001). Matching identities of familiar and unfamiliar faces caught on CCTV images. *Journal of Experimental Psychology: Applied, 7*, 207–218.

Dodson, C. S., Johnson, M. K., & Schooler, J. W. (1997). The verbal overshadowing effect: Why descriptions impair facial recognition. *Memory and Cognition, 25*, 129–139.

Finger, K. (2002). Mazes and music: Using perception processing to release verbal overshadowing. *Applied Cognitive Psychology, 16*, 887–896.

Kimchi, R. (1992). Primacy of wholistic processing and global/local paradigm: A critical review. *Psychological Bulletin, 112*, 24–38.

MacLin, M. K. (2002). The effects of exemplar and prototype descriptors on verbal overshadowing. *Applied Cognitive Psychology, 16*, 929–936.

Macrae, C. N., & Lewis, H. L. (2002). Do I know you? Processing orientation and face recognition. *Psychological Science, 13*, 194–196.

Meissner, C. A., & Brigham, J. C. (2001). A meta-analysis of the verbal overshadowing effect in face identification. *Applied Cognitive Psychology, 15*, 603–616.

Meissner, C. A., Brigham, J. C., & Kelley, C. M. (2001). The influence of retrieval processes in verbal overshadowing. *Memory and Cognition, 29*, 176–186.

Mueller, J. H., Courtois, M. R., & Bailis, K. L. (1981). Self-reference in face recognition. *Bulletin of the Psychonomic Society, 17*, 85–88.

Navon, D. (1977). Forest before the trees: The precedence of global features in visual perception. *Cognitive Psychology, 9*, 353–383.

Schooler, J. W. (2002). Verbalization produces a transfer inappropriate processing shift. *Applied Cognitive Psychology, 16*, 989–997.

Schooler, J. W., & Engstler-Schooler, T. Y. (1990). Verbal overshadowing of visual memories: Some things are better left unsaid. *Cognitive Psychology, 22*, 36–71.

Schooler, J. W., Fiore, S. M., & Brandimonte, M. A. (1997). At a loss from words: Verbal overshadowing of perceptual memories. In D. L. Medlin (Eds.), *Advances in research and theory: Vol. 37. The psychology of learning and motivation* (pp. 291–340). London: Academic Press.

Weston, N. J., & Perfect, T. J. (2005). Effects of processing bias on the recogniton of composite face halves. *Psychonomic Bulletin and Review, 12*, 1038–1042.

Young, A. W., Hellawell, D., & Hay, D. C. (1987). Configurational information in face perception. *Perception, 16*, 747–759.

EUROPEAN JOURNAL OF COGNITIVE PSYCHOLOGY
2008, 20 (3), 587–611

Navon processing and verbalisation: A holistic/featural distinction

Nicola J. Weston and Timothy J. Perfect
University of Plymouth, Plymouth, UK

Jonathan W. Schooler
University of British Columbia, Vancouver, Canada

Ian Dennis
University of Plymouth, Plymouth, UK

Three experiments compared face recognition performance following global and local Navon processing and verbalisation, and explored the extent to which the effects of these tasks were influenced by encoding processes. Experiment 1 used the Navon letter task at encoding, whereas Experiments 2 and 3 used personality and physical feature judgements to induce holistic and featural encoding. Accuracy and response latencies were measured for stimuli of own- and other-race faces. Results showed that both the Navon and verbal overshadowing effects were not influenced by the Navon encoding task; however, the judgement task used in Experiments 2 and 3 eliminated all impairment caused by local processing but not by providing a verbal description. These results are discussed with regards to the holistic and featural explanations of Navon processing and verbalisation effects.

There is agreement amongst researchers that optimal face recognition is achieved through holistic processing where the information about specific features (featural information) is combined with information about the spatial relationships between features (configural information) (Bartlett & Searcy, 1993; Tanaka & Farah, 1993; Thompson, 1980; Yin, 1969). This claim has been supported by research using a variety of different tasks, for example, the recognition of facial composites (Young, Hellawell, & Hay, 1987), comparing the recognition of whole faces and face parts (Tanaka &

Correspondence should be addressed to Miss Nicola J. Weston, School of Psychology, Cardiff University, Tower Building, Park Place, Cardiff CF10 3AT, UK. E-mail: westonn1@cardiff.ac.uk

This research was supported by sponsorship from the Economic and Social Research Council.

http://www.psypress.com/ecp DOI: 10.1080/09541440701728557

Farah, 1993) and the recognition of inverted faces (Bartlett & Searcy, 1993; Thompson, 1980; Yin, 1969).

Research has shown that any task or process that disrupts or reduces the amount of holistic information used in face recognition substantially reduces recognition accuracy. The transfer appropriate processing theory provides one explanation of why this occurs. Transfer appropriate processing theory (TAP; Morris, Brandsford, & Franks, 1977; Roediger, 1990) claims that optimal memory performance is achieved when encoding processes match retrieval processes. With regard to face recognition, this theory suggests that optimal face recognition is achieved when holistic processing is used at both encoding and retrieval stages. Any task that disrupts the use of holistic information, at either stage, reduces face recognition accuracy.

THE ROLE OF ENCODING STRATEGIES

The TAP theory of memory highlights the importance of encoding and retrieval strategies for optimal performance. Therefore, it is surprising that only a few studies have investigated the influence of different encoding strategies on face recognition performance (Coin & Tiberghien, 1997; Hanley, Pearson, & Howard, 1990; Wells & Hryciw, 1984). Despite the small number of studies conducted, the results support the claim that performance is optimal when encoding processes match retrieval processes. For example, Wells and Hryciw (1984) induced holistic and featural encoding strategies by asking participants to make judgements about faces based on either abstract traits (holistic) or physical features (featural). The retrieval tasks were either to identify someone from a lineup or to create a photofit. They found that lineup identification was more accurate following trait judgements, whereas photofit creations were more accurate following judgements about physical features. They concluded that accurate lineup identifications were based on holistic retrieval strategies and thus benefited from holistic encoding. Furthermore, optimal photofit creations were based on a more featural strategy and thus benefited from featural encoding processes. In line with TAP these results highlight the importance of similar encoding and retrieval strategies for optimal performance.

THE CROSS-RACE EFFECT

Holistic face processing requires access to, and the use of, both featural and configural information. The contribution of both featural and configural information has been demonstrated using a number of techniques. One notable advance in the face memory literature has involved work on the face inversion effect; the finding that inverted faces are identified with less accuracy than upright faces (Bartlett & Searcy, 1993; Thompson, 1980; Yin, 1969). The consensus within the literature points towards a reduction in the access to configural information when faces are inverted. Diamond and Carey (1986) hypothesised that this effect was the result of a lack of expertise with the inverted stimulus. This, they claimed, stemmed from experienced participants' reliance on configural information, which was not present in novice participants. Research investigating the role of expertise in face recognition has concluded that expert processing relies on access to configural information (e.g., Diamond & Carey, 1986; Rhodes, Brake, Taylor, & Tan, 1989).

A line of research linking reliance on configural information to that of expertise comes from research comparing own-race and other-race face recognition. Studies examining cross-race identifications have shown that individuals are better at recognising faces of their own race than faces of another race (Brigham & Malpass, 1985; Ellis & Deregowski, 1981; Rhodes et al., 1989). One common explanation for this advantage is that individuals have more expertise with own-race face recognition (Ellis, Deregowski, & Shepherd, 1975; Rhodes et al., 1989), and thus greater access to configural properties. Rhodes et al. (1989) explored the lack of configural information used in other-race face recognition using inversion techniques. They found that reduced performance following inversion of own-race faces was not present with other-race faces and concluded that their results provide evidence for the importance of configural information in expert face recognition. This lack of configural information in identifying other-race faces points towards a greater reliance on featural properties.

THE VERBAL OVERSHADOWING EFFECT

Tasks such as the recognition of inverted faces and recognition of other-race faces have demonstrated that a lack of configural information reduces face recognition accuracy. In addition to these face recognition tasks, it has been shown that other tasks such as providing a verbal description of a face can also reduce the amount of configural information used in the recognition process.

Research has shown that under some circumstances providing a verbal description of a face prior to a face recognition task significantly reduces face recognition accuracy (Brown & Lloyd-Jones, 2002, 2003; Dodson, Johnson, & Schooler, 1997; Fallshore & Schooler, 1995; Schooler & Engstler-Schooler, 1990). This effect, known as verbal overshadowing, has a number of possible explanations with the most recent rendering it as a change in processing style (Fallshore & Schooler, 1995; Schooler, 2002). This suggests that the act of verbalisation causes the transfer of inappropriate processing (TIP) to the final test. The TIP account claims that faces are encoded using a holistic strategy and that providing a verbal description changes the processing style from holistic, used at encoding, to a more featural-based strategy brought on by the verbal description process. Therefore, when presented with a recognition task, the featural processing strategy used to provide the verbal description is transferred to the retrieval process, reducing face recognition accuracy.

This processing account of verbal overshadowing has been supported in the literature by a number of studies. For example, research has shown that verbally describing a face that is not the target stimulus also reduces face recognition accuracy (Brown & Lloyd-Jones, 2002; Dodson et al., 1997), and even describing a car can have a negative impact on face recognition accuracy (Westerman & Larsen, 1997). This finding provides support for a generalised processing shift and cannot be explained by interference from the verbalised account (Schooler & Engstler-Schooler, 1990). The verbal overshadowing effect has been tested using multiple trials, with mixed results (e.g., Brown & Lloyd-Jones, 2002, 2003; Fallshore & Schooler, 1995; Lloyd-Jones, Brown, & Clarke, 2006; Melcher & Schooler, 1996; Ryan & Schooler, 1998). A small number of studies demonstrated a detrimental effect of verbal description over a series of trials (Brown & Lloyd-Jones, 2002, 2003; Lloyd-Jones et al., 2006) with the remainder only finding a verbal overshadowing effect for the first trial following a verbal description (Fallshore & Schooler, 1995; Melcher & Schooler, 1996; Ryan & Schooler, 1998). Furthermore, other studies have used different stimuli to highlight the generality of the effect of verbalisation. For example, negative effects of verbalisation have also been demonstrated using colours (Schooler & Engstler-Schooler, 1990), taste (Melcher & Schooler, 1996), voices (Perfect, Hunt, & Harris, 2002), and shapes (Brandimonte, Schooler, & Gabbino, 1997).

PROCESSING BIAS THEORY

The processing bias account of the verbal overshadowing effect states that providing a verbal description reduces the amount of configural information attended to at retrieval, which is the result of a shift in processing style from holistic to a more feature-based style. A study conducted by Macrae and Lewis (2002) attempted to investigate the processing style account of verbal overshadowing, using the global and local responses to the Navon letter task (Navon, 1977) to induce holistic and featural processing styles. Their study used a lineup task as a test of recognition and they asked participants to either engage in global processing of Navon stimuli, local processing of Navon stimuli, or a control task prior to the recognition test. They found that engaging in global processing significantly improved recognition accuracy (83%) compared with control (60%) and local processing significantly decreased accuracy (30%). The aim of their experiment was to investigate whether engaging in local processing would impair recognition accuracy the same as providing a verbal description. They concluded that local processing, like verbalisation, caused a transfer inappropriate processing shift to a more featural based strategy and thus reduced performance. Furthermore, they claimed that the global Navon task encouraged a more appropriate holistic strategy which led to better performance. Although a possible explanation for the results, this claim that the effects of verbalisation and local Navon processing are caused by the same processing deficit is, as yet, unsupported. A number of studies have found evidence for the effects of Navon processing on face recognition performance (Perfect, 2003; Weston & Perfect, 2005); however, to date these effects have not been directly compared to the effects of verbalisation.

THE LINK BETWEEN VERBALISATION AND PROCESSING BIAS

There are some consistencies in the literature between the effects of verbalisation and local Navon processing. For example, research has shown that the effects of verbalisation are limited to a short number of recognition judgements following the verbalisation process (Fallshore & Schooler, 1995). In line with these results, similar findings of a trial effect have been demonstrated using the Navon processing task (Weston & Perfect, 2005). However, despite these similarities, no study to date has investigated the similarities between the effects of verbalisation and Navon processing. The present studies aim to bridge this gap.

The present work aimed to bring together the findings of Macrae and Lewis (2002) and Fallshore and Schooler (1995) by investigating the effects of Navon processing and verbalisation across multiple trials. In order to compare the processing styles used in both the Navon letter task and verbalisation, face recognition performance was tested following both holistic and featural encoding strategies and for own- and other-race faces. All experiments presented in this paper used a four-stage procedure. In Stage 1, participants engaged in either the holistic or featural encoding task. In Experiment 1 holistic and featural encoding was encouraged with the Navon letter task whereas in Experiments 2 and 3 participants were asked to focus on either personality traits or facial features. In Stage 2, participants were asked to remember eight images of faces presented on the screen (Caucasian or Asian). Multiple images were presented at encoding because a multiple encoding paradigm has been used in previous research to demonstrate the effects of Navon processing (e.g., Weston & Perfect, 2005). Stage 3 was a between-subjects interval task where they completed either the global or local version of the Navon letter task, provided a verbal description or read aloud from a book. In Stage 4 they were presented with two face images at a time and asked to decide which face had been presented before (Caucasian or Asian). Given that only two alternatives were presented at retrieval in this paradigm there is a possibility that the strategies used at test when presented with only two alternatives differ to the strategies used when presented with an array of 6–8 faces. Although a two-alternative paradigm differs from previous paradigms used to investigate the verbal overshadowing effect, a two-alternative paradigm has reliably demonstrated effects of Navon processing (e.g., Weston & Perfect, 2005). The four stages were repeated four times to make four blocks so that each participant completed all combinations of the encoding and race factors. A number of predictions follow from the literature.

Predictions

Encoding processes. The TAP account states that optimal face recognition accuracy is achieved through the use of holistic processing at encoding and retrieval. Therefore, based on the assumption that global Navon processing induces a holistic strategy, three predictions regarding the encoding manipulation were made. First, holistic encoding would lead to better face recognition accuracy compared with faces encoded featurally. Predictions were also made regarding the interaction between the encoding task and interval task effects. Following holistically encoded stimuli, it was predicted that both the local Navon processing and verbalisation conditions would produce performance below that of the control condition. Furthermore, it was predicted that the global Navon interval task would produce performance rates equal to controls, given that stimuli had been encoded using a holistic strategy. Following featurally encoded stimuli, it was predicted that both the local Navon processing and verbalisation conditions would produce performance equal to that of the control condition. Furthermore, it was predicted that the global Navon interval task would improve performance compared to control.

Cross-race effects. In order to investigate the link between global and local Navon processing and holistic and featural processing styles both own- and other-race faces were used as stimuli. Research has shown that own- and other-race faces are processed differently using holistic and featural strategies, respectively. Given this distinction the following predictions were made. First, own-race faces would be recognised more accurately than other-race faces, thus confirming the race effect found in the literature. Second, the recognition of own-race faces would benefit from holistic encoding strategies whereas the recognition of other-race faces would benefit from more featural encoding strategies.

Furthermore, research which has investigated the effect of verbalisation on own- and other-race faces has provided support for the claim that verbalisation results in a processing shift (Fallshore & Schooler, 1995). They found that reliance on featural information in other-race faces reduced the impact of verbalisation compared with own-race faces. Therefore, based on this finding this experiment makes the final prediction that the processing shifts due to Navon processing and deficits following verbalisation would only be evident for own-race and not other-race faces.

EXPERIMENT 1

The aim of Experiment 1 was to compare the effects of verbalisation and Navon processing for both own-race and other-race faces following both holistic and featural encoding. Results found by Macrae and Lewis (2002) suggest that the impact of global and local versions of the Navon processing task was the result of encouraging holistic and featural processing styles. Based on this claim we decided to use the Navon letter task to encourage the use of holistic and featural processing at the encoding stage.

Method

Participants. Eighty participants (from the University of British Columbia, Vancouver and the University of Plymouth, UK took part in this experiment for course credit. Fourteen were male and sixty-six were female (age range 17–45 years). Half of the participants were of Asian origin and half were of Caucasian origin.

Stimuli and design. The experiment used a 2 (encoding: global, local) × 2 (race of stimuli: own race, other race) × 4 (interval task condition: control, global, local, verbal) mixed-design with two within-subjects factors, encoding strategy and race of stimuli, and one between-subjects factor, interval task condition. The task used a repeated measures design with multiple stimuli where participants were asked to make a series of judgements based on faces previously encountered.

The face stimuli were digital colour photographs taken of female students from the University of British Columbia. Both full-face and three-quarter pose images were used. All images were of the head only and the background of each image was neutral. The stimulus set comprised of 64 images, 32 three-quarter pose images used at the encoding stage and 32 full-face images used at the test stage. Half of the people in the images were Asian and half were Caucasian.

A multiple trial design was used in this experiment where face recognition accuracy was tested over four blocks. Each block contained an encoding manipulation (global or local), eight faces for encoding (own race or other race), an interval task which was either global or local Navon processing, a control task or verbal description task, and four two-alternative forced choice test trials. In each block, and for each participant, one combination of encoding and race of stimuli was tested, for example global encoding with own-race faces, global encoding with other-race faces, local encoding with own-race faces and local encoding with other-race faces. The order of the encoding/race of stimuli combination was counterbalanced across participants.

The experiment was programmed in E-Prime and run on a PC. The face stimuli at encoding and test were presented in a surface area of 5 cm wide × 7 cm high. The experiment took 45 min to complete.

Procedure. All participants were briefed as to the nature of the experiment and asked to provide their informed consent. Participants were told that there were four stages to the experiment. In Stage 1, they were asked to complete a version of the Navon letter task. In Stage 2, they were asked to remember eight images of faces presented on the screen. Stage 3 was the between subjects interval task where they completed either the global or local version of the Navon letter task, provided a verbal description or read aloud from a book. In Stage 4 they were presented with two face images and asked to decide which face had been presented before. These four stages were repeated four times to make four blocks so that each participant completed all combinations of the encoding and race factors.

During Stage 1 all participants were asked to complete either the global or local version of the Navon letter task (Navon, 1977), for 3 min. For both global and local processing, participants were presented with 90 Navon letters each for 2 s. During the 2 s that the letter was on the screen participants were asked to say aloud either the large letter (global processing) or the small letter (local processing). Following this they were shown eight three-quarter pose faces presented simultaneously on the screen for 12 s and asked to remember these faces. These faces were either eight Caucasian faces or eight Asian faces.

Before the experiment began participants were randomly assigned to one of four interval task conditions; in Stage 3 they engaged in one of these four tasks. Participants in the global processing condition engaged in the global version of the Navon letter task. Participants in the local condition engaged in the local version of the Navon letter task. Participants in the verbal description condition were shown another face (not one of the eight presented at encoding) and asked to provide a verbal description of this face. To encourage a more featural analysis of the face participants were asked to write down everything they could about the shape, size, and the appearance of different features such as the eyes, nose, mouth, etc., for the full 3 min. Participants in the control condition were asked to read aloud from a book. All participants engaged in one of these tasks for 3 min.

In Stage 4 participants were presented with four two-alternative forced choice test trials. Each trial presented two faces simultaneously. Both were full-face images where one face had been presented at encoding and the other a new face. The "new" image presented on each trial was determined by the degree of similarity to the old image. This similarity was determined by asking a sample of 20 independent reviewers to choose which image, out of a collection of 10 possible images was most similar to a target image. The image which was selected most often was deemed most similar to the target was selected as a pairing at test. A high degree of similarity between old and new images at test was important to avoid ceiling effects in the data. In Stage 4 the participants' task was to indicate using the keys "c" and "m" on the keyboard which face they had seen before. On two trials the old face appeared on the left and on two trials the old face appeared on the right; the presentation order was randomised.

These four stages were repeated four times to create four blocks. Four blocks were used to ensure a completely counterbalanced design with different stimuli in each block. All participants completed all four blocks. The four blocks consisted of: global processing at encoding and own-race faces, global processing at encoding and other-race faces, local processing at encoding and own-race faces, and local processing at encoding and other-race faces.

Results and discussion

Both accuracy and latency data were used in the analysis as both have been used in previous research to demonstrate the effects of verbalisation and Navon processing (e.g., Brown & Lloyd-Jones, 2002, 2003; Macrae & Lewis, 2002; Schooler & Engstler-Schooler, 1990; Weston & Perfect, 2005). Although both measures are reported here, for the purpose of this paper, the accuracy measure was used as the main dependent variable. This measure was chosen for two reasons: (1) The majority of research in this area uses accuracy as a measure of performance; and (2) given the nature of the paradigm, the below ceiling accuracy rates reduced the reliability of the latencies as the most accurate measure of performance.

Results based on the multiple trial analysis revealed that the effects were strongest in the first trial following the interval task manipulation. A mean comparison of all trials did not show any differences in performance between interval task conditions (global, $M = 0.71$; control, $M = 0.71$; local,

$M = 0.68$; verbal, $M = 0.66$). However, means from the first trial only revealed a different pattern (global, $M = 0.80$; control, $M = 0.73$; local, $M = 0.60$; verbal, $M = 0.61$). Based on this finding and results of previous studies (Fallshore & Schooler, 1995; Melcher & Schooler, 1996; Ryan & Schooler, 1998; Weston & Perfect, 2005), showing that the effects of verbalisation and Navon processing were limited to a short number of trials, we report the results from the first trial only.

Two separate analyses were carried out. The first was to investigate how effective the Navon encoding task was in encouraging holistic and featural processing styles. To test this we compared the effects of both encoding tasks on the ability to recognise own- and other-race faces, in the control condition only. Only the control condition was used in this analysis because it was predicted that the Navon and verbalisation manipulations would interfere with processing at test. Given that own- and other-race stimuli have been shown to use holistic and featural processes respectively, this enabled us to measure the effectiveness of the holistic and featural encoding tasks. Second, we examined the influence of the interval tasks on recognition performance.

Cross-race effects in the control condition

A 2 (encoding: global, local) × 2 (race of stimuli: own, other) factor ANOVA, carried out on the accuracy scores in the control condition, did not find any significant main effects of race, $F < 1$, or encoding, $F < 1$, nor a significant interaction between race of face and encoding, $F < 1$.

A 2 (encoding: global, local) × 2 (race of stimuli: own, other) factor ANOVA, carried out on the latency scores in the control condition did not find any significant main effects of race, $F < 1$, or encoding, $F(1, 19) = 2.17$, $MSE = 3{,}254{,}227$, nor a significant interaction between race of face and encoding, $F < 1$.

Interval task effects

A 2 (encoding: global, local) × 2 (race of stimuli: own, other) × 4 (interval task: control, global, local, verbal) factor ANOVA carried out on the accuracy scores found a significant main effect of interval task, $F(3, 76) = 3.53$, $MSE = 0.728$, $p < .05$ (control, $M = 0.73$; global processing, $M = 0.80$; local processing, $M = 0.60$; verbalisation, $M = 0.61$). Bonferroni pairwise comparisons revealed that accuracy scores following local processing, $p = .04$, and verbalisation, $p = .06$, were significantly lower than accuracy following global processing. No significant differences were found between the Navon or verbalisation condition compared with control. The main effects of race, $F < 1$, and encoding, $F < 1$, did not reach significance. The interactions between interval task and encoding, $F(3, 76) = 1.02$, $MSE = 0.253$, $p > .10$, race and interval task, $F(3, 76) = 1.57$, $MSE = 0.303$, $p > .10$, race and encoding, $F(1, 76) = 1.24$, $MSE = 0.253$, $p > .10$, and race, encoding, and interval task, $F < 1$, did not reach significance.

Although the interaction between race, encoding, and interval task did not reach significance, the pattern of means were in the direction predicted. Figure 1 shows the mean accuracy scores for each condition following global and local encoding for both own- (Figure 1a) and other-race (Figure 1b) faces. Figure 1a shows an advantage of global processing across both encoding manipulations. Moreover, the graph shows a differential effect of verbalisation and local Navon processing following global and local encoding. For globally encoded faces both verbalisation and local processing

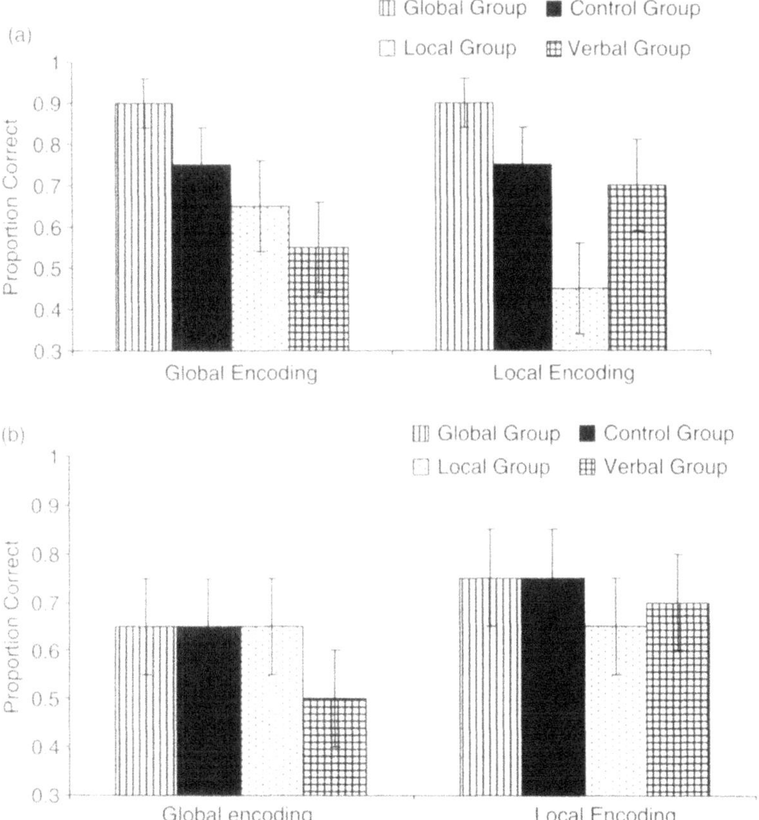

Figure 1. Mean accuracy scores and standard errors for (a) own-race faces and (b) other-race faces, across all conditions following holistic and featural encoding in Experiment 1.

reduced accuracy; however, for locally encoded faces accuracy was reduced far more following local Navon processing compared with verbalisation. Furthermore, as shown by Figure 1b, the advantage of global processing and detriment of local Navon processing and verbalisation were not apparent for other-race faces.

Analysis of the mean latency scores (in ms) revealed a significant main effect of race, $F(1, 76) = 4.61$, $MSE = 11{,}824{,}913$, $p < .05$, with faster reaction times for own-race faces (own race, $M = 3407$, other race, $M = 3791$) and a significant main effect of interval task, $F(3, 76) = 6.50$, $MSE = 56{,}169{,}371$, $p < .01$ (control, $M = 2745$; global processing, $M = 3096$; local processing, $M = 3961$; verbalisation, $M = 4595$). Bonferroni pairwise comparisons revealed that reaction times following local processing, $p = .06$, and verbalisation, $p = .001$, were significantly slower compared with control. Also reaction times following verbalisation, $p = .011$, were significantly slower than those following global processing. The main effect of encoding did not reach significance, $F < 1$. The interactions between interval task and encoding, $F < 1$, race and interval task, $F(3, 76) = 1.19$, $MSE = 3{,}038{,}681$, $p > .10$, race and encoding, $F < 1$, and race, encoding, and interval task, $F(3, 76) = 1.40$, $MSE = 5{,}299{,}669$, $p > .10$, did not reach significance.

The accuracy data from Experiment 1 showed that although local processing and verbalisation tasks appeared to impair performance, the only significant impairment was observed when compared with the global processing condition. Furthermore, global Navon processing improved performance; however, again the difference in means between global processing and control conditions did not reach significance. Results from the latency data were consistent with the accuracy data. Individuals were significantly slower to respond at test following local processing and verbal description. Marginal differences were found between interval tasks; however, no significant interactions were found in performance between interval task, race, and encoding, as predicted. This result was surprising given that previous research has found that the effects of verbal description were eliminated when recognising faces of another race (Fallshore & Schooler, 1995).

Analysis of the cross-race data from the control condition and the lack of an interaction between race of stimuli and encoding task indicate that the global and local Navon task used at encoding might not have successfully induced the holistic and featural styles used in own- and other-race face recognition. This could explain why the encoding task did not significantly interact in the predicted way with own- and other-race stimuli. Furthermore, if holistic and featural strategies were not induced at encoding the predictions regarding the effects of verbalisation and Navon processing would not be upheld. To test this we conducted a second experiment where we changed the encoding task to a task in which participants were asked to think about either personality traits or physical features of face images.

EXPERIMENT 2

Method

Participants. Eighty participants from the University of Plymouth, UK took part in this experiment for course credit. Twenty-three were male and fifty-seven were female (age range 18–38 years). Half of the participants were of Asian origin and half were of Caucasian origin.

Stimuli and design. The stimuli used and the design of Experiment 2 were the same as that used in Experiment 1.

Procedure. The only change made to the procedure was during encoding. For the holistic encoding manipulation participants were told "past research has shown that focusing on personality traits of faces can help you remember them, therefore whilst the eight faces are on the screen I would like you to think about which face you think is the most honest". For the featural encoding manipulation participants were told "past research has shown that focusing on a person's eyes can help you remember them, therefore whilst the eight faces are on the screen I would like you to focus your attention on the eyes of each face". All other procedures were the same as in Experiment 1.

Results and discussion

In line with the results of Experiment 1, the data from Experiment 2 were analysed using the first trial only following the interval task as this is where the effects were strongest.

Cross-race effects in the control condition. A 2 (encoding: holistic, featural) × 2 (race of stimuli: own, other) factor ANOVA carried out on the accuracy scores in the control condition did not reveal a significant main effect of race, $F < 1$, or a significant main effect of encoding, $F < 1$. However, results showed a significant interaction between race of face and the encoding manipulation, $F(1, 19) = 8.88$, $MSE = 1.51$, $p < .01$. A paired samples t-test found that following holistic encoding, own-race faces were recognised with more accuracy than other-race faces, $t(19) = 2.52$, $p = .021$. This pattern was reversed following featural encoding; other-race faces were recognised more accurately than own-race faces, $t(19) = -0.204$, $p = .05$. This significant interaction is displayed in Figure 2.

A 2 (encoding: holistic, featural) × 2 (race of stimuli: own, other) factor ANOVA, carried out on the latency scores in the control condition found no significant main effects of race, $F < 1$, or encoding, $F(1, 19) = 1.70$, $MSE = 3{,}551{,}137$, $p > .10$, or any significant interaction between the two factors, $F < 1$.

Interval task effects. A 2 (encoding: holistic, featural) × 2 (race of stimuli: own, other) × 4 (interval task: control, global, local, verbal) factor ANOVA carried out on the accuracy scores found a significant main effect of interval task, $F(3, 76) = 6.60$, $MSE = 1.37$, $p < .01$ (control, $M = 0.54$; global processing, $M = 0.79$, local processing, $M = 0.78$; verbalisation, $M = 0.83$). Bonferroni pairwise comparisons revealed that accuracy scores following the control task were significantly lower than accuracy scores following global processing, $p = .005$, local processing, $p = .009$, and verbalisation, $p = .001$. The main effect of race was approaching significance, $F(1, 76) = 2.82$, $MSE = 0.450$, $p < .10$, where own-race faces ($M = 0.77$) were recognised with more accuracy than other-race faces ($M = 0.69$). There was no main effect of encoding, $F(1, 76) = 2.29$, $MSE = 0.312$, $p > .10$. Results revealed a significant race by interval task interaction, $F(3, 76) = 2.98$, $MSE = 0.475$, $p < .05$, and a significant encoding by interval task interaction, $F(3, 76) = 3.21$, $MSE = 0.437$, $p < .05$. This two-way interaction between encoding and interval task was further investigated by examining the interval task effects following holistic and featural encoding trials separately using one-way ANOVAs. Bonferroni pairwise comparisons showed that for stimuli encoded holistically, global processing, $p < .001$,

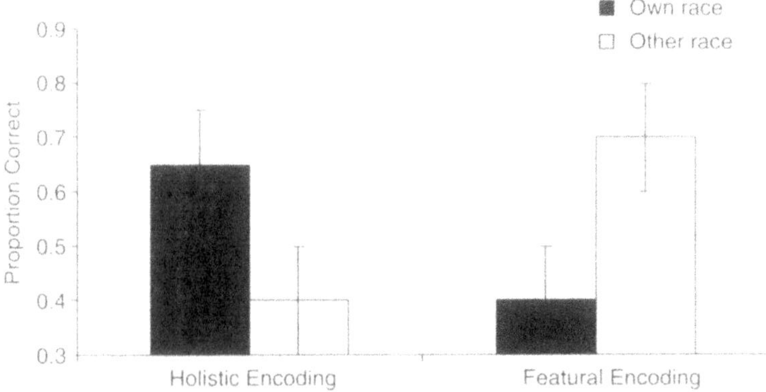

Figure 2. Mean accuracy scores and standard errors for own-race faces and other-race faces, following holistic and featural encoding for the control condition in Experiment 2.

and verbalisation, $p = .005$, both improved performance compared with control. For stimuli that had been encoded featurally, both local processing, $p = .048$, and verbalisation, $p = .048$, improved performance compared with control. The interaction between race and encoding did not reach significance, $F < 1$. However, analysis did reveal a significant three-way interaction between race, encoding, and interval task, $F(3, 76) = 3.06$, $MSE = 0.608$, $p < .05$. This three-way interaction is displayed in Figure 3. This interaction was analysed further by splitting the data by race of stimuli.

For own-race faces there was a significant main effect of interval task condition, $F(3, 76) = 8.88$, $MSE = 0.136$, $p < .001$. There was no interaction between encoding and interval task, $F(3, 76) = 1.06$, $MSE = 0.179$, $p > .10$. Figure 3a shows that accuracy scores improved, compared with control,

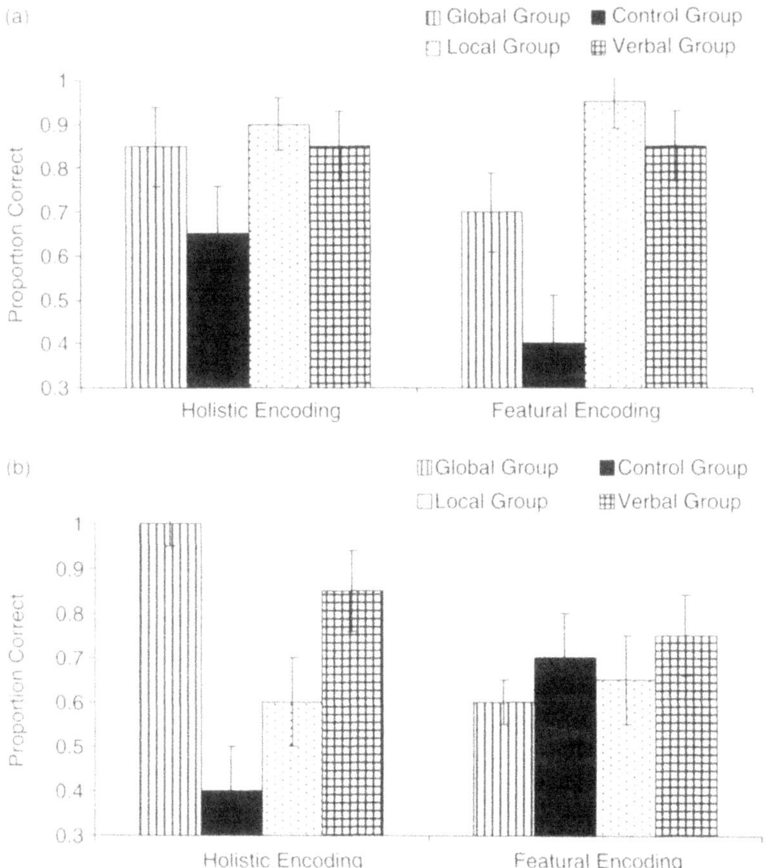

Figure 3. Mean accuracy scores and standard errors for (a) own-race faces and (b) other-race faces, across all conditions following holistic and featural encoding in Experiment 2.

following all interval task conditions for both holistic and featural encoding tasks. For other-race faces there was a significant main effect of interval task, $F(3, 76) = 2.77$, $MSE = 0.231$, $p < .05$, and a significant interaction between encoding and interval task, $F(3, 76) = 5.48$, $MSE = 0.156$, $p < .01$. One-way ANOVAs showed that there were significant differences between interval task conditions following holistic encoding, $F(3, 76) = 8.84$, $p < .01$. Bonferroni pairwise comparisons revealed that global processing, $p < .001$, and verbalisation, $p = .004$, improved performance compared with control. No significant differences were found between interval tasks following featural encoding, $F < 1$. This interaction is displayed in Figure 3b.

Analysis of the mean latency scores revealed a significant main effect of encoding, $F(1, 76) = 5.41$, $MSE = 34{,}974{,}174$, $p < .05$ (holistic encoding, $M = 4386$; featural encoding, $M = 3724$) and a significant main effect of interval task, $F(3, 76) = 3.77$, $MSE = 84{,}347{,}724$, $p < .05$ (control, $M = 3718$; global processing, $M = 3753$, local processing, $M = 3201$; verbalisation, $M = 5548$). Bonferroni pairwise comparisons revealed that reaction times following verbalisation were significantly slower compared with reaction times following local processing, $p = .015$. The main effect of race did not reach significance, $F < 1$. None of the interactions reached significance; race by interval task, $F < 1$; encoding by interval task, $F(3, 76) = 2.54$, $MSE = 16{,}396{,}983$, $p > .05$; race by encoding, $F < 1$; race by encoding by interval task, $F(3, 76) = 1.32$, $MSE = 9{,}689{,}135$, $p > .10$.

The only difference between the design of Experiment 2 and that of Experiment 1 was the nature of the encoding task used to induce holistic and featural strategies. Instead of the global and local versions of the Navon letter task used in Experiment 1, Experiment 2 used holistic and featural tasks which asked participants to focus on either personality traits (holistic) or physical features (featural) prior to the initial face presentation.

The results from the control condition were consistent with the claim that own-face faces and other-race faces are recognised by different processing styles. Analysis showed that holistic encoding benefited the recognition of own-race faces, whereas featural encoding benefited the recognition of other-race faces. This manipulation not only provided a test of the reliability of the encoding task but also provided a measure of the holistic and featural processes used in the recognition of own- and other-race faces.

The interval task analysis on the accuracy data showed that all three manipulations—global processing, local processing, and verbalisation—improved performance compared with control. The significant interaction between encoding and interval task showed that following holistic encoding both global processing and verbalisation improved performance. However, following featural encoding, local processing and verbalisation improved performance. It was predicted that local processing and verbalisation would both have a negative effect on performance due to the transfer of an inappropriate processing style and that this effect would greater following holistic encoding. Consequently, the improvement in accuracy following local processing and verbalisation was surprising given the results found in the Navon and verbal overshadowing literature. However, the latency data were somewhat inconsistent with the accuracy data. Whilst reaction times following local processing did not differ from control, verbalisation significantly increased the time taken to respond at test. However, the high accuracy and slow reaction times found in this experiment could be explained by a speed–accuracy tradeoff in that participants were compromising speed for high accuracy in the verbalisation condition.

Given previous findings in the literature which have shown a clear advantage of global processing and disadvantage of local processing, the results following the Navon task in Experiment 2 were unexpected and not in line with predictions. A third experiment was conducted to test the results found in Experiment 2. Experiment 3 used the same holistic and featural encoding task as Experiment 2; however, in order to increase power in the data the race factor was removed from the design. Furthermore, due to the limited research conducted on the Navon processing task it was decided to remove the verbalisation interval task condition from the design and focus on the effects of Navon processing. In order to add to the reliability and generality of the results different face stimuli were used in Experiment 3 to those used in Experiments 1 and 2.

EXPERIMENT 3

Method

Participants. Sixty participants from the University of Plymouth, UK took part in this experiment for course credit. Twenty-one were male and fifty-nine were female (age range 19–35 years).

Stimuli and design. The face stimuli were digital colour photographs of male faces. Both full-face and three-quarter pose images were used. All images were of the head only and the background of each image was neutral. The stimulus set comprised of 64 images, 32 three-quarter pose images used at the encoding stage and 32 full-face images used at the test stage.

The experiment used a 2 (encoding: holistic, featural) × 3 (interval task: control, global, local) mixed-design with one within-subjects factor, encoding strategy, and one between-subjects factor, interval task.

Procedure. The experiment procedure was the same as in Experiments 1 and 2; however, with the race factor removed the four experimental blocks consisted of two holistic encoding blocks and two featural encoding blocks with own-race face stimuli.

Results and discussion

Interval task effects. A 2 (encoding: holistic, featural) × 3 (interval task: control, global, local) factor ANOVA carried out on the accuracy scores found a significant main effect of interval task, $F(2,\ 57) = 8.86$, $MSE = 0.752$, $p < .001$ (control, $M = 0.54$; global, $M = 0.80$; local, $M = 0.74$) where performance improved following both global Navon processing, $p < .001$, and local Navon processing, $p < .01$, compared with control. Figure 4 shows the means for each interval task condition following both holistic and featural encoding. There was no significant main effect of encoding, $F(1,\ 57) = .2.52$, $MSE = 0.300$, $p > .10$, or encoding by interval task interaction, $F < 1$.

The two-factor ANOVA carried out on the latency scores did not reveal any significant main effects of encoding, $F(1,\ 45) = 2.02$, $MSE = 2{,}277{,}284$, $p > .10$, or interval task, $F < 1$. The two-way interaction between encoding and interval task did not reach significance, $F < 1$.

This experiment aimed to investigate the effect of holistic and featural encoding strategies and the influence encoding strategy has on the Navon effect. As in Experiment 2, Experiment 3 manipulated holistic and featural encoding strategies by asking participants to focus on either personality traits or featural aspects of a face. In line with the results of Experiment 2, both global and local Navon processing increased accuracy scores compared with control. Furthermore, this beneficial effect following both global and local Navon processing was sustained for both holistic encoding trials and featural encoding trials. The results of Experiment 3 support the global

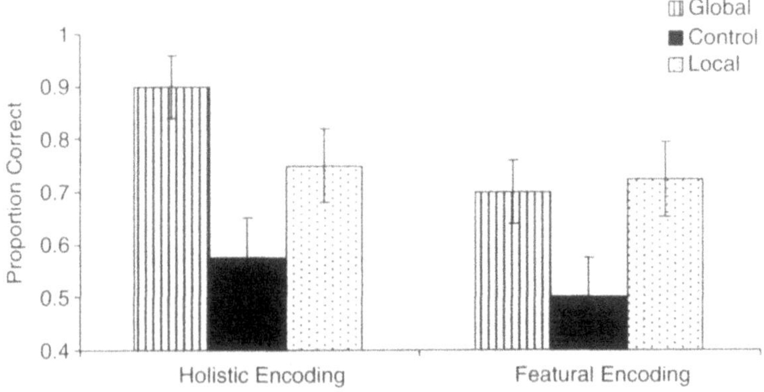

Figure 4. Mean accuracy scores and standard errors across all conditions following holistic and featural encoding in Experiment 3.

processing advantage found in Experiment 2 and in previous literature. However, the increased accuracy following local Navon processing found in both Experiments 2 and 3 raises questions about the reliability of the effects of local processing and the relationship between the Navon letter task and holistic and featural processing styles. This point is discussed further in the General Discussion.

GENERAL DISCUSSION

The aim of this paper was to investigate the effects of Navon processing and verbalisation on face recognition performance following both holistic and featural encoding. The results, from three experiments, although unexpected, have questioned the claim that the effects of Navon processing and verbalisation can both be explained using a holistic and featural processing framework.

Encoding and race effects

The TAP account of face recognition, which states that optimal performance is achieved through similarity between encoding and retrieval strategies, gained some support from the results of these studies. In Experiments 1 and 3 the effects of the Navon task were the same regardless of the type of processing engaged in at encoding. However in Experiment 2, the positive effects of global processing, local processing, and verbalisation differed depending on the encoding task participants engaged in. For example, effects were found for global processing and verbalisation following holistic encoding, whereas the effects of local processing and verbalisation were found following featural encoding. One explanation for these results relates to the potential differences between the processes evoked by the encoding task and the processes evoked by the Navon processing task. The reliability of the encoding task was tested by comparing performance for both own- and other-race faces following holistic and featural encoding. Given that own- and other-race faces have been shown to elicit different processing styles, this comparison enabled a test of the encoding task in evoking holistic and featural processes. Experiment 1, which used the global and local Navon task at encoding, did not find any significant differences in performance due to the type of encoding process in either the control condition analysis or the interval task analysis. However, when the personality and physical judgement task was used at encoding in Experiment 2, the control condition results showed a clear interaction between encoding process and race of stimuli. This interaction demonstrated that holistic encoding was beneficial for own-race faces (65%) compared with other-race faces (40%), whereas featural encoding was beneficial for other-race faces (70%) compared with own-race faces (40%). The only difference between Experiments 1 and 2 was the type of encoding task used. Therefore, the differential findings of Navon processing and verbalisation across Experiments 1 and 2 suggests that the Navon encoding task and the holistic/featural encoding task did not encourage the same processing style.

If one assumes that the own-race effect found in the literature is the result of a holistic and featural processing distinction then the results of Experiment 2 indicate that the holistic and featural encoding task used in this experiment successfully induced the holistic and featural processing styles used in face recognition. To date, evidence for the holistic account of the cross-race effect has come from tasks such as inversion which assume that poor performance equates to a lack of configural information. The results of Experiment 2 have provided a measure of the type of holistic and featural information used in the recognition of own- and other-race faces by manipulating processing style at encoding. One explanation therefore for the lack of any encoding effects in Experiment 1 is that the global and local encoding task did not evoke the necessary holistic and featural processing styles used in face recognition.

Past research has posed a strong link between global and local Navon processing and holistic and featural face processing strategies (Macrae & Lewis, 2002). However, the results of Experiment 1 do not support this strong claim as the Navon processing task, when presented at encoding did not affect performance on the face recognition task. However, the lack of any encoding effects in Experiment 1 does not rule out an explanation based on holistic and featural processing. It is possible that any effects of global and local processing only occur prior to test and not at encoding. We consider this explanation in the next section.

Navon processing as an interval task

It appears that the influence of Navon processing on face recognition performance is not as clear as first thought. Results from a number of studies have provided support for a global processing advantage and local processing disadvantage on face recognition performance (Macrae & Lewis, 2002; Perfect, 2003). However, the inconsistent results found across Experiments 1 and 2 in this paper cast doubt on the generality of the effect. Some possible explanations for the different results found across experiments are described next.

The consistent increase following global processing and decrease following local processing in past research has led researchers to posit a possible link between holistic and featural face processing and the global and local

Navon letter task. But the link between Navon processing and face processing strategies has not yet been extensively tested in the literature. It seems that the Navon letter task, when presented at encoding does not influence performance (Experiment 1). When presented as an interval task between encoding and retrieval global and local Navon processing produced means in line with predictions. Although not significantly different from control, the means observed in Experiment 1 were consistent with past research. Therefore, one explanation for the results found in Experiment 1 is that Navon processing does influence holistic and featural processing styles; however, these effects are most influential postencoding just prior to retrieval.

However, the results of Experiment 2, which used a facial judgement task at encoding provides evidence for the differences between global and local Navon processing and holistic and featural face processing. Contrary to predictions all interval task conditions improved performance compared with control. Improvements in performance were consistent across both holistically encoded and featurally encoded stimuli. This unexpected improvement following local processing was replicated in Experiment 3 where again accuracy scores improved following both the global and local processing interval task regardless of the encoding strategy used.

If one assumes that the holistic and featural encoding task used in Experiments 2 and 3 successfully induced holistic and featural encoding strategies, then the positive effects of global and local processing when presented prior to retrieval are difficult to explain in terms of a holistic and featural processing bias. For example, based on a combination of TAP and processing bias theory, local processing when presented prior to retrieval should impair performance due to the featural nature of the task. However the results of Experiments 2 and 3 showed a strong advantage following local processing. As mentioned earlier, it is possible that the effects caused by engaging in the global and local versions of the Navon letter task were not the result of a shift towards holistic and featural processing strategies. This leaves the Navon effect open to alternative explanations, which are discussed later in this section.

Verbalisation as an interval task

In addition to the effects of Navon processing, another aim of this paper was to explore the similarities between the effect of verbalisation and the effect of local Navon processing. Despite the limited number of studies carried out that directly test the relationship between verbal overshadowing and local processing, similarities between the two tasks have been reported, such as the longevity of both effects (Fallshore & Schooler, 1995; Weston & Perfect, 2005).

The processing bias account of verbalisation suggests a change in processing from a holistic to a more feature-based style. Based on this account larger effects of verbalisation were predicted following holistic encoding. Although the pattern of means in Experiment 1 supported this prediction, the interaction between encoding and interval task did not reach significance. As mentioned earlier, this interaction may have been due to the discrepancy between Navon encoding and holistic and featural processing styles. The results of Experiment 2 showed that, in line with the effects of the local processing interval task, verbalisation improved accuracy following both holistic and featural encoding. The latency data, however, showed the opposite results.

Whilst reaction times to make a response following local processing did not differ from control, reaction times following verbalisation increased significantly. The different effects found between local processing and verbalisation in terms of latencies highlights possible differences between the two effects. However, it could be argued that the lengthy latencies shown in the verbalisation condition can be attributed to a speed–accuracy tradeoff in that participants were sacrificing speed of responding for high accuracy. Therefore, the high accuracy found in the verbalisation group may not have been an accurate measure of performance given the length of time it took participants to respond, compared with participants in the other conditions. However, the data did not support this prediction. In order to investigate this explanation we removed the participants whose response times were more than two standard deviations from the mean. Whilst the mean response latencies dropped to around 3500 ms, the accuracy only dropped to 80%, which was still better than control.

One further explanation for the increase reaction time found following verbalisation in Experiment 2 relates to potential interference of the verbalised face. Participants in the verbalisation condition were exposed to a "ninth" face which they were asked to verbalise; this stimuli was not shown to participants in all other conditions. Therefore, it could be argued that this caused proactive interference with the time it took participants to make a decision. However, whilst this theory explains the effects found in Experiment 2, the results of Experiment 1 are not consistent with this explanation as no significant differences were found between the effects of verbalisation and the other three conditions.

Whilst it is clear that Navon processing and verbalisation influence face recognition performance, we still have a lot to learn regarding the processes involved in each task. This paper investigated the holistic and featural explanation of the Navon processing task and verbal overshadowing effect and has demonstrated a potential discrepancy between these two processes.

Whilst we need to investigate the processes involved in the Navon letter task in more depth, this paper has provided evidence for a possible distinction between Navon processing and verbalisation.

Navon processing: A holistic/featural explanation

One explanation for these findings relates to the cognitive processes involved in the Navon letter task and the processes involved in face recognition. Engaging in both a holistic processing style and a global Navon processing task has been shown to improve face recognition accuracy. However, there is no direct evidence to suggest that they actually elicit the same cognitive processes. There are many cognitive operations involved in face recognition and many tasks have been shown to influence face recognition accuracy. The personality and physical judgements used to induce holistic and featural processing styles at encoding have shown beneficial for different face recognition tasks such as lineup recognition and photofit creations (Wells & Hryciw, 1984). The benefits observed from using both personality and physical attributes at encoding highlights the importance both types of information have in recognition. However, the Navon letter task has not been tested with the same scrutiny. The main body of evidence for the influence of Navon processing has come from the perception literature, which explores the perceptual nature of the task in terms of the precedence and hierarchy of information (Navon, 1977). Therefore, the claim that global and local Navon processing influences the holistic and featural processing styles necessary for face recognition remains to be tested.

A final consideration—why did local processing increase accuracy?

Why did local processing increase accuracy in Experiments 2 and 3 and not in Experiment 1? The answer to this question warrants further investigation; however, we provide some possible explanations.

First, a featural recognition strategy may have been beneficial to the type of recognition task used. Past research (e.g., Macrae & Lewis, 2002; Perfect, 2003) has measured face recognition accuracy using an eight person array or lineup, where holistic processing has been shown to be the optimal strategy (Dunning & Stern, 1994). Other experiments which have used two-alternative forced choice tasks required participants to recognise composite face halves—a less holistic approach (e.g., Weston & Perfect, 2005). The experiments conducted in this paper used a two-alternative forced choice task whereby individuals had to make a decision based on only two alternatives in which the optimal strategy was holistic. It is possible that given only two alternatives, individuals were able to use a more featural-based comparative strategy as this was not so cognitively demanding. Given that both holistic and featural processing could be used, it follows that either global or local processing would improve performance on this task. However, we acknowledge the circularity of this argument.

The differences found between Experiment 1 and Experiments 2 and 3 can also be explained by the differential processes involved in the Navon letter task and holistic and featural processing tasks. For example, local processing only improved performance when the personality and physical judgement task was used at encoding and not when the Navon task was used at encoding. It is possible that the specificity of the holistic and featural task used in Experiments 2 and 3 allowed participants to encode particular facial characteristics which could be used in the later recognition task. This suggests that the improvement following global processing and impairment following local processing, observed in the literature, only occurs when no specific holistic or featural information has been encoded.

REFERENCES

Bartlett, J. C., & Searcy, J. (1993). Inversion and configuration of faces. *Cognitive Psychology, 25*, 281–316.

Brandimonte, M. A., Schooler, J. W., & Gabbino, P. (1997). Attenuating verbal overshadowing through visual retrieval cues. *Journal of Experimental Psychology: Learning, Memory, and Cognition, 23*, 915–931.

Brigham, J. C., & Malpass, R. S. (1985). The role of experience and contact in the recognition of faces of own- and other-race persons. *Journal of Social Issues, 41*(3), 139–155.

Brown, C., & Lloyd-Jones, T. J. (2002). Verbal overshadowing in a multiple face presentation paradigm: Effects of description instruction. *Applied Cognitive Psychology, 16*, 873–885.

Brown, C., & Lloyd-Jones, T. J. (2003). Verbal overshadowing of multiple face and car recognition: Effects of within- versus across-category verbal descriptions. *Applied Cognitive Psychology, 17*(2), 183–202.

Coin, C., & Tiberghien, C. (1997). Encoding activity and face recognition. *Memory, 5*(5), 545–568.

Diamond, R., & Carey, S. (1986). Why faces are and are not special: An effect of expertise. *Journal of Experimental Psychology: General, 115*, 107–117.

Dodson, C. S., Johnson, M. K., & Schooler, J. W. (1997). The verbal overshadowing effect: Why descriptions impair face recognition. *Memory and Cognition, 25*, 129–139.

Dunning, D., & Stern, L. B. (1994). Distinguishing accurate from inaccurate eyewitness identifications via inquiries about decision processes. *Journal of Personality and Social Psychology, 67*, 818–835.

Ellis, H. D., & Deregowski, J. B. (1981). Within-race and between-race recognition of transformed and untransformed faces. *American Journal of Psychology, 94*, 27–35.

Ellis, H. D., Deregowski, J. B., & Shepherd, J. W. (1975). Descriptions of white and black faces by white and black subjects. *International Journal of Psychology, 10*, 119–123.

Fallshore, M., & Schooler, J. W. (1995). Verbal vulnerability of perceptual expertise. *Journal of Experimental Psychology: Learning, Memory, and Cognition, 21*, 1608–1623.

Hanley, J. R., Pearson, N. A., & Howard, L. A. (1990). The effects of different types of encoding task on memory for famous faces and names. *Quarterly Journal of Experimental Psychology, 42A*(4), 741–762.

Lloyd-Jones, T. J., Brown, C., & Clarke, S. (2006). Verbal overshadowing of perceptual discrimination. *Psychonomic Bulletin and Review, 13*(2), 269–274.

Macrae, C. N., & Lewis, H. L. (2002). Do I know you? Processing orientation and face recognition. *Psychological Science, 13*(2), 194–196.

Melcher, J. M., & Schooler, J. W. (1996). The misremembrance of wines past: Verbal and perceptual expertise differentially mediate verbal overshadowing of taste memory. *Journal of Memory and Language, 35*, 231–245.

Morris, C. D., Brandsford, J. D., & Franks, J. J. (1977). Level of processing versus transfer-appropriate processing. *Journal of Verbal Learning and Verbal Behavior, 16*, 519–533.

Navon, D. (1977). Forest before trees: The precedence of global features in visual perception. *Cognitive Psychology, 9*, 353–383.

Perfect, T. J. (2003). Local processing bias impairs line-up performance. *Psychological Reports, 93*, 393–394.

Perfect, T. J., Hunt, L. J., & Harris, C. M. (2002). Verbal overshadowing in voice recognition. *Applied Cognitive Psychology, 16*, 973–980.

Rhodes, G., Brake, S., Taylor, K., & Tan, S. (1989). Expertise and holistic coding in face recognition. *British Journal of Psychology, 80*, 313–331.

Roediger, H. L., III. (1990). Implicit memory: Retention without remembering. *The American Psychologist, 45*, 1043–1056.

Ryan, R. S., & Schooler, J. W. (1998). Whom do words hurt? Individual differences in the susceptibility to verbal overshadowing. *Applied Cognitive Psychology, 12*, S105–S125.

Schooler, J. W. (2002). Verbalization produces a transfer inappropriate processing shift. *Applied Cognitive Psychology, 16*, 989–998.

Schooler, J. W., & Engstler-Schooler, T. Y. (1990). Verbal overshadowing of visual memories: Some things are better left unsaid. *Cognitive Psychology, 22*, 36–71.

Tanaka, J. W., & Farah, M. J. (1993). Parts and wholes in face recognition. *Quarterly Journal of Experimental Psychology, 46A*, 225–245.

Thompson, P. (1980). Margaret Thatcher: A new illusion. *Perception, 9*, 483–484.

Wells, G. L., & Hryciw, B. (1984). Memory for faces: Encoding and retrieval operations. *Memory and Cognition, 12*(4), 338–344.

Westerman, D. L., & Larsen, J. D. (1997). Verbal overshadowing effect: Evidence for a general shift in processing. *American Journal of Psychology, 110*(3), 417–428.

Weston, N. J., & Perfect, T. J. (2005). Effects of processing bias on the recognition of composite face halves. *Psychonomic Bulletin and Review, 12*(6), 1038–1042.

Yin, R. K. (1969). Looking at upside-down faces. *Journal of Experimental Psychology, 81*(1), 141–145.

Young, A. W., Hellawell, D., & Hay, D. C. (1987). Holistic information in face perception. *Perception, 16*, 747–759.

EUROPEAN JOURNAL OF COGNITIVE PSYCHOLOGY
2008, 20 (3), 612–631

Verbal overshadowing in visual imagery is due to recoding interference

Maria A. Brandimonte and Simona Collina
Università Suor Orsola Benincasa, Naples, Italy

Verbal overshadowing reflects the impairment in memory performance following verbalisation of nonverbal stimuli. A recent debate has concerned the mechanisms that govern the verbal overshadowing phenomenon in different domains. In the present paper, we explore the dynamics of verbal overshadowing in the imagery domain, by manipulating the presence of visual and verbal cues at retrieval. In particular, the role of self-generated names as retrieval cues was investigated to contrast the Transfer-Inappropriate Processing (TIP) and the Recoding Interference (RI) accounts of verbal overshadowing. Results from three experiments revealed that verbal overshadowing in visual imagery can be attenuated by any cues (visual or verbal) that trigger the activation of featural representations necessary to complete an image transformation task. Counterintuitively, like visual cues, self-generated common nouns, but not proper nouns or nonwords, significantly improved visual imagery performance, hence supporting a recoding interference account of VO.

It has long been known that verbalising visual stimuli can interfere with subsequent memory performance (Bahrick & Boucher, 1968; Carmichael, Hogan, & Walter, 1932; Nelson & Brooks, 1973). More recently, this effect has been termed *verbal overshadowing* (Schooler & Engstler-Schooler, 1990) and, although it has occasionally proved difficult to replicate, since the influential paper by Schooler and Engstler-Schooler (1990) it has been documented in many different domains of nonverbal cognition known to rely on nonverbal knowledge. In fact, while the focus of the research has largely been in examining the overshadowing effect within the face

Correspondence should be addressed to Maria A. Brandimonte, Laboratory of Experimental Psychology, Università degli Studi Suor Orsola Benincasa, Via Suor Orsola, 10, 80134 Naples, Italy. E-mail: maria.brandimonte@unisob.na.it

This research was supported by a USOB grant (2004) to Maria A. Brandimonte. The present results were presented at the Symposium on Verbalizing Visual Memories at the BBCS conference, Montreal, Canada, July 2005. We are grateful to Lucia Maione for data collection and to Peter Walker for his helpful comments and suggestions at the initial stages of the research.

http://www.psypress.com/ecp DOI: 10.1080/09541440701728441

recognition paradigm, the basic phenomenon has also been observed when participants attempt to verbalise other types of visual stimuli such as colors (Schooler & Engstler-Schooler, 1990), abstract shapes (Brandimonte, Schooler, & Gabbino, 1997), spatial environments (Fiore & Schooler (2002), or even with nonvisual tasks such as wine tasting (Melcher & Schooler, 1996), insight problem-solving (Schooler, Ohlsson, & Brooks, 1993), decision making (Wilson & Schooler, 1991), voice recognition (Perfect, Hunt, & Harris, 2002), music recognition (Houser et al., unpublished manuscript, cited in Schooler, 2002), and discrimination of analogies (Lane & Schooler, 2004).

To date, two major theoretical explanations exist for verbal overshadowing. Compelling evidence exists in support of each of the primary accounts, yet no single explanation can accommodate all of the extant findings. As already noticed by several researchers in the field, multiple mechanisms may be involved and more than one form of VO may exist (Meissner, Sporer, & Schooler, 2007; Schooler, Fiore, & Brandimonte, 1997).

The first account goes under the rubric of *recoding interference* (RI, or retrieval-based interference, RBI) and suggests that VO corresponds to the dominance of the verbal trace over a visual trace at the time of retrieval. The recoding interference explanation was initially proposed by Schooler and Engstler-Schooler (1990) in the face recognition domain and by Brandimonte et al. (1997; see also Schooler et al., 1997) in the imagery domain. More recently, it has been formally elaborated by Meissner, Brigham, and Kelley (2001) in the face recognition domain, following the findings of a study in which they manipulated the nature of people's verbalisation.

Contrary to some recent interpretations (e.g., Clare & Lewandowski, 2004), one of the central predictions of the original recoding interference account of verbal overshadowing is that "verbalisation does not reduce the amount of visual information that is encoded, but rather interferes with subjects' use of the visual code" (p. 39). According to this interpretation, verbalisation produces a verbally biased representation that overshadows but does not eradicate the original visual memory, thereby excluding any alteration of the original memory trace. This was termed "the accessibility assumption" and implies that, under appropriate conditions, verbal interference should be alleviated, hence allowing the use of the original visual information. In accordance with this prediction, Brandimonte et al. (1997) found that VO of mental image manipulation can be reduced by reintroducing visual cues (e.g., colour of the background) present at encoding.

Another fundamental prediction of the recoding interference account is that there should be a relationship between the quality of the verbal descriptions and recognition performance. Occasionally this correlation has proved difficult to replicate. However, a meta-analysis by Meissner and Brigham (2001) showed that when participants are encouraged to guess or are forced to provide a detailed description, even when uncertain (recently called "elaborative description"; see Clare & Lewandowski, 2004), the size of the VO effect is much greater than when participants are discouraged from guessing, hence explaining the selective presence and absence of the correlation between description quality and identification accuracy by means of the type of descriptions encouraged at retrieval. Although the recoding interference account can explain most of the extant findings across different domains, the failure to find a systematic relationship between verbalisation quality and visual performance may be problematic for this account (see Meissner et al., 2007, for a similar view).

The second major explanation of VO is known as the Transfer-Inappropriate Processing Shift (TIPS). According to Schooler and colleagues (Lane & Schooler, 2005; Schooler, 2002; Schooler et al., 1997), the interference caused by the verbalisation of visual stimuli in the domain of face recognition is due to a switching over from nonverbal to verbal processes. More specifically, the TIPS hypothesis, which refined the former Transfer-Inappropriate Retrieval (TIR) account (Schooler et al., 1997) in that it reduced emphasis on the retrieval aspects, proposes that verbal overshadowing in face recognition involves a general processing shift from non verbal to verbal operations (Lane & Schooler, 2004; Schooler, 2002). Activation of the verbal processes required for the description inhibits the subsequent application of nonverbal face recognition processes. Accordingly, verbal overshadowing occurs because "verbalisation induces inappropriate processing operations which, when carried over at the time of test, are incommensurate with the processes required for successful recognition performance" (Schooler, 2002, p. 992). In Meissner et al.'s (2007, p. 24) words, "verbal description causes participants to become 'stuck' in a verbal mode of processing faces, which is then applied (inappropriately transferred) to the recognition test, resulting in disruption". Several other studies (Brown & Lloyd-Jones, 2002, 2003; Dodson, Johnson, & Schooler, 1997) supported the TIPS hypothesis on the basis of the observation that verbal overshadowing often extends beyond the particular stimulus that is verbalised, a result that is hard to accommodate within a recoding interference account.

Thus, overall, the TIPS account nicely accommodates many results across different domains of visual cognition. However, it runs into some difficulties in explaining why sometimes a relationship between verbalisation quality and visual performance is observed, as well as in explaining some results in the visual imagery domain (see Schooler, 2002). In addition, within the face recognition domain, most recent studies by Brown and Lloyd-Jones (2005) documented verbal facilitation when participants described each face in a series and were later asked to recognise the *same faces* that they had previously described. The result that the facilitative effects of verbalisation are tied to the face that is described as well as the finding that for featural descriptions, the number of descriptors was positively correlated with discrimination performance, leave room for an interpretation in terms of memory representations rather than processing.

Most recently, a novel account of VO effects in the face recognition domain has been proposed (Clare & Lewandowski, 2004), which suggests that VO effects may reflect a change in recognition criterion rather than a changed processing style (TIPS) or the negative effects of recoding (RI). These authors found that verbal description of a previously presented face impaired recognition performance on suspect present lineups when participants were provided a "not present" option, but not when they were forced to select from among the faces presented. The explanation of this result is based on a shift in people's recognition criterion; that is, an increased reluctance to choose someone from the lineup. Thus, according to the *criterion shift account*, verbalisation leads witnesses to adopt a more stringent recognition criterion, thus reducing identification rates. However, a number of studies have found verbal overshadowing effects with paradigms that either did not include a "not present" option (e.g., Fallshore & Schooler, 1995) or assessed performance on target-absent lineups (e.g., Meissner, 2002). In addition, the criterion shift account cannot explain the bulk of extant evidence of VO effects in the domain of visual mental imagery, where recognition paradigms were not used.

VO effects in visual mental imagery

In the domain of visual imagery, several studies by Brandimonte and colleagues (Brandimonte & Gerbino, 1993; Brandimonte, Hitch, & Bishop, 1992a, 1992b, 1992c; Brandimonte et al., 1997; Hitch, Brandimonte, & Walker, 1995; Pelizzon, Brandimonte, & Favretto, 1999; Pelizzon, Brandimonte, & Luccio, 2002; Walker, Hitch, Dewhurst, Whiteley, & Brandimonte, 1997) have shown that the ability to manipulate visual mental images is vulnerable to the negative effects of verbalisation. The basic paradigm used by Brandimonte and colleagues involves first having participants study a set of visual forms. After participants learn the forms under either verbal or nonverbal conditions, they are given an imagery task that requires them to manipulate their visual images. For example, in one of these studies (Brandimonte et al., 1992b), participants were asked to mentally rotate the forms and identify, in their mind's eye, the constituent letters contained in the rotated forms. The standard result from these studies is that individuals' ability to successfully complete the memory-based imagery task critically depends on whether the prior encoding conditions encouraged or discouraged verbalisation. Under conditions in which verbal recoding of visual stimuli occurs (e.g., with easy-to-name forms or labelled hard-to-name forms), visual imagery performance is impaired relative to conditions in which verbal recoding is discouraged (e.g., with articulatory suppression or with unlabelled hard-to-name forms). To summarise, different manipulations can either induce or counteract verbal overshadowing in mental imagery. In particular, verbal overshadowing is fostered by easy nameability of the stimuli or by labels assigned to otherwise hard-to-name figures. However, it is prevented by articulatory suppression at encoding and released by the introduction of appropriate cues at retrieval (Brandimonte et al., 1992a, 1992b, 1997; Pelizzon et al., 2002).

Taken together, the data gathered by Brandimonte and colleagues (Brandimonte et al., 1997; Pelizzon et al., 2002) seem to indicate that in imagery tasks, verbal overshadowing is due to a conflict between representations, the assumption being that verbal recoding encourages the formation of a visual representation corresponding to the stimulus verbal label which, in turn, can influence performance at the time of retrieval.

This view is supported by considerable research demonstrating that the use of verbal labels during encoding systematically influences subsequent memory performance such that subjects tend to emphasise details consistent with the label and deemphasise information inconsistent with the label (e.g., Carmichael et al., 1932; Daniel, 1972; see also Meissner & Brigham, 2001, and Meissner & Memon, 2002, in the face recognition domain). The exact nature of this representational shift, however, is far from being clear. What is it about verbalisation that impairs imagery performance? Is the verbal overshadowing effect observed in imagery tasks different from that observed with the face recognition paradigm?

A face is a very special stimulus. It is encoded as a single unit and, when visualised, it is activated all of a piece (Kosslyn, 1994, p. 305). Accordingly, global processing should favour face recognition, whereas featural processing should not. Recent research (Macrae & Lewis, 2002) has investigated this issue and concluded that it is not verbalisation per se that impairs face recognition; rather it is the shift from global to local processing that disrupts recognition accuracy by inducing a featural strategy. In contrast, multipart images are encoded by inspecting individual parts as well as the spatial relations among them. These images are then formed starting with a global image and then adding the details (Kosslyn, 1994). Because the initial global image does not contain all information, if one needs high resolution parts to manipulate the image, additional elaboration is necessary and the exact features must be activated (Kosslyn, 1994). Accordingly, featural representations should favour image transformations, while global, configural representations should not. Thus, if one takes into account the featural/global distinction as related to representations, it appears that face recognition and image transformation processes benefit from different (may be opposite) types of representation. Though there is some support to this claim (Pelizzon et al., 1999), to date, this intuition has not been directly related to the featural/global and verbal/nonverbal dichotomies. In fact, the way in which these dichotomies have been associated with one another in the VO literature is somewhat unclear (see General Discussion).

According to the recoding interference hypothesis developed in previous work (e.g., Brandimonte et al., 1992a, 1992b, 1997; Pelizzon et al., 1999) and more directly tested here, verbal overshadowing in mental imagery is more than verbal. In fact, it reflects a transition from featural to global *visual* representations *by means* of verbalisation. In this view, verbalisation fosters the use of the visuospatial representations that are more closely related to verbal material (Kosslyn, 1994, p. 298; Paivio, 1986). However, "verbalisation" is a label for a wide class of phenomena that may differ markedly from one another. Consider, for example, picture naming. It is well known that people name pictures more quickly when the name has a higher frequency of occurrence in the language (Oldfield & Wingfield, 1965) and when the pictured objects are familiar rather than unfamiliar (Jolicoeur, 1985). Moreover, they tend to name pictures of familiar objects spontaneously, while viewing them (Brandimonte et al., 1992a, 1992b; Mazard, Laou, Joliot, & Mellet, 2005). Thus, if one not only encounters the name frequently but also sees the object frequently, their joint representations become more accessible in associative memory (Kosslyn, 1994). These mechanisms imply that when people are presented with easy-to-name (familiar) pictures, they make no effort to find a name (which is automatically accessed in associative memory) and that name is sufficient to later generate a global, prototypical image that will prove inappropriate if the imagery task requires featural manipulations. Analogously, it appears that a global image is formed when people are presented with labelled hard-to-name figures and the names for the figures are not generated by the participants, but chosen on the basis of "objective" criteria (e.g., independent judges' agreement on a name) (Brandimonte et al., 1992a, 1992b). However, the mechanisms of picture naming and their effects on the nature of imagery representations are presumably different if, rather than providing people with labels, participants are required to generate names for hard-to-name pictures. In fact, it has been shown that object naming is greatly impaired if parts or arbitrarily determined fragments are in unusual positions (Cave & Kosslyn, 1993) because the initial input does not match a stored representation of an object and its name. However, individual parts can be matched and, possibly, named (de Winter & Wagemans, 2006). Indeed, when people look at objects, they often spontaneously segment them into parts and then use these parts as perceptual units to determine object encoding and subsequent recognition (Barenholtz & Feldman, 2003; Bertamini & Farrant, 2005; Biederman, 1987; Hoffman & Richards, 1984).

The present study is a first attempt to explore the dynamics of visual image verbal overshadowing by means of verbal cues. In particular, we know nothing about the fate of visual representations and of VO when the names associated with hard-to-name figures are self-generated by the participants and the same names are then used as retrieval cues. Extending research on the above general topics, we reasoned that when required to generate a name for hard-to-name pictures people may find it difficult to come up with a name or a category for the whole object. They may then allocate attention to specific parts or characteristics that they consider as "relevant portions" of the figure, and find a satisfactory name for the figure, based on those parts, but then extended to the whole picture (de Winter & Wagemans, 2006). The extraction of such parts requires a visual routine based on a serial algorithm (Ullman, 1979/1984), which may allow, at retrieval, high spatial resolution necessary to discern the stimulus structure. It should be noted, however, that the resulting representation does not carry per se information on the specific exemplar, though it contains specific subrepresentations of parsed regions that might work as effective cues for the featural representation of the whole picture, if they are reactivated at retrieval. According to this reasoning, a necessary condition for such a reactivation is that the cue at retrieval matches the memory trace of parts or characteristics of the representation as they have been encoded (Thomson & Tulving, 1970; Tulving & Thomson, 1973). Counterintuitively, for the mechanisms outlined above, such a cue should be the self-generated name associated to each hard-to-name figure.

A first issue addressed in Experiment 1 is therefore whether verbal overshadowing occurs when the names for the hard-to-name forms are self-generated and no cue is provided at retrieval. A related, most important, question is whether—provided verbal overshadowing effects are observed—a self-generated name can work as an effective retrieval cue in attenuating verbal overshadowing by reactivating the subrepresentations of parts and characteristics associated at encoding with the name.

From a Transfer-Inappropriate Processing Shift view (Schooler, 2002), when no cue is present, verbal overshadowing should occur because of the processing shift fostered by verbalisation from nonverbal to verbal processing. However, re-presenting the name the participant has generated at encoding should in no way determine release from verbal overshadowing, because of the verbal nature of the cue.

Predictions are different if the verbal overshadowing effects observed in the imagery domain are due to a representational shift caused by verbal recoding. In particular, it is predicted that, in the absence of any cue, naming a hard-to-name figure should not be sufficient per se to induce, at retrieval, the generation of an image of the specific exemplar so as to prevent verbal overshadowing. Therefore, this view too predicts verbal overshadowing in the no cue condition. However, re-presenting the name self-generated by the participant should help reactivate the subrepresentations of portions of the stimulus associated with the name, hence producing a shift to featural representations and consequently attenuating verbal overshadowing (as measured by a higher performance in the presence of the self-generated-name cue).

In Experiment 2, the self-generation hypothesis was contrasted with a context reinstatement hypothesis and tested through the introduction of labels at encoding that were then used as retrieval cues at test. To the extent that only self-generated verbal cues help reactivate the features of the visual stimulus associated with each name, in Experiment 2, no beneficial effects of re-presenting the labels at retrieval should emerge.

Finally, in Experiment 3, we examined whether the beneficial effect of representing at retrieval self-generated verbal stimuli is specific to objects names or it is apparent with any self-generated words (e.g., proper nouns) and/or with nonwords. Indeed, a recoding interference account of verbal overshadowing would predict an improvement in visual imagery performance only with self-generated object names but not with self-generated proper nouns or with self-generated nonwords.

EXPERIMENT 1

Method

Participants learned hard-to-name line drawings that were drawn on coloured cards. After studying the shapes visually, they were asked to find a name for each shape. Participants were then asked to complete a mental rotation task and to discover the letters compounding each shape (Brandimonte et al., 1992b). Just before performing the mental rotation and discovery task, participants were presented with the following cues, according to conditions: (a) the colour of the card on which each picture was drawn, (b) the name generated by the participant for each correspondent picture, (c) a name generated by others, (d) a name generated by others and the colour of the card; or (e) the self-generated name and the colour of the card. A sixth group of participants (control condition) performed only the imagery task, without receiving any retrieval cue. In accordance with prior results, we expected verbal overshadowing effects in the no cue condition. However, as originally reported by Brandimonte et al. (1992b, 1997), if the long-term visual representations used in mental imagery can preserve surface characteristics, then re-presenting the colour of the card (a visual cue) on which the figure was drawn should allow the participant to contact their intact visual representation, hence attenuating verbal overshadowing. The manipulation of interest in the present research was, however, the introduction of self-generated names as retrieval cues. We predicted that, when used as cues, the names generated by the participant should help reactivate the subrepresentations of portions of the stimulus associated with them, hence improving imagery performance. No such improvement should be observed when names generated by other participants are used as retrieval cues. Finally, the conditions in which the visual and the verbal cues were both present served as further controls for additive effects.

Participants and design. One hundred and twenty undergraduates at Università Suor Orsola Benincasa (USOB), Naples, participated in this experiment as volunteers. Verbal and visual cues at retrieval were provided in a 3 (self-generated verbal cue, others generated verbal cue, no verbal cue) × 2 (presence vs. absence of visual cues) between-participants design. The dependent variable was accuracy in a rotation and discovery imagery task.

Procedure and stimulus material. The procedure for the image rotation task was modelled after Brandimonte et al. (1992b). Participants were asked to memorise a series of six hard-to-name figures drawn on cards having different colours, which were presented at a rate of 5 s per picture, for a total of three presentations (Figure 1). Pilot work with an independent group of participants had shown that 90 s was a sufficient time for participants to memorise all six figures with 100% accuracy (see Brandimonte et al., 1992a, 1992b).

Participants were not forewarned about the task they would be requested to perform thereafter, so as reduce the possibility that they might spontaneously rotate the stimuli during acquisition. Pictures were displayed face down in a row on a table in front of the participant with the experimenter sitting at the opposite side. Presentation of the stimuli was fully randomised across participants. Immediately after learning, participants were asked to check, in their mind, whether they could remember the members of the series exactly in the order in which they had learned them. All participants reported that they could do so. Each figure was then showed again for 1 s, and the participants were asked to find a name for each shape. A practice trial in the mental rotation task followed the naming phase. After practice, participants were requested to form a mental image of the first picture, to mentally rotate it 90% counterclockwise, and to identify and report the two capital letters compounding the original stimulus. Just before performing the mental rotation and discovery task, each participant was

Figure 1. Examples of the stimuli used in the experiments.

presented with the cues, according to conditions. After naming the two letters, he/she was asked to form an image of the second stimulus, and so on. Participants were given as much time as they needed.

Six independent judges rated the goodness of the names given by the participants on a 4-point scale. Three of them were asked to evaluate whether the names were appropriate for the whole figure, while three were required to evaluate whether the names were appropriate for any of the parts of the figure. For example, suppose the two stimuli illustrated in Figure 1 were named as "roof" and "main door", respectively. The judges' task was to evaluate how well the names matched either the whole figure or any of its parts.

Results and discussion

Scoring reflected the number of letters correctly identified in mental imagery (0, 1, 2, max. 12). Figure 2 shows the results for performance in the rotation task, expressed as the proportion of letters correctly identified in the imagery task. A two-way ANOVA by items showed an effect of verbal cue type, $F(2, 10) = 10.512$, $p = .0035$, $MSE = 0.103$, an effect of visual cue, $F(1, 5) = 22.839$, $p = .005$, $MSE = 0.326$, and an interaction between verbal and visual cue, $F(2, 10) = 10.46$, $p = .0035$, $MSE = 0.104$.

Planned comparisons revealed that imagery performance was higher in the visual cue condition than in the no cue condition, $F(1, 5) = 49.176$, $p = .0001$, hence replicating previous results in the literature (Brandimonte et al., 1997). Analogously, imagery performance was higher in the self-generated

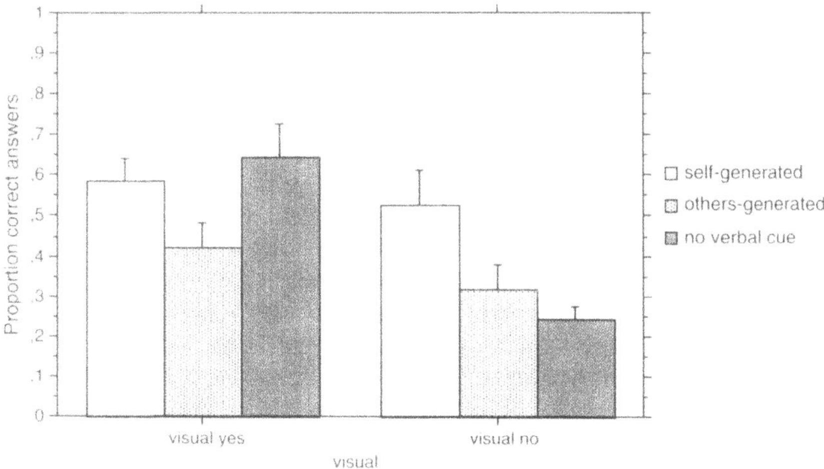

Figure 2. Proportion of correct answers in the imagery task as a function of type of retrieval cues in Experiment 1.

name condition than in the no cue condition, $F(1, 5) = 24.167$, $p = .0006$. Most important, imagery performance was significantly better when the self-generated names were given as retrieval cues rather than when the names given by other participants were re-presented as cues, $F(1, 5) = 12.5492$, $p = .0053$. Interestingly, the simultaneous presence of visual and self-generated cues did not improve performance as compared to the self-generated cue condition. In contrast, participants performed significantly worse when the visual and the others generated cue were both present than when the visual and the self-generated cue were present, $F(1, 5) = 7.95$, $p = .018$.

An additional analysis was carried out on the relationship between quality of the names (as rated by the judges) and imagery performance. There was no correlation, $r = .15$, between the quality of the names—as related to the whole figure—and imagery performance (interrater reliability was higher than 95%). However, a positive correlation was found between imagery performance and the quality of the names as related to parts of the figure, $r = .26$, $p = .017$.

In the imagery domain, the disruptive effect of naming nonverbal memories plausibly derives from the formation of a verbally recoded memory representation that interferes with access to the original memory (Meissner, 2002; Meissner et al., 2001; Pelizzon et al., 2002). Results from Experiment 1 support the recoding interference account in that re-presenting the names generated by the participant improved imagery performance. From a Transfer-Inappropriate retrieval account, no benefit of re-presenting a verbal cue at retrieval should be observed because, according to this view, engaging in retrieval processes that emphasised one class of operations (i.e., verbal) but not another (i.e., nonverbal) may inhibit the deemphasised operations on subsequent retrieval attempts (Schooler, 2002, p. 991).

One of the central predictions of a recoding interference account of verbal overshadowing is that there should be a relationship between the quality of the verbal description and performance. Although it is difficult to ascribe verbal overshadowing effects to the poor quality of verbal descriptions when no relationship between description quality and visual performance is observed, it seems quite plausible that inaccurate verbal descriptions may contribute to verbal overshadowing by inducing the use of a global representation when a relationship between verbal descriptions and performance is observed (see Schooler, 2002). Correlational data from Experiment 1 strongly support the recoding interference hypothesis, in that the poorer the quality of the names given to the visual forms on the basis of their relevant parts, the worse the performance in the imagery task (see also Meissner & Brigham, 2001). Importantly, no such correlation was found when the names reflected the whole figure, replicating previous results in the literature and providing even stronger support to the present analysis of the implications of the recoding interference account.

Theoretically, the results of Experiment 1, while clearly in accordance with the retrieval based, recoding interference view, do not disentangle the self-generation hypothesis from a hypothesis based on context reinstatement. In fact, in Experiment 1, those participants who received their self-generated names as retrieval cues were also the only participants who saw the same verbal stimulus at encoding and at retrieval. To evaluate this issue, we conducted Experiment 2. If only self-generated verbal cues can help reactivate the visual stimulus associated with each name, in Experiment 2, no beneficial effects of re-presenting the labels at retrieval should emerge.

EXPERIMENT 2

Method

Participants and design. One hundred and twenty undergraduates at USOB, Naples, participated in this experiment as volunteers. The design was a 2 (labels vs. self-generation at encoding) × 3 (labels, self-generated names, no cue at retrieval) between-participants design.

Procedure. Participants performed the same imagery task as in Experiment 1, with the modification that, at learning, either labels representing names of the pictures were applied below each shape (see Brandimonte et al., 1992b, Exp. 2) or participants were asked to generate a name for each shape, as in Experiment 1. The labels were chosen from the list obtained by Brandimonte et al. (1992b) through a nameability agreement test. Those names that obtained the highest percentage of agreement on a single name were used as labels.

At retrieval, either the label or the self-generated name were used as cues and crossed by encoding conditions in order to obtain "same name" versus "different name" retrieval conditions. The no cue conditions served as control. It should be noticed that when names different from encoding were given to participants at retrieval, the names were simply names generated by others, hence replicating some of the conditions of Experiment 1, namely, the others generated conditions. Three independent judges were required to evaluate, on a 4-point scale, whether the names were appropriate for any of the parts of the figure.

Results and discussion

As in Experiment 1, scoring reflected the number of letters correctly identified in mental imagery (0, 1, 2, max. 12). A two-way ANOVA by items revealed an effect of generation at encoding, $F(1, 5) = 8.12$, $p = .035$,

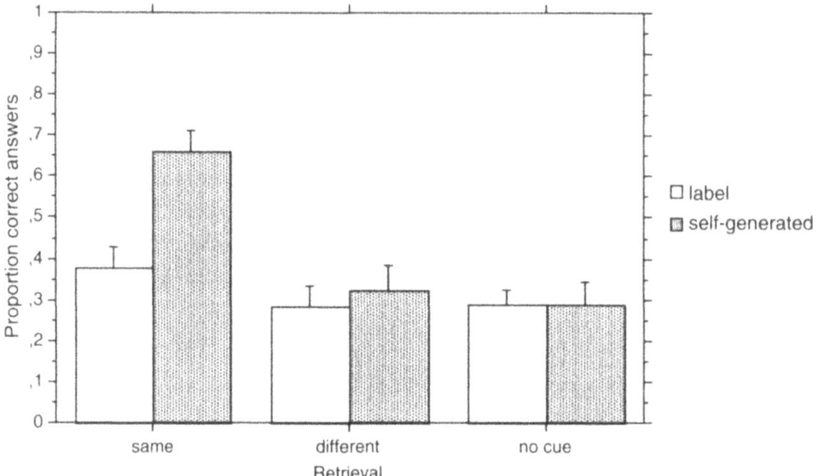

Figure 3. Proportion of correct answers in the imagery task as a function of self-generation and type of retrieval cues in Experiment 2.

$MSE = 0.013$, an effect of type of cue, $F(2, 10) = 37.25$, $p = .0001$, $MSE =$ 0.005, and an interaction between encoding and retrieval conditions, $F(2, 10) = 17.73$, $p = .0005$, $MSE = 0.004$ (Figure 3), with a beneficial effect of verbal cues only when self-generated names were re-presented at retrieval. Planned comparisons showed a significant difference between same label and same self-generated names re-presentation at retrieval, $F(1, 5) = 60.84$, $p = .0001$). Re-presenting the label used at encoding had no effect whatsoever on imagery performance in all cue conditions (all Fs < 1).

Once again, a positive correlation was found between imagery performance and the quality of the names *as related to parts* of the figure, $r = .38$. Interrater reliability was higher than 90%.

The pattern of results that emerged from Experiment 2 clearly rules out the hypothesis that the beneficial effect of re-presenting the names participants had self-generated might be due to context reinstatement. In fact, the most important result here is the interaction between encoding and retrieval conditions showing that while re-presenting the same label participants had viewed at encoding had no beneficial effect on imagery performance, re-presenting their self-generated names greatly improved mental image manipulation.

EXPERIMENT 3

Having established that it is not re-presentation per se that causes release from VO, in Experiment 3, we examined whether the beneficial effect of re-presenting at retrieval self-generated verbal stimuli is specific to objects names or it is apparent with any self-generated words (e.g., proper nouns) and/or with nonwords. We reasoned that a recoding interference account of verbal overshadowing would predict an improvement in visual imagery performance only with self-generated object names but not with self-generated proper nouns or with self-generated nonwords. Indeed, if verbal overshadowing in visual imagery is mediated by a verbally biased, global representation, which nonetheless maintains some correspondence with the original stimulus (Schooler & Engstler-Schooler, 1990, p. 62), then the higher the correspondence of the name with characteristics of the original stimulus (as indicated by the positive correlation found in previous experiments), the more likely their effectiveness as cues that may attenuate verbal overshadowing. No such improvement should be expected with other types of verbalisation (proper nouns and nonwords), even though they are self-generated by the participant.

Method

Participants and design. One hundred and eighty undergraduates at USOB, Naples, participated in this experiment as volunteers. The design was a 3 (common nouns, proper nouns, nonwords, at encoding) × 4 (visual cue, same, different, no cue, at retrieval) between-participants design.

Procedure. Participants performed the same imagery task as in previous experiments, with the modification that, at learning, participants were asked to generate either a common noun (e.g., "roof" as in Experiments 1 and 2), a proper noun (e.g., Maria, Giovanni, etc.), or a nonword to be associated to each figure. For the nonwords, there were two constraints: (a) each nonword had to contain three syllables in a consonant/vowel/consonant/vowel structure, so as to produce pronounceable strings (e.g., sarofa); (b) the string should not result from the substitution of a single letter in a word (for example, *badana* from *banana*). Participants were briefly trained on this. Postexperimental interviews showed that no participant found nonword generation difficult to perform. At retrieval, either the same name/string, a different name/string, or a visual cue was presented. The no cue conditions served as control.

Results and discussion

As before, scoring reflected the number of letters correctly identified in mental imagery (0, 1, 2, max. 12). A two-way ANOVA by items revealed an effect of type of generation at encoding, $F(2, 10) = 29.69$, $p = .0001$, $MSE = 0.038$, an effect of type of cue, $F(3, 15) = 102.72$, $p = .0001$, $MSE = 0.007$,

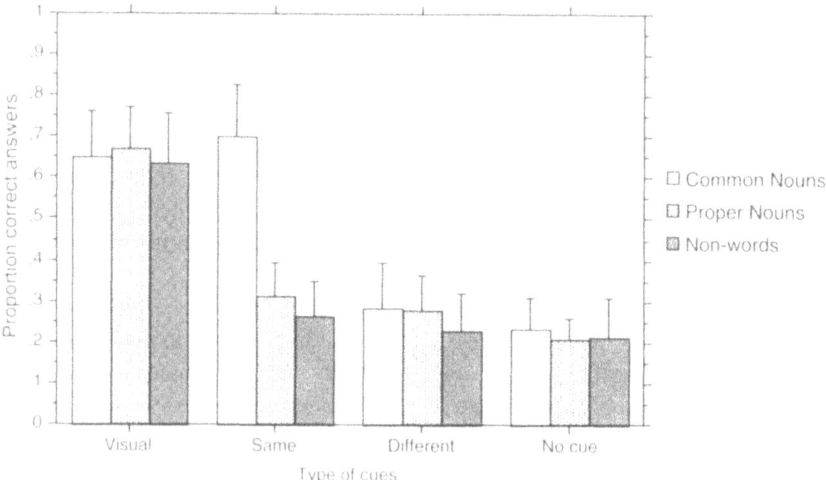

Figure 4. Proportion of correct answers in the imagery task as a function of type of naming and type of cues in Experiment 3.

and an interaction between encoding and retrieval conditions, $F(6, 30) = 21.46$, $p = .0001$, $MSE = 0.004$ (Figure 4), with a beneficial effect of verbal cues only when the same self-generated common nouns were re-presented at retrieval. As expected, re-presenting a visual cue released VO in all three verbalisation conditions. Planned comparisons showed a significant difference between the "same common name" condition and all the remaining retrieval conditions (all $ps < .0001$), which, in turn, did not differ from one another (all $Fs < 1$).

This experiment aimed to investigate the effect of verbal and nonverbal retrieval cues on imagery performance following self-generation of common nouns, proper nouns, and nonwords to be associated to hard-to-name figures at encoding. The manipulation of interest here was the re-presentation, at retrieval, of the same names/nonwords participant had generated at encoding, to establish whether any self-generated verbal cue may facilitate image manipulation for the mere fact that the name/letter string has been associated, at encoding, with the specific picture. Results clearly indicate that this is not the case and add some important refinements to the picture emerging from Experiments 1 and 2. In fact, it appears that self-generation per se is not enough to make the generated string a good retrieval cue, as neither self-generated proper nouns nor self-generated nonwords improved visual imagery performance. Rather, in order to be as an effective cue as a visual cue, the verbal cue has to maintain some correspondence with the object features (e.g., with some of its parts). Interestingly, in the control, no cue conditions, performance was equally low under common nouns, proper nouns, and nonwords, hence indicating that nonwords generation, like proper nouns generation, produces VO by means of an inappropriate verbal label (the nonword), associated to the figure, which interferes with the retrieval of the original figure. However, re-presenting the proper nouns or the nonwords generated at encoding is not sufficient to alleviate VO. On the other hand, re-presenting the self-generated figure's name produces the same beneficial effect on imagery performance as re-presenting the colour of the figure's background (i.e., the visual cue).

If one accepts the core assumption of the recoding interference account, i.e., that verbalisation fosters the use of the visuospatial representations that are more closely related to verbal material, then the logical implication—supported by the present results—is that the more verbalisation reflects features of the stimulus, the more the verbal material can be used as an effective cue for the retrieval of the original visual memory and the higher the correlation between quality of verbalisation and performance. On the other hand, the farther verbalisation from the characteristics of the original stimulus, the less verbal material can be used as a retrieval cue and the lower the correlation between quality of verbalisation and performance.

GENERAL DISCUSSION

The aim of the present research was to investigate the dynamics of verbal overshadowing in the imagery domain, by manipulating the nature of stimulus processing at encoding and the presence of visual and verbal cues at retrieval. In particular, we explored the role of self-generated names as retrieval cues to contrast the Transfer-Inappropriate Processing (TIP) and the Recoding Interference (RI) accounts of verbal overshadowing. Results from three experiments strongly support a retrieval-based, recoding interference account of verbal overshadowing in that re-presenting, at retrieval, the figure's name generated by the participant at encoding improved imagery performance, hence attenuating VO. No other self-generated verbal material alleviated VO if re-presented at retrieval. Most important, a positive correlation was found between imagery performance and the quality of the names *as related to parts* of the figure. In this perspective, the impairment in imagery performance documented in the literature under verbalisation conditions can be plausibly attributed to an inappropriate representational shift from featural to global representations via verbal recoding of the original picture. From a Transfer-Inappropriate Processing Shift view, re-presenting the name the participant has generated at encoding should in no way determine release from verbal overshadowing, because persisting in verbal processing (with the re-presentation of the figure's name) should inhibit the application of those nonverbal processes needed for completing the imagery task. In contrast, as demonstrated in the present research, verbal overshadowing in visual imagery can be attenuated by any cues (visual or verbal) that trigger the activation of featural representations, which are necessary to complete an image transformation task.

The featural/global and the verbal/nonverbal dichotomies

In accordance with previous results (Brandimonte et al., 1997), in the present paper, we showed that featural representations favour image transformations, while configural, prototypical representations do not, hence supporting the notion that face recognition and image transformation processes may rely on opposite types of representation (Pelizzon et al., 1999). We also showed that VO in visual imagery is due to a transition from featural to global/prototypical representations by means of verbalisation (naming) at encoding, which shows its effects at retrieval. Finally, the present results showed that VO effects in visual imagery can be attenuated by reactivating the featural aspects of the stimulus.

The featural/configural dichotomy has recently emerged as one explanation of VO that may reduce the role of verbalisation in the VO effects observed in face recognition (Macrae & Lewis, 2002). The present results, though in a different domain, speak against such an interpretation, as they clearly indicate that the type of representation (featural or global) used at retrieval for image transformation is mediated by the type of verbalisation generated at encoding.

Past research has posed a strong link between the featural/global and the verbal/nonverbal dichotomies, often treating them as synonyms and using the terms interchangeably (e.g., Fiore & Schooler, 2002; Schooler, 2002). In particular, because often features are easier to verbalise (e.g., Fiore & Schooler, 2002), the term "featural" has been associated with "verbal" or "propositional" and the term "global" (or "configural") has been associated with "nonverbal". However, such a correspondence may be confusing, as in the realm of visual cognition it is commonly accepted that nonverbal representations may include featural as well as global aspects. Rather, the core question is which of these aspects—and related representations—are susceptible to or fostered by verbalisation. Indeed, Fiore and Schooler (2002) found that verbalising one's memory for the route on a map impaired later performance on a measure of the configural aspects of that map (Euclidean distance estimations), while having no effect on a measure of the featural aspects (route distance estimations). Such a result hints to an explanation in terms of different forms of visuospatial *representations*, which are differentially susceptible to verbalisation. The results reported in the present paper mirror the Fiore and Schooler results in that they show that whenever the visuospatial task requires the use of the featural aspects of a hard-to-name stimulus, naming it impairs later imagery performance. However, these results also confirm that the original representation has not been eradicated by verbalisation and that with appropriate cues it can be retrieved (Brandimonte et al., 1997). The novel result, which responds to the long-standing question of whether VO in visual imagery is due to TIPS or to RI, is that re-presenting, at retrieval, the figure's name generated by the participant at encoding improved imagery performance, hence attenuating VO.

Interestingly, the self-generated figure's name typically derived from one's naming a part of the hard-to-name stimulus. Therefore, re-presenting the name self-generated by the participant fostered the reactivation of the subrepresentations of portions of the stimulus associated with the name, hence allowing retrieval of the featural representation and consequently attenuating verbal overshadowing.

CONCLUDING REMARKS

So far, the precise mechanisms responsible for the VO effect in visual imagery were somewhat unclear. We hope that the results reported in this paper can help depict a more coherent picture, which reconciles previous results in the imagery literature documenting VO, lack of the effect, and its attenuation through appropriate cues. Our findings may also have considerable practical interest as they identify some new conditions under which memory for shapes and image transformation processes can be improved. Further research along this line may contribute to our knowledge regarding the theoretical mechanisms that govern the verbal overshadowing phenomenon in this domain by identifying some boundary conditions that might define when the VO effect is due to a switching over from featural to configural *representations.*

REFERENCES

Bahrick, H. P., & Boucher, P. (1968). Retention of visual and verbal codes of the same stimuli. *Journal of Experimental Psychology, 78*, 417–422.

Barenholtz, E., & Feldman, J. (2003). Visual comparisons within and between object parts: Evidence for a single part superiority effect. *Vision Research, 43*, 1655–1666.

Bertamini, M., & Farrant, T. (2005). Detection of change in shape and its relation to part structure: An advantage for changes in part structure. *Acta Psychologica, 120*, 35–54.

Biederman, I. (1987). Recognition-by-components: A theory of human image understanding. *Psychological Review, 94*, 115–147.

Brandimonte, M. A., & Gerbino, W. (1993). Mental image reversal and verbal recoding: When ducks become rabbits. *Memory and Cognition, 21*, 23–33.

Brandimonte, M. A., Hitch, G. J., & Bishop, D. V. M. (1992a). Influence of short-term memory codes on visual image processing: Evidence from image transformation tasks. *Journal of Experimental Psychology: Learning, Memory, and Cognition, 18*, 157–165.

Brandimonte, M. A., Hitch, G. J., & Bishop, D. V. M. (1992b). Manipulation of visual mental images in children and adults. *Journal of Experimental Child Psychology, 53*, 300–312.

Brandimonte, M. A., Hitch, G. J., & Bishop, D. V. M. (1992c). Verbal recoding of visual stimuli impairs mental image transformations. *Memory and Cognition, 20*, 449–455.

Brandimonte, M. A., Schooler, J. W., & Gabbino, P. (1997). Attenuating verbal overshadowing through color retrieval cues. *Journal of Experimental Psychology: Learning, Memory, and Cognition, 23*, 915–931.

Brown, C., & Lloyd-Jones, T. J. (2002). Verbal overshadowing in a multiple face presentation paradigm: Effects of description instruction. *Applied Cognitive Psychology, 16*, 873–885.

Brown, C., & Lloyd-Jones, T. J. (2003). Verbal overshadowing of multiple face and car recognition: Effects of within- versus across-category verbal descriptions. *Applied Cognitive Psychology, 17*, 183–201.

Brown, C., & Lloyd-Jones, T. J. (2005). Verbal facilitation of face recognition. *Memory and Cognition, 33*(8), 1442–1456.

Carmichael, L., Hogan, H. P., & Walter, A. A. (1932). An experimental study of the effect of language on the reproduction of visually perceived forms. *Journal of Experimental Psychology, 15*, 73–86.

Cave, C. B., & Kosslyn, S. M. (1993). The role of parts and spatial relations in object identification. *Perception, 22*, 229–248.

Clare, J., & Lewandowski, S. (2004). Vebalizing facial memory: Criterion effects in verbal overshadowing. *Journal of Experimental Psychology: Learning, Memory, & Cognition, 30*:44, 739–755.

Daniel, T. C. (1972). Nature of the effect of verbal labels on recognition memory for forms. *Journal of Experimental Psychology, 96*, 152–157.

De Winter, J., & Wagemans, J. (2006). Segmentation of object outlines into parts: A large-scale integrative study. *Cognition, 99*, 275–325.

Dodson, C. S., Johnson, M. K., & Schooler, J. W. (1997). The verbal overshadowing effect: Why descriptions impair face recognition. *Memory and Cognition, 25*, 129–139.

Fallshore, M., & Schooler, J. W. (1995). The verbal vulnerability of perceptual expertise. *Journal of Experimental Psychology: Learning, Memory, and Cognition, 21*, 1608–1623.

Fiore, S. M., & Schooler, J. W. (2002). How did you get here from there? Verbal overshadowing of spatial mental models. *Applied Cognitive Psychology, 16*, 897–910.

Hitch, G. J., Brandimonte, M. A., & Walker, P. (1995). Two types of representation in visual memory: Evidence from the effects of stimulus contrast in image combination. *Memory and Cognition, 23*, 147–154.

Hoffman, D. D., & Richards, W. A. (1984). Parts of recognition. *Cognition, 18*, 65–96.

Jolicoeur, P. (1985). The time to name disoriented natural objects. *Memory and Cognition, 13*(4), 289–303.

Kosslyn, S. M. (1994). *Image and brain: The resolution of the imagery debate.* Cambridge, MA: MIT Press.

Lane, S. M., & Schooler, J. W. (2004). Skimming the surface: Verbal overshadowing of analogical retrieval. *Psychological Science, 15*, 715–719.

Macrae, C. N., & Lewis, H. L. (2002). Do I know you? Processing orientation and face recognition. *Psychological Science, 13*, 194–196.

Mazard, A., Laou, L., Joliot, M., & Mellet, E. (2005). Neural impact of the semantic content of visual mental images and visual percepts. *Cognitive Brain Research, 24*, 423–435.

Meissner, C. A. (2002). Applied aspects of the instructional bias effect in verbal overshadowing. *Applied Cognitive Psychology, 16*, 911–928.

Meissner, C. A., & Brigham J. C. (2001). A meta-analysis of the verbal overshadowing effect in face identification. *Applied Cognitive Psychology, 15*(6), 603–616.

Meissner, C. A., Brigham, J. C., & Kelley, C. M. (2001). The influence of retrieval processes in verbal overshadowing. *Memory & Cognition, 29*, 176–186.

Meissner, C. A., & Memon, A. (2002). Verbal overshadowing: A special issue exploring theoretical and applied issues. *Applied Cognitive Psychology, 16*, 869–872.

Meissner, C. A., Sporer, S. L., & Schooler, J. W. (2007). Person descriptions as eyewitness evidence. In R. Lindsay, D. Ross, J. Read, & M. Toglia (Eds.), *Handbook of eyewitness psychology: Memory for people.* Lawrence Erlbaum and Associates.

Melcher, J. M., & Schooler, J. W. (1996). The misremembrance of wines past: Verbal and perceptual expertise differentially mediate verbal overshadowing of taste memory. *Journal of Memory and Language, 35*, 231–245.

Nelson, D. L., & Brooks, D. H. (1973). Functional independence of pictures and their verbal memory codes. *Journal of Experimental Psychology, 98*(1), 44–48.

Oldfield, R. C., & Wingfield, A. (1965). Response latencies in naming objects. *Quarterly Journal of Experimental Psychology, 17*, 273–281.

Paivio, A. (1986). *Mental representations: A dual coding approach.* New York: Oxford University Press.

Pelizzon, L., Brandimonte, M. A., & Favretto, A. (1999). Imagery and recognition: Dissociable measures of memory? *European Journal of Cognitive Psychology, 3*, 429–443.

Pelizzon, L., Brandimonte, M. A., & Luccio, R. (2002). The role of visual, spatial, and temporal cues in attenuating verbal overshadowing. *Applied Cognitive Psychology, 16*, 947–961.

Perfect, T. J., Hunt, L. J., & Harris, C. M. (2002). Verbal overshadowing in voice recognition. *Applied Cognitive Psychology, 16*, 973–980.

Schooler, J. W. (2002). Verbal overshadowing produces a transfer inappropriate processing shift. *Applied Cognitive Psychology, 12*, S105–S125.

Schooler, J. W., & Engstler-Schooler, T. Y. (1990). Verbal overshadowing of visual memories: Some things are better left unsaid. *Cognitive Psychology, 17*, 36–71.

Schooler, J. W., Fiore, S. M., & Brandimonte, M. A. (1997). At a loss from words: Verbal overshadowing of perceptual memories. In D. L. Medin (Ed.), *Psychology of learning and motivation* (Vol. 37, pp. 291–340). San Diego, CA: Academic Press.

Schooler, J. W., Ohlsson, S., & Brooks, K. (1993). Thoughts beyond words: When language overshadows insight. *Journal of Experimental Psychology: General, 122*, 166–183.

Thomson, D. M., & Tulving, E. (1970). Associative encoding and retrieval: Weak and strong cues. *Journal of Experimental Psychology, 86*, 255–262.

Tulving, E., & Thomson, D. (1973). Encoding specificity and retrieval processes in episodic memory. *Psychological Review, 80*, 352–373.

Ullman, S. (1984). *The interpretation of visual motion* (Russian ed.). Cambridge, MA: MIT Press. (Original work published 1979)

Walker, P., Hitch, G. J., Dewhurst, S., Whiteley, H. E., & Brandimonte, M. A. (1997). The representation of non-structural information in visual memory: Evidence from image combination. *Memory and Cognition, 25*, 484–491.

Wilson, T. D., & Schooler, J. W. (1991). Thinking too much: Introspection can reduce the quality of preferences and decisions. *Journal of Personality and Social Psychology, 60*, 181–192.

EUROPEAN JOURNAL OF COGNITIVE PSYCHOLOGY
2008, 20 (3), 632–648

Object naming induces viewpoint-independence in longer term visual remembering: Evidence from a simple object drawing task

Peter Walker, Helen Blake, and J. Gavin Bremner
Department of Psychology, University of Lancaster, Lancaster, UK

The impact of object naming on object drawing confirms an association between object categorisation and viewpoint-independence in longer term visual remembering. Adult participants viewed a novel object from a viewpoint from which it would not normally be drawn from memory. The experimenter either labelled the object with a novel count noun ("Look at this dax") or did not ("Look at this object"). Participants then drew the object from immediate, short-term, or longer term memory, with no constraints being imposed on how they should depict the object. When the object was named at presentation, but not otherwise, the transition from immediate to longer term remembering increased the likelihood that the object was depicted from a viewpoint from which it had not been seen. This trend was reversed when participants were asked to depict the object in the orientation in which it had appeared to them. These results are discussed in relation to an account of the conditions under which visual category representations become established and may be used preferentially over image-like visual representations.

Evidence is accumulating to suggest that short-term and longer term visual remembering can rely on representations that preserve contrasting information about objects. For example, compared to short-term remembering, longer term remembering is more likely to utilise visual information about object categories than about specific objects (Avons & Phillips, 1987; Burgund & Marsolek, 2000; Marsolek, 1995), and information that specifies object shape categorically rather than with metric accuracy (Rosielle & Cooper, 2001). It is less likely to utilise information about the specific viewpoints from which objects were originally seen (Biederman & Cooper, 1991, 1992; Biederman & Gerhardstein, 1993; Cooper, 1994; Cooper & Schacter, 1992; Ellis, Allport, Humphreys, & Collis, 1989; Seamon &

Correspondence concerning this article should be addressed to Peter Walker, Department of Psychology, Lancaster University, Lancaster LA1 4YF, UK. E-mail: P.Walker@lancaster.ac.uk

http://www.psypress.com/ecp DOI: 10.1080/09541440601056539

Delgado, 1999; Seamon et al., 1997; Stankiewicz & Hummel, 2002; Stankiewicz, Hummel, & Cooper, 1998), or visual information about the colours of objects (Brandimonte, Schooler, & Gabbino, 1997; Cooper, 1994; Hitch, Brandimonte, & Walker, 1995; Seamon et al., 1997; Walker, Hitch, Dewhurst, Whiteley, & Brandimonte, 1997).

These contrasting aspects of objects, which are differentially associated with short-term and longer term remembering, might be preserved in two distinct types of visual representation. Candidate representations are images, such as those proposed by Tarr (e.g., Tarr, 1995), and structural descriptions, such as the geon structural descriptions (GSDs) proposed by Biederman (e.g., Biederman, 1995). Images are object-specific, preserve information about the object's orientation in depth relative to the viewer, and are likely to capture all the visible features of an object (e.g., its surface colour). In contrast, GSDs represent object categories at an intermediate level of abstraction, and focus on the shape of category relevant object parts in their spatial configuration, to the exclusion of information about an object's material properties (including colour).[1] With shape being encoded categorically, rather than with metric accuracy, GSDs are tolerant to the variation in shape among exemplars from a category. They are also largely insensitive to orientation in depth, and so can tolerate variations in the viewpoint from which an exemplar is observed. Perhaps, therefore, it is because these different forms of representation are differentially associated with short-term and longer term remembering that information about contrasting aspects of objects has varying relevance depending on memory delay. The proposal is not that short-term and longer term remembering are exclusively dependent on different types of representation, but rather that, though both types of representation can support visual remembering in most situations, there is a tendency for longer term remembering to rely on GSD-like structural descriptions when these are available.

If the various features of objects associated with longer term visual memory are preserved in a single representation, then their involvement in visual remembering should be highly correlated. For example, when participants appear to rely on visual category representations in longer term remembering, their performance should also confirm the

[1] As a referee has correctly pointed out, a GSD could have an associative link to a representation of the typical colour for a category of object, and evidence from neuropsychology indicates this to be the case. However, notwithstanding the presence of such links, structural descriptions and colour will still be separately represented, allowing stored information about structure to be accessed selectively, without information about colour being accessed at the same time. Our argument is that the same selectivity is not an option when images are accessed, because images do not represent structure and colour separately, but rather in an integrated manner. In addition, of course, many object categories, especially artefacts, do not have a typical colour, so their GSDs will not be linked to representations of colour.

viewpoint-invariance of these representations. Conversely, when participants are deprived of the opportunity to rely on category representations, longer term remembering should reveal the same sensitivity to viewpoint that is observed in short-term remembering, because in both cases viewpoint-specific object representations will mediate performance.

The experiment reported here was designed to assess this particular prediction. It did so by exploiting the impact object naming has on the creation of visual category representations. Thus, naming novel objects with novel count nouns[2] induces infants and young children to establish shape-based category representations for the objects (e.g., Baldwin, 1989; Hall, 1993; Hall & Moore, 1997; Hall, Quantz, & Persoage, 2000; Hall & Waxman, 1993; Landau, 1994; Smith, Jones, & Landau, 1992; Waxman, 1999; Waxman & Booth, 2001; Waxman & Hall, 1993), and it does so at an intermediate taxonomic level (Hall, 1993; Hall & Waxman, 1993; Waxman, 1999; Waxman & Hall, 1993; Xu, Carey, & Welch, 1999).

With this evidence in mind, the potential for a three-way association between longer term remembering, object categorisation, and viewpoint-independence was assessed by examining the impact of object naming on visual memory for a novel object at varying memory delays. It was expected that increasing evidence for viewpoint-independence would emerge with the shift from immediate to longer term remembering, but only when the object was named, because only then would a visual category representation for the object be established.

A simple drawing task was employed to determine if object naming and memory delay combine to increase the viewpoint-independence evident in adults' drawings of a novel object from memory. Participants drew a novel object from immediate, short-term, or longer term memory. Prior to drawing, the object was presented for inspection from a single viewpoint, at which time the experimenter either named the object with a novel count noun, or did not name it. The restricted viewpoint from which participants inspected the object was not one from which participants would normally depict the object. Depicting the object from a viewpoint other than this restricted viewpoint was to be taken as evidence for viewpoint-independence in visual remembering. No constraints were placed on how participants were to draw the object, and in particular, whether they should draw it in the orientation from which it had been seen by them (e.g., participants were simply instructed to "Draw the dax" or "Draw the first/second object"). It was predicted that the combined effect of naming the novel object at

[2] A count noun is a noun for a single entity, including objects (*lamp*) and mental entities (*image*), that can be counted. Hence, count nouns appear with indefinite articles in phrases referring to a single instance of a type of entity (*a lamp*), and in phrases referring to multiple instances of a type of entity (*six lamps*, *many images*).

presentation and testing longer term remembering, would be to increase the viewpoint-independence evident in participants' drawings, as revealed by a reduced tendency to depict the object from the restricted viewpoint from which it had been seen. Finally, to check if participants in this condition could still remember how the object had appeared to them, an additional control condition was run where participants were specifically asked to draw the object in the orientation in which it had appeared to them.

METHOD

Participants

One hundred and sixty one students at Lancaster University, aged between 18 and 32 years, completed the experiment. They were not paid for their participation.

Materials

Two novel objects were constructed out of wood. They each comprised an 18 cm cube, with a smaller wooden part attached to the centre of one face. For one object, the attached part was a pyramid, with an 11 cm square base and a vertex of 10 cm. For the other object, the attached part was a 7.5 cm diameter sphere.

Design

A 3 × 2 independent-groups design was created by crossing two factors. The factors were memory delay (immediate, short-term, and longer term remembering) and object naming (object named versus object unnamed). An equal number of participants ($n = 23$) was assigned randomly to each of these six groups. An additional, control group of participants ($n = 23$) was assigned to a longer term remembering with object naming condition, with the constraint that they should depict the object in the orientation it had appeared to them. The groups had similar mean ages and male:female ratios. For the object named conditions, the mean ages (in years) and male:female ratios (in parentheses) were 19.8 (5:18), 19.4 (4:19), 19.7 (6:17), and 20.3 (4:19), for the immediate, short-term, longer term, and longer term control conditions, respectively. The corresponding values for the object unnamed conditions were 19.6 (4:19), 20.4 (5:18), and 19.7 (5:18), for the immediate, short-term, and longer term conditions, respectively. Only four of the participants drew with their left hand (one male in each of the immediate remembering with object naming and longer term remembering with object naming conditions, and one female in each of the immediate remembering without object naming and short-term remembering without object naming conditions).

Procedure

Each object in turn was presented for visual inspection for 20 s, and then immediately removed from sight for the remainder of the experiment (see Figure 1). In all conditions, between presentation of the two objects, participants engaged in a visual imagery task for 1 min. This was intended to ensure participants were unable to hold the first object in mind by continually visualising it (cf. Phillips, 1983, for discussion of the link between visualisation and visual memory). The imagery task was

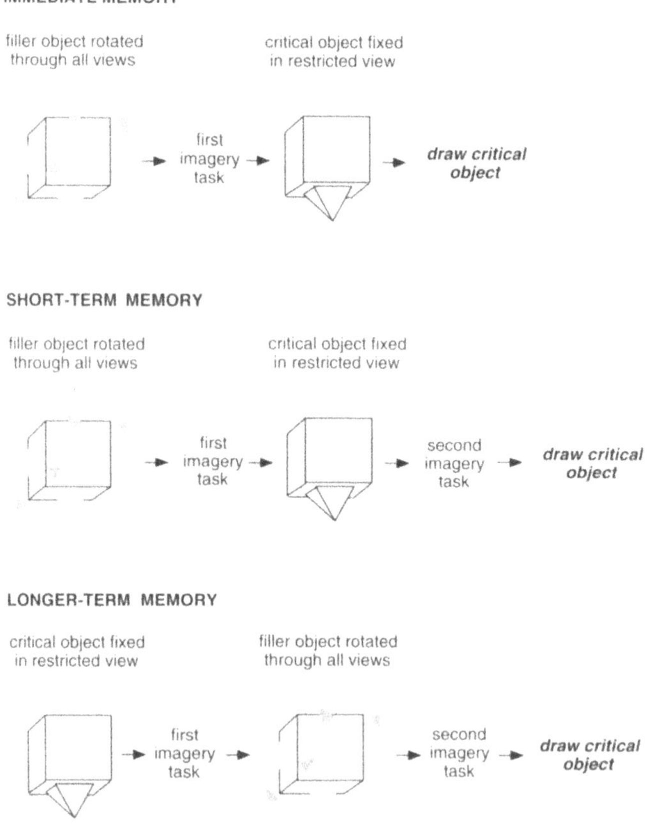

Figure 1. The sequence of visual events in each memory condition.

taken from Finke, Pinker, and Farah (1989), and required participants to imagine transforming and combining two letters of the alphabet to discover an emerging object. In the immediate memory condition, participants were asked to draw the second object immediately after it had been removed. In the short-term and longer term memory conditions, after the second object had been inspected and removed from view, participants were asked to engage in the imagery task for a second time, again for 1 min. In the short-term memory condition, participants were then asked to draw the second object. In the longer term memory condition, they were asked to draw the first object. The order of presentation of the two objects was arranged to ensure that it was always the object with the pyramid attachment that was drawn. Thus, whereas this object was the first object to be presented in the longer term memory condition, it was the second object to be presented in the immediate and short-term memory conditions. This object was always inspected by participants from a restricted view. Specifically, the experimenter held the object in front of the participant with the attached part always pointing down. Previous research has shown that this is rarely an orientation in which this type of object will be drawn after it has been seen from all major viewpoints (cf., Walker et al., 2006). Viewing of the other object was unrestricted, with the experimenter rotating the object in front of the participant following a carefully rehearsed routine that exposed the object equally from every major viewpoint. Participants did not know in advance which object they would be asked to draw, or how they would be asked to draw it. In the object named condition, as the experimenter presented each object for inspection, she named it using one of two novel count nouns (i.e., "This is a riff/dax. Please look at this riff/dax.") A different label was assigned to the two objects. When later requesting participants in this condition to draw one of the objects, she said "Do you remember the first/second object? It was a riff/dax. Please now draw it for me." In the object unnamed condition, as the experimenter presented each object for inspection, she said "This is an object. Please look at this object." When later requesting participants in this condition to draw one of the objects, she said "Do you remember the first/second object? Please now draw the first/second object for me." In the additional control condition, which combined longer term remembering and object naming, the experimenter requested participants to draw the first object in the orientation in which it had appeared to them, saying "Do you remember the first object? It was a riff/dax. Please now draw it for me in the orientation in which it had appeared to you."

RESULTS

The view from which the object was depicted in each drawing was assessed by a colleague who was ignorant of the purpose of the study and of the conditions under which each drawing had been produced. In every case, it was clear that the attached part had been including in the drawing, and in which direction the object (i.e, the attached part) was pointing.

Figure 2 presents the number of drawings in each condition where the object was depicted either from the restricted viewpoint from which it had been seen, or from some other viewpoint. For all statistical analyses, an alpha level of .05 was adopted.

Changes in the likelihood of depicting the object from the restricted viewpoint, versus some other viewpoint, confirmed the combined impact of object naming and memory delay. Aggregating across levels of memory delay, there were significantly more drawings in the object named condition, than in the object unnamed condition, that depicted the object from a viewpoint other than the one from which it had been seen, Fisher's Exact $p = .002$. In the object unnamed condition, the likelihood of depicting the object from the restricted viewpoint did not change as memory delay was extended, Linear-by-Linear Association $(1, N = 69) = 0.76$, $p = .385$. In the object named condition, the likelihood of depicting the object from the restricted viewpoint decreased as

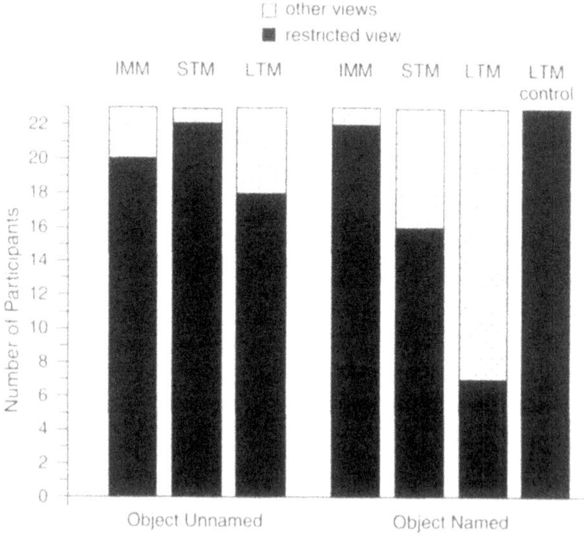

Figure 2. The number of participants depicting the novel object from the restricted viewpoint from which it had been seen, or from some other viewpoint, as a function of whether or not the object was named with a novel count noun at encoding, and according to whether it was drawn from immediate memory (IMM), short-term memory (STM), or longer term memory (LTM).

memory delay was extended, Linear-by-Linear Association (1, $N = 69$) = 21.25, $p < .001$. Two separate analyses of the results from the object named condition confirmed that the likelihood of depicting the object from the restricted viewpoint decreased significantly with both the transition from immediate to short-term remembering, Fisher's Exact $p = .023$, and with the transition from short-term to longer term remembering, Fisher's Exact $p = .009$. Neither of these transitions had a significant impact in the object unnamed condition, Fisher's Exact $p = .61$ and .19, for the immediate to short-term and short-term to longer term transitions, respectively.

The results from the longer term remembering control condition were clear. Despite having heard the experimenter name the object, all the participants drew the object in the orientation in which it had appeared to them.

DISCUSSION

The results confirm that with the transition from immediate to longer term remembering, object naming reduces the likelihood that participants will be constrained to depict a remembered object from the viewpoint from which it had been seen. Given the evidence linking object naming with object categorisation, this result is consistent with the proposal that two distinct types of visual representation are differentially associated with short-term and longer term remembering. More specifically, though both image-like and GSD-like representations can support remembering across a full range of circumstances, there is a tendency for longer term remembering to utilise GSD-like representations when these are available. Object naming can be a critical factor determining the availability of GSD-like representations and, because of this, the extent to which visual remembering is viewpoint-independent.[3]

---

[3] With regard to why, when an orientation has to be specified for a category of object, certain orientations become preferred, we presume there are many contributing factors. Frequency of exposure to particular orientations would be the most obvious, though this cannot apply here. The ease with which the constituent geons can be discriminated from a particular orientation is claimed to be another factor. In addition, as a referee pointed out, the stability of an object in a particular orientation is likely to be another factor, in part because an unstable orientation is an unlikely orientation from which to encounter the same type of object in the future. Having said this, however, we might note the overwhelming tendency for people to draw bicycles in an unstable orientation (i.e., upright, and with no apparent support being depicted). The functional significance of certain orientations also is likely to be very important. Thus, drinking mugs can only serve their usual function from a limited range of orientations, and they normally do this best when their handles are pointing to the viewer's right (so that a right-handed person can grasp the mug easily). We intend to run a study in which we explain an intended function for our novel object. In one condition, this function will require the object to be oriented with the attached part pointing down (e.g., so that indentations can be made in pastry). We then expect this orientation to become the preferred one, and the one towards which drawers will shift when object naming is combined with longer term remembering.

Walker et al. (2006) also have shown that naming a similar novel object (a cube with a cone attachment) with a novel count noun can impact on young children's drawings of the object. In their study, however, the object remained available for inspection during drawing. Specifically, after it had been shown to the children from every major angle, it was placed in position for drawing with the cone hidden from view (i.e., pointing directly away from the children). It is known that young children are inclined to depict an object part that is currently hidden from view (e.g., Freeman & Janikoun, 1972), and such intellectual realism can be seen as another example of viewpoint-independence in drawing. It is relevant to note, therefore, that Walker et al. confirmed that if the object was labelled with a novel count noun as it was being inspected prior to drawing, the likelihood that the children would be constrained by the viewpoint from which they could see the object was reduced. When the object was named, the children showed an increased tendency to depict the object from a viewpoint that revealed the hidden part, but only if the name chosen indicated that this part was category relevant. In the present context, these results confirm that, despite their differential association with longer term remembering, visual object category representations can impact on live drawing (i.e., drawing an object that remains available for inspection). It seems, therefore, that when young children engage in live drawing, they behave as if they were adults drawing from longer term visual memory.

According to the current proposal, whenever a task requires participants to refer to those aspects of an object that are best preserved in an image-like representation, object naming will have the potential to impact negatively on performance, especially if this involves longer term, rather than short-term, remembering. The task might require participants to draw an object from its current viewpoint, or from the viewpoint from which it was last seen. Alternatively, it might require them to reproduce the colour and shape of the object with high fidelity.

Detrimental effects of object naming on longer term visual remembering have already been demonstrated in studies of visual image combination (cf. Brandimonte, Hitch, & Bishop, 1992; Hitch, Brandimonte, & Walker, 1995; Walker et al., 1997). In these studies, participants were asked to combine a visual image of a recently presented line drawing with an image of a current line drawing. They were then to discover the identity of the object resulting from this combination. The nature of the to-be-combined drawings required the superimposition of the two images in the mind's eye to be metrically accurate. In some situations, the recently presented visual stimulus was either still available in short-term memory (because no other item had been presented in the interim), or it was available only in longer term memory (because other task-relevant items had been presented in the interim). In addition, it was arranged that when the memory item depicted a familiar object, it was either named or unnamed at presentation. In agreement with the results of the present study, participants were *less* able to complete the image combination task if the object depicted in the first drawing was named at presentation. Moreover, this detrimental effect of naming was observed only with longer term remembering, and not with short-term remembering. Walker et al. (1997) proposed that performance was impaired by object naming because this induced participants to increase their reliance on a visual representation of the category to which the object belonged, with the effect that the shape of the object became less accurately described (i.e., there was a shift towards shape being described categorically rather than with metric accuracy). Finally, additional support for the current proposal emerged with the observation that performance in the image combination task was insensitive to the colour congruity of the to-be-combined stimuli, but only when longer term remembering was being assessed and the first figure had been named (Hitch et al., 1995; Walker et al., 1997). With short-term remembering, image combination was impaired when the two figures to be combined appeared in different colours (e.g., black-on-grey and white-on-grey), rather than the same colour (e.g., both black-on-grey), regardless of whether or not the first figure was named. In other words, whereas the visual representation supporting longer term remembering resembled a GSD-like representation insofar as it did not preserve object colour, the visual representation supporting short-term remembering resembled an image-like representation insofar as it preserved object colour independently of object naming.

Much of the evidence confirming the impact of distinct types of visual representation in longer term remembering has involved the contrast between implicit and explicit tests of memory (see, for example, Cooper, 1994, and Srinivas, 1996). For example, though longer term priming in both object naming and the possible-impossible object decision task has been shown to involve visual representations that do not preserve information about viewpoint and object colour, explicit recognition memory for the same stimuli has been shown to involve visual representations that do preserve information about these two features (Biederman & Cooper, 1991, 1992; Cooper, 1994; Cooper & Schacter, 1992; Seamon & Delgado, 1999; Seamon et al., 1997; Srinivas, 1996). Clearly, therefore, a full account of the representational basis of visual remembering, and of the moderating influence of object naming, will need to acknowledge the distinction between implicit and explicit tests of memory. Nevertheless, the present results confirm that, as an explicit test of memory, object drawing tasks can reveal the varying contributions of different types of visual representation and the moderating influence of object naming.[4]

Figure 3 illustrates the conceptual framework developed here to accommodate the results of the present study and related findings (e.g., Hitch et al., 1995; Walker et al., 1997). It is proposed that when an object is encountered, distinct visual processes support the derivation of the two types of visual representation. These are labelled simply as type A and type B processes, so as to remain mute regarding their nature.[5] It is assumed that image-like visual representations are always established, whereas certain conditions have to be satisfied for a visual category representation to be established. Combining object naming (i.e., naming a novel object with a novel count noun in the present study) with longer term remembering creates a sufficient condition for this to occur. These two component conditions are seen to impact on different aspects of the cognitive resources supporting object drawing. Whereas object naming facilitates the derivation of a visual category representation, longer term remembering increases the likelihood that this representation will be used to support performance. Neither of these component conditions is thought to be *necessary* for a category representation to impact on performance. Indeed, Biederman and Bar (1999) and Coltheart, Mondy, and Coltheart (2005) have revealed that, on the basis of encountering a single view of a novel object, a viewpoint-independent visual representation can be established quickly, even in the absence of object naming. And in their studies of viewpoint-independent visual priming in the possible-impossible object decision task, Schacter and Cooper have revealed a number of visual encoding conditions, other than

[4] A good illustration that object drawing can reveal the varying contributions of different types of visual representation according to memory delay is provided by Bozeat et al. (2003). They presented geometric designs and pictures of familiar objects to patients with semantic dementia. They asked the patients either to copy the pictures, or to draw them some time after they had been removed from view. With regard to the pictures of familiar objects, the patients produced good copies, but their drawings after a delay were much less good. In addition, the quality of an individual patient's delayed drawings was correlated with the severity of their dementia, and with the quality of the drawings they produced of the same objects in response to being given their names. There was no unusual deterioration with delay in their drawings of the geometric designs. The point to note in the context of the present study is that whereas immediate object drawing was uninfluenced by category representations in long-term memory, and hence by the dementia, delayed object drawing was.

[5] It is beyond the scope of the present paper to explore either the nature of the processes required to derive each type of visual representation, or the interdependencies between them. Though they are likely to share very early visual encoding pathways, it is not clear at what point they dissociate. It is also unclear if the processes dissociate to operate in parallel of each other, as illustrated in Figure 3, or if the processes responsible for deriving a viewpoint-independent structural description follow in sequence those responsible for deriving the corresponding viewpoint-specific image(s).

WITHOUT OBJECT NAMING

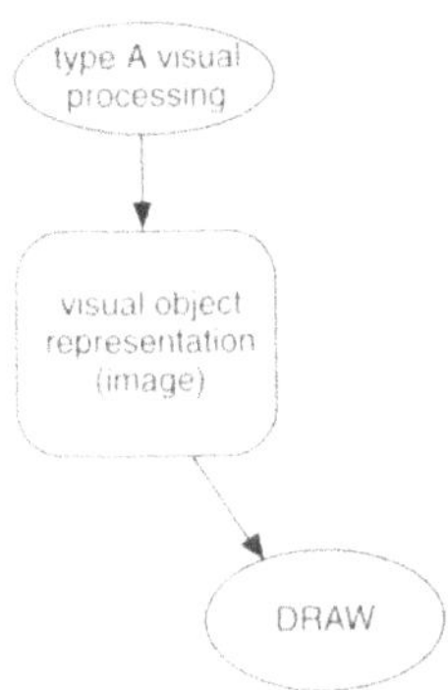

WITH OBJECT NAMING

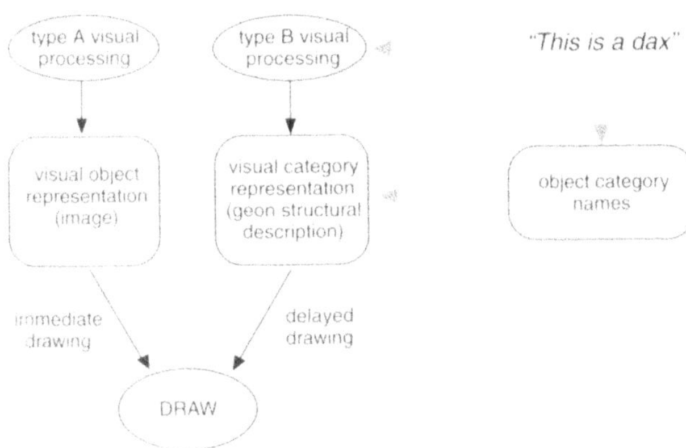

Figure 3. The conceptual framework developed to accommodate the results of the present study and related findings. The information provided by the two types of visual representation is depicted as converging on common production mechanisms. This is intended to reflect the fact that a single drawing need not be based exclusively on one type of representation, but can be based on a mix of representations, including viewpoint-specific object representations and category representations (for evidence, see Walker et al., 2006).

object naming, that lead to the derivation of viewpoint-independent structural descriptions of novel objects (e.g., deciding if a novel object depicted in a simple line drawing faces left or right, deciding how the object might be used as a tool, or deciding if the object resembles an item of household furniture) (Schacter & Cooper, 1993; Schacter, Cooper, & Delaney, 1990). Schacter and Cooper argue that the need to derive a global structural description of the novel object is common to all encoding conditions yielding viewpoint-independent visual priming.

It is proposed that image-like representation(s) do not become unavailable or inaccessible when a visual category representation is established. Indeed, even when naming was combined with longer term remembering in the control condition of the present study, participants were able to draw the critical object in the restricted viewpoint from which it had been seen when asked to do so. Brandimonte et al. (1997) have also shown that the detrimental effects of object naming in longer term visual remembering can be reversed by providing colour as a visual cue to facilitate access to the original visual representation. And in an earlier study of verbal overshadowing, Schooler and Engstler-Schooler (1990) demonstrated that requiring participants to make their face recognition judgements quickly removed the verbal overshadowing effect, confirming that the original visual representation of the face had not been eradicated when participants provided a verbal description of the face. Finally, Schacter and colleagues (e.g., Cooper & Schacter, 1992; Schacter & Cooper, 1993; Schacter et al., 1990) and Burgund and Marsolek (2000) have confirmed that viewpoint-specific and viewpoint-independent visual representations can coexist in memory, and that particular task conditions can determine which type of representation impacts on performance (e.g., whether the test stimulus is presented directly to the left or right cerebral hemisphere).

Although the focus has been on viewpoint in the present study, the conceptual framework being proposed implies that other visual features will correlate with object naming and longer term remembering. It is predicted that whenever conditions are such as to encourage the drawer to rely on an image-like representation, their drawings will be more likely to reflect object shape with metric accuracy, and to reproduce the object's material properties (e.g., surface texture and colour). Conversely, these features will be less apparent when conditions are such as to encourage the drawer to rely on a GSD. Further work is required to assess these predictions, and to see if these other features of drawings will cooccur with viewpoint-dependence.

When a person names a *familiar* object with its category label, they are required to categorise the object visually, and in many situations this in turn will require them to derive a structural description. But why should hearing someone else name a novel object with a novel count noun induce a person to visually categorise the object? That it should do so is often assumed in discussions of language acquisition. According to Waxman (1999), for example, object naming by someone else (typically by an adult, who also gestures towards the object) is perceived by young children to be an act of object categorisation, encouraging the children themselves to categorise the object. In this way, children learn to associate a visual representation of the object's category with a verbal representation of the name provided by the adult, which typically is the name of the object's category. The claim being made here is that these processes, which are so important in early language development, remain influential in later life. Thus, just like young children, adults who hear an experimenter name a novel object with a novel count noun also perceive the experimenter to be categorising the object and also, therefore, are induced to derive a visual category representation for the object. On this account, verbal recoding has a significant impact on visual information processing, including visual remembering, even when it is someone else who is heard to do the verbal recoding.

Verbal overshadowing

Much of the work on verbal overshadowing has focused on using faces as stimuli, has required participants to provide verbal descriptions of the faces, and has then examined the impact of this on explicit, forced-choice visual recognition memory for the faces. Of course, providing a verbal description of an item is not the same as naming it, and faces are a distinct class of stimuli with distinct systems of visual categorisation. Despite these differences, however, it is worth reflecting on some implications of the conceptual framework presented here for studies of verbal overshadowing.

The first point to make is that because distinct forms of visual processing support the derivation of distinct types of representation, the present conceptualisation allows either the type of encoding, or the type of representation, to be emphasised in accounts of verbal overshadowing. That is, explanations of overshadowing based on representational competition (e.g., Schooler & Engstler-Schooler, 1990) are not incompatible with explanations based on the transfer of inappropriate processing (e.g., Schooler, 2002).

A second point to make relates to the fact that early accounts of verbal overshadowing emphasise the contrast between verbal and visual representations of the same item, and how the relative utility of these forms of representation varies according to context. Accordingly, these accounts require that the foils for the recognition test are selected carefully, so that it is clear if, and to what extent, recognition can be supported by verbal representations. If it cannot, because the target and foils share similar verbal descriptions, then any verbal overshadowing that occurs will have to be explained without reference to the availability/accessibility of verbal representations. The present conceptualisation indicates that it is also important to know the extent to which visual recognition can be supported by visual category representations, and again the nature of the foils is critically important. To give one example, if all the foils were to share the same basic geon structural description as the target, then visual category representations would be precluded from supporting visual recognition memory, which instead would have to rely exclusively on visual representations that are capable of discriminating among exemplars from the same visual category (i.e., rely on visual images).

Studies of the impact of verbal recoding on visual image manipulation were designed to preclude verbal representations from mediating performance, so that interest could be focused on alternative forms of visual representation and their differential association with object naming and memory delay (see, for example, Hitch et al., 1995, and Walker et al., 1997). But is performance in the current object drawing task supported exclusively by visual memory representations, or can verbal representations make a contribution? In principle, verbal representations have the potential to support object drawing. However, it is important to note that the novel count noun assigned to the object participants in the present study had to draw carried no information about the nature of the object, and so could not contribute directly to drawing.

A final point to make is that unconstrained verbal descriptions can include the names of different types of visual category to which an item belongs, although they need not. Indeed, in some studies of verbal overshadowing, participants have been instructed to include category labels in their descriptions (e.g., personality type, occupational category, age group, gender, weight category, and hair colour). However, control over the inclusion of category labels is not normally exercised, nor are the foils for the recognition test selected with the potential utility of category representations in mind. Uncertainty often remains, therefore, regarding the involvement of category representations in supporting visual recognition memory. From a purely procedural point of view, therefore, the present conceptual framework, and the success of the present study, indicates that there might be considerable merit in providing participants with a verbal description, rather than asking them to generate their own. The fact that the description is provided by someone else might not be critical, allowing control to be exercised over the nature of the verbal description that might lead to verbal overshadowing.

REFERENCES

Avons, S. E., & Phillips, W. A. (1987). Representation of matrix patterns in long- and short-term visual memory. *Acta Psychologica*, *65*, 227–246.

Baldwin, D. A. (1989). Priorities in children's expectations about object label reference: Form over colour. *Child Development*, *60*, 1291–1306.

Biederman, I. (1995). Visual object recognition. In S. M. Kosslyn & D. N. Osherson (Eds.), *Visual cognition: An invitation to cognitive science* (2nd ed., Vol. 2, pp. 121–165). Cambridge, MA: MIT Press.

Biederman, I., & Bar, M. (1999). One-shot viewpoint invariance in matching novel objects. *Vision Research, 39*, 2885–2899.

Biederman, I., & Cooper, E. E. (1991). Evidence for complete translational and reflectional invariance in visual object priming. *Perception, 20*, 585–593.

Biederman, I., & Cooper, E. E. (1992). Size invariance in visual object priming. *Journal of Experimental Psychology: Human Perception and Performance, 18*, 121–133.

Biederman, I., & Gerhardstein, P. C. (1993). Recognizing depth-rotated objects: Evidence and conditions for 3D viewpoint invariance. *Journal of Experimental Psychology: Human Perception and Performance, 19*, 1162–1182.

Bozeat, S., Lambon Ralph, M. A., Graham, K. S., Patterson, K., Wilkin, H., Rowland, J., et al. (2003). A duck with four legs: Investigating the structure of conceptual knowledge using picture drawing in semantic dementia. *Cognitive Neuropsychology, 20*, 27–47.

Brandimonte, M. A., Hitch, G. J., & Bishop, D. V. M. (1992). Influence of short-term memory codes on visual image processing: Evidence from image transformation tasks. *Journal of Experimental Psychology: Learning, Memory and Cognition, 18*, 157–165.

Brandimonte, M. A., Schooler, J. W., & Gabbino, P. (1997). Attenuating verbal overshadowing through visual retrieval cues. *Journal of Experimental Psychology: Learning, Memory and Cognition, 23*, 915–931.

Burgund, E. D., & Marsolek, C. J. (2000). Viewpoint-invariant and viewpoint-dependent object recognition in dissociable neural subsystems. *Psychonomic Bulletin and Review, 7*, 480–489.

Coltheart, V., Mondy, S., & Coltheart, M. (2005). Repetition blindness for novel objects. *Visual Cognition, 12*, 519–540.

Cooper, L. A. (1994). Probing the nature of the mental representation of visual objects: Evidence from cognitive dissociations. In S. Ballesteros (Ed.), *Cognitive approaches to human perception* (pp. 199–221). Hillsdale, NJ: Lawrence Erlbaum Associates, Inc.

Cooper, L. A., & Schacter, D. L. (1992). Dissociations between structural and episodic representations of visual objects. *Current Directions in Psychological Science, 1*, 141–146.

Ellis, R., Allport, D. A., Humphreys, G. W., & Collis, J. (1989). Varieties of object constancy. *Quarterly Journal of Experimental Psychology, 41*, 775–796.

Finke, R. A., Pinker, S., & Farah, M. J. (1989). Reinterpreting visual patterns in mental imagery. *Cognitive Science, 13*, 51–78.

Freeman, N. H., & Janikoun, R. (1972). Intellectual realism in children's drawings of a familiar object with distinctive features. *Child Development, 43*, 1116–1121.

Hall, D. G. (1993). Basic-level individuals. *Cognition, 48*, 199–221.

Hall, D. G., & Moore, C. E. (1997). Red bluebirds and black greenflies: Preschoolers' understanding of the semantics of adjectives and count nouns. *Journal of Experimental Child Psychology, 67*, 236–267.

Hall, D. G., Quantz, D. H., & Persoage, K. A. (2000). Preschoolers' use of form class cues in word learning. *Developmental Psychology, 36*, 449–462.

Hall, D. G., & Waxman, S. R. (1993). Assumptions about word meaning: Individuation and basic-level kinds. *Child Development, 64*, 1550–1570.

Hitch, G. J., Brandimonte, M. A., & Walker, P. (1995). Two types of representation in visual memory: Evidence from the effects of stimulus contrast on image combination. *Memory and Cognition, 23*, 147–154.

Landau, B. (1994). Object shape, object name, and object kind: Representation and development. *Psychology of Learning and Motivation, 31*, 253–304.

Marsolek, C. J. (1995). Abstract visual-form representations in the left cerebral hemisphere. *Journal of Experimental Psychology: Human Perception and Performance, 21*, 375–386.

Phillips, W. A. (1983). Short-term visual memory. *Philosophical Transactions of the Royal Society of London, Series B, 302*, 295–309.

Rosielle, L. J., & Cooper, E. E. (2001). Categorical perception of relative orientation in visual object recognition. *Memory and Cognition, 29*, 68–82.

Schacter, D. L., & Cooper, L. A. (1993). Implicit and explicit memory for novel visual objects: Structure and function. *Journal of Experimental Psychology: Learning, Memory and Cognition, 19*, 995–1009.

Schacter, D. L., Cooper, L. A., & Delaney, S. M. (1990). Implicit memory for unfamiliar objects depends on access to structural descriptions. *Journal of Experimental Psychology: General, 119*, 5–24.

Schooler, J. W. (2002). Verbalization produces a transfer inappropriate processing shift. *Applied Cognitive Psychology, 16*, 989–997.

Schooler, J. W., & Engstler-Schooler, T. Y. (1990). Verbal overshadowing of visual memories: Some things are better left unsaid. *Cognitive Psychology, 22*, 36–71.

Seamon, J. G., & Delgado, M. R. (1999). Recognition memory and affective preference for depth-rotated solid objects: Part-based structural descriptions may underlie the mere exposure effect. *Visual Cognition, 6*, 145–164.

Seamon, J. G., Ganor-Stern, D., Crawley, M. J., Wilson, S. M., Weber, W. J., O'Rourke, C. M., & Mahoney, J. K. (1997). A mere exposure effect for transformed three-dimensional objects: Effects of reflection, size, or color changes on affect and recognition. *Memory and Cognition, 25*, 367–374.

Smith, L. B., Jones, S. S., & Landau, B. (1992). Count nouns, adjectives, and perceptual properties in children's novel word interpretations. *Developmental Psychology, 28*, 273–286.

Srinivas, K. (1996). Contrast and illumination effects on explicit and implicit measures of memory. *Journal of Experimental Psychology: Learning, Memory, and Cognition, 22*, 1123–1135.

Stankiewicz, B. J., & Hummel, J. E. (2002). Automatic priming for translation- and scale-invariant representations of object shape. *Visual Cognition, 9*, 719–739.

Stankiewicz, B. J., Hummel, J. E., & Cooper, E. E. (1998). The role of attention in priming left-right reflections of object images: Evidence for a dual representation of object shape. *Journal of Experimental Psychology: Human Perception and Performance, 24*, 732–744.

Tarr, M. J. (1995). Rotating objects to recognize them: A case study on the role of viewpoint dependency in the recognition of three-dimensional objects. *Psychonomic Bulletin and Review, 2*, 55–82.

Walker, P., Bremner, J. G., Merrick, K., Coates, S., Cooper, E., Lawley, R., et al. (2006). Visual mental representations supporting object drawing: How naming a novel object with a novel count noun impacts on young children's object drawing. *Visual Cognition, 13*, 733–788.

Walker, P., Hitch, G. J., Dewhurst, S. A., Whiteley, H. E., & Brandimonte, M. A. (1997). The representation of nonstructural information in visual memory: Evidence from image combination. *Memory and Cognition, 25*, 484–491.

Waxman, S. R. (1999). The dubbing ceremony revisited: Object naming and categorization in infancy and early childhood. In D. L. Medin & S. Atran (Eds.), *Folkbiology* (pp. 233–284). Cambridge, MA: Bradford.

Waxman, S. R., & Booth, A. E. (2001). Seeing pink elephants: Fourteen-month-olds' interpretations of novel nouns and adjectives. *Cognitive Psychology, 43*, 217–242.

Waxman, S. R., & Hall, D. G. (1993). The development of a linkage between count nouns and object categories: Evidence from 15- to 21-month-old infants. *Child Development, 64*, 1224–1241.

Xu, F., Carey, S., & Welch, J. (1999). Infants' ability to use object kind information for object individuation. *Cognition, 70*, 137–166.

Subject index

accessibility assumption 613
articulatory suppression 389–390, 478–496

cognitive interview, eyewitness descriptions 500, 529, 531–556
conceptual processing 400, 404, 473
configural processing 570–574, 579, 585, 587–611, 628
content account 388, 392, 396, 399–403, 408–409
context 389, 406, 423
reinstatement 504–507, 521, 531, 543–545, 549, 619, 623–624
criterion shift account 396, 407–408, 410–411
not present option 421, 615
person descriptions and identifications 389, 390, 497–528, 533, 551, 556
cues, retrieval 392, 441, 612–629
cultural differences 404, 406, 423–424, 587, 588–610

decision making 396, 398, 403
decision processes 390, 497–528
dual coding theory 479, 485–487

encoding processes
  see also recoding
  description-identification delay 414, 419–424, 432–445, 550–551
  dual coding theory 479, 485–487
  face recognition memory 389–390, 478–496, 587–611
  multiple face recognition 471
  Navon letters 391, 587–611
  person description 510–511, 530
  verbalisation effect 402, 481–482, 587–611
eyewitness identification 390, 414–417, 422–424, 443–445, 497–498, 529–560

face recognition
  see also person memory
  accuracy 414–455, 506–507, 511–521, 525, 565, 588–589, 609–610
  content account 401–402
  description and processing effects 391, 577–586
  description-identification relationship 389, 414–455, 506
  facilitation effects 388, 416–422, 438, 440, 504–505, 521, 577, 579–585
  levels of processing framework 421–422, 438
  meta-analysis study 416, 417–418, 424–455
  multiple faces 389, 417–418, 421, 423, 433, 443, 456–477
  Navon processing and verbalisation 391, 587–611
  same and other-races 404, 423–424, 587, 588–589, 592–610
  spatial frequency information 570–574
  transfer-inappropriate processing shift 403–407, 420–421, 438–439, 471, 561–576, 577, 584–585
  verbal interference effects 388, 416–422, 438–439, 493, 561
  verbal processing role 389–390, 478–496
facilitation, face recognition 388, 416–422, 438, 440, 504–505, 521, 577, 579–585
false “know” judgements 389, 456, 471, 473–474
familiarity-based judgements 440, 456, 459, 464, 469–474, 617, 644
featural information
  description and processing 392, 577–586, 616, 628

description–identification relationship 418, 420, 422, 506–507
eyewitness descriptions 542, 553–554
face recognition 403
Navon processing 391, 563, 570–575, 587–611
verbalisation effect 457

forced recall 401–403, 407, 423, 500–502, 521, 554
fuzzy trace theory 474

geon structural descriptions (GSDs) 392, 633, 639, 641, 644
global processing 403–407, 563, 573, 575, 577–586, 587–611, 616–617, 628

holistic information 403, 406, 418, 420, 422, 439, 577–586, 587–611

imagery 388, 543, 545, 555, 612–631
individual differences 400
interval tasks 391, 404–405, 414, 579, 584–585, 596–599, 602–609

letter identification *see* Navon task
levels of processing framework 421–422, 438
local processing 403–407, 563, 573, 575, 577–586, 587–611, 616
long-term memory
eyewitness identification 415
visual objects 392, 619, 632–648

meta-analysis studies 416, 417–418, 424–455
misinformation account 457, 473, 554

Navon task
face description and processing effects 391, 561–576, 577–586
processing and verbalisation 391, 587–611
transfer-inappropriate processing shift 403–404, 410, 561–576

nonverbal processing 585, 612–629
not present option 421, 441, 474, 501, 512, 533, 615
nouns 612, 619, 624–627, 632, 634
novel objects 392, 632–648

object memory 392, 619, 632–648
optional-choice procedure 501–502
orientation 392, 632–648
output encoding 419–420, 422, 438, 441
outshining hypothesis 419

perceptual processing 400, 404, 473, 584–585
person memory
see also face recognition
eyewitness descriptions 390, 414–417, 422–424, 529–560
non-visual information 555
verbal overshadowing 390, 497–528

police, eyewitness identification performance 390, 499–500, 529–560
postencoding
delay 551
retention interval 390, 552–553, 556
verbal processes role 478, 481–482, 485, 490–494

problem solving 396, 398, 403, 405–406
processing bias theory 590–593, 606–607, 608
processing shift hypothesis *see* transfer-inappropriate processing shift

reasoning 388, 396, 398, 406
recoding
see also retrieval-based interference
content account 399, 401, 402
interference account 399, 401, 419, 533, 551–554, 556, 612–631

recollection-based processes 440, 456, 459, 464, 471–472, 473–474
retrieval
face recognition memory 389–390, 478, 492–494

forced recall 401–403, 407, 423, 500–502, 521, 554
long-term memory 632
retrieval-based interference 401, 419–420, 422, 439, 500–501, 521, 613
visual imagery 392, 612–631

semantic information 421, 573–574, 579
sensory information 398, 399–400, 417, 555
shape 632–633, 641, 644
short-term memory 392, 632–648
stress 529, 548

taste 398, 399–400, 417, 555
transfer-appropriate processing theory 403, 405, 499, 588, 592, 605, 607
transfer-inappropriate processing shift
face recognition
description and processing types 577, 580, 584–585
encoding and retrieval 589–590, 593
Navon processing 561–576, 588
verbal overshadowing 388, 396, 403–410, 420–421, 438–439, 471, 499, 521
visual imagery 612, 614–615, 618, 622, 627–629

verbal ability 400–401, 404, 408, 539
verbal overshadowing
accounts evaluation 388, 396–413
content account 388, 396, 399–403, 408–409
criterion shift account 389, 396, 407–408, 410–411, 421
eyewitness identification 390, 416–417, 422–424, 443–445, 529–560
face encoding/retrieval 389–390, 424, 438–439, 478–496, 589–590, 605–606
face recognition 388, 389–390, 417–418, 481–482, 561–576
misinformation account 457
multiple face recognition 389, 456–477
Navon processing 587, 589–590
not present option 421, 441, 474, 501, 512, 533, 615
object naming 645–646
person description/identification 390, 497–528, 529, 532–535
recoding interference account 399, 419–420, 612–631
transfer-inappropriate processing shift 396, 403–410, 420–421, 438–439, 471, 561–576, 577, 584–585
visual imagery encoding 392, 612–631
verbalisation
description/testing delay 390, 414, 419, 467–468, 470–472, 498–500, 522–523, 547, 551–552, 556
eyewitness identification 390, 422–424, 443–445, 529–560
face description and processing effects 577–586
face recognition 389–390, 414–455, 478–496
Navon processing 587–611
object memory 392, 632–648
repeated description effects 390, 541, 552–553, 556
self-generated 399, 401, 423, 612–629
visual information influence 613, 628–629
viewpoints, novel 392, 632–648
visual memory
encoding 389–390, 391, 392, 402, 478, 587–611
imagery 543, 545, 555
Navon shapes 566–570, 575
non-visual information 555
objects 392, 632–648
postencoding retention interval 390, 552–553

recoding interference account 399, 612–631
retrieval processes 389–390, 392, 401, 478, 612–631, 632
storage processes 392, 632–648
verbalisation effect 391–392, 397–398, 401, 612
visuospatial representations 628–629

wine tasting 399–400

For Product Safety Concerns and Information please contact our EU representative GPSR@taylorandfrancis.com
Taylor & Francis Verlag GmbH, Kaufingerstraße 24, 80331 München, Germany

www.ingramcontent.com/pod-product-compliance
Lightning Source LLC
Chambersburg PA
CBHW050413280326
41932CB00013BA/1843

* 9 7 8 1 1 3 8 8 7 7 7 9 5 *